In the Name of God, the Lord _of_ C---

Sayyid

IN THE SHADE OF
THE QUR'ĀN

Fī Ẓilāl al-Qur'ān

VOLUME XIV

SŪRAHS 33–39

Al-Aḥzāb – Al-Zumar

Translated and Edited by
Adil Salahi

THE ISLAMIC FOUNDATION
AND
ISLAMONLINE.NET

Published by

THE ISLAMIC FOUNDATION,

Markfield Conference Centre,
Ratby Lane, Markfield, Leicestershire LE67 9SY, United Kingdom
Tel: (01530) 244944, Fax: (01530) 244946
E-mail: i.foundation@islamic-foundation.org.uk
Website: www.islamic-foundation.org.uk

Quran House, PO Box 30611, Nairobi, Kenya

PMB 3193, Kano, Nigeria

ISLAMONLINE.NET,
PO Box 22212, Doha, Qatar
E-mail: webmaster@islam-online.net
Website: www.islamonline.net

Distributed by: Kube Publishing

British Library Cataloguing-in-Publication Data
Qutb, Sayyid, 1903–1966
    In the shade of the Qur'an = Fi zilal al-Qur'an
    Vol. 14: Surahs 33–39
    1. Koran – Commentaries
    I.   Title
    II. Salahi, M.A.
    III. Islamic Foundation (Great Britain)
    297.1'229

ISBN 13: 978 0 86037 431 2
ISBN 13: 978 0 86037 426 8 (pbk)

Typeset by: N.A.Qaddoura
Cover design by: Imtiaze A. Manjra
Printed and bound by: Antony Rowe Ltd, Chippenham, Wiltshire

Contents

Transliteration Table

Arabic Consonants

Initial, unexpressed medial and final:

ء ʾ	د d	ض ḍ	ك k
ب b	ذ dh	ط ṭ	ل l
ت t	ر r	ظ ẓ	م m
ث th	ز z	ع ʿ	ن n
ج j	س s	غ gh	هـ h
ح ḥ	ش sh	ف f	و w
خ kh	ص ṣ	ق q	ي y

Vowels, diphthongs, etc.

Short: ــَ a ــِ i ــُ u

Long: اـَ ā ـِي ī ــُو ū

Diphthongs: ــَوْ aw

ــَىْ ay

Introduction
Where to Turn in Hard Situations

Sayyid Quṭb was one of the best Arabic writers of his generation. His literary talent made of him a poet, a novelist, a literary critic and a prose writer of distinction. His style was lucid and powerful. He was very dextrous at driving his point home, particularly when he felt that a basic idea had largely been ignored by people. Indeed he felt duty bound to put it to them in all possible ways, so that even a casual reader would not miss its import. At times, he dwells at length on a particular point because he wants his readers to share with him its significance, effects and ramifications. This is why some accuse him of repetitiveness. Yet when we read Sayyid Quṭb in Arabic, we rarely feel the sort of repetitiveness that causes boredom. This is mainly because of his exceptional ability in using an inexhaustible wealth of words, expressions and images. When he discusses a central idea, he is without peers.

In the present volume, the author comments at length on the second verse in *Sūrah* 35, The Originator, speaking on how God's grace changes even the hardest situation into one of ease and comfort. The verse states: "*Whatever grace God opens up to man, none can withhold it; and whatever He withholds, none other than Him can release. He alone is Almighty, Wise.*" He takes up every aspect of hardship and shows how it is transformed by God's grace into something that brings no pain, worry, anxiety or suffering. He also tells us how a believer feels God's mercy even when encountering what most people would describe as intolerable. As we read we may take this as the word of a firm believer whose contribution in intellectual debate is very useful. Yet at the same time, we feel that there is more to it than this. We soon realize what he is driving at when he tells us about his personal experience. We see him at this point a firm believer who is full of humility. He has no desire to speak about himself, yet he feels duty bound to express his gratitude to God and to present to us what gives greater credence to the ideas he has just explained.

Here Sayyid Qutb speaks of a time when he himself was at a very low ebb, under immense stress, with no expectation of a change that would end this hardship. The people around him also suffered. He does not tell us the details of this situation, nor what sort of distress he suffered. Yet it is not difficult to determine to what hardship he is referring. The *Sūrah* occurs in Volume 22 of the Arabic edition, which was one of the early volumes after he resumed writing. He had published 19 volumes before his second imprisonment in 1954, which lasted for ten years. He resumed publication after the situation had settled down and when the severe restrictions that did not allow giving him books or writing materials could be circumvented. These could then be smuggled to him during infrequent family visits, or when his health deteriorated and he had to be moved to hospital. Resumption of publication thus took place in 1958.

Sayyid Qutb's early period of imprisonment was extremely hard. Tens of thousands of the Muslim Brotherhood were rounded up. The Brotherhood puts the number at 61,000, while Nasser himself referred to these mass arrests in one of his speeches, in 1968, saying that "in 1954 we arrested 18,000 in one day." Torture was inflicted on all prisoners, without exception. Conditions in prison were very poor. Often there was no room in the cells for all the inmates to lie down at night, and they had to take turns at standing while the others slept. Early in 1955, Sayyid Qutb was due for trial, but this could not take place because of a severe chest infection that caused him to discharge blood from his mouth when he tried to speak. The great protest throughout the Muslim world against the execution of four of the leaders of the Brotherhood and two of its members caused the Egyptian government to announce that there would be no more death sentences. It was only because of this announcement that Sayyid Qutb escaped death at that time, receiving instead a sentence of 15 years imprisonment.

The way he describes the hardship he endured, referring to the fact that everyone around him suffered great distress, points clearly to this period. Depression is infectious in the same way as mirth and happiness are. If one finds oneself in the midst of a large group of people, everyone of whom is in pain, sadness, grief and distress, one cannot help but be distressed. If we add to this that Sayyid Quṭb was unjustly imprisoned, with no end to this in sight, and if we add that he was tortured to the point when he felt that his tormentors were trying to destroy his dignity and self respect, we realize that he and all around him were greatly distressed.

He tells us that in this situation God let him feel His grace through contemplation of the following Qur'ānic verse: "*Whatever grace God opens up to man, none can withhold it; and whatever He withholds, none other than Him can release. He alone is Almighty, Wise.*" (35: 2) The way he comments on this verse suggests two things: the first that he wants everyone of his readers to understand it fully, realizing that God's grace is closer to us than even the distress we may actually be suffering. We should trust to His mercy and realize that whatever adversity we go through is only momentary and can be turned into a positive situation if we would only appreciate God's grace, which is with us all at every moment of our lives. Its gates are wide open, if only we would enter.

Secondly, Sayyid Quṭb did not lose sight of this truth of the permanent availability of God's grace, even in the most stressful situations, for the rest of his life. When I met him in 1964, a few months after his release from prison, my clearest impression was that this one man, on his own, was stronger than Nasser with all his police state and security apparatus. Later in 1965, when he was offered several chances to leave Egypt, escaping the inevitable mass arrests, torture and death, he refused preferring to share all the hardship of this second wave of oppression.[1] He felt that should he leave Egypt, he would be in the same position as a commanding officer deserting his troops when things go wrong on the battlefield.

---

1. Details of these offers to leave Egypt are given in the Introduction to Volume 6. – Editor's Note.

Sayyid Quṭb was very clear as to the nature of the battle he was fighting. He never entertained the idea of seizing power by force to establish an Islamic state. He was out to win the hearts and minds of people, particularly the young, in order to bring about a new Islamic revival through education, not military training; using the pen, not the gun; changing attitudes through books and speeches, rather than tanks and artillery. He considered the battle of education to be harder and to take longer than any plan to seize power by force and establish a revolutionary government. Besides, he did not accept that a true Islamic state could be established by force, even though its government might have the support of the armed forces. To him, Islamic government is assigned a heavy trust which it must deliver, and this can only be done by people of unshakeable belief abiding by the teachings of their faith. The only method that can produce such people is education. The hard tests which the Muslim Brotherhood in Egypt went through were part of that education process. These tests separated the truly committed to Islam among its members from the weaker elements. A committed movement that works for Islamic revival must always be ready to make sacrifices. Its members must be clear that they can expect nothing in this life, not even victory for Islam through their own efforts. These efforts are a long term investment which matures in the life to come. Its returns are very rich indeed, but these returns are not due here in this life.

However, there is one return on this investment, in which one pledges everything including one's life, which is given here and now. This is the grace God opens up to His servants. It comes in all situations. We feel it in our hearts and we experience it even when we are going through very hard and stressful times. When we look up to God appealing for His grace, with sincerity and devotion, it never fails to come. God's promise is very clear as He says: "*God's grace is ever near to the righteous.*" (7: 56)

It is important, however, to remember that tests and hardships can be experienced by the whole Muslim community. The great hardship suffered by the Muslim Brotherhood in Egypt was indeed far-reaching, but its target was only one group of the population. It is true that others who were not members of the Brotherhood were also victims, either because they advocated Islamic revival by different methods when the Nasser government was opposed to any such revival, or because they were simply taken by mistake. Still, the sufferers only represented a section of the population. There may come times when the entire Muslim community suffers. *Sūrah* 33, The Confederates, which is the first in this volume, speaks of such a time experienced by the first Muslim community, in Madinah. This was when the rest of Arabia, idolaters and Jews, collaborated against them, declaring their aim as the final extermination of Islam and the Muslims. A force of 10,000 fighters from the major tribes of Quraysh and Ghaṭafān, as well as other Arabian tribes, laid siege to Madinah where the Muslim community lived. They were only prevented from storming the city by the moat dug by the Muslims to defend their city when they realized the approaching danger. Then the Jewish tribe of Qurayẓah, who lived at the other end of the city and were bound by a treaty of friendship with the Muslims, broke their pact to join the attacking forces. The siege continued for nearly a month. In describing the situation in Madinah at the time, I wrote:

> Skirmishes on the Quraysh front were now much more frequent. Parades of forces taken in turn by the Quraysh commanders were a daily occurrence. One has to remember here that each time a division of the enemy forces went on parade, the Muslims went on full alert. Their position was a defensive one. They, therefore, had to guard against any action their enemies might take. Every movement was watched and every eventuality was prepared for.
>
> While these parades attracted the Muslims' attention for a time, skirmishes of an ever-increasing intensity presented an imminent danger. One such engagement took place when a battalion of the Quraysh army launched an attack on the position where the Prophet himself stood. He and his Companions fought hard to repel it. The fighting continued all day and well into the night. The fighting was so fierce that neither the Prophet nor any of his Companions was able to offer any of the obligatory prayers on that day. All of them missed the three prayers of *Ẓuhr*, *ʿAṣr* and *Maghrib*...

The Qurayẓah themselves took part in the systematic intensification of the pressure on the Muslims. It seems that they were creating impressions that they were ready to launch an attack on the Muslims at any moment in order to divert their attentions and make it easy for the Quraysh to cross the moat and put their plan into operation. The situation was so critical as far as the Muslims were concerned that the Prophet did not allow any of his Companions to go back to Madinah for any reason without carrying his full armour. This was a precaution against any trap the Qurayẓah might have set for the Muslim soldiers.

One evening, it was reported to the Prophet that the Qurayẓah were about to launch a night attack on Madinah and its civilian population. This was not just idle talk. The Prophet had to treat the report seriously. He sent two units of his Companions to guard Madinah that night. The first unit of 200 men was commanded by Salamah ibn Aslam and assigned the task of guarding one side of the city. The other unit was even larger: Zayd ibn Ḥārithah commanded 300 men and was given the task of providing a guard for the rest of Madinah. Some of the Prophet's Companions described the difficulty of their situation in those days by saying that they were much more worried about their women and children being attacked by the Qurayẓah than about facing the much larger force of the Quraysh and the Ghaṭafān. It was apparently a time when every moment brought something to worry about. The Jews of the Qurayẓah had easy access to Madinah and apparently they sent some of their men to frighten the Muslim women and children. One of them was killed by Ṣafiyyah bint 'Abd al-Muṭṭalib, the Prophet's aunt, when she saw the man moving suspiciously very close to the quarters of the Muslim women.[2]

During that period, the entire Muslim community faced a sustained threat of annihilation. There was no safe position to be had. No man,

2. Adil Salahi, *Muhammad: Man and Prophet*, Leicester: The Islamic Foundation, 2002, pp. 445–446.

woman or child was secure. Yet God's grace was ever near. When they demonstrated their readiness to face the situation squarely, and not to compromise in the face of danger, God granted the Muslims victory without even the need to fight. This victory was consummate, as it marked a major turning point in the fortunes of this fledgling community. It was now the major power in Arabia, and it could no longer be easily challenged. One year later, a peace treaty was concluded that allowed the Muslims to advocate their faith in peace throughout Arabia, and within a further four years, the whole of Arabia was transformed into the land of Islam. All this was accomplished because God opened the gates of His grace to the Muslim community after they had amply demonstrated their commitment, steadfastness in the face of adversity, and dedication to their cause. They would brook no compromise on any point of their faith. They were ready to sacrifice all: wealth, self and family. When all this was clear to all, the gates of God's grace were opened wide. The pincer attack carefully strategized by the opposing forces did not materialize, and instead the attacking armies left of their own accord, the treacherous Qurayẓah surrendered unconditionally, and the Muslims held the initiative.

Here was a case of the whole Muslim community enduring great hardship but remaining steadfast. In Sayyid Qutb's case, it was an individual going through a period of great personal distress but firmly holding to his faith. In both cases God's grace was not slow in coming. When it was bestowed, it soon overflowed, enriching the life of both individual and community.

Today, Muslims all over the world are going through a long period of stress. Poor economic conditions have continued in most Muslim countries since the days of colonialism. Dictatorial governments, which are common in the great majority of Muslim countries, have weakened the social fabric of the community and caused much hardship. Corruption, which mushrooms and flourishes under dictatorship, has ensured that the wealth of many a Muslim country is plundered, while the majority of the population live in dire poverty. Injustice is practised at every level. In too many countries, large numbers of ordinary people have to flee in order to escape imprisonment, torture and even death, for no crime they commit other than expressing a point of view that is at variance with the policy of the dictatorial regime. Indeed many suffer such a fate without even entertaining such a point of view: they are the victims of false reports or unfortunate circumstances. Many are taken by mistake in the all too eager hurry of government security forces to round up suspected opponents.

When the two waves of mass arrests of Muslim Brotherhood members took place in Egypt, in 1954 and 1965, a number of Christian Egyptians found themselves in prison accused of being members of the Brotherhood. When they managed to persuade the prison authorities that they were Christian, and could not possibly be members of that organization, some were released, but others were still incarcerated. They were told that they had been placed with the Muslim Brotherhood by mistake; they should have been placed with the Communists. Ironic as this may be, it is not uncommon. It happens under all dictatorial regimes. People are taken by mistake, stay in prison for many years, and are then released without even being told why they had been held. One former prisoner told me: "I was released after spending 13 months in prison. Only when I was discharged, did they ask me my name." Does this sound shocking? I know another prisoner in a different country who was summoned to the prison office where he was surprised to see a smile on the director's face. As he was offered a seat, a cup of coffee was placed before him. He was then told the good news: "Your case was submitted to a tribunal which looked into it and found you innocent. You are now a free man." He was released, having spent ten years in prison. He was judged innocent by a tribunal which did not find it necessary to ask him a single question.

At the same time, major powers forge alliances against Muslim countries, destroying them one by one. Three wars have recently been waged against three separate Muslim countries with flimsy and concocted pretexts. Afghanistan and Lebanon were destroyed by much superior firepower, with the population in both countries screaming: why? Iraq was occupied, with scores of its civilian population meeting their death day after day. The world stood watching, unable or unwilling to lift a finger as peaceful women, children and civilians of all creeds died under the rubble of their homes. We are told that this is all part of the war on terrorism. To many free thinking people everywhere in the world, the phrase now sounds obscene. It is no more than a thin cover for the war on Islam. Some may dispute this, saying that it is only an American bid to control all oil resources. This is only a secondary reason, because Saddam Hussein would have placed Iraqi oil under American control in return for staying in power. Besides, Afghanistan and Lebanon had no oil.

The ills that beset the Muslim world are numerous, and it is no wonder that in many Muslim countries the way out seems exceedingly obscure. When one is struggling against adverse circumstances on several fronts, one can hardly think of a partial, let alone total solution. The same is the case with countries and communities. Unless something gives, or a ray of light appears from somewhere, the darkness will inevitably increase. Yet Muslims everywhere should learn that the light is available to them at all times. They only need to seek it and it will soon begin to remove all their troubles. They should begin by understanding the Qur'ānic verse we stated at the outset: "*Whatever grace God opens up to man, none can withhold it; and whatever He withholds, none other than Him can release. He alone is Almighty, Wise.*" (35: 2) What they need is for God's grace to be forthcoming, and it will certainly be forthcoming once they mend their relations with the Almighty, trust in Him alone, and look nowhere else for help. They certainly need to do all they can to deal with their various situations. They must, however, adhere to their Islamic values and standards. They cannot say that the US fights an immoral war against us, so we can be similarly immoral in fighting back its aggression. If a bomber belonging to the US and its allies drops its deadly bombs on people celebrating a wedding, as happened in both Iraq and Afghanistan, Muslims cannot use this as justification for planting a bomb on a train in Madrid or London. Muslims must abide by Islamic teachings which are clear in prohibiting any digression from moral values. They must remember what 'Umar told his army commander as he set out on an expedition: "Muslims win victory because of their enemy's disobedience of God's laws. If we were equal to them in such disobedience, we would be no match for them."

Again I say that God's grace is available, and it can remove all the problems faced by the Muslim community everywhere. With God's grace, no situation is too hard to tolerate, as Sayyid Quṭb admirably explains in his commentary on the above verse. In order to qualify for an abundance of God's grace, Muslims must adhere to their faith and its principles, and they must remain patient in adversity, realizing that all these troubles are part of the test they should pass. They cannot pass it by any means other than remaining true to their faith, being patient in adversity, placing their full trust in God, the Lord of Grace, the Ever Merciful. They have numerous precedents in their own history, and in the history of the divine message and all God's messengers, from Noah to Muḥammad, (peace be upon them all).

London   **Adil Salahi**
Rajab 1428 H.
August 2007.

Note on the translation of the opening of the Qur'ānic *sūrahs*

All *sūrahs* of the Qur'ān except one start with the phrase *Bismillāh al-Rahmān al-Rahīm*, which, starting with this volume, we are rendering in a different way from that we have so far used. This phrase is composed of four Arabic words, the first two of which mean 'In the Name of God'. The other two words add two of God's attributes derived from the same root, *Rahima*, which signifies grace and mercy. While the second of these attributes, *al-Rahīm*, is commonly used as a superlative form of granting mercy, the first, *al-Rahmān*, is used only to refer to God. In fact, it was never used in Arabic before Islam.

Commentators on the Qur'ān have often spoken on this usage, trying to show why *al-Rahmān* is a divine quality that cannot be attributed to any human being. Their clearest point is that *al-Rahmān* should be treated as a proper noun and a name of God, just like His most common Arabic name, *Allah*. Translators of the Qur'ān have always struggled to produce a translation of the phrase that distinguishes the two attributes, yet retains their common connotations. Drawing mostly on the terms of compassion, grace and mercy, they came up with forms like, "the merciful, the compassionate" (Arberry); "most gracious, most merciful" (Yusuf Ali); "most gracious, dispenser of grace" (Asad); "Lord of mercy, giver of mercy" (Abdel Haleem); "all merciful, most merciful" (Abdalhaqq and Bewley). The Saheeh International translation opted to retain the Arabic form without giving a translation. The form we have used so far, "the merciful, the beneficent", shares this approach.

In a recent discussion with Dr Muhammad Haitham al-Khayat, a scholar whom I greatly admire and respect, he pointed out that use of *al-Rahmān* in its frequent occurrences in the Qur'ān consistently bears connotations of power, might and dominion alongside those of grace and mercy. Therefore, an accurate translation of the term should bring out these additional connotations. This is perhaps most clearly apparent where it is employed in *surahs* 50 *Qāf*, 67 *al-Mulk*, and 19 *Maryam*. The word occurs once in the first of these *surahs*, four times in the second and on no less than fourteen occasions in the third. A discerning look at these instances will not fail to see that the connotations of power and ability to punish, smite and destroy are equally, if not more, prominent than those of grace, mercy and compassion. Therefore, we can say that *al-Raḥmān* connotes "the exercise of mercy on the basis of free choice by one who is able to inflict severe punishment without fear of any consequence".

By contrast *al-Raḥīm* stresses the availability of God's mercy in all situations and to all creatures. People only need to appeal for it and it is certain to be granted. Indeed it is given at all times without such appeals. There are numerous aspects of God's mercy that people enjoy, and often without appreciation or gratitude.

After long reflection and consideration of all these aspects I have now settled on a new form of translating these two attributes of God. Thus, from here on *al-Raḥmān* will be rendered as 'Lord of Grace' and *al-Raḥīm* as 'the Ever Merciful'. Thus, the opening of each *surah* of the Qur'ān, except *Surah* 9, will be given as:

"In the Name of God, the Lord of Grace, the Ever Merciful"

Adil Salahi

SŪRAH 33

Al-Aḥzāb

(The Confederates)

Prologue

This *sūrah* describes a practical aspect of the first Muslim community's life over a period stretching from shortly after the Battle of Badr in year 2 to shortly before the signing of the al-Ḥudaybiyah Peace Treaty four years later. In this respect it gives a true and direct description of the Muslim community in Madinah. It refers to many of the events that took place during that period and outlines certain regulations which it either initiates or endorses for the fledgling Muslim community.

The comments on events and regulations are relatively few, constituting only a small portion of the *sūrah*. Indeed, these comments serve only to link these events and regulations to the central concept of faith and submission to God. This is how we read the opening verses: *"Prophet! Have fear of God and do not yield to the unbelievers and the hypocrites. God is certainly All-Knowing, Wise. Follow what is revealed to you by your Lord; for God is well aware of all that you do. Place your trust in God; for God alone is worthy of all trust. Never has God put two hearts in one man's body."* (Verses 1–4) Early on, the *sūrah* comments on some social regulations: *"This is written down in God's decree. We did accept a solemn pledge from all the prophets: from you, [Muḥammad], and from Noah, Abraham, Moses and Jesus son of Mary. From all did We accept a weighty, solemn pledge. God will question the truthful about the truth [entrusted to them]. He has prepared painful suffering for the unbelievers."* (Verses 6–8) A little further on we are shown the attitude of the weak-hearted when the confederate tribes laid siege to Madinah: *"Say: 'Flight will benefit you nothing. If you flee from natural death or from being slain, you will only be left to enjoy life for a little while. Say: 'Who can keep you away from God if it be His will to harm you, or if it be His will to show you mercy?' Other than God they can find none to protect them or to bring them support."* (Verses 16–17) A piece of social legislation that went against the familiar practice in pre-Islamic days is followed by the comment: *"Whenever God and His Messenger have decided a matter, it is not for a believing man or a believing woman to claim freedom of choice in that matter."* (Verse 36) Finally, we have a statement that sets the human mission against a universal background: *"We offered the trust to the heavens and the earth and the mountains, but they refused to bear it and were afraid to receive it. Yet man took it up. He has always been prone to be wicked, foolish."* (Verse 72)

The *sūrah* depicts a period of time when the Islamic character of both the community and the state had begun to take shape but had not yet developed sufficiently or acquired its full authority. That took place after Makkah fell to Islam and people began to embrace the new faith in large numbers allowing the Muslim state and its new system to establish their roots.

The *sūrah* undertakes an important part of social reorganization imparting the distinctive Islamic features of family and community life, outlining their basis in Islamic teachings. It also modifies or outlaws certain practices and traditions, bringing all these within the framework of the Islamic concept of life and society.

It is within the overall discussion of these situations and regulations that the confrontation with the confederate tribes and the Qurayẓah expedition are discussed. We are informed of the attitudes of the unbelievers, the hypocrites and the Jews during these events, their schemes to weaken the Muslim community and how they always tried to undermine Islamic moral standards, even in Muslim homes. It was precisely this sort of derogatory behaviour that aimed at undermining the Muslim community either through direct military action and a corresponding defeatism or through efforts to erode the social and moral fabric of Muslim society. Moreover, these events left clear marks on the Muslim community to the extent that certain social aspects and particular concepts required modification. Thus the *sūrah* appears to be an integrated unit with a common thread running through its subject matter. Moreover, the time frame around which it works also constitutes a unifying factor.

The *sūrah* begins with a directive issued to the Prophet that he must fear God and pay no heed to the unbelievers and the hypocrites. On the contrary, he should obey God and rely on Him alone. This opening relates all that the *sūrah* includes to the central principle that forms the basis of all Islamic teachings, legislation, its social system and morality. It is the principle that formulates the Islamic concept of God and the requirements to submit to Him, implement the code He has outlined and place all our trust in Him.

A decisive word is then given on certain social traditions and practices. This starts with outlining a basic fact: *"Never has God put two hearts in one man's body."* (Verse 4) This alludes to the fact that man cannot live in two different universes or follow two different systems. Should he do so he would stumble and become a hypocrite. Since he has only one heart, he must look up to One God and follow one system to the exclusion of all other things, familiar and well established as these may be.

The *sūrah* immediately moves on to abolish the practice of *ẓihār*, which involves a man swearing to his wife that she is to him like his mother's back, meaning that she is as unlawful to him to marry as his mother: *"Nor does He make your wives whom you declare to be as unlawful to you as your mothers' bodies truly your mothers."* (Verse 4) It makes clear that these are mere words that cannot establish a fact. They do not make a mother out of a wife; the wife remains the man's wife. It follows this with abolishing the practice of child adoption: *"Likewise, He does not make your adopted sons truly your sons."* (Verse 4) Thus inheritance within an adopting family is no longer valid. (We will

3

discuss this in detail later on.) In contrast, the *sūrah* establishes the overall authority God assigns to His Messenger over all Muslims, placing his authority above what they may wish for themselves. It further establishes a sense of motherly relation between the Prophet's wives and all believers: *"The Prophet has more claim on the believers than they have on their own selves; and his wives are their mothers."* (Verse 6) The practical effects of the bond of brotherhood established between Muslim individuals shortly after the migration of Makkan Muslims to Madinah are terminated, so as to restrict inheritance and the payment of blood money to real kinsfolk: *"Blood relatives have, according to God's decree, a stronger claim upon one another than other believers [of Madinah] and those who have migrated [for God's sake]."* (Verse 6) Thus, earlier temporary measures are abrogated in favour of natural and permanent ones.

The following comment makes clear that the new system derives from the Islamic code and from God's ruling. It is written in God's book and established in the covenant made with all prophets, particularly those of them endowed with stronger resolve. In this way the Qur'ān gives Islamic legislation and principles their appropriate place within people's thoughts and consciences.

This then outlines the first part of the *sūrah*. The second part shows God's great favour as He repelled the attacking forces of the confederates who besieged Madinah. It describes the confrontation with confederate forces and the Qurayẓah Expedition vividly, painting successive images that show inner feelings, outward action and dialogue between groups and individuals. Within the overall picture of the battle and its events relevant directives are issued at the proper junctures. Furthermore, the reporting of events is followed by comments aimed at establishing sound values for the Muslim community. The Qur'ānic method is to paint the action exactly as it took place, stating both apparent and inner feelings, and bringing these into sharp relief. It then gives believers its verdict about their actions, criticizing any deviation and praising what is sound and correct. It also gives directives to avoid error and confirm right practice and values. It relates all this to God's will, human nature and universal laws.

4

Thus, the discussion of the confrontation and the battle starts with the following verse: *"Believers! Remember the blessings God bestowed on you when hosts came down upon you. We let loose against them a windstorm and hosts that you could not see. Yet God sees all that you do."* (Verse 9) In the middle of the discussion, the following facts are highlighted: *"Say: 'Flight will benefit you nothing. If you flee from natural death or from being slain, you will only be left to enjoy life for a little while. Say: 'Who can keep you away from God if it be His will to harm you, or if it be His will to show you mercy?' Other than God they can find none to protect them or to bring them support."* (Verses 16–17) *"In God's Messenger you have a good model for everyone who looks with hope to God and the Last Day, and always remembers God."* (Verse 21) The discussion is finally concluded thus: *"God will surely reward the truthful for having been true to their word, and will punish the hypocrites, if that be His will, or accept their repentance. God is indeed Much-Forgiving, Merciful."* (Verse 24)

Alongside its discussion of events the *sūrah* shows how the true believers looked at the situation as it developed and portrays the contrasting feelings of the hypocrites. This enables us to distinguish sound values from false ones: *"The hypocrites and the sick at heart said: 'God and His Messenger promised us nothing but delusions'."* (Verse 12) *"When the believers saw the Confederate forces they said: 'This is what God and His Messenger have promised us! Truly spoke God and His Messenger.' This only served to strengthen their faith and their submission to God."* (Verse 22) The outcome is then given in decisive terms: *"God turned back the unbelievers in all their rage and fury; they gained no advantage. He spared the believers the need to fight. God is Most Powerful, Almighty."* (Verse 25)

When this second part is concluded we are introduced to the decision that gave the Prophet's wives a choice. They had asked him for a more comfortable standard of living after the Muslim community became more prosperous, having gained much booty as a result of the siege of Qurayẓah. They were asked to choose either the fine things of life or relinquish these in preference for pleasing God and His Messenger and earning a better position in the life to come. They all chose to be with

5

God and His Messenger, preferring this to all worldly riches. They were also told that they would have double the reward if they maintained the path of goodness and remained God-fearing, and double the punishment should they commit any gross indecency. The *surah* explains that this doubling of reward and punishment was a result of their noble status, their relation with the Prophet and the revelation and recitation of the Qur'ān in their own homes, as well as the wisdom they received from the Prophet. This third part of the *surah* concludes with an outline of the reward given to all believers, men and women.

The fourth part makes an indirect reference to the case of Zaynab bint Jaḥsh, a cousin of the Prophet belonging to a noble Qurayshī family and her marriage to Zayd ibn Ḥārithah, a former slave given as a gift to Muḥammad long before his prophethood. The first thing it says about Zayd makes it clear that all believers, men and women, are subject to God's decision in any matter; they do not even have a say in their own personal business. It is God's will that determines everything, and they have to submit to it fully: *"Whenever God and His Messenger have decided a matter, it is not for a believing man or a believing woman to claim freedom of choice in that matter. Whoever disobeys God and His Messenger strays far into error."* (Verse 36)

This marriage soon ends in divorce and the situation provides a practical example for the abolition of the effects of child adoption. God's Messenger himself is chosen to provide this example, because adoption was a deeply rooted tradition in the Arabian environment, and its practical effects were very difficult to break. Hence, God's Messenger was to bear this new burden as part of his mission to shape the new Muslim society: *"Then, when Zayd had come to the end of his union with her, We gave her to you in marriage, so that no blame should attach to the believers for marrying the spouses of their adopted sons when the latter have come to the end of their union with them. God's will must be fulfilled."* (Verse 37) A clear statement of the nature of the relation between the Prophet and the believer then follows: *"Muḥammad is not the father of any one of your men, but is God's Messenger and the seal of all prophets."* (Verse 40)

6

This part concludes with clear directives to the Prophet and the believers: "*Do not yield to the unbelievers and the hypocrites, and disregard their hurting actions. Place your trust in God; for God alone is worthy of all trust.*" (Verse 48)

The fifth part begins by making a statement on the status of a woman who gets divorced before the consummation of her marriage. It moves on to organize the Prophet's marital life, stating which women are lawful for him to marry and which are not. This is followed by directives defining the relation between Muslims and the Prophet's homes and wives, both during his lifetime and after his death. It requires them not to mix with any men other than their fathers, sons, brothers, paternal and maternal nephews, other women and their slaves. It states that those who sought to disparage the Prophet and his wives would face severe punishment; they would be punished both in this life and the life to come. This gives us an impression that the hypocrites and others frequently resort to such disparagement.

Then follows a directive to the Prophet's wives, daughters and all Muslim women, to draw some of their outer garments over their bodies. "*This will be more conducive to their being recognized and not affronted.*" (Verse 59) It warns the hypocrites and others similar to them that they may be made to evacuate Madinah in a similar way as the two Jewish tribes of Qaynuqāʿ and al-Naḍīr were made to do, or that they might be dealt with in the same way as the Qurayẓah Jews. All this implies that these people resorted to foul methods to harm the Muslim community in Madinah.

The final part of the *sūrah* mentions that people frequently ask about the Last Hour. Such questions are answered simply by saying that its knowledge belongs to God. They only need to know that it could be very close. This is followed by an image of the punishment meted out on the Day of Judgement. "*On the day when their faces shall be tossed about in the fire, they will say: 'Would that we had obeyed God and obeyed His Messenger.'*" (Verse 66) It also describes how unbelievers then feel towards their leaders for having led them astray: "*And they shall say: 'Our Lord! We have paid heed to our masters and our leaders, but they have led us astray from the right path. Our Lord! Give double suffering, and banish them utterly from Your grace.'*" (Verses 67–68)

The *sūrah* ends on a highly powerful note that leaves a strong and lasting effect: "*We offered the trust to the heavens and the earth and the mountains, but they refused to bear it and were afraid to receive it. Yet man took it up. He has always been prone to be wicked, foolish. So it is that God will punish the hypocrites, men and women, as well as the men and women who associate partners with Him; and He will turn in mercy to the believers, both men and women. God is Much-Forgiving, Merciful.*" (Verses 72–73)

This conclusion illustrates the heavy burden placed on humanity in general and the Muslim community in particular, since it is this community that shoulders this great trust of faith as well as its advocacy and implementation at individual and community levels. This is in perfect harmony with the particular atmosphere of the *sūrah*, and with the nature of the social system Islam lays down.

I

False Relations Abolished

Al-Aḥzāb (The Confederates)

In the Name of God, the Lord of Grace, the Ever Merciful

بِسْمِ اللَّهِ الرَّحْمَنِ الرَّحِيمِ

Prophet! Have fear of God and do not yield to the unbelievers and the hypocrites. God is certainly All-Knowing, Wise. (1)

يَـٰٓأَيُّهَا ٱلنَّبِيُّ ٱتَّقِ ٱللَّهَ وَلَا تُطِعِ ٱلۡكَـٰفِرِينَ وَٱلۡمُنَـٰفِقِينَ إِنَّ ٱللَّهَ كَانَ عَلِيمًا حَكِيمًا ١

Follow what is revealed to you by your Lord; for God is well aware of all that you do. (2)

وَٱتَّبِعۡ مَا يُوحَىٰٓ إِلَيۡكَ مِن رَّبِّكَ إِنَّ ٱللَّهَ كَانَ بِمَا تَعۡمَلُونَ خَبِيرًا ٢

Place your trust in God; for God alone is worthy of all trust. (3)

وَتَوَكَّلۡ عَلَى ٱللَّهِ وَكَفَىٰ بِٱللَّهِ وَكِيلًا ٣

Never has God put two hearts in one man's body. Nor does He make your wives whom you

مَّا جَعَلَ ٱللَّهُ لِرَجُلٍ مِّن قَلۡبَيۡنِ فِي جَوۡفِهِ وَمَا جَعَلَ أَزۡوَٰجَكُمُ ٱلَّـٰٓـِٔي

declare to be as unlawful to you as your mothers' bodies truly your mothers. Likewise, He does not make your adopted sons truly your sons. These are only words you utter with your mouths, but God says the truth and He alone shows the right path. (4)

تَظَٰهِرُونَ مِنۡهُنَّ أُمَّهَٰتِكُمۡ وَمَا جَعَلَ أَدۡعِيَآءَكُمۡ أَبۡنَآءَكُمۡ ذَٰلِكُمۡ قَوۡلُكُم بِأَفۡوَٰهِكُمۡ وَٱللَّهُ يَقُولُ ٱلۡحَقَّ وَهُوَ يَهۡدِي ٱلسَّبِيلَ ٤

Call them by their fathers' names; that is more just in God's sight. If you do not know who their fathers are, then treat them as your brethren in faith and your protégés. You shall not be blamed if you make a mistake, but for what your hearts intend. God is indeed Much-Forgiving, Merciful. (5)

ٱدۡعُوهُمۡ لِأٓبَآئِهِمۡ هُوَ أَقۡسَطُ عِندَ ٱللَّهِ فَإِن لَّمۡ تَعۡلَمُوٓاْ ءَابَآءَهُمۡ فَإِخۡوَٰنُكُمۡ فِي ٱلدِّينِ وَمَوَٰلِيكُمۡ وَلَيۡسَ عَلَيۡكُمۡ جُنَاحٌ فِيمَآ أَخۡطَأۡتُم بِهِۦ وَلَٰكِن مَّا تَعَمَّدَتۡ قُلُوبُكُمۡ وَكَانَ ٱللَّهُ غَفُورٗا رَّحِيمًا ٥

The Prophet has more claim on the believers than they have on their own selves; and his wives are their mothers. Blood relatives have, according to God's decree, a stronger claim upon one another than other believers [of Madinah] and those who have migrated [for God's sake]. None the less, you are to act with kindness towards your close friends. This is written down in God's decree. (6)

ٱلنَّبِيُّ أَوۡلَىٰ بِٱلۡمُؤۡمِنِينَ مِنۡ أَنفُسِهِمۡ وَأَزۡوَٰجُهُۥٓ أُمَّهَٰتُهُمۡ وَأُوْلُواْ ٱلۡأَرۡحَامِ بَعۡضُهُمۡ أَوۡلَىٰ بِبَعۡضٖ فِي كِتَٰبِ ٱللَّهِ مِنَ ٱلۡمُؤۡمِنِينَ وَٱلۡمُهَٰجِرِينَ إِلَّآ أَن تَفۡعَلُوٓاْ إِلَىٰٓ أَوۡلِيَآئِكُم مَّعۡرُوفٗا كَانَ ذَٰلِكَ فِي ٱلۡكِتَٰبِ مَسۡطُورًا ٦

We did accept a solemn pledge from all the prophets: from you, [Muḥammad], and from Noah, Abraham, Moses and Jesus son of Mary. From all did We accept a weighty, solemn pledge. (7)

وَإِذْ أَخَذْنَا مِنَ ٱلنَّبِيِّـۧنَ مِيثَـٰقَهُمْ وَمِنكَ وَمِن نُّوحٍ وَإِبْرَٰهِيمَ وَمُوسَىٰ وَعِيسَى ٱبْنِ مَرْيَمَ وَأَخَذْنَا مِنْهُم مِّيثَـٰقًا غَلِيظًا ٧

God will question the truthful about the truth [entrusted to them]. He has prepared painful suffering for the unbelievers. (8)

لِّيَسْـَٔلَ ٱلصَّـٰدِقِينَ عَن صِدْقِهِمْ وَأَعَدَّ لِلْكَـٰفِرِينَ عَذَابًا أَلِيمًا ٨

Setting the Scene

"Prophet! Have fear of God and do not yield to the unbelievers and the hypocrites. God is certainly All-Knowing, Wise. Follow what is revealed to you by your Lord; for God is well aware of all that you do. Place your trust in God; for God alone is worthy of all trust." (Verses 1–3) Thus begins the *sūrah* which regulates certain aspects of the social and moral life of the newly born Muslim community. It is a beginning that tells us something about the nature of the Islamic system and its underlying principles. Islam is not merely a set of directives and admonitions, or manners and moral values, or a collection of laws and regulations, or traditions and practices. All these are included in Islam, but they do not make up Islam in its totality. Islam means submission to God's will, a willingness to obey its orders, observe its prohibitions, looking up to no other system and adopting no other way. It is essentially an acceptance that mankind are subject to the overall divine code that governs their life and the earth they live on, as well as other planets and stars, and indeed governs the whole universe including the realms we know nothing about. It is also a certainty that as humans the only choice we should make is to do what God orders, refrain from what He forbids, take what He makes available and await the results He brings about. This is the basic rule on which are then established laws,

11

regulations, traditions, manners and moral values. All these represent the practical manifestation of faith and submission to God. Islam is a faith that lays down a code which puts in place a specific social order. In their close interaction, these three make up Islam.

It is in this light that we should understand that the first directive in this *sūrah*, concerned as it is with the regulation of the Islamic social order, is addressed to the Prophet, requiring him to remain God-fearing. To stand in awe of God and remember that He watches over us, makes us alert, urging us to abide by every rule and implement every directive: "*Prophet! Have fear of God.*" (Verse 1)

The second directive prohibits yielding to the unbelievers and hypocrites, following their suggestions or adopting their views and methods: "*and do not yield to the unbelievers and the hypocrites.*" (Verse 1) This directive is given before the order to follow God's revelation, which suggests that the pressures brought to bear by the hypocrites and the unbelievers in Madinah and its surrounding area were very strong. Nevertheless this directive remains applicable in all situations, warning the believers against following the hypocrites and the unbelievers, particularly in questions of faith, law and social order. This guarantees for the Muslim community that its system remains pure, unadulterated by directives other than God's.

No one should be deceived by the wealth of knowledge and experience the unbelievers and hypocrites appear to possess, as were some Muslims in periods of weakness and deviation from the Islamic system. It is God who has perfect knowledge and infinite wisdom. The Islamic system is His own choice, established by His knowledge and wisdom: "*God is certainly All-Knowing, Wise.*" (Verse 1) However rich human knowledge and experience appear to be, they are only scanty.

The third direct order given at the outset is: "*Follow what is revealed to you by your Lord.*" (Verse 2) This defines the authority that issues directives that must be followed. The phrasing of this directive is particularly inspiring: the revelation is made 'to *you*' specifically, and its source is '*your* Lord', both of which add a specially personal element to the need to follow these orders even though they must be obeyed because they are issued by the One commanding obedience. This verse ends with the comment: "*for God is well aware of all that you do.*"

(Verse 2) His revelation is based on full awareness of you, your deeds and motives.

The last order in these three opening verses states: "*Place your trust in God; for God alone is worthy of all trust.*" (Verse 3) There is no need to worry about others or their scheming against you. You should place all your concerns in God's hands and He will look after them in accordance with His knowledge and wisdom. Trusting to God alone is ultimately what gives us complete reassurance. It helps us to know our limitations and leave what lies beyond our ability to the One who controls and conducts everything.

Thus, along with the instruction to disobey the unbelievers and the hypocrites we have three directives: to always remain God-fearing, to follow His revelation and to place our trust in Him alone. It is these three elements that provide the advocates of Islam with all the resources they need. Furthermore, it clearly defines the system of Islamic advocacy: from God, for God's sake, and relying on God: "*for God alone is worthy of all trust.*" (Verse 3)

These opening directives end on a strong note that refers to practical situations: "*Never has God put two hearts in one man's body.*" (Verse 4) Since it is only one heart, it needs one system providing one complete and full concept of life. It requires one standard to give consistent values and judge events and actions. Otherwise, it will be pulled apart and will have different motives and considerations. It could easily fall into the trap of hypocrisy.

Man cannot have one source for his manners and morality, another for his laws and legislation, a third for his social and economic values, and a fourth for his art and philosophy. Such a mixture does not produce a man with a sound heart: it only produces a confused medley that lacks solid form or basis. A person with faith cannot truly hold to his faith and abandon its values and requirements in any situation in life, serious or not. He cannot say a word, take an action, formulate a concept, make a decision unless he remains within the limits established by his faith, which must always be a reality in his life. This is because God has not given him more than one heart, one law and one standard of values. A person of faith cannot say of anything he does: 'I am doing this in my personal capacity and I am doing that in my Islamic

13

capacity', as we frequently hear politicians, businessmen, academics and others say. Since he is one person with one heart, he has one faith and one standard that govern all that he does and says in any and every situation. With this one heart he lives as an individual, a family man, a member of the community, a citizen of the state and the world; he lives in public and private, employer or employee, ruler or ruled, in situations of comfort or distress; having the same values and standards at all times: "*Never has God put two hearts in one man's body.*" (Verse 4)

In short, we have a single system outlined by the same revelations and submitting to the One God. A single heart cannot worship two deities, serve two masters and move in two directions.

No False Relations

The *sūrah* now moves on to abolish certain practices in order to make the family the basis of the community: "*Nor does He make your wives whom you declare to be as unlawful to you as your mothers' bodies truly your mothers. Likewise, He does not make your adopted sons truly your sons. These are only words you utter with your mouths, but God says the truth and He alone shows the right path. Call them by their fathers' names; that is more just in God's sight. If you do not know who their fathers are, then treat them as your brethren in faith and your protégés. You shall not be blamed if you make a mistake, but for what your hearts intend. God is indeed Much-Forgiving, Merciful.*" (Verses 4–5)

In pre-Islamic days a man would say to his wife, 'you are to me like my mother's back', which meant that she was forbidden for him to marry. From that moment sex between them was regarded as incestuous. Yet she remained suspended: she was neither divorced such that she could marry another man, nor married having a lawful relationship with her husband. This was one aspect of the cruelty to which women were subjected in pre-Islamic days. As Islam started to reorganize social relations, making the family the basic social unit where each new generation grows in a sound environment, it attached great importance to removing such injustices against women and to giving family relations a basis of fairness and an easy, relaxed atmosphere. One of its new laws was "*Nor does He make your wives whom you declare to be as unlawful to you as your mothers' bodies truly your mothers."* (Verse 4) The words a man utters do not change facts. Mothers and wives are totally different, and the nature of a relationship cannot be changed by the uttering of a word. Therefore, a pronouncement like this, or *zihār*, did not make a wife permanently forbidden to her husband as if she were his mother.

Some reports suggest that *zihār* was outlawed by other verses in *Sūrah* 58, The Pleading, when Aws ibn al-Ṣāmit pronounced *zihār* against his wife Khawlah bint Mālik ibn Thaʿlabah. She complained to the Prophet, saying: "Messenger of God! He took my money and used me throughout my years of strength, and I have given him children. Now when I have grown old and can no longer bear children, he makes me like his mother!" The Prophet said to her: "I am afraid you are no longer lawful to him." [Related by Ibn Mājah, al-Ḥākim and al-Bayhaqī]. She repeated her complaint several times. God then revealed the following verses:

> *God has heard the words of the woman who pleads with you concerning her husband, and complained to God. God has heard what you both had to say. God is All-Hearing, All-Seeing. Even if any of you say to their wives, 'You are to me like my mother's bodies,' they are not their mothers; their only mothers are those who gave them birth. What they say is iniquitous and false. Yet God pardons and forgives. Those who separate themselves from their wives by saying, 'You are as unlawful to me as my mother,' and then go back on what they have said, must atone by freeing a slave before the couple may resume their full marital relation. This you are enjoined to do, and God is fully aware of all that you do. However, he who does not have the means shall fast instead for two consecutive months before the couple may resume their full marital relation; and he who is unable to do it shall feed sixty needy people; this, so that you may prove your faith in God and His Messenger. Such are the bounds set by God. Grievous suffering awaits those who will not believe.* (58: 1–4)

Thus, *zihār* is treated as a temporary prohibition of marital relations; it is neither permanent nor a divorce. It must be atoned for by the freeing of a slave, or fasting for two consecutive months, or feeding 60 needy people. When such atonement is made full marital relations can be resumed, retaining the practical facts as they are. The statement in the present *sūrah* is very clear: "*Nor does He make your wives whom you declare to be as unlawful to you as your mothers' bodies truly your mothers.*" (Verse 4) The family is thus safeguarded against this unfair practice, something that represented an aspect of the maltreatment of women in pre-Islamic Arabian society.

Adoption Abolished

Similarly, the practice of adopting a child reflected flaws in the foundation of the family and society. Although chastity was highly valued by the Arabs who, as is widely known, took pride in their ancestry, there were other phenomena that moved in the opposite direction. These were generally accepted, but not in the prominent families and clans. Indeed, some individuals could not tell who their fathers were. Furthermore, if a man liked one of these 'off-spring', he could adopt him, calling him his son, and the two would then inherit each other. The same applied to some people whose real fathers were even known. In this respect, they too could be adopted. This was particularly so with captives, when children or adolescents were taken captive in a raid on a clan or during a war. If a man then wished to adopt such a captive, he would declare such adoption, and the captive would then be known as a son of his adopting father. He would then enjoy the privileges of being a son and was required to fulfil his duties as a son.

One of these was Zayd ibn Ḥārithah, of the Arab tribe of Kalb. He was taken captive when young in pre-Islamic days, then sold to Ḥakīm ibn Ḥizām who gave him as a gift to his aunt Khadījah. When she was married to the Prophet, she gave him Zayd as a gift, but Zayd's father and uncle appealed to him for Zayd's release. The Prophet then decided to give him a choice, and he chose to remain with the Prophet. Therefore, the Prophet set him free and adopted him as his son. He was then called Zayd ibn Muḥammad. When Islam started several years later, he was the first man to accept Islam from among the lower classes in society.

Subsequently, when Islam began to set family relations on their natural basis and strengthen family bonds, purging these of any distortion, it abolished adoption, making the true blood relation the only cause for a son and father to be so called. Therefore, the Qur'ān states: *"Likewise, He does not make your adopted sons truly your sons. These are only words you utter with your mouths."* (Verse 4) Words can neither change reality nor can they establish a substitute relation to that of blood, which allows for hereditary qualities resulting from conception, pregnancy and birth, and which then allows for natural feelings to be engendered. The fact is that a child is seen as a living part of its natural parents.

"But God says the truth and He alone shows the right path." (Verse 4) God says the absolute truth which admits no falsehood whatsoever. It is only right that family relations should be established on facts of marriage and birth, not on mere words. God indeed shows the right path that is in harmony with sound, undistorted human nature and which cannot be substituted by any man-made system. Needless to say, the word of truth stated by God is far stronger and more solid.

"Call them by their fathers' names; that is more just in God's sight." (Verse 5) It is only fair that a child should be called by its father's name: it is fair to the father from whom the child comes into existence, and fair to the child to take his father's name, inherit and be inherited by him, cooperate with him and provide a continuation of the lineage that relates him to his ancestors. It is also fair to put everything in its proper place and establish every relation on its natural basis, allowing no child or parent to be deprived of any special or distinctive quality. Moreover, it is only fair that no one other than the natural parent should shoulder the parental responsibility or enjoy its benefit, and no one other than a natural child should have the rights and duties of being a son or daughter.

Islam provides a system which ensures balance in family relations and gives the family a strong and real foundation. At the same time, it gives society a solid foundation that combines reality with nature. Any system that ignores the natural family is bound to fail, because it is weak and based on forgery.

Since there was much confusion in family relations in pre-Islamic Arabian society, and because of the prevalent sexual permissiveness that led to some family relations being unknown, Islam made things easy, providing certain concessions. For example, should the true father of an adopted child be unknown, the child still had its place in the Muslim community; a relation based on brotherhood in faith and patronage: *"If you do not know who their fathers are, then treat them as your brethren in faith and your protégés."* (Verse 5) This is, then, a moral relation that does not create practical commitments, such as inheritance and sharing in the payment of blood money. In pre-Islamic days, these family commitments were extended so as to apply to relations through adoption. The purpose of creating this moral relation is to give the formerly adopted child a bond in society after the abolition of adoption. The reference in the verse to those adopted children whose fathers were unknown gives us a clear picture of the prevalent confusion in family relations and the loose morality that held sway in pre-Islamic Arabia. Islam put an end to all this by establishing a society on the basis of the family unit which, in turn, is based on real marital and blood relations.

When Muslims have carefully endeavoured to call everyone by their fathers' names, they are not to be blamed for cases where they are unable to establish the true facts: *"You shall not be blamed if you make a mistake, but for what your hearts intend."* (Verse 5) This benevolent attitude results from the fact that God forgives and bestows mercy on His servants, and He never charges them with more than they can reasonably do: *"God is indeed Much-Forgiving, Merciful."* (Verse 5)

The Prophet placed a strong emphasis on the need to establish real parenthood so that the new Islamic system could put an end to the social chaos that prevailed before Islam. Those who suppress true relations are warned that they could be considered as unbelievers. A report by al-Ṭabarī mentions that Abū Bakr once recited this verse and a man called 'Abd al-Raḥmān declared: "I am one of those whose fathers are not known. I am your brother in faith." The report quotes 'Abd al-Raḥmān's son, 'Uyaynah, as saying of his father: "By God! I believe that had he known that his father was an ass, he would have

18

declared himself the son of that ass." The Prophet says: "Whoever knowingly claims to be the son of someone other than his father is not a believer."

Ending Brotherhood

Having abolished adoption, the *surah* moves on to put an end to the brotherhood institution, established by Islam following the migration of the Muslims from Makkah to Madinah. This was a practical measure to address the situation of those immigrants who had abandoned their relations and property in Makkah, and the situation of Muslims in Madinah whose relations with their families were severed as a result of their embracing Islam. At the same time, the Prophet's personal authority over all believers is emphasized and given a higher position than all blood relations, while his wives are to be seen as the spiritual mothers of all believers: "*The Prophet has more claim on the believers than they have on their own selves; and his wives are their mothers. Blood relatives have, according to God's decree, a stronger claim upon one another than other believers [of Madinah] and those who have migrated [for God's sake]. None the less, you are to act with kindness towards your close friends. This is written down in God's decree.*" (Verse 6)

When the Muhājirīn, i.e. the Muslims from Makkah, left for Madinah, they had to leave everything behind, preferring their faith to their relatives, clans, property, livelihood, friends, and life memories. They abandoned all this for their faith. Their migration in this way, abandoning all that was dear, including their own families, provided an example of how faith grips one's whole being. They provided the practical example of the integrity of the Islamic personality, confirming the Qur'ānic statement: "*Never has God put two hearts in one man's body.*" (Verse 4)

A different situation, however arose in Madinah as Islam began to infiltrate homes. The result was that some members of a family became Muslims while others did not. Relations between people were often severed; family bonds became shaky; and there was an even greater disruption of social bonds. The Muslim society was still in its infancy and the Muslim state was still more of an idea than a solid regime with lasting roots.

This gave the new faith a strong moral impetus that superseded all emotions, traditions, social institutions and bonds, making faith the only bond that unites hearts. At the same time it united the small units that separated from their natural roots in the family and the clan, thus replacing the ties of blood, family, interest, friendship, race and language. It united these Muslim units into a well-knit and coherent block that showed a high degree of solidarity, cooperation and mutual care. This was not initiated by legislative texts or government orders; instead, it was based on an inner impetus that was stronger than anything that was familiar in ordinary human life. This provided the basis for the rise of the Muslim community, which could not be otherwise established.

The Muhājirīn [i.e. the migrants from Makkah] were welcomed in Madinah by its Muslim residents, the Anṣār. They were made so welcome that the Anṣār opened their hearts and homes for them and gave them shares in their property. In fact they were so keen to make the Makkan Muslims feel welcome in their new abode that the Anṣār drew lots to decide who would take each of the Muhājirīn: this because there were only a few of the latter as compared with the great many Anṣār who were keen to host them. They, in fact, shared with the Muhājirīn everything they had, willingly and with warm hearts that betrayed no trace of avarice or showing off.

The Prophet established a bond of brotherhood between individuals of the Muhājirīn and individuals of the Anṣār, naming each two brothers, thereby giving rise to a unique bond in the history of mutual solidarity between believers in the same ideology. Indeed this brotherhood superseded the blood relationship, as it included rights of inheritance and other commitments between relatives. The resulting moral impetus was strong because the Prophet's Companions took to the new bond seriously, in the same way as their attitude towards everything Islam laid down. This impetus was essential to the rise of Islamic society and its protection, providing all, if not more than what could have been provided by a state that enjoyed stability and well established laws. Thus, the bond of Islamic brotherhood was necessary to safeguard and consolidate the new Muslim community in its exceptional and highly complicated circumstances. A similarly strong impetus is essential for the rise of any community facing equally unusual circumstances, until it begins to have a stable state with well defined laws that give it normality.

Although Islam welcomes such a strong impetus, it nonetheless wants Islamic society to have a foundation that relies on the normal resources its people can give in ordinary situations, not on what people are ready to sacrifice in exceptional circumstances. This is essential because once an emergency is over, people should return to their normal and ordinary standards. Therefore, once circumstances in Madinah began to settle after the Battle of Badr when the new Muslim state became more stable, social conditions and means of livelihood improved, and all were able to earn their living, the Qur'ān amended the system of brotherhood. It abrogated the commitments attached to it, which normally arise from family and blood relations, but retained it as a moral bond of brotherhood that can be reactivated in reality whenever needed. Thus, the Muslim community returned to a normal situation in which inheritance and other binding commitments are limited to blood relatives as they have always been in God's original decree and natural law: "*Blood relatives have, according to God's decree, a stronger claim upon one another than other believers [of Madinah] and those who have migrated [for God's sake]. None the less, you are to act with kindness towards your close friends. This is written down in God's decree.*" (Verse 6)

The Prophet's Authority

At the same time, it re-emphasized the Prophet's authority over all Muslims, which gave him a higher claim than that of blood, indeed one that is higher than one's own wishes and desires: "*The Prophet has more claim on the believers than they have on their own selves.*" (Verse 6) Islam also makes the Prophet's wives spiritual mothers to all believers: "*and his wives are their mothers.*" (Verse 6)

The Prophet's authority over all Muslims is comprehensive. Inevitably, this includes charting a complete way of life for them. They cannot choose for themselves anything other than what he chooses for them in accordance with what God reveals to him. In an authentic *ḥadīth*, the Prophet is quoted as saying: "No one of you is a true believer until his preferences are subject to my message." This is so pervasive as to include their own feelings whereby the Prophet (peace be upon him) is dearer to them than their own lives. Thus, believers do not prefer their own safety to his, and they do not place anyone ahead of him in their hearts. Authentic *aḥādīth* speaking of this are many, and here we give just two examples: "None of you attains to true faith until I am dearer to him than his own soul, his property, offspring and all mankind." "'Umar said to the Prophet: 'By God! I love you more than I love anyone other than my own self.' The Prophet said: 'No, 'Umar! I should be dearer to you than your own self.' Then 'Umar rejoined: 'Messenger of God! I love you more than anyone else, including myself.' The Prophet said: 'You have got it now, 'Umar.'"

This is not some mere utterance of a word. It is a standard, an extremely high one that people cannot attain to without possessing a special touch that opens a sublime horizon before their hearts, purging them of the self love that is deeply rooted in their very natures. Indeed, human beings love themselves far more than they can imagine. We may think that we have managed to bring our self love under control. Yet should anyone say a derogatory word to us, we will react as though we have been bitten by a snake. So much so that we may not be able to rein in our reactions, and even if we do restrain ourselves sufficiently so as not to react visibly, we will still feel the injury keenly. We may be willing to sacrifice our lives for what we believe in, and we may claim that are free of self interest, but we still find it impossible to accept insults or derogatory criticism. Once more, this is a high standard which is difficult to attain without long training, constant alertness and the seeking of God's help. This is what the Prophet called the greater *Jihād*, or striving for God's cause. We need only to remember that even 'Umar ibn al-Khaṭṭāb needed instruction by the Prophet to open his pure heart to it.

The Prophet's authority over the believers also includes their commitments. An authentic *ḥadīth* quotes the Prophet as saying: "I am the patron of every believer, both in this life and in the life to come. Read, if you will, [God's revelation]: *'The Prophet has more claim on the believers than they have on their own selves.'* (Verse 6) Therefore, whoever leaves behind any property, his kinsfolk will inherit him, but if he leaves an outstanding debt or neglected children, let them come to me, for I am his guardian." What the *ḥadīth* implies is that the Prophet would repay the debts of any Muslim who died leaving outstanding debts and no repayment facility, and that he would also look after any young children until they came of age.

Apart from this, life was to run normally, without the need for any special charge or exceptional moral impetus. Yet the close relationship between good friends remained intact after the abrogation of the brotherhood system. A Muslim may make a bequest in favour of a close friend, or give generous gifts during their lifetimes: *"None the less, you are to act with kindness towards your close friends."* (Verse 6)

All these measures relate to the original bond, making it clear that this has always been God's will as recorded in His permanent decree: *"This is written down in God's decree."* (Verse 6) Thus people are reassured as they rely on an original and natural status to which all laws and systems refer. Life then takes its natural line, moving easily and comfortably, with no need to overcharge oneself as happens during special times of emergency or to meet exceptional needs. After all, such periods are few and of limited duration in human life. Yet should the need arise, the overflow can always be tapped.

A Binding Covenant

Referring to God's decree that He willed it to be the permanent system, the *sūrah* refers to His covenant with prophets in general, and with the Prophet Muḥammad and other messengers of firm resolve in particular. This covenant commits them to deliver God's message containing His code for human life, and to implement and advocate it among the communities to which they were sent. When they have done so, people will then be responsible for their own attitudes towards divine guidance, and for their belief or disbelief. They are now accountable for themselves having no justification whatsoever for not following divine guidance after God's messengers delivered His message to them: "*We did accept a solemn pledge from all the prophets: from you, [Muḥammad], and from Noah, Abraham, Moses and Jesus son of Mary. From all did We accept a weighty, solemn pledge. God will question the truthful about the truth [entrusted to them]. He has prepared painful suffering for the unbelievers.*" (Verses 7–8)

It is a single covenant or pledge that remained the same from Noah to Muḥammad, the seal of all prophets (peace be upon them all). It is one covenant, one system and one trust taken up by each and every one of them. The following two verses outline the covenant in general: "*We did accept a solemn pledge from all the prophets.*" A specific reference to the Messenger who received the Qur'ān and whose message is addressed to all mankind then follows: "*from you, [Muḥammad],*" and then makes mention of other messengers endowed with strong and firm resolve. These were the ones entrusted with the major divine messages prior to Muḥammad, the last one: "*and from Noah, Abraham, Moses and Jesus son of Mary.*" Then the *sūrah* describes the covenant itself: "*From all did We accept a weighty, solemn pledge.*" The description of the covenant here gives it a tangible, solid form. It was indeed a pledge between God and the individuals He chose to receive His revelations, deliver His messages and establish His code, being all the time faithful to what He had entrusted them with.

"*God will question the truthful about the truth [entrusted to them].*" The truthful are the believers. They are the ones who said the word of truth and believed in the message of truth. All others are liars because they believe in and say what is false. Describing the believers as truthful here is significant as it carries a clear meaning. They will be asked about the truth on the Day of Judgement in the same way as a teacher asks a top student to state the answer which earned him high marks. It is a question asked to honour those being asked. It informs all those present that the truthful deserve to be honoured on the great day when all mankind are assembled.

As for those who believed in what is false and made false claims concerning the most important issue of all, the issue of faith, a totally different result awaits them: "*He has prepared painful suffering for the unbelievers.*" (Verse 8)

2

Rallying All Hostile Forces

Believers! Remember the blessings God bestowed on you when hosts came down upon you. We let loose against them a windstorm and hosts that you could not see. Yet God sees all that you do. (9)

يَٰٓأَيُّهَا ٱلَّذِينَ ءَامَنُوا ٱذۡكُرُوا نِعۡمَةَ ٱللَّهِ عَلَيۡكُمۡ إِذۡ جَآءَتۡكُمۡ جُنُودٌ فَأَرۡسَلۡنَا عَلَيۡهِمۡ رِيحًا وَجُنُودًا لَّمۡ تَرَوۡهَا وَكَانَ ٱللَّهُ بِمَا تَعۡمَلُونَ بَصِيرًا ۝

They came upon you from above and from below you. Your eyes rolled [with fear] and your hearts leapt up to your throats, and confused thoughts about God passed through your minds. (10)

إِذۡ جَآءُوكُم مِّن فَوۡقِكُمۡ وَمِنۡ أَسۡفَلَ مِنكُمۡ وَإِذۡ زَاغَتِ ٱلۡأَبۡصَٰرُ وَبَلَغَتِ ٱلۡقُلُوبُ ٱلۡحَنَاجِرَ وَتَظُنُّونَ بِٱللَّهِ ٱلظُّنُونَا۠ ۝

That was a situation when the believers were sorely tested and severely shaken. (11)

هُنَالِكَ ٱبۡتُلِيَ ٱلۡمُؤۡمِنُونَ وَزُلۡزِلُوا زِلۡزَالًا شَدِيدًا ۝

The hypocrites and the sick at heart said: 'God and His Messenger promised us nothing but delusions.' (12)

وَإِذۡ يَقُولُ ٱلۡمُنَٰفِقُونَ وَٱلَّذِينَ فِى قُلُوبِهِم مَّرَضٌ مَّا وَعَدَنَا ٱللَّهُ وَرَسُولُهُۥٓ إِلَّا غُرُورًا ۝

Some of them said: 'People of Yathrib! You cannot withstand [the attack] here, so go back.' And a group of them asked the Prophet's permission to leave, saying: 'Our houses are exposed,' while they were not exposed. They only wanted to run away. (13)

وَإِذْ قَالَت طَّآئِفَةٌ مِّنْهُمْ يَٰٓأَهْلَ يَثْرِبَ لَا مُقَامَ لَكُمْ فَٱرْجِعُواْ وَيَسْتَـٔذِنُ فَرِيقٌ مِّنْهُمُ ٱلنَّبِيَّ يَقُولُونَ إِنَّ بُيُوتَنَا عَوْرَةٌ وَمَا هِيَ بِعَوْرَةٍ إِن يُرِيدُونَ إِلَّا فِرَارًا ۝

Had their city been stormed from all sides, and had they been asked to renounce their faith they would have done so without much delay. (14)

وَلَوْ دُخِلَتْ عَلَيْهِم مِّنْ أَقْطَارِهَا ثُمَّ سُئِلُواْ ٱلْفِتْنَةَ لَأَتَوْهَا وَمَا تَلَبَّثُواْ بِهَآ إِلَّا يَسِيرًا ۝

They had previously vowed before God that they would never turn their backs in flight. A vow made to God must surely be answered for. (15)

وَلَقَدْ كَانُواْ عَٰهَدُواْ ٱللَّهَ مِن قَبْلُ لَا يُوَلُّونَ ٱلْأَدْبَٰرَ وَكَانَ عَهْدُ ٱللَّهِ مَسْـُٔولًا ۝

Say: 'Flight will benefit you nothing. If you flee from natural death or from being slain, you will only be left to enjoy life for a little while.' (16)

قُل لَّن يَنفَعَكُمُ ٱلْفِرَارُ إِن فَرَرْتُم مِّنَ ٱلْمَوْتِ أَوِ ٱلْقَتْلِ وَإِذًا لَّا تُمَتَّعُونَ إِلَّا قَلِيلًا ۝

Say: 'Who can keep you away from God if it be His will to harm you, or if it be His will to show you mercy?' Other than God they can find none to protect them or to bring them support. (17)

قُلْ مَن ذَا ٱلَّذِي يَعْصِمُكُم مِّنَ ٱللَّهِ إِنْ أَرَادَ بِكُمْ سُوٓءًا أَوْ أَرَادَ بِكُمْ رَحْمَةً وَلَا يَجِدُونَ لَهُم مِّن دُونِ ٱللَّهِ وَلِيًّا وَلَا نَصِيرًا ۝

God is indeed aware of those of you who hold others back; and those who say to their brethren: 'Come and join us,' while they themselves hardly ever take part in the fighting, (18)

قَدْ يَعْلَمُ ٱللَّهُ ٱلْمُعَوِّقِينَ مِنكُمْ وَٱلْقَآئِلِينَ لِإِخْوَٰنِهِمْ هَلُمَّ إِلَيْنَا وَلَا يَأْتُونَ ٱلْبَأْسَ إِلَّا قَلِيلًا ۝

begrudging you all help. But then, when danger threatens, you see them looking to you for help, their eyes rolling as though they were overshadowed by death. Yet when the danger has passed, they will assail you [believers] with sharp tongues, begrudging you all that is good. Such people have not experienced faith. God will bring their deeds to nothing. That is all too easy for God. (19)

أَشِحَّةً عَلَيْكُمْ فَإِذَا جَآءَ ٱلْخَوْفُ رَأَيْتَهُمْ يَنظُرُونَ إِلَيْكَ تَدُورُ أَعْيُنُهُمْ كَٱلَّذِى يُغْشَىٰ عَلَيْهِ مِنَ ٱلْمَوْتِ فَإِذَا ذَهَبَ ٱلْخَوْفُ سَلَقُوكُم بِأَلْسِنَةٍ حِدَادٍ أَشِحَّةً عَلَى ٱلْخَيْرِ أُوْلَٰٓئِكَ لَمْ يُؤْمِنُوا۟ فَأَحْبَطَ ٱللَّهُ أَعْمَٰلَهُمْ وَكَانَ ذَٰلِكَ عَلَى ٱللَّهِ يَسِيرًا ۝

They think that the Confederates have not withdrawn. Should the Confederates return, they would wish they were in the desert, among the Bedouins, asking for news about you. Even if they were with you, they would take but little part in the fighting. (20)

يَحْسَبُونَ ٱلْأَحْزَابَ لَمْ يَذْهَبُوا۟ وَإِن يَأْتِ ٱلْأَحْزَابُ يَوَدُّوا۟ لَوْ أَنَّهُم بَادُونَ فِى ٱلْأَعْرَابِ يَسْـَٔلُونَ عَنْ أَنۢبَآئِكُمْ وَلَوْ كَانُوا۟ فِيكُم مَّا قَٰتَلُوٓا۟ إِلَّا قَلِيلًا ۝

In God's Messenger you have a good model for everyone who looks with hope to God and the Last Day, and always remembers God. (21)

لَّقَدْ كَانَ لَكُمْ فِى رَسُولِ ٱللَّهِ أُسْوَةٌ حَسَنَةٌ لِّمَن كَانَ يَرْجُوا۟ ٱللَّهَ وَٱلْيَوْمَ ٱلْءَاخِرَ وَذَكَرَ ٱللَّهَ كَثِيرًا ۝

When the believers saw the Confederate forces they said: 'This is what God and His Messenger have promised us! Truly spoke God and His Messenger.' This only served to strengthen their faith and their submission to God. (22)

وَلَمَّا رَءَا ٱلْمُؤْمِنُونَ ٱلْأَحْزَابَ قَالُواْ هَٰذَا مَا وَعَدَنَا ٱللَّهُ وَرَسُولُهُۥ وَصَدَقَ ٱللَّهُ وَرَسُولُهُۥ وَمَا زَادَهُمْ إِلَّآ إِيمَٰنًا وَتَسْلِيمًا ٢٢

Among the believers are people who have always been true to what they have vowed before God. Some have already fulfilled their pledges by death, and some are still waiting. They have not changed in the least. (23)

مِّنَ ٱلْمُؤْمِنِينَ رِجَالٌ صَدَقُواْ مَا عَٰهَدُواْ ٱللَّهَ عَلَيْهِ فَمِنْهُم مَّن قَضَىٰ نَحْبَهُۥ وَمِنْهُم مَّن يَنتَظِرُ وَمَا بَدَّلُواْ تَبْدِيلًا ٢٣

God will surely reward the truthful for having been true to their word, and will punish the hypocrites, if that be His will, or accept their repentance. God is indeed Much-Forgiving, Merciful. (24)

لِّيَجْزِىَ ٱللَّهُ ٱلصَّٰدِقِينَ بِصِدْقِهِمْ وَيُعَذِّبَ ٱلْمُنَٰفِقِينَ إِن شَآءَ أَوْ يَتُوبَ عَلَيْهِمْ إِنَّ ٱللَّهَ كَانَ غَفُورًا رَّحِيمًا ٢٤

God turned back the unbelievers in all their rage and fury; they gained no advantage. He spared the believers the need to fight. God is Most Powerful, Almighty. (25)

وَرَدَّ ٱللَّهُ ٱلَّذِينَ كَفَرُواْ بِغَيْظِهِمْ لَمْ يَنَالُواْ خَيْرًا وَكَفَى ٱللَّهُ ٱلْمُؤْمِنِينَ ٱلْقِتَالَ وَكَانَ ٱللَّهُ قَوِيًّا عَزِيزًا ٢٥

He brought down from their strongholds those of the people of earlier revelations who aided them, casting terror in their hearts: some you slew, and some you took captive. (26)

وَأَنزَلَ ٱلَّذِينَ ظَٰهَرُوهُم مِّنْ أَهْلِ ٱلْكِتَٰبِ مِن صَيَاصِيهِمْ وَقَذَفَ فِى قُلُوبِهِمُ ٱلرُّعْبَ فَرِيقًا تَقْتُلُونَ وَتَأْسِرُونَ فَرِيقًا ٢٦

And He passed on to you their land, their houses and their goods, as well as a land on which you had never yet set foot. God has power over all things. (27)

وَأَوْرَثَكُمْ أَرْضَهُمْ وَدِيَٰرَهُمْ وَأَمْوَٰلَهُمْ وَأَرْضًا لَّمْ تَطَئُوهَا وَكَانَ ٱللَّهُ عَلَىٰ كُلِّ شَىْءٍ قَدِيرًا ٢٧

Overview

In the early days of Islam, it was in the midst of events that the Muslim personality was moulded. With every new day and every new situation, this personality came closer to maturity, presenting its distinctive features. Furthermore this Muslim community, reflecting the total sum of its members' personalities, also had its own unique qualities and values that distinguished it from all other communities. At times, the predicaments the Muslim community faced presented its members with an acid test that separated the true from the false and which also proved everyone's true mettle.

Qur'ānic revelations were given either before or after a particular test, describing events and throwing light on the difficulties involved. This brought into focus the attitudes taken as the event unfolded, and what intentions and motives were behind these attitudes and feelings. The Qur'ān then addressed people's hearts as they lay open to the light, with no screen to cover them. It touched them at precisely the right spot so as to ensure the right response. This was a continuous educational exercise making use of events and experiences, one after the other, day after day.

29

The Muslims were not given the Qur'ān in its totality in one go so that they could study it, understand its directives, observe its prohibitions and fulfil its commands. Instead, God put them to a variety of tests because He is fully aware that man does not attain full maturity except through practical experience and it is this that drives lessons home and moulds characters. The Qur'ān then tells people the truth about what has taken place and its significance. Thus, it issues its directives only when people have gone through the ordeal.

The experiences the Muslims went through during the Prophet's lifetime were truly remarkable. For it was a period of direct contact between heaven and earth, reflected in both events and words. When a Muslim went to bed he was aware that God watched and heard him, and that his every action, word, thought or intention could be exposed and commented upon by the Qur'ān. Similarly, all Muslims felt a direct contact with their Lord: if they faced a problem or a hardship, they hoped that the gates of heaven would open with a ruling that removed their difficulties. It was a period when God, in His majesty, said to one or the other: 'You have done, intended, declared or said this and that; or you must do this or should refrain from that.' It is infinitely awesome that God should address Himself to a particular person when that person and all who live on earth, and indeed the whole earth with all that it contains, do not represent more than a tiny particle in His glorious kingdom. Hard as we may find it to reflect on that period and its events we can hardly imagine how it was in practice. This is indeed beyond imagination.

Yet God did not leave the education of the Muslims and the moulding of their personalities to be accomplished through feelings only. He put them to practical tests necessitating their interaction. He is infinite in His wisdom, and He knows best the creation He has created. We need to reflect long on this wisdom so that we can better understand what we may encounter of tests during our own lives.

Difficulties in Abundance

The present passage analyses one of the great events in the history of the Muslim community, indeed, one of its hardest tests. The event was the attack launched by confederate forces on Madinah, which took place in the fourth or fifth year of the Prophet's migration.[1] A thorough reading of this passage and the way it portrays the events and comments on them, highlighting certain scenes and bringing out certain thoughts and feelings experienced by some Muslims, will enable us to understand how God shaped the personality of the Muslim community through both the events themselves and the Qur'ān. In order to understand this we will explain the Qur'ānic text after we have briefly related the events as given in books on the Prophet's life and history. This will demonstrate the great difference between how God relates historical events and the narrative man gives of them.

An Encounter with Allied Forces

Muḥammad ibn Isḥāq relates: "The beginning of events leading to the Encounter of the Moat started when a number of Jews, including Sallām ibn Abī al-Ḥuqayq, Ḥuyay ibn Akhṭab and Kinānah ibn Abī al-Ḥuqayq, all of the al-Naḍīr tribe, and Ḥūwathah ibn Qays and Abū 'Ammār of Wā'il, as well as others of both Jewish tribes travelled to Makkah and spoke with the Quraysh. It was these Jews who worked hard to forge the alliance against God's Messenger. When they met the Quraysh elders they called on them to join them in fighting the Prophet. They said to them: 'We will join forces with you until we have exterminated him and his followers.' The Quraysh put the following question to them: 'You, the Jews, are the people who follow the first divine book, and you know the issues over which we differ with Muḥammad: which is better, our religion or his?' Those Jewish elders answered: 'Your religion is better than his, and you are closer to the truth than him.' It is concerning these people that God revealed in the Qur'ān:

Are you not aware of those who, having been granted a share of Divine revelations, now believe in falsehood and arrogant deviation

---

1. Although biographers of the Prophet differ on whether this event was in year 4 or 5, it was most probably in year 5, as a careful reading of the events during the Prophet's lifetime indicates. – Editor's note.

[from Divine faith], and they say to the unbelievers that they are better guided than the believers. These are the ones whom God has rejected; anyone whom God rejects shall find none to succour him. Have they, perchance, a share in (God's) dominion? If so, they would not give other people so much as [would fill] the groove of a date-stone. Do they, perchance, envy other people for what God has given them out of His bounty? We have indeed given revelation and wisdom to the House of Abraham, and We did bestow on them a mighty dominion. Some of them believe in him and some turn away from him. Sufficient scourge is the fire of Hell. (4: 51–55)

The Quraysh were very happy with this answer and expressed a readiness to join the Jews in battle against the Prophet.

"Then this Jewish delegation travelled to meet the leaders of the Ghaṭafān, another leading Arabian tribe, and they urged them to fight the Prophet, assuring them that they would be joining them as well as the Quraysh. The Ghaṭafān agreed and they all marshalled their forces. The Quraysh marched under the leadership of Abū Sufyān ibn Ḥarb, while the Ghaṭafān were led by 'Uyaynah ibn Ḥisn of the Fizārah clan, al-Ḥārith ibn 'Awf of Murrah and Mis'ar ibn Rukhaylah of Ashja'.

"When the Prophet heard of what they had plotted, he ordered the digging of a moat to prevent their entrance into Madinah. The Prophet himself and his Companions worked hard to dig the moat. However, a number of hypocrite men put little effort into the work. They would put up a show of working, but then sneak off, going back home, without asking permission from the Prophet. By contrast, if any good believer needed to leave for some urgent matter, he would mention this to the Prophet and ask his permission to absent himself for a while. The Prophet gave such people leave. Any of these would then go home, attend to the emergency and return, knowing that he would be rewarded by God for such work. Concerning the believers, God revealed in the Qur'ān: "*They only are true believers who believe in God and His Messenger, and who, whenever they are with him upon a matter requiring collective action, do not depart unless they have obtained his leave. Those who ask leave of you are indeed the ones who believe in God and His Messenger. Hence, when they ask your leave to attend to some business of theirs, grant you this leave to whomever of them you choose, and pray to God to forgive them. God is indeed Much-Forgiving, Merciful.*" (24: 62) And He also said about the hypocrites who sneaked away: "*Do not address God's Messenger in the manner you address one another. God certainly knows those of you who would slip away surreptitiously. So, let those who would go against His bidding beware, lest some affliction or grievous suffering befall them.*" (24: 63)

"When the Muslims had completed digging the moat, the Quraysh arrived and encamped at a place called Majma' al-Asyal near Rawmah. They numbered 10,000 including their slaves and affiliates as well as those who followed them from the people of Kinānah and Tihāmah. The Ghaṭafān and their followers from Najd marched to their camping place near Uḥud. The Prophet marshalled his troops, numbering 3,000, camping at a spot where their backs were to Mount Sala', with the moat separating them from their attackers. He also ordered that the women and children should stay in sheltered homes.

"Ḥuyay ibn Akhṭab, God's enemy, went up to Ka'b ibn Asad, the Rabbi of the Jewish tribe of Qurayẓah, who had signed, on behalf of his tribe, a friendship treaty with the Prophet, pledging support to the Muslims. Ḥuyay wanted him to break his treaty and join the attacking forces. He used all his powers of persuasion and brought much pressure to bear on Ka'b, all of which culminated with a pledge of honour that should the Quraysh and Ghaṭafān withdraw without defeating Muḥammad, he would come and join Ka'b in his fort and share his fate with him. At this point Ka'b ibn Asad decided to join the attacking forces, thereby breaking his treaty with the Prophet.

"This was an extremely testing time for the believers. People were truly in fear of the outcome. The enemy was also preparing for a pincer attack from the front and the rear. Inevitably, the believers started to have all types of thoughts and doubts, while the hypocrites capitalized on the situation by speaking out against the Prophet. One of them, Mut'ib ibn Qushayr, said: 'Muḥammad used to promise us that we would eat of the treasures of the Persian and Byzantine Emperors, while today we feel unsafe to go to the toilet.' Another, Aws ibn Qayẓī, said to the Prophet in front of a number of his clansmen: 'Messenger of God! Our homes are vulnerable. So permit us to leave and go home, as our homes are outside Madinah.'

"The Prophet remained steadfast with his Companions, while the idolaters laid siege for nearly a month, without war breaking out between them, except for exchanges of arrows across the moat.

"When things got worse and the Muslims were in real trouble, the Prophet sent a message to 'Uyaynah ibn Ḥiṣn and al-Ḥārith ibn 'Awf, the Ghaṭafān leaders offering them one third of Madinah's crops if they withdrew their forces. This was agreed and written down, but neither signed nor witnessed. It was essentially a proposed arrangement. When the Prophet wanted to conclude the agreement, he called in Sa'd ibn Mu'ādh, the Chief of the Aws tribe, and Sa'd ibn 'Ubādah, the Chief of the Khazraj tribe, consulting them on his proposal. They asked him: 'God's Messenger! Is this something you like and we would willingly do it, or something God has instructed you to do and we have no choice but to do it, or something you are doing for our sake?' He said: 'I am doing it for you, because I see that the Arabs are united against you, attacking you from all sides. I only want to break the unity of your enemy for the present.' Sa'd ibn Mu'ādh said: 'Messenger of God, when we were, like these people, idolaters, unaware of any religion other than the worship of idols, they did not hope to get a single fruit from Madinah except as a present from us or if we sold it to them. Now that God has honoured us with Islam and guided us to it and has given us the honour and strength of having you in our midst, would we willingly give them our goods? We have no need for this agreement. We will give them nothing but the sword until God makes His judgement between us.' The Prophet replied: 'The matter is entirely up to you.' Then Sa'd took the sheet on which the agreement was written and erased the writing. He said: 'Let them do their worst.'"

Thereafter, the Prophet and his Companions remained steadfast despite their fear of their enemies and the impending pincer attack they were sure would come.

Then a man from the Ghaṭafān called Nu'aym ibn Mas'ūd came over to the Muslim camp and said to the Prophet: "Messenger of God, I am now a Muslim and my people are not aware of the fact. You may give me whatever orders you wish." Keenly aware of the situation the Muslims were in, the Prophet said to Nuʿaym: "If you join us, you increase our number by one. But try, if you can, to dissuade the people from attacking us. War is but a successful trick." [Nuʿaym did a splendid job creating mistrust between the three groups forming the confederate forces, the Quraysh, Ghaṭafān and Qurayẓah. This is related in detail in books documenting the history of the period. Hence, we confine ourselves to simply referring to the results of his efforts.]

It was through God's grace that the hostile forces' unity of purpose did not last long. Furthermore, God sent them a very strong wind on a severely cold and wet night. Nothing remained stable in their tents.

When the Prophet learnt of the doubts now casting shadows in the minds of his enemy, which meant that God had actually split them and that mutual mistrust had replaced their former unity, he sent one of his Companions, Ḥudhayfah ibn al-Yamān, to their camp at night to gather intelligence on what they intended to do.

Ibn Isḥāq relates: "Ḥudhayfah ibn al-Yamān, a Companion of the Prophet who belonged to the Anṣār, was with a group of people in the city of Kūfah in Iraq many years later when he was asked by someone from that city: 'Did you people really see God's Messenger, and were you truly in his company?' When Ḥudhayfah answered in the affirmative, the man asked: 'How did you serve him?' Ḥudhayfah said: 'We used to try our best.' The man said: 'Had it been our fortune to be his Companions we would not have let him walk. We would have carried him on our shoulders.' Ḥudhayfah said: 'My nephew! We were one night with God's Messenger during the Encounter of the Moat when he stood up praying for a part of the night. He then turned to his Companions and asked: "Who is willing to go and find out what our enemies are doing and return [to return was a condition the Prophet attached to that particular mission]. I shall pray to God to make any volunteer for this mission my Companion in Heaven." No one volunteered because of our great fear and hunger on that very cold night. When no one answered, the Prophet called me forward. I then had no choice but to go. He said to me: 'Ḥudhayfah, go inside their camp and find out what they are doing. Do not do anything on your own initiative until you return.' I went into their quarters to see the wind and God's other soldiers playing havoc in their camp. No pot or pan stood upright, no fire could be maintained and no structure stood up. Abū Sufyān then addressed his people: 'People of the Quraysh, let everyone make sure of the person sitting next to him.'

"I took the man next to me by the hand and asked him who he was. He answered me, mentioning his name and his father's name. Abū Sufyān then said: 'People of the Quraysh, you realize that we cannot stay much longer. We have endured great hardship and the Jews of the Qurayẓah have not fulfilled their promises to us. Indeed, we have received highly disturbing reports about their position. You see what these strong winds are doing to us. We cannot stay much longer in these conditions, and my advice to you is to go back home where I am now going." He then mounted his camel, which was tied to a peg. He hit the camel, which jumped on its feet, and released itself as it stood up. Had it not been for the Prophet's clear instructions to me that I must not do anything serious before I returned, I could have killed Abū Sufyān with my arrow."

Ḥudhayfah then returned to the Prophet to deliver his report. He found the Prophet praying, and sat very close to him. Continuing his prayers, the Prophet drew Ḥudhayfah closer to him until he was sitting between his legs and he covered him with his robe. When he finished his prayers, he listened to Ḥudhayfah's report. The Ghaṭafān decided to follow the Quraysh's decision when they learned that their allies were leaving.

The Qur'ānic Report

In its reporting of the events and its comments on them and the directives it gives to the Muslim community, the *sūrah* neither mentions people by name nor specifies positions; rather it describes types of people and patterns of character. It gives few details but highlights constant values and consequences. It focuses on the elements that remain after the events are over and their actors have departed. In this way, its focus serves to draw lessons for future generations and different communities. The Qur'ānic text also relates events to God's will that controls both the event and those who participate in it. It shows how God's will operates gently and smoothly to bring about the end He wants. The *sūrah* also pauses after each stage in the story to give a directive or to make comments reminding the listeners of the essential truth.

Although the *sūrah* relates the story to the people who took part in it in the first place, it does not only give them more information about it, but also lays before them certain aspects which they were unaware of. In this way, it brings to light people's inner thoughts, feelings, intentions and what was hidden within their hearts.

Added to all this is the fine style, vividness and freshness of the images drawn. Furthermore, the *sūrah* paints the hypocrites' cowardice with acid derision as also describes their twisted nature. This contrasts with the profoundly inspiring picture of faith that is drawn and the qualities it imparts to believers.

The Qur'ānic text is a manual for action, not only by those who witnessed the event but also in every environment and generation. It is a guide for Muslims whenever they face circumstances similar to those faced by the first Muslim community and at any time in the future. It aims to give them the same determination and motivation as the Prophet's Companions possessed.

No one will understand Qur'ānic texts fully unless they face circumstances similar to those faced by the first Muslim community. It is in such circumstances that texts reveal their meanings fully and hearts open up to understand them in depth. When this takes place, the text is no longer words and sentences, but rather a source of power and energy. The events described come alive: inspiring, motivating and urging action both in real life and in the depths of the human heart.

The Qur'ān is not merely a book to be read and understood: it is a motivating force. Its texts are ready for implementation at every point. It only needs a heart that warms to it in circumstances that enable its resources to be fully tapped. We may read a particular Qur'ānic text tens or hundreds of times, then we look at it again when we are facing a particular situation only to discover that it gives us what it had not given before. It provides a straight answer to our complex problem, shows a way that we overlooked, clears our doubts and replaces these with firm and perfect reassurance. Nothing else, old or new, gives us what the Qur'ān gives.

A Test Too Hard

The *surah* begins its discussion of the encounter with the confederate forces by reminding the believers of God's favours when He repelled the armies that were intent on exterminating them. The first verse in the passage sums up the nature of the event, its beginning and end, before giving any details or explaining any attitudes. Thus, God's favour is brought into focus so that the Muslims will always remember it. It also makes it clear that as God commands the believers to follow His revelations, place their trust in Him and not yield to the unbelievers or the hypocrites, it is also He who protects those advocating His message and code for human life against aggression: *"Believers! Remember the blessings God bestowed on you when hosts came down upon you. We let loose against them a windstorm and hosts that you could not see. Yet God sees all that you do."* (Verse 9)

In this short opening verse we have a picture of the beginning and end of the battle, along with the decisive factors that combine to produce its result: the arrival of the enemy forces; God's sending strong winds and other troops unseen by the believers; and His support which is dependent on their attitude and action as God is fully aware of all that they do.

The *surah* then gives details of the situation:

> *They came upon you from above and from below you. Your eyes rolled [with fear] and your hearts leapt up to your throats, and confused thoughts about God passed through your minds. That was a situation when the believers were sorely tested and severely shaken. The hypocrites and the sick at heart said: 'God and His Messenger promised us nothing but delusions.' Some of them said: 'People of Yathrib! You cannot withstand [the attack] here, so go back.' And a group of them asked the Prophet's permission to leave, saying: 'Our houses are exposed,' while they were not exposed. They only wanted to run away.* (Verses 10–13)

The verses paint an image of the whole of Madinah in the grip of great alarm and distress, with the idolaters of the Quraysh and Ghatafān allied with the Jews of Qurayẓah moving in from all sides. These feelings of alarm and distress affected all of the people, but their reactions

38

and responses differed. Needless to say, people's thoughts about God, their behaviour, and their evaluation of causes and results were much at variance. Therefore, the test was extremely difficult and the distinction between believers and hypocrites was decisive.

We can see today the whole situation: its elements, feelings, actions and reactions as if it were happening before our eyes. We see it though from the outside: "*They came upon you from above and from below you.*" (Verse 10) We also see people's reactions to what was unfolding: "*Your eyes rolled [with fear] and your hearts leapt up to your throats.*" (Verse 10) This is a picture of profound fear, anxiety and distress, imparted through people's expressions and feelings. "*Confused thoughts about God passed through your minds.*" (Verse 10) The *sūrah* does not tell us about these thoughts in detail. In fact the adjective 'confused' is implied rather than stated in the Arabic text. This gives a more vivid picture of the confusion in people's feelings and ideas, leaving minds bewildered and perplexed. Such a state of fear and confusion is then further heightened: "*That was a situation when the believers were sorely tested and severely shaken.*" (Verse 11)

A test that left the believers severely shaken must have been truly fearful. Muḥammad ibn Maslamah and others said: "During the Moat Encounter our nights were days. The unbelievers took it in turns to confront us, with Abū Sufyān showing up at the head of his troops one day, Khālid ibn al-Walīd with his forces the next day, ʿAmr ibn al-ʿĀṣ the next, Hubayrah ibn Wahb the next, followed by ʿIkrimah ibn Abī Jahl, and lastly by Ḍirār ibn al-Khaṭṭāb. This was very hard for us, and people were really in fear."

A further description of the state in which the Muslims found themselves is given by al-Maqrīzī in *Imtāʿ al-Asmāʿ*: "The idolaters appeared at dawn, and the Prophet mobilized his Companions and the two sides engaged in fighting throughout the day and part of the night. Neither the Prophet nor any Muslim could move out of position. The Prophet could not offer any of the *Ẓuhr*, *ʿAṣr*, *Maghrib* and *ʿĪshāʾ* prayers. His Companions said to him: 'Messenger of God! We have not prayed.' He said: 'Nor have I.' Then the idolaters withdrew and each side went back to their encampments. On another day, Usayd ibn Ḥuḍayr stood guard on the edge of the moat, at the head of 200

Muslims. Mounted forces of idolaters, commanded by Khālid ibn al-Walīd tried to take them unawares, but the two sides were engaged in fighting for some time. Waḥshī, who had killed Ḥamzah, the Prophet's uncle, during the Battle of Uḥud, stabbed al-Ṭufayl ibn al-Nu'mān al-Anṣārī with a spear and killed him. On that day, the Prophet said: 'The idolaters have kept us from our middle prayer of 'Aṣr. May God fill their bellies and hearts with fire.'"[2]

Two Muslim reconnaissance units went out one night, and they met by accident, each thinking the other to belong to the enemy. They clashed, with some from both groups being injured or killed. When one of them shouted the Muslim battle slogan: '*Ḥā Mīm*. They will not triumph', they realized their mistake and stopped fighting. The Prophet advised the two parties: 'Whoever of you is wounded should consider it an injury incurred for God's sake, and whoever of your men has been killed is a martyr.'

The worst distress the Muslims faced during the siege was the treachery of the Qurayẓah Jews, who were to their rear. They feared that at any time a concerted attack by the idolaters and Jews could be mounted and that they would be heavily outnumbered by the herds intent on exterminating Islam and the Muslims.

On top of all this, the Muslims also faced the schemes concocted by the hypocrites, who, as usual, tried to raise doubts in their minds and so split their ranks: "*The hypocrites and the sick at heart said: God and His Messenger promised us nothing but delusions.*" (Verse 12) In this way, the hypocrites saw in the Muslims' distress a chance to speak out without being blamed. They felt they could now undermine the believers' morale, raising doubts about the promises given by God and His Messenger, without accusing fingers being raised against them. The overall situation, or so it seemed, confirmed the doubts they were raising. Moreover, they were consistent with what they felt deep inside. Such testing times, however, removed the thin cover by which the hypocrites tried to hide their reality. They were in such a state of fear

---

2. In a *hadīth* reported by Jābir, the Prophet was kept from offering 'Aṣr prayer that day. It appears that this took place on more than one occasion, with the Muslims unable once to pray 'Aṣr, while on another occasion, they could not pray any of the other prayers.

themselves that this in itself shattered all their claims to be believers. In short, their truth was out.

In every community there will always be hypocrites and doubters who will, in times of difficulty, adopt the same attitude. Theirs is a state of mind encountered in all communities and across all generations.

"*Some of them said: People of Yathrib! You cannot withstand [the attack] here, so go back.*" (Verse 13) Thus they tried to encourage the people of Madinah to desert and go home, arguing that standing guard behind the moat was meaningless when their homes were exposed to danger. This was a wicked attempt to exploit a natural weakness in people's hearts: their concerns about their women and children at times of great danger. "*And a group of them asked the Prophet's permission to leave, saying: 'Our houses are exposed.'*" (Verse 13) Such people tried to give the appearance of being with the Muslims, whilst all they wanted was leave to go home under the pretext that their homes were vulnerable to attack. The Qur'ān, however, states their true motives, refutes their arguments and confronts them with their lies and tricks: "*while they were not exposed. They only wanted to run away.*" (Verse 13)

One report mentions that the Ḥārithah clan sent one of their people, Aws ibn Qayẓī, to the Prophet with a message saying: "Our homes are exposed. There is none among the Anṣār whose quarters are as vulnerable as ours. There is nothing to repel the Ghaṭafān from directing an attack against our quarters. Could you please give us permission to return home so that we can protect our women and children." The Prophet gave them permission. However, Saʿd ibn Muʿādh said to him: "Messenger of God! Do not give them such permission. Whenever we faced a hardship in the past, they would do the same." Thereafter the Prophet issued an order that they should return to Madinah. It was such people that the Qur'ān put face to face with their inner motives: "*They only wanted to run away.*" (Verse 13)

Where to Escape Death

The *sūrah* pauses a little here in order to draw a mental picture for those hypocrites as to how hollow their faith was and how they were always ready to break ranks, even for the slightest reason. They would not even try to cover their weaknesses: "*Had their city been stormed from all sides, and had they been asked to renounce their faith they would have done so without much delay.*" (Verse 14) The attitude described in the previous verses was the one they adopted when the enemy were still outside Madinah, unable to storm it. No matter how hard and stressful a situation is, a potential danger is far less than a real one. Should their worst fears come true and Madinah be stormed from all sides, and should they be asked to renounce Islam, they would do so with little hesitation, or a few would hesitate for a while before then reverting to disbelief. In essence, their claimed faith lacked firm roots while their cowardice made them unable to resist.

Thus the Qur'ān exposed their reality and put them naked before the mirror to see themselves as they truly were. It then accused them of breaking their clear pledges which they had earlier given to none other than God. Yet they were heedless of their promises and pledges: "*They had previously vowed before God that they would never turn their backs in flight. A vow made to God must surely be answered for.*" (Verse 15)

Ibn Hisham reports: "This is a reference to the Ḥārithah clan who, together with the Salamah clan, were about to desert the Muslim camp before the Battle of Uḥud. They subsequently vowed before God they would never do so again. Therefore, the *sūrah* reminds them of their earlier undertaking.

At Uḥud, God saved them and spared them from the consequences of desertion. This was one example of the practical lessons of the early days of *Jihād*. Now, with the lapse of time ensuring greater experience, they had to be put face to face against their reality.

At this point the Qur'ān restates an important value, one that corrects their notions about life and death, which had caused them to break their pledges and try to desert:

> *Say: Flight will benefit you nothing. If you flee from natural death or from being slain, you will only be left to enjoy life for a little while. Say: Who can keep you away from God if it be His will to harm you, or if it be His will to show you mercy? Other than God they can find none to protect them or to bring them support.* (Verses 16–17)

It is God's will that determines events and destinies, directing them along a certain way that leads to a definite result. Death, whether in battle or by natural causes, is inevitable and occurs at the appointed moment: it comes neither a second early nor a moment late. Flight from battle will not spare the deserter what God has willed. Should they flee from battle, they are certain to meet their inevitable death soon, at the appointed time. All times in this present life are soon, and all life extensions are short. No one can protect anyone else against God's will; no one can prevent it running its course. Should He will to harm someone or show them mercy, His will shall be done. Hence, the only proper attitude for anyone is to submit to God, obey His orders, and honour the vows given to Him in all situations of comfort and hardship. It is far better to place oneself in God's hand, placing one's trust completely in Him. He will, in any case do what He pleases.

Inner Feelings Laid Bare

The *sūrah* then clearly states that God knows the inner thoughts of those who not only stay behind at times of *Jihād*, but who also try to dissuade others from joining the battle. It draws a very truthful picture of their mentality, yet it provokes laughter and derision at such people who are encountered in all communities. It is a picture of cowardice composed of lines of fright and panic in times of hardship, arrogance and presumptuousness in times of ease, a begrudging nature of every good thing, a reluctance to participate in anything good, yet a state of utter terror and hysteria when danger looms from afar. The Qur'ān paints this picture with some fascinating touches that can neither be substituted nor replaced:

> God is indeed aware of those of you who hold others back; and those who say to their brethren: 'Come and join us,' while they themselves hardly ever take part in the fighting, begrudging you all help. But then, when danger threatens, you see them looking to you for help, their eyes rolling as though they were overshadowed by death. Yet when the danger has passed, they will assail you [believers] with sharp tongues, begrudging you all that is good. Such people have not

experienced faith. God will bring their deeds to nothing. That is all too easy for God. They think that the Confederates have not withdrawn. Should the Confederates return, they would wish they were in the desert, among the Bedouins, asking for news about you. Even if they were with you, they would take but little part in the fighting. (Verses 18–20)

These verses begin with the statement that God is fully aware of those who try to weaken the Muslim community by persuading others to stay behind. They themselves hardly, if ever, take part in any battle. Their attitude is well known to Him, and their scheming is exposed. The miraculous brush then begins to delineate the main lines that depict this type of people. They 'begrudge you all help.' They are very tight against the Muslims, unwilling to help them with effort or money, or even with sympathy and feeling. Yet *"when danger threatens, you see them looking to you for help, their eyes rolling as though they were overshadowed by death."* (Verse 19) This is a true-to-life, vibrant image of a cowardly people, yet it fills us with laughter when we look at their limbs shaking with fear. Worse still is the shadow they cast when the danger is over and security is assured: *"Yet when the danger has passed, they will assail you [believers] with sharp tongues."* (Verse 19) They come out of their holes, swelling with false pride, unashamedly making all sorts of claims about their bravery, determination, unwavering effort, etc. Not only so, but they *"begrudge you all that is good."* (Verse 19) Despite all their wild claims, they are unwilling to make any effort or donation in order to help with good works.

There will always be people belonging to this type in all generations and communities: boasting, cowardly, miserly and abusive: *"Such people have not experienced faith. God will bring their deeds to nothing."* (Verse 19) This is then the basic reason for their attitude. Their hearts have never experienced faith and they never saw its guiding light, or recognized its guidance. Hence, all their endeavours will end up in ruin. They cannot succeed because the basic element of success is absent from their lives. *"That is all too easy for God."* (Verse 19) Nothing is difficult for God, and His will is certain to be done.

The *sūrah* paints another derogatory picture of their condition on the day when the confederate forces acknowledged their failure and departed: "*They think that the Confederates have not withdrawn.*" (Verse 20) They still tremble with fear, refusing to believe that those large forces have gone and all are now safe and secure. "*Should the Confederates return, they would wish they were in the desert, among the Bedouins, asking for news about you.*" (Verse 20) How pathetic and laughable! If those forces did return, these hypocrites would wish that they were Bedouins, and that they never lived in Madinah. They would rather not have anything to do with the people of Madinah, not even know anything about them. They only want to enquire of travellers about what happened to them, but this would only be a casual enquiry, as when one stranger asks about another.

They wish all this despite the fact that they have been left behind, away from the battle, unexposed to danger. It is all fear at a distance. Hence, "*Even if they were with you, they would take but little part in the fighting.*" (Verse 20) Such was the condition of the hypocrites, the sick at heart, and those who spread lies to weaken the Muslim community.

The Opposite Image

Such severely testing times did not make all people look about in such an ugly way. Indeed, there was a totally different scenario going on, one casting light within all this darkness, one that remained stable despite the hardship, one that trusted to God, accepted His will, was reassured that His help would be forthcoming, and one that remained unshaken despite all the fear and confusion. The Qur'ān begins drawing this delightful image by citing the example given by the Prophet: "*In God's Messenger you have a good model for everyone who looks with hope to God and the Last Day, and always remembers God.*" (Verse 21)

In the midst of all the worry, stress and fear, the Prophet provided shelter for the Muslims: he was the source of their hope, confidence and reassurance. Studying his attitude during the unfolding events of this period is necessary for leaders of Muslim communities and revivalist organizations today so that they can chart the way ahead. His attitude provides a good example for those who hope to earn God's pleasure on the Day of Judgement, and for those who always remember God. We should perhaps look at some aspects of his attitude, by way of example, though we cannot discuss this at any great length in this commentary.

The Prophet went out to work with the Muslims in digging the moat, using the axe and removing the earth and carrying the dust in a basket. As his Companions worked, they sang some rhymes, which they composed on the spot, deriving the same from whatever was taking place. The Prophet repeated their rhyming words at the end of the lines. For example, one of his Companions was called Ju'ayl, but the Prophet did not like his name as it meant 'a small dung beetle', so he renamed him 'Amr. So the people around composed a rhyming couplet about this very thing of giving a man a better name. The Prophet repeated with them the two rhyming words. We can imagine the atmosphere the Prophet's participation gave them and how it could fill them with reassurance and enthusiasm.

Zayd ibn Thābit, a young Muslim, was carrying the dust away, and the Prophet said of him: 'He is certainly a good lad.' At one point Zayd was too tired and he fell asleep. It was very cold, but as he was sleeping another person, 'Imārah ibn Hazm, took Zayd's sword away. When he woke up, he was upset. The Prophet said to Zayd: 'Father of sleep! You slept and your weapon is gone!' Then the Prophet asked his Companions: 'Who of you knows where the sword belonging to this young man is?' 'Imārah said: 'It is with me.' The Prophet told him to return it to Zayd and prohibited anyone from taking the weapon of a sleeping man even in jest.

This little episode shows how the Prophet was aware of all those who were with him, young and old, and that he cared for them all. We see him ready to joke with everyone in a pleasant way: 'Father of sleep! You slept and your weapon is gone!' This also tells us much about the general atmosphere in which the Muslims lived as the Prophet took care of them, even during the hardest of circumstances.

The Prophet's pure soul looked forward to assured victory, distant as it might have been. He could see it as axes hit hard rocks to produce rays of light. He speaks about this to his Companions giving them reassurance. Ibn Isḥāq reports: "Salmān mentioned that as he was digging in his area, a rock was too hard for him. The Prophet was nearby and when he saw Salmān's difficulty he took the axe from him and struck the rock three times, with each strike producing a flash of light. Salmān asked him: 'Messenger of God! What is this I have just seen: a flash of light from under the axe?' The Prophet said to him: 'Have you seen that? At the first strike, God opened to me the land of Yemen; at the second, He opened Syria and the west for me; and at the third, He opened the land to the east for me.'" In *Imtāʿ al-Asmāʿ*, al-Maqrīzī mentions that this happened to 'Umar in front of Salmān. We can imagine what effect these words from the Prophet would have had on his Companions' hearts at the time when they felt danger approaching.

We should add to these delightful scenes the report we mentioned earlier when Ḥudhayfah returned from his dangerous night mission, gathering intelligence about the enemy and what they were doing. The night was exceedingly cold, and on his return the Prophet was in prayer. Yet on seeing Ḥudhayfah he realized how he felt, and he drew him to himself so that he was sitting by his side, near his feet, and then the Prophet covered him with his robe to let him warm himself a little while he continued his prayer. After he had finished his prayer, he sat listening to Ḥudhayfah's report confirming the good news he had anticipated.

As for the Prophet's courage, perseverance and unshaken belief throughout this severely testing time, this is evident at every point in the story. We do not need to give details here, as they can be easily and clearly recognized: "*In God's Messenger you have a good model for everyone who looks with hope to God and the Last Day, and always remembers God.*" (Verse 21)

Strengthening Faith

The *sūrah* then depicts an image of firm faith and believers confronting real danger, one which is great enough to make even believers' hearts tremble. Yet the believers transform this trembling into something that gives them hope and reassurance: "*When the*

47

believers saw the Confederate forces they said: 'This is what God and His Messenger have promised us! Truly spoke God and His Messenger.' This only served to strengthen their faith and their submission to God." (Verse 22)

The situation the Muslims faced on this occasion was so testing and stressful that it is described as such by none other than God: *"That was a situation when the believers were sorely tested and severely shaken."* (Verse 11) They were ordinary people, and people have limited ability. God does not charge them with more than they can bear. Despite being assured of God's eventual support and the good news the Prophet gave them, going beyond their immediate problems to tell them of where Islam would soon expand to, spreading into Yemen and Syria and even further east and west, danger was staring them in the eye, giving them almost too much stress to cope with.

Ḥudhayfah's story is perhaps the most accurate in relaying how the Muslims felt. The Prophet sensed this fear and apprehension. Therefore, when he wanted an assignment to be taken up, he made its reward clear. He said: 'Who is willing to go and find out what our enemies are doing and return. I shall pray to God to make any volunteer for this mission my Companion in Heaven.' Yet despite this certain promise of returning safely and being assured of a high place in heaven, there were still no volunteers. When the Prophet called Ḥudhayfah by name, he said: 'I then had no choice but to go.' This could not have happened except in a situation of extreme stress and hardship.

However, side by side with the rolled eyes and shaken hearts there was an unseverable bond with God, a firm awareness of divine rules, and an unshakeable belief that these rules cannot be changed, and that their results are bound to come about once they have been set in motion. Hence, the Muslims felt that their being so severely tested heralded their victory, because they knew that they had been true to their trust: *"Do you reckon that you will enter paradise while you have not suffered like those [believers] who passed away before you? Affliction and adversity befell them, and so terribly shaken were they that the Messenger and the believers with him would exclaim, 'When will God's help come?' Surely, God's help is close at hand."* (2: 214) They felt that they themselves had also been terribly shaken. Hence, God's help must be close at hand. This is what prompted them to say: "*This is what God and His Messenger have promised us! Truly spoke God and His Messenger. This only served to strengthen their faith and their submission to God.*" (Verse 22)

"*This is what God and His Messenger have promised us.*" Such trouble and distress is the preamble to the help we have been promised. Therefore, God's help is bound to come: "*Truly spoke God and His Messenger.*" They have spoken the truth in as far as both the indication and the result are concerned. Therefore, they were certain of the outcome: "*This only served to strengthen their faith and their submission to God.*"

Those Muslims were ordinary human beings subject to all the qualities and weaknesses that distinguish humans. Nor was it required of them that they surpass the limitations of the human race or shed its characteristics. God had created them such and they were meant to remain such. They were not expected to transform themselves into another race: angels, *jinn,* or animals. Therefore, as humans, it was inevitable that they would be afflicted by hardship and shaken when facing extreme danger, but they remained nevertheless faithful to their bond with God. This was the bond that stopped them from falling, renewed their hope and prevented their despair. This is what made the generation of the Prophet's Companions unique, having no parallel in history. We need to understand this very clearly and recognize that they attained their summit while retaining all their human strengths and weaknesses. At the same time, they also held tight to their bond with God.

When we see ourselves weaken under stress, shaken by danger or worry at what lies ahead, we must not allow despair to overwhelm us, or feel that we are lost, unfit to achieve any high standard. What we must not do is hold on to our weak feelings thinking that this must be so because it happens to others who are better than ourselves. We must remember our bond with God and hold to this, because it is through this that we can shed our weakness, and regain our confidence and reassurance. We should look at our worry and fear as a signal that help is on its way. Then we will find renewed strength and self belief.

It was such balance that moulded that unique generation in the early days of Islam, which the *sūrah* praises in the following terms: "*Among the believers are people who have always been true to what they have vowed before God. Some have already fulfilled their pledges by death, and some are still waiting. They have not changed in the least.*" (Verse 23) This is set against the other type of person who pledged to God that they would never run away, but who were untrue to their vows: "*They had previously vowed before God that they would never turn their backs in flight. A vow made to God must surely be answered for.*" (Verse 15)

One of the young Companions of the Prophet reports: "I was named after my uncle Anas ibn al-Naḍr. He did not take part in the Battle of Badr, and he was sad. He thought: 'This was the first major battle the Prophet fights and I was absent. Should I live to fight in another battle with the Prophet, God will see what I will do.' He then felt that this was a serious pledge and he feared to say anything more. He was later in the Muslim army in the Battle of Uḥud. Before the battle, he saw Saʿd ibn Muʿādh and said to him: 'Abū ʿAmr! I can smell heaven! I smell it coming from the side of Uḥud.' He fought hard until he was killed. He received 80 odd strikes variously from a sword, spear and arrow. Indeed, he was unrecognisable. His sister, my aunt, al-Rubayyiʿ bint al-Naḍr, said: 'I could only identify my brother by his finger.' When the verse saying, '*Among the believers are people who have always been true to what they have vowed before God,*' was revealed, people felt that this referred to him and others who did as he did." [Related by Aḥmad, Muslim, al-Tirmidhī and al-Nasāʾī.]

The *sūrah* then includes a comment stating the purpose of testing believers and the outcome of honouring a vow or breaking it: "*God will surely reward the truthful for having been true to their word, and will punish the hypocrites, if that be His will, or accept their repentance. God is indeed Much-Forgiving, Merciful.*" (Verse 24) Comments like this, which are often found within the description of events, serve to outline the purpose behind what takes place, making it clear that everything is determined by God's will. Nothing occurs by coincidence. Everything is according to plan and for a definite purpose. All events reflect God's grace and confirm that His forgiveness and mercy are always close at hand. "*God is indeed Much-Forgiving, Merciful.*" (Verse 24)

The *sūrah's* discussion of the Encounter of the Moat concludes by stating its outcome which confirmed the believers' expectations and showed how far in error the unbelievers and hypocrites had gone: "*God turned back the unbelievers in all their rage and fury; they gained no advantage. He spared the believers the need to fight. God is Most Powerful, Almighty.*" (Verse 25)

From start to finish, God was in control of the battle, turning it the way He wished. The *sūrah* confirms this in its presentation, attributing to God every event and its outcome, so that we can understand this fact making it part of our overall Islamic concept.

The Other Enemy

It was not only the Quraysh and the Ghaṭafān that suffered a miserable defeat. Their allies, the Jews of Qurayẓah also shared the same outcome: "*He brought down from their strongholds those of the people of earlier revelations who aided them, casting terror in their hearts: some you slew, and some you took captive. And He passed on to you their land, their houses and their goods, as well as a land on which you had never yet set foot. God has power over all things.*" (Verses 26–27) However, before we discuss these verses we need to throw some light on the attitude the Jews in Madinah adopted towards Islam.

When Islam arrived in Madinah, the Jews there maintained peaceful relations with it for only a short period. Shortly after his arrival in Madinah, the Prophet signed a treaty with them with mutual obligations of support against outside enemies and clear conditions that they would never be in breach of their commitments, or aid any enemy, or take any hostile action against the Muslims.

The Jews, however, soon felt that Islam represented a threat to their traditional position as followers of the divine faith. Indeed they enjoyed much respect by the people of Madinah on account of this fact. Moreover, they felt that the new social system Islam established in Madinah under the leadership of the Prophet also constituted a threat to their position. Previously, they had very cleverly exploited the conflict between the two main Arab tribes in Madinah, the Aws and the Khazraj, to ensure that they themselves had the upper hand. The Prophet united the two tribes in a new social system which deprived the Jews of the chance to sew discord between them.

Perhaps the last straw that broke the camel's back for them was that the rabbi they considered to be their master and leading scholar, 'Abdullāh ibn Sallām, converted to Islam with all his family members. However, he feared that should he announce his conversion to Islam in public, the Jews might level false accusations against him. Therefore, he requested that the Prophet ask them about him and his standing among them before telling them that he had become a Muslim. When the Prophet asked the Jews as 'Abdullāh had requested him, they said: 'He is our master as his father was; and he is our rabbi and leading scholar.' It was at this point that 'Abdullāh came out to tell them that Islam was God's message to mankind and he asked them to follow his example and become Muslims. They immediately turned against him, speaking ill of him and warning all the other Jews against him. Clearly they felt that Islam represented an imminent threat to their religious and political standing. They were determined to scheme against God's Messenger allowing him no respite. This, then, was the beginning of the war between Islam and the Jews, which has never subsided.

At first, the war started as a cold war, as we say these days. That is to say, it began as propaganda against both Muḥammad (peace be upon him) and Islam. The tactics they employed varied from raising doubts about the message and the new faith, to sowing discord and creating division between the Muslims, as between the Aws and the Khazraj one day and between the Muhājirīn and the Anṣār another day. They also spied on the Muslims for their idolater enemies, and befriended a group of hypocrites who pretended to be Muslim manipulating them to create trouble within the Muslim community. Ultimately, they openly urged other groups to unite against the Muslims, as happened in the encounter with the confederate tribes.

The major Jewish groups in Madinah were the tribes of the Qaynuqāʿ, al-Naḍīr and Qurayẓah. Each had its own ongoing situation with the Prophet and the Muslim community. The Qaynuqāʿ tribe, who were the best fighters among the Jews, begrudged the Muslims their victory at Badr. Therefore, they started to exploit little events against the Muslims, so demonstrating that they had little respect for their treaty with the Prophet, fearing that he would soon gather strength and gain mastery over them. Ibn Hishām mentions in his biography of the Prophet: "One aspect of the case of the Qaynuqāʿ Jews was that the Prophet addressed them in their market place, saying: 'Take warning from what happened to the Quraysh and adopt Islam. You already know that I am a prophet sent by God with a message. You read this in your own scriptures and you are committed to believe in me by God's promise to you.' They replied: 'Muḥammad! Do not take it as something great that you met people who have no knowledge of war and fighting and that you got the upper hand against them. Should we fight you, you will learn that we are the true fighters.'"

Ibn Hishām also reports on the authority of ʿAbdullāh ibn Jaʿfar: "Behind the problem of the Qaynuqāʿ was an Arab woman who had brought some milk and sold it in the Qaynuqāʿ Market. She then sat at a jeweller's shop. People there wanted her to uncover her face, but she refused. The jeweller took the edge of her dress and tied it to her back, without her noticing. When she rose, her bottom was exposed and people laughed at her. She shouted for help. A Muslim attacked the Jewish jeweller, and killed him. The Jews then attacked the Muslim and killed him. His people shouted for other Muslims to come and help. The Muslims were very angry and trouble so erupted between them and the Qaynuqāʿ clan."

Ibn Isḥāq continues this report of the events: "The Prophet laid siege to them until they agreed to accept his judgement. ʿAbdullāh ibn Ubayy [the chief of the hypocrites who was still accepted as a Muslim] went to the Prophet saying: 'Be good to my allies.' The Qaynuqāʿ were formerly allied to the Khazraj. The Prophet made no reply. ʿAbdullāh repeated this but the Prophet turned away. ʿAbdullāh then put his hand inside the Prophet's armour and the Prophet asked him to let him go. ʿAbdullāh did not listen. The Prophet became angry and said: 'Let me go!' ʿAbdullāh then said: 'I will not let you go until you are good to my allies. They are 700 fighters who protected me against all my enemies and you come to finish them off in one day. I am a man who fears the turn of fortune.' The Prophet then said to him: 'They are yours.'

'Abdullāh ibn Ubayy was clearly still held in high esteem by his clan. Furthermore, the Prophet accepted his intercession in favour of the Qaynuqāʿ Jews, provided they agreed to leave Madinah, taking their property with them, but not their weapons. Thus Madinah was rid of a powerful Jewish section.

As for the al-Naḍīr tribe, the Prophet went to their quarters in the fourth year of his migration to Madinah, after the Battle of Uḥud, seeking their help in raising funds to pay the blood money for two people killed accidentally by one of his Companions. According to the provisions of the agreement between them and the Muslim state, they were bound to make such a contribution. When he explained his purpose, they said: 'Yes, we will certainly make a contribution.' He sat with his back to the wall of one of their houses. Then they consulted among themselves, and some suggested: 'You will never again find this man in such a vulnerable state. Who can get to the roof of this house and throw a large rock to rid us of him?'

So they set about carrying out their wicked plot. The Prophet was informed of what they were planning; so he returned to Madinah. Once there, he ordered his community to prepare to fight the Jewish tribe of al-Naḍīr. They retreated to their forts. 'Abdullāh ibn Ubayy, the chief of the hypocrites, sent them word to remain steadfast promising to give them his full support. He added: 'We will never let you down. If war is waged against you, we will fight alongside you; and if you are made to leave, we will go with you.' The hypocrites, however, did not fulfil their promise to the Jews. Instead, God struck fear into the hearts of the al-Naḍīr and they surrendered without a fight. They asked the Prophet to spare their lives in return for their departure. He agreed and allowed them a camel load each of their property, provided they surrendered any arms. They thus left Madinah, most settling in Khaybar, whilst others went further north to Syria. Among their leaders were Sallām ibn Abī al-Ḥuqayq, Kinānah ibn al-Rabīʿ ibn Abī al-Ḥuqayq and Ḥuyay ibn Akhṭab, the three who had played a leading role in forging the alliance between the Quraysh and Ghaṭafān and so forming the confederate tribes that sought to exterminate Islam and the Muslims.

Treachery of Great Magnitude

This left only the Qurayzah, the third major Jewish tribe in Madinah. As we now know, they too had sided with the confederate tribes against the Muslims, this at the instigation of the al-Nadīr chiefs, particularly Huyay ibn Akhtab. This treachery by the Qurayzah, in violation of their treaty with the Prophet, was a much harder test for the Muslims than the external attack they faced from the confederates.

To be absolutely sure of this new situation, the Prophet sent four of his Companions – Saʿd ibn Muʿādh, the chief of the Aws, Saʿd ibn ʿUbādah, the chief of the Khazraj, ʿAbdullāh ibn Rawāhah and Khawāt ibn Jubayr – to the Qurayzah to ascertain their position: "If you find out that the intelligence we have received is true, give me a hint which I will understand. Try to avoid affecting the Muslims' morale. If, on the other hand, you find that the Qurayzah remain faithful to their treaty with us, make the news known to everyone." This shows how seriously he expected the news of treachery to affect the Muslim community as a whole.

The delegation went to the Qurayzah and met the people there, calling on them to maintain their peaceful relations and to confirm their alliance with the Prophet. However, they found that the Qurayzah had adopted a worse position than what they had heard about. Defiantly, they said: "You want us to confirm the alliance now, when we have been weakened by the departure of al-Nadīr. Who is God's Messenger? We do not know him. We have no treaty or agreement with Muhammad."

The Muslim delegation then left the Qurayzah, returning to the Prophet with the bad news that the Jews no longer recognized their peace treaty with him. On arrival, they found the Prophet with a group of his Companions. Following his advice, they gave him a clear hint of the Qurayzah's treachery rather than deliver the fact publicly. The Prophet was not perturbed. On the contrary, he said: "God is Supreme. Rejoice, you Muslims, for the end will be a happy one."

In his report of these events, Ibn Ishāq says: "This test was too hard for the Muslims: fear mounted; the enemy came upon them from the front and the rear; the Muslims' thoughts went in all directions; hypocrisy was now in the open, etc."

When God gave the Prophet His support so as to make his enemies withdraw without gaining any advantage, sparing the believers the need to fight, the Prophet returned to Madinah victorious. People put down their arms. Back in his wife, Umm Salamah's home, the Prophet was washing himself after the long ordeal. Jibrīl, the angel, came to him saying: "The angels have not put down their arms yet. I have just come back from chasing the enemy." He then said to him: "God commands you to march to the Qurayẓah." Their quarters were a few miles away from Madinah. This was after the noon *Ẓuhr* prayer. The Prophet issued an order to all his Companions: "He who obeys God must not pray *'Aṣr* except at the Qurayẓah." People started marching. On the way, the *'Aṣr* prayer became due. Some of them stopped to offer it arguing that the Prophet had only wanted them to start marching immediately. Others said they would prefer to delay it until they had arrived, taking the Prophet's order at face value. Neither party blamed the other.

The Prophet marched behind them, having asked Ibn Umm Maktūm, his blind Companion, to deputize for him in Madinah. He also gave the banner to his cousin 'Alī ibn Abī Ṭālib. The Prophet laid siege to the Qurazah quarter for 25 days. When they were in despair, they sent word to the Prophet saying that they would accept the judgement of Sa'd ibn Mu'ādh, the chief of the Aws tribe of the Anṣār, as he was their ally in pre-Islamic days. They felt that he was bound to be lenient towards them, just like 'Abdullāh ibn Ubayy had been lenient towards the Qaynuqā' Jews when he sought their release by the Prophet. They did not know, however, that Sa'd had received an injury to his arm during the earlier siege of Madinah and that the Prophet had the wound cauterized to stop it bleeding. He had also placed him in a tent close by where he was nursed. When he received his injury, Sa'd had prayed: "My Lord! If we are to fight the Quraysh again, spare me now for that fight. If you have willed that this encounter between us be the last, I pray to You, my Lord, to make this wound of mine my way to martyrdom, but spare me until I see our affair with the Qurayẓah have a happy ending for Islam.' God answered his prayer, making them choose him as their judge.

When the Qurayẓah Jews intimated that they would accept Saʿd's judgement, the Prophet gave instructions for him to be brought in. He came riding a donkey that had been saddled for him. On his way, his tribesmen, the Aws, tried to persuade him to be lenient. They said: 'Be kind to your allies. The Prophet has chosen you to judge them in order that you be kind to them.' Saʿd first chose to be silent. When he was tired of their insistence, he said: 'It is time for Saʿd to disregard all criticism when it comes to something through which he hopes to please God.' His tribesmen realized then that he would not be lenient.

As Saʿd approached the Prophet's tent, the Prophet said to those who were with him: 'Stand up to greet your master.' This was to give Saʿd extra respect in his position as judge and to make his judgement binding. When he sat down, the Prophet said to him that the Qurayẓah had agreed to accept his judgement in their case. Saʿd said: "Will my judgement be binding on them?" He was answered in the affirmative. He asked again: "And on all who are present [meaning the Muslims]?" Again he received a positive answer. He then lowered his head in deference to the Prophet, pointing his hand in the direction where the Prophet was sitting, without looking at him, and said: "Does this also apply to those who are on this side?" The Prophet answered: "Yes." Saʿd said: "I hereby rule that all the men of the Qurayẓah are to be killed, their properties to be divided and their women and children to be enslaved." The Prophet endorsed the ruling and said to him: "You have given God's own verdict."

At the Prophet's orders, moats were dug in the marketplace and the Qurayẓah men were brought there with their hands tied. They were all executed. According to different reports they constituted somewhere between 700–800 people. Ḥuyay ibn Akhṭab was among them, remaining faithful to his promise to stay with them and share their fate. Whoever of their young men was below the age of puberty was spared.

That day not only marked the humiliation of the Jews but also the weakness of hypocrisy. Thereafter, the hypocrites were reluctant to continue with their earlier trickery. Moreover, the idolaters no longer thought of attacking the Muslims in Madinah. In fact it was the Muslims who were now able to go on the offensive. Events thus moved in such a way as to lead to the fall of the two main cities in Arabia, Makkah and Ṭā'if, to Islam. It may be said that the actions of the Jews, the hypocrites and the idolaters were interlinked, and that the expulsion of the Jews from Madinah put an end to such affiliations. The whole episode thus marked a totally new stage in the history of the Muslim state.

This was the practical development to which God refers in the Qur'ānic verses:

> *He brought down from their strongholds those of the people of earlier revelations who aided them, casting terror in their hearts: some you slew, and some you took captive. And He passed on to you their land, their houses and their goods, as well as a land on which you had never yet set foot. God has power over all things."* (Verses 26–27)

The phrase, 'a land on which you had never yet set foot,' can refer either to a land that the Qurayẓah owned outside their quarters, and which the Muslims took over along with the rest of their property, or it may refer to the fact that the Qurayẓah surrendered their land without fighting. In this second sense, the Arabic phrase *taṭa'ū*, meaning, 'to set foot,' indicates fighting, which involves taking land by force.

"*God has power over all things.*" This comment is taken from what takes place in reality. It refers all matters to God. The *sūrah*'s presentation of the battle and its commentary on events are altogether consistent with this. It attributes all matters and actions to God, so that this essential truth is firmly rooted in the hearts of all Muslims. We see how God establishes it in people's hearts using first the actual events and then the Qur'ān as it makes a record of these events. Thus it takes its place at the centre of the overall Islamic concept.

In this way, the events become the subject matter of education, and the Qur'ān a manual and guide for life and all that relates to it. Values are well established and hearts reassured, using both the practical test and the Qur'ān as the means.

3

Unlike All Women

Prophet! Say to your wives: 'If you desire the life of this world and its charms, I shall provide for you and release you in a becoming manner; (28)

يَـٰٓأَيُّهَا ٱلنَّبِيُّ قُل لِّأَزْوَٰجِكَ إِن كُنتُنَّ تُرِدْنَ ٱلْحَيَوٰةَ ٱلدُّنْيَا وَزِينَتَهَا فَتَعَالَيْنَ أُمَتِّعْكُنَّ وَأُسَرِّحْكُنَّ سَرَاحًا جَمِيلًا ۝

but if you desire God and His Messenger and the life of the hereafter, know that God has readied great rewards for those of you who do good.' (29)

وَإِن كُنتُنَّ تُرِدْنَ ٱللَّهَ وَرَسُولَهُۥ وَٱلدَّارَ ٱلْأَخِرَةَ فَإِنَّ ٱللَّهَ أَعَدَّ لِلْمُحْسِنَٰتِ مِنكُنَّ أَجْرًا عَظِيمًا ۝

Wives of the Prophet! If any of you were to be guilty of manifestly immoral conduct, her punishment would be doubled. That is easy for God. (30)

يَـٰنِسَآءَ ٱلنَّبِيِّ مَن يَأْتِ مِنكُنَّ بِفَٰحِشَةٍ مُّبَيِّنَةٍ يُضَٰعَفْ لَهَا ٱلْعَذَابُ ضِعْفَيْنِ وَكَانَ ذَٰلِكَ عَلَى ٱللَّهِ يَسِيرًا ۝

But if any of you devoutly obeys God and His Messenger and does good deeds, We shall grant her a double reward, and We have prepared for her most excellent provisions. (31)

وَمَن يَقْنُتْ مِنكُنَّ لِلَّهِ وَرَسُولِهِۦ وَتَعْمَلْ صَٰلِحًا نُّؤْتِهَآ أَجْرَهَا مَرَّتَيْنِ وَأَعْتَدْنَا لَهَا رِزْقًا كَرِيمًا ۝

59

Wives of the Prophet! You are unlike any other women: if you truly fear God, do not speak too soft, lest any who is sick at heart should be moved with desire; but speak in an appropriate manner. (32)

يَٰنِسَآءَ ٱلنَّبِىِّ لَسْتُنَّ كَأَحَدٍ مِّنَ ٱلنِّسَآءِ إِنِ ٱتَّقَيْتُنَّ فَلَا تَخْضَعْنَ بِٱلْقَوْلِ فَيَطْمَعَ ٱلَّذِى فِى قَلْبِهِۦ مَرَضٌ وَقُلْنَ قَوْلًا مَّعْرُوفًا ﴿٣٢﴾

And stay quietly in your homes, and do not display your charms as they used to display them in the old days of pagan ignorance. Attend regularly to your prayers, and pay the obligatory charity, i.e. zakāt, and pay heed to God and His Messsenger. God only wants to remove all that is loathsome from you, you members of the [Prophet's] household, and to purify you fully. (33)

وَقَرْنَ فِى بُيُوتِكُنَّ وَلَا تَبَرَّجْنَ تَبَرُّجَ ٱلْجَٰهِلِيَّةِ ٱلْأُولَىٰ وَأَقِمْنَ ٱلصَّلَوٰةَ وَءَاتِينَ ٱلزَّكَوٰةَ وَأَطِعْنَ ٱللَّهَ وَرَسُولَهُۥٓ إِنَّمَا يُرِيدُ ٱللَّهُ لِيُذْهِبَ عَنكُمُ ٱلرِّجْسَ أَهْلَ ٱلْبَيْتِ وَيُطَهِّرَكُمْ تَطْهِيرًا ﴿٣٣﴾

Bear in mind all that is recited in your homes of God's revelations and wisdom; for God is unfathomable in His wisdom, all aware. (34)

وَٱذْكُرْنَ مَا يُتْلَىٰ فِى بُيُوتِكُنَّ مِنْ ءَايَٰتِ ٱللَّهِ وَٱلْحِكْمَةِ إِنَّ ٱللَّهَ كَانَ لَطِيفًا خَبِيرًا ﴿٣٤﴾

For all men and women who have submitted themselves to God, all believing men and believing women, all truly devout men and truly devout women, all men and women who are true to their word, all men and women who are patient in adversity, all

إِنَّ ٱلْمُسْلِمِينَ وَٱلْمُسْلِمَٰتِ وَٱلْمُؤْمِنِينَ وَٱلْمُؤْمِنَٰتِ وَٱلْقَٰنِتِينَ وَٱلْقَٰنِتَٰتِ وَٱلصَّٰدِقِينَ وَٱلصَّٰدِقَٰتِ وَٱلصَّٰبِرِينَ وَٱلصَّٰبِرَٰتِ

men and women who humble themselves before God, all men and women who give in charity, all men and women who fast, all men and women who are mindful of their chastity, and all men and women who always remember God – for them all God has prepared forgiveness of sins and a mighty reward. (35)

وَٱلْخَٰشِعِينَ وَٱلْخَٰشِعَٰتِ
وَٱلْمُتَصَدِّقِينَ وَٱلْمُتَصَدِّقَٰتِ
وَٱلصَّٰٓئِمِينَ وَٱلصَّٰٓئِمَٰتِ
وَٱلْحَٰفِظِينَ فُرُوجَهُمْ
وَٱلْحَٰفِظَٰتِ وَٱلذَّٰكِرِينَ
ٱللَّهَ كَثِيرًا وَٱلذَّٰكِرَٰتِ
أَعَدَّ ٱللَّهُ لَهُم مَّغْفِرَةً وَأَجْرًا
عَظِيمًا ﴿٣٥﴾

Overview

This third passage in the *sūrah* speaks specifically of the Prophet's wives, except for the last verse which tells of the reward for all Muslims, men and women, for their good actions. At the beginning of the *sūrah*, they were called *'mothers of the believers'*, and this motherhood establishes certain duties. Their noble position, which earned them this status, also establishes certain duties. Further duties are also made obligatory on them because of their relationship to the Prophet. The present passage outlines some of these duties and states the values God wants the Prophet's home, with all its purity, to represent and uphold so as to serve as a beacon of light guiding travellers.

A Choice is Offered

Prophet! Say to your wives: 'If you desire the life of this world and its charms, I shall provide for you and release you in a becoming manner; but if you desire God and His Messenger and the life of the hereafter, know that God has readied great rewards for those of you who do good.' (Verses 28–29)

The Prophet chose for himself and his household a standard of living which was just about enough to meet their essential needs. The reason for so doing was not that he could not afford a better standard of living. Indeed, enormous tracts of land came under his control, yielding great wealth, and availing him of great riches if he so chose. Yet there were times when a month would pass without a fire being lit for cooking in any of his homes. At the same time, the Prophet was extremely generous when it came to giving gifts and charitable donations. Essentially, then, he made this choice so as to rise above material and worldly needs, and to sincerely seek what God keeps for believers. It was a question of preference. Neither his faith nor the law it lays down required that the Prophet lead such a life of austerity. Comfort and luxury are not disdained in Islam. Indeed, the Prophet did not turn his back on them when they were offered normally, without being sought after. Yet, he neither excessively indulged in them nor was he so preoccupied. We do not find any instruction from the Prophet requiring that any of his followers live the sort of life he chose for himself. He left it entirely to them, should they choose to emulate him in freeing themselves from the pressures of seeking life's comforts.

The Prophet's wives were ordinary women who shared all human feelings and desires. Noble, virtuous and close to the Prophet as they all were, their natural desire for life's comforts remained strong. When they felt that circumstances had changed and, by God's grace, prosperity had replaced poverty in the Muslim society, they spoke to the Prophet about their standard of living. He did not welcome this. In fact it was unpleasant to him, because his noble soul preferred to live without any such preoccupation. He appreciated the freedom and sublimity such a life provides. It was not a matter of whether life's comforts were lawful or not: there was no question of prohibition as Islam made it clear that such comforts were not prohibited for Muslims. It was rather a question of being free from material pressures.

The Prophet was so upset at this turn of events that he did not go out to meet his Companions. That he stayed away was very hard for them. They, therefore, went to see him, but were not admitted. Imām Aḥmad relates on Jābir's authority: "Abū Bakr went to the Prophet when people were sitting near his door, but he was not admitted. 'Umar also went, sought permission to enter but no such permission was given. Later on though, he admitted both Abū Bakr and 'Umar. As they went in, they saw the Prophet surrounded by his wives but he was silent. 'Umar thought that he should say something to make the Prophet laugh. He said: 'Messenger of God! I wish you had seen how last night my wife was asking me for more money and I thrust my fingers into her neck.' The Prophet laughed heartily and said: 'You see them surrounding me asking for more money.' Abū Bakr rose to hit his daughter, 'Ā'ishah, while 'Umar sought to do the same to Ḥafṣah, his daughter. Both said to them: 'Are you asking the Prophet to give you what he has not?' The Prophet told them not to hit their daughters, and both 'Ā'ishah and Ḥafṣah said: 'By God! We will never again ask the Prophet for anything he does not have.' God then revealed the verses offering them the choice. The Prophet started with 'Ā'ishah saying to her: 'I am going to tell you something which I would like you to consider carefully and consult your parents before you decide.' He then read to her the two verses: *"Prophet! Say to your wives: 'If you desire the life of this world and its charms, I shall provide for you and release you in a becoming manner; but if you desire God and His Messenger and the life of the hereafter, know that God has readied great rewards for those of you who do good."* She said to him: 'Would I consult my parents about staying with you? I certainly choose God and His Messenger. However, I would request you not to mention my choice to any of your other wives.' He said to her: 'God has not sent me to adopt a hard attitude, but He has made me a teacher and a facilitator. If any of them asks me about your choice, I will tell her.'" [This *ḥadīth* is also related by Muslim on the authority of Zakariyyā ibn Isḥāq, and related in a slightly different wording by al-Bukhārī.]

The Qur'ān defines the principal values in the Islamic concept of human life. These values must be practically reflected in the Prophet's home and in his own private life. His home remains a beacon of light for Muslims throughout human life. Hence it should provide the best and most accurate example of Islamic values.

The two verses gave the Prophet's wives a choice: either world luxuries and life comforts or God, His Messenger and the life to come. No single heart can accommodate two different value systems. The

Prophet's wives had already said that they would never again ask the Prophet for what he did not have. The Qur'ānic verses were revealed to define the principle involved. It is not a question of whether the Prophet has such luxuries or not: it is a question of choosing between God, the Prophet and the life to come on the one hand and the luxuries and adornments of the present life on the other. The Prophet's wives were to choose whether they had worldly treasures at their disposal or their homes were without food. When this decisive choice was offered, they all made their preference clearly and absolutely, choosing God, the Prophet and success in the life to come. They proved themselves fit for the sublime standard their high position as the Prophet's wives required. One report also mentions that the Prophet was delighted with their choice.

All Were Human

We need to pause a little to reflect on some aspects of this event which defines the Islamic concept of values. It leaves our hearts with no room for hesitation between worldly values and those of the life to come; between the world we live in and the world of heaven. It purges our hearts of any influence that hinders us from purely seeking God's pleasure, to the exclusion of everything else.

From another point of view, the event describes to us the nature of the Prophet's lifestyle, as well as those who lived with him and were closely related to him. The most beautiful thing about this lifestyle is the fact that it was chosen by ordinary people who never lost sight of their human feelings, desires and preferences, despite rising to sublime standards of devotion and dedication. Their human feelings and emotions did not die; they only rose to an exalted level and were purged of impurity while retaining their natural human beauty. Thus, they enabled them to attain the highest standard of perfection possible.

We often err when we give the Prophet and his Companions an untrue or incomplete image that does not consider all their human characteristics and emotions. We think that in this way we put them above what we consider to be a weakness. Our mistake renders the Prophet and his Companions opaque, devoid of their essential human features and characteristics. The human relation between us and them is severed, and we begin to see them as ghosts lacking a tangible reality. We begin to think of them as belonging to a different species: angels or a similar type of creature above human feelings and emotions. In this way they are removed from our lives and if we permit this they will no longer provide us with an example to follow or to be influenced by. When we read the history of the Prophet and his Companions we no longer find in this something for us to emulate, but instead we find ourselves looking at their lives with an awe and admiration that produces only vague feelings without practical effect. We also lose our ability to identify with such great personalities, because we no longer see them as ordinary humans who experienced the same emotions, feelings and reactions as we ourselves experience.

We can clearly understand God's wisdom in assigning His messages to ordinary men to deliver. This task was not assigned to angels or to creatures from any other species. This provides a real bond between the lives of the messengers and the lives of their followers. The latter continue to feel that the messengers' feelings and emotions, exalted as they were, were always those of humans. Thus, they love them and try to emulate them in the same way as children try to emulate adults.

In the question of the choice offered to the Prophet's wives we note their natural desire for comforts and luxuries. We also see an image of the Prophet's home life, with his wives asking their husband for more money. He is upset, but he does not allow Abū Bakr and 'Umar to beat 'Ā'ishah and Ḥafṣah, their daughters for their requests. The whole question is one of feelings and inclinations, which need to be refined, not suppressed. The question remains at this level until God orders the Prophet to give his wives the choice and they make their free choice without pressure or the suppression of any feelings. That his wives opted for the sublime standard he preferred greatly delighted the Prophet.

We also need to reflect for a moment on what we see of sweet emotion in the Prophet's heart. He shows that he loves 'Ā'ishah and that he would love it if she rose to the standard of values God wants for him and his household. He therefore offers her the choice. He wants to help her rise to the sublime, so he asks that she does not make a decision until she has consulted her parents. He knows that her parents would never ask their daughter to leave him. 'Ā'ishah does not overlook the Prophet's sweet emotion towards her. She is delighted with it, and she mentions this in her report. In this *ḥadīth* we see the Prophet as a man in love with his young wife, and as someone who would be delighted to see her rise to, and maintain the standard he has adopted for his life. We also see her delighted to recognize her place in her husband's heart, reporting his love and desire to keep her, which is manifested by his request that she consult her parents. We also see the woman in her as she requests him not to tell his other wives of her choice. She wants to be the one who makes that choice, ahead of at least some of them. But we also see the Prophet's greatness as he tells her: 'God has not sent me to adopt a hard attitude, but He made me a teacher and facilitator. If any of them asks me about your choice, I will tell her.' He does not want to deprive any of them of what could help them make the right choice. He is not testing them to see who might fail; rather he is helping those who request help, so that they can rise above worldly attractions.

All these are noble human elements which we must never ignore, suppress or undervalue as we read the Prophet's life story. To understand them as they truly are establishes a strong and active bond between us and the Prophet's person, as well as the personalities of his Companions. We can thus interact with them in a way that motivates us into emulation.

A Unique Position

The *sūrah* then outlines some special features for the Prophet's wives, giving them special privileges and responsibilities, which suit their noble status and their relation to the Prophet:

> *Wives of the Prophet! If any of you were to be guilty of manifestly immoral conduct, her punishment would be doubled. That is easy for God. But if any of you devoutly obeys God and His Messenger and does good deeds, We shall grant her a double reward, and We have prepared for her most excellent provisions.* (Verses 30–31)

This is a responsibility commensurate with their status as wives of the Prophet and mothers of all believers. Both positions impose on them heavy duties and protect them against immorality. If, for argument's sake, any of them is guilty of some manifestly immoral conduct, she would deserve double punishment. This relates to the responsibility associated with their position and status. *"That is easy for God."* It is in no way more difficult as a result of their status as the Prophet's wives, as some people might think. *"But if any of you devoutly obeys God and His Messenger and does good deeds, We shall grant her a double reward,"* just as We double her punishment in the opposite situation. *"And We have prepared for her most excellent provisions."* (Verse 31) It is all ready, waiting for her, by God's grace.

The *sūrah* then explains what distinguishes the Prophet's wives from all other women, outlining their duties in dealing with other people, worshipping God, their conduct at home, and the special care God takes of the Prophet's noble household:

> *Wives of the Prophet! You are unlike any other women: if you truly fear God, do not speak too soft, lest any who is sick at heart should be moved with desire; but speak in an appropriate manner. And stay quietly in your homes, and do not display your charms as they used to display them in the old days of pagan ignorance. Attend regularly to your prayers, and pay the obligatory charity, i.e. zakāt, and pay heed to God and His Messsenger. God only wants to remove all that is loathsome from you, you members of the [Prophet's] household, and to purify you fully. Bear in mind all that is recited in your homes of God's revelations and wisdom; for God is unfathomable in His wisdom, all aware. (Verses 32–34)*

At the dawn of Islam, Arabian society looked upon women as a means of enjoyment and physical fulfilment. In this, it was like most other societies at the time. From a purely human angle, Arabian society simply looked upon women as inferior. Islam also found in Arabian society much confusion in sexual relations. The family system, moreover, was unsound, as already explained in this *sūrah*. Moreover, sex was looked at in a carnal way that disregarded beauty and purity and endorsed a wild, physical approach. This is clear in pre-Islamic poetry which focused on the woman's body, and expressed carnal thoughts.

Islam began to change the social attitude towards women, emphasizing the human aspect in relations between the two sexes. It is not merely a physical relation that seeks to satisfy a carnal urge. It is rather the meeting of two people, created from one soul, connected with a tie based on affection and mercy, and bringing both of them comfort and reassurance. Their meeting has a goal related to God's will that brought man into being, gave the earth its population and assigned to man the charge of taking care of the earth.

Islam also paid attention to family ties, making the family the central unit of its social structure. The precursor for this was a caring home where future generations start life and find a healthy atmosphere free from negative influences that contaminate feelings and ideas. Family law constitutes a sizeable portion of Islamic legislation and takes up a considerable number of Qur'ānic verses. In addition to enacting legislation, Islam continually directs its followers to the need to strengthen this societal base, particularly ensuring its spiritual purity, keeping relations between the sexes clean, respectable and free from vulgarity, even in the gratification of sexual urges. In fact, the organization of society and family matters takes up a large part of the present *sūrah*. The passage we are currently discussing now includes an address to the Prophet's wives giving them instructions concerning their relations with other people, their own status and their relations with God. This address also includes a gentle directive expressed in fine style: "*God only wants to remove all that is loathsome from you, you members of the [Prophet's] household, and to purify you fully.*" (Verse 33)

What are the means to remove what is loathsome and ensure the purity of those women married to the Prophet, living in his home and who were in any case the purest women in the whole world? Needless to say, other women are in greater need of such means.

Initially, the *sūrah* makes them aware of their high positions and the advantages they have over all other women, making it clear that this is unique to them and cannot be shared by any other women in history. Hence, it is their duty to ensure that they can meet the obligations attendant with their status: "*Wives of the Prophet! You are unlike any other women, if you truly fear God.*" (Verse 32) They are told that their unique position is dependent on their being God-fearing. It is not their mere relation to the Prophet that gives them their status. Hence, they have to be up to the task, doing what this entails.

This is the plain truth that forms the basis of this religion of Islam. It is stated in absolute clarity by the Prophet as he addresses his own family, telling them that their close relation to him should not make them oblivious of their duties; he cannot benefit them anything unless they redeem themselves through their own actions: "Fāṭimah bint Muḥammad! Ṣafiyyah bint 'Abd al-Muṭṭalib! All you of the 'Abd al-Muṭṭalib clan! I can in no way benefit you against God. You can ask me whatever you wish of my own money." [Related by Muslim.] Another version quotes the Prophet as broadening his address so as to include first the entire Quraysh tribe, and narrowing it gradually to his own small clan and finishing it by addressing his own daughter: "You the Quraysh people! Save yourselves from hell. You the Ka'b people! Save yourselves from hell. You the Hāshim clan! Save yourselves from the fire. You the 'Abd al-Muṭṭalib clan! Save yourselves from the fire. Fāṭimah bint Muḥammad! Save yourself from the fire. By God! I can benefit you nothing against God. However, you are my relations and I will honour this relation and foster it." [Related by Muslim and al-Tirmidhī.]

Having outlined their status which they earn through being God-fearing, the *surah* outlines the means by which God removes what is loathsome from the members of the Prophet's household: "*do not speak too soft, lest any who is sick at heart should be moved with desire.*" (Verse 32) When they speak to strangers, they must not use the sort of softness in their speech which arouses men's desires and make those who are sick at heart feel their urge.

It is pertinent to ask who are those women to whom God issues this warning? They are the Prophet's own wives and the mothers of all believers. Our minds cannot imagine that anyone would be tempted to think of them in terms of physical desire. When then is this warning issued? During the Prophet's own lifetime and in the best of human societies. However, God who created men and women knows that

69

when a woman speaks too softly, with yielding tones, she touches upon man's desire and awakens his urge. He also knows that in all societies there are people who are sick at heart, and who think of every woman in carnal terms, even though she may be married to the Prophet and has the status of a mother of all believers. God is perfectly aware that loathsomeness can only be purged when the causes that awaken desire are removed.

How about our own society which deliberately awakens desire and plays on it? Everything around us aims to bring sexual desire into full play, and encourages promiscuity. In modern society, women are encouraged to use speech, appearance, attractions, in order to move men to desire and let loose their urge. How can purity find a place in this polluted atmosphere when people's movements, speech and appearance serve to encourage the very loathsome thing that God wants to remove from His chosen servants?

"But speak in an appropriate manner." (Verse 32) They were first ordered not to speak in a soft way; now they are ordered to confine their talk to what is appropriate. Indeed the subject matter of a conversation may encourage certain thoughts. Therefore, there must not be in the conversation between men and women anything that leads to what is improper. This applies to the tone of voice, jokes and ordinary chatting. We should remember that it is God, the Creator who knows His creation and what affects and influences them, who gives these instructions to the Prophet's wives who were already exemplary in their purity. They were required to observe these instructions with the people of their own society, which was the best human society ever.

"And stay quietly in your homes." (Verse 33) The Arabic word used here, *qarna*, connotes having weight that facilitates stability. This order does not mean staying permanently at home so as not to go out at all. It only indicates that to be at home is the normal situation, and whatever else is the exception that meets a need. In the home a woman finds herself as fits her nature: sound, undistorted and uncontaminated. She fulfils her role without being overburdened with duties God has not equipped her to fulfil.

In order to give the family home its proper atmosphere that is suited for the upbringing of young children, God made it a binding duty of the man to support the woman financially. Thus, the mother has the energy, time and freedom to look after her young ones and give the family its congenial and relaxed atmosphere. A mother who has to work in order to earn her living, giving her job her time and energy cannot bring freshness and a pleasant ambience into her family home. She cannot give her children what is due to them of care and attention. The homes of women who go out to work every day are akin to hotels in their atmosphere. They have but little of the pleasant atmosphere of a proper family home. In fact a home can only be established by a woman; its pleasant congeniality can only be ensured by a wife, and its tenderness and care can only be generated by a mother. A wife and mother who spends her time and energy, physical and spiritual, at work cannot bring anything into her home other than her tiredness and boredom.

When a woman goes out to work, that constitutes a disaster for her home, which may be allowed by necessity. That people should resort to it when they have no need for it is a setback affecting souls and minds at a time when too many social ills are encountered.[3]

When a woman goes out frequently, for something other than work, such as visiting places of entertainment, clubs and the like, then this represents a setback for humanity. During the Prophet's lifetime, women used to go to the mosque, as there was no directive to prohibit them from so doing. However, that was a time when moral standards were high and most people were God-fearing. Moreover, a woman went out for prayer, and no one could recognize her. She revealed nothing of her charms. Nevertheless, after the Prophet died 'Ā'ishah preferred that they did not go to the mosque. An authentic *hadīth* related by al-Bukhārī and Muslim quotes 'Ā'ishah as saying: "Muslim

---

3. Sayyid Qutb, *Al-Salām al-'Ālamī wa'l-Islām*, or 'Islam and World Peace', Cairo and Beirut, 6th edition, 1982, pp. 69–70.

71

women used to attend Fajr, or the dawn prayer with God's Messenger and then go back home wrapped in their outer garments, unrecognizable in the darkness." Another report quotes her as saying: "Had God's Messenger seen what women have introduced into their behaviour, he would have disallowed them in mosques, just as Israelite women were disallowed." [Related by al-Bukhārī and Muslim.]

What could women have introduced into their lives during 'Ā'ishah's lifetime to make her think that God's Messenger would have not allowed them in the mosques? How does this compare with what we see in our own time?

"And do not display your charms as they used to display them in the old days of pagan ignorance." (Verse 33) This applies when a woman needs to go out, and it follows the order to stay quietly at home. In pre-Islamic days in Arabia, women used to display their charms, but all reports about such displays appear trifling, or even decent when compared with how women reveal their charms in our present climate. Mujāhid defines it as women walking alongside men and among them, while Qatādah says that they used to walk in a coquettish way. Muqātil ibn Ḥayyān, on the other hand, says that a display of charms meant that a woman would throw her head cover over her head without tightening it to cover her necklace, earrings or neck. Indeed, all this could be seen. Ibn Kathīr mentioned that a woman could walk among men, revealing her chest. She might also reveal her neck, plaits and earrings. Hence, God ordered female believers to cover themselves.

Such were the displays in ignorant Arabia and with which the Qur'ān dealt, purging the Muslim community from their effects and removing the elements that could lead to immoral behaviour. In so doing, the Qur'ān elevated thoughts, manners and feelings and it refined the senses of the Muslim community.

We say, 'senses' because the type of taste which admires the naked human body is vulgar, uncouth and lacks refinement. It is certainly less civilized than one which admires the beauty of modest appearance and what it indicates of beauty of soul, feeling and morality. This is a true measure of civilized human standards. Modesty has its own refined beauty which cannot be appreciated by people with coarse taste who only admire the naked flesh.

The Qur'ānic text speaks of such displays of women's charms as belonging to *'the old days of pagan ignorance,'* using the Arabic term *jāhiliyyah* which, in Islamic usage, refers to pre-Islamic days. Thus, it implies that displaying physical charms belongs to the old days of ignorance. People who have left such ignorance behind and attained a higher standard of ideals and concepts will ignore such vulgarity.

We need to explain here that the term *jāhiliyyah* describes social conditions and a philosophy of life, not a particular period of time. Therefore, *jāhiliyyah* could exist at any time and in any society. Hence we can say that we live today in a period of blind *jāhiliyyah*, which reflects vulgar tastes and unrefined concepts, pulling humanity to a humiliating and lowly level of civilization. When society accepts such standards, it cannot enjoy purity or blessings. Only a society that adopts the means of purification which the Prophet and the members of his household were the first to practise will attain such purity and blessings. The Qur'ān directs the Prophet's wives to these means, and then turns their eyes towards the sublime, giving them light and helping them to rise to the high standards their bond with God requires: *"Attend regularly to your prayers, and pay the obligatory charity, i.e. zakāt, and pay heed to God and His Messsenger."* (Verse 33)

Worship is not divorced from social and moral behaviour. It is indeed the means by which to attain those high standards. The tie with God is indispensable, because it gives strength, purity of heart and immunity to social pressures. With such a tie, a believer feels that he follows better guidance than his community, and that he can lead others to the light he sees, rather than following their lead to the darkness they live in. In fact, mankind sinks into the ignorance of *jāhiliyyah* whenever they deviate from God's path.

Islam is a fully integrated whole that includes rituals, manners, morality, systems and laws, placing them all within the framework of faith. Each aspect has its role in putting this faith into practice. They work in full harmony. It is such integrated unity and harmony that provides the overall structure of Islam in practice. Hence, the order to attend to prayer, pay *zakāt* and obey God and His Messenger comes as the last of the moral and behavioural directives given to members of the Prophet's household. In fact, none of those directives can work fully in practice without worship and obedience. In fact, all this serves a definite purpose: "*God only wants to remove all that is loathsome from you, you members of the [Prophet's] household, and to purify you fully.*" (Verse 33)

The way this statement is phrased imparts gentle and tender feelings. They are described here as *'members of the household'*, without defining which household. In the text's translation we added in brackets the word 'Prophet' for explanation. By omitting it, the Qur'ān refers to it as if it is the only household in the world that deserves to be called as such. Once the word 'household', or *bayt* in Arabic, is used, then it has been defined. A similar usage applies to the Ka'bah, God's house. It is often called *al-bayt*, or 'The House'. Hence this reference to the Prophet's household adds an element of special honour.

The *sūrah* says: "*God only wants to remove all that is loathsome from you, you members of the [Prophet's] household, and to purify you fully.*" (Verse 33) We note the very kindly and gentle approach adopted here. It tells them that God in all His majesty is the One to ensure their purification and the removal of all that is loathsome from them. This is direct care from God shown to the members of this household. We appreciate this care more fully when we remember that it is said by none other than God Almighty, who said to the universe, 'Be', and it came into existence, and who is in control of everything, the Lord of all majesty and glory. Furthermore, He says this in His book which is recited on high and recited in every place on earth, at all times, by millions in their devotion. Furthermore, these directives are given as a means of purification and removing what is loathsome. These are goals achieved by means which people adopt in their practical lives. This is the method Islam prefers, combining feelings of consciousness of God with action and behaviour. Together they reflect Islamic life and achieve its goals in human society.

These directives to the Prophet's wives are concluded, as they started, with a reminder of their high position and special privileges over other women. This they earn by their relation to God's Messenger and the grace with which God has favoured them when He made their homes the place where revelation is bestowed from on high, providing light, guidance and wisdom: "*Bear in mind all that is recited in your homes of*

God's revelations and wisdom; for God is unfathomable in His wisdom, all aware." (Verse 34) That is certainly a great privilege which is fully appreciated once it is mentioned. We should remember that this reminder is given at the conclusion of the address that started with offering the Prophet's wives a choice between the luxuries of this life on the one hand and God, His Messenger and the life to come on the other. This helps us to appreciate the great favour God has granted them and to recognize the triviality of the present life with all its attractions and luxuries.

Values in Islamic Life

When it comes to the purification of the Muslim community and establishing its life on the basis of Islamic values, men and women are equal and have the same role. Therefore, the *sūrah* gives these in detail:

> *For all men and women who have submitted themselves to God, all believing men and believing women, all truly devout men and truly devout women, all men and women who are true to their word, all men and women who are patient in adversity, all men and women who humble themselves before God, all men and women who give in charity, all men and women who fast, all men and women who are mindful of their chastity, and all men and women who always remember God – for them all God has prepared forgiveness of sins and a mighty reward.* (Verse 35)

These qualities grouped together in this one verse work together to form a Muslim's character. These are: self surrender to God, faith, devotion, being true to one's word, patience in adversity, humility before God, being charitable, fasting, being mindful of one's chastity, and remembering God at all times. Each quality has its own role to play in a Muslim's life.

The first two qualities are expressed in the two Arabic words *islām* and *īmān*, which mean 'submission' and 'belief' respectively. There is a strong interrelation between the two, or we can say that both are two sides of the same coin. Submission is the outcome of belief and true belief gives rise to submission. 'Devotion' means obedience that results from submission and belief, through inner acceptance, not external pressure. 'Truthfulness' is the quality essential for every Muslim. Whoever does not possess this quality cannot be within the ranks of the Muslim community. God says in the Qur'ān: "*It is only those who do not believe in God's revelations that invent falsehood.*" (16: 105) Thus, a liar is expelled from the ranks of the community which always remains true to its word, the Muslim community.

The next quality is 'patience in adversity'. In fact a Muslim cannot fulfil the requirements and duties of his faith without this quality. Islam needs patience in adversity at every step. Muslims have to be patient, resisting desire, bearing the harm inflicted by others, overcoming impediments, patiently addressing weaknesses and crookedness in other people, and going through the tests of either an easy life or hardship. Essentially, both are difficult predicaments.

'Humility before God' is an inner quality that reflects how we feel God's majesty deep in our hearts and how truly and willingly we obey and fear Him. 'Being charitable' indicates purification from greed and self indulgence. It also reflects care for others and kindness to them, as well as mutual security within the Muslim community. It is an act of gratitude to God for what He gives us and represents our discharging our duty on wealth.

'Fasting' is considered a quality because of its regular and consistent nature. It reflects an attitude that rises above the essential needs of life, enhancing man's willpower and giving supremacy within man's constitution to human qualities. 'Being mindful of one's chastity' involves not only the element of purity but also the proper control of the most profound and powerful desire in man. In fact, no one can achieve such proper control except one who is a God-fearing believer and who seeks God's help. This quality also regulates relations between people and aims to elevate the meeting between man and woman to a level that is higher than that of the urge of the flesh. It makes this meeting subject to God's law and serves the purpose of creating both sexes to populate the earth and build human life on it.

'Remembering God at all times' provides the link between all human activity and man's faith. It makes man mindful of God at every moment.

He thus constantly retains his strong bond with Him. Moreover, his mind and heart beam with happiness and the light of life. Those who reflect all these qualities, essential as they are for the building of Islamic character, are the ones for whom *"God has prepared forgiveness of sins and a mighty reward."* (Verse 35)

In conclusion we should note how the *sūrah* gives an account of the qualities of all Muslims, men and women, after it paid special attention at the beginning of this part to the Prophet's wives. Women are mentioned side by side with men, as part of the Islamic effort to give women their rightful position in society and establish society's attitude to women on the right basis. In their bond with God and in the Islamic duties of purification, worship and practical conduct, men and women are seen to be in the same position.

4

Fearing Social Reaction

Whenever God and His Messenger have decided a matter, it is not for a believing man or a believing woman to claim freedom of choice in that matter. Whoever disobeys God and His Messenger strays far into error. (36)

وَمَا كَانَ لِمُؤْمِنٍ وَلَا مُؤْمِنَةٍ إِذَا قَضَى اللَّهُ وَرَسُولُهُۥ أَمْرًا أَن يَكُونَ لَهُمُ الْخِيَرَةُ مِنْ أَمْرِهِمْ وَمَن يَعْصِ اللَّهَ وَرَسُولَهُۥ فَقَدْ ضَلَّ ضَلَالًا مُّبِينًا ۝

You did say to the one to whom God had shown favour and you had shown favour, 'Hold on to your wife and have fear of God.' And thus you would hide in your heart that which God wanted to bring to light. You stood in awe of people, whereas it was God alone of whom you should have stood in awe. Then, when Zayd had come to the end of his union with her, We gave her to you in marriage, so that no blame should attach to the believers for marrying the spouses of their adopted sons when the latter have come to the end of their union with them. God's will must be fulfilled. (37)

وَإِذْ تَقُولُ لِلَّذِىٓ أَنْعَمَ اللَّهُ عَلَيْهِ وَأَنْعَمْتَ عَلَيْهِ أَمْسِكْ عَلَيْكَ زَوْجَكَ وَاتَّقِ اللَّهَ وَتُخْفِى فِى نَفْسِكَ مَا اللَّهُ مُبْدِيهِ وَتَخْشَى النَّاسَ وَاللَّهُ أَحَقُّ أَن تَخْشَىٰهُ فَلَمَّا قَضَىٰ زَيْدٌ مِّنْهَا وَطَرًا زَوَّجْنَٰكَهَا لِكَىْ لَا يَكُونَ عَلَى الْمُؤْمِنِينَ حَرَجٌ فِىٓ أَزْوَٰجِ أَدْعِيَآئِهِمْ إِذَا قَضَوْا مِنْهُنَّ وَطَرًا وَكَانَ أَمْرُ اللَّهِ مَفْعُولًا ۝

79

No blame whatsoever attaches to the Prophet for doing what God has ordained for him. Such was God's way with those who went before him. God's will is always destiny absolute. (38)

مَّا كَانَ عَلَى ٱلنَّبِيِّ مِنْ حَرَجٍ فِيمَا فَرَضَ ٱللَّهُ لَهُ ۖ سُنَّةَ ٱللَّهِ فِي ٱلَّذِينَ خَلَوْا۟ مِن قَبْلُ ۚ وَكَانَ أَمْرُ ٱللَّهِ قَدَرًا مَّقْدُورًا ﴿٣٨﴾

Those are the ones who convey God's messages and stand in awe of Him, and hold none but God in awe. Sufficient is God to reckon all things. (39)

ٱلَّذِينَ يُبَلِّغُونَ رِسَٰلَٰتِ ٱللَّهِ وَيَخْشَوْنَهُۥ وَلَا يَخْشَوْنَ أَحَدًا إِلَّا ٱللَّهَ ۗ وَكَفَىٰ بِٱللَّهِ حَسِيبًا ﴿٣٩﴾

Muḥammad is not the father of any one of your men, but is God's Messenger and the seal of all prophets. God has indeed full knowledge of everything. (40)

مَّا كَانَ مُحَمَّدٌ أَبَآ أَحَدٍ مِّن رِّجَالِكُمْ وَلَٰكِن رَّسُولَ ٱللَّهِ وَخَاتَمَ ٱلنَّبِيِّـۧنَ ۗ وَكَانَ ٱللَّهُ بِكُلِّ شَىْءٍ عَلِيمًا ﴿٤٠﴾

Believers! Remember God always, (41)

يَٰٓأَيُّهَا ٱلَّذِينَ ءَامَنُوا۟ ٱذْكُرُوا۟ ٱللَّهَ ذِكْرًا كَثِيرًا ﴿٤١﴾

and glorify Him morning and evening. (42)

وَسَبِّحُوهُ بُكْرَةً وَأَصِيلًا ﴿٤٢﴾

It is He who bestows His blessings upon you, with His angels, so that He might take you out of the depths of darkness into the light. He is truly merciful to the believers. (43)

هُوَ ٱلَّذِى يُصَلِّى عَلَيْكُمْ وَمَلَٰٓئِكَتُهُۥ لِيُخْرِجَكُم مِّنَ ٱلظُّلُمَٰتِ إِلَى ٱلنُّورِ ۚ وَكَانَ بِٱلْمُؤْمِنِينَ رَحِيمًا ﴿٤٣﴾

On the day when they meet Him, they will be greeted with 'Peace', and He will have prepared for them a most generous reward. (44)

تَحِيَّتُهُمْ يَوْمَ يَلْقَوْنَهُۥ سَلَـٰمٌ وَأَعَدَّ لَهُمْ أَجْرًا كَرِيمًا ۝

Prophet! We have sent you as a witness, a bearer of good news and a warner; (45)

يَـٰٓأَيُّهَا ٱلنَّبِيُّ إِنَّآ أَرْسَلْنَـٰكَ شَـٰهِدًا وَمُبَشِّرًا وَنَذِيرًا ۝

one who calls people to God by His leave and a light-giving beacon. (46)

وَدَاعِيًا إِلَى ٱللَّهِ بِإِذْنِهِۦ وَسِرَاجًا مُّنِيرًا ۝

Give to the believers the good news that a great bounty from God awaits them. (47)

وَبَشِّرِ ٱلْمُؤْمِنِينَ بِأَنَّ لَهُم مِّنَ ٱللَّهِ فَضْلًا كَبِيرًا ۝

Do not yield to the unbelievers and the hypocrites, and disregard their hurting actions. Place your trust in God; for God alone is worthy of all trust. (48)

وَلَا تُطِعِ ٱلْكَـٰفِرِينَ وَٱلْمُنَـٰفِقِينَ وَدَعْ أَذَىٰهُمْ وَتَوَكَّلْ عَلَى ٱللَّهِ وَكَفَىٰ بِٱللَّهِ وَكِيلًا ۝

Overview

This passage represents another stage in reorganizing the Muslim community on the basis of Islamic teachings, addressing in particular the adoption system to which reference was made at the beginning of the *sūrah* and annulling its effects. God has willed that His Messenger, Muhammad (peace be upon him), be the one who undertakes in practice the annulment of this tradition. The Arabs used to treat the divorcee of an adopted son in the same way as if he was one's own son, i.e. she was permanently forbidden in marriage to the father. They could not accept that a woman who had previously been married to an adopted son was lawful for them to marry and this situation held until there was a precedent giving practical application to the new rule. Hence, the Prophet was chosen to undertake this new responsibility in addition to his burden of delivering God's message. When we examine this more closely, it is immediately apparent that no one other than the Prophet could have discharged this very heavy responsibility, facing as he did the community with an action that challenged its accepted norms. We also see that the Qur'ānic comment on this situation is long, stressing the believers' bond with God and His Messenger and clarifying the role of the Prophet in their community. All this is stated so as to make things easier for people to accept and make them more willing to implement God's orders outlining this new social system.

Before this specific case is discussed, a rule is put in place giving God and His Messenger all authority over the Muslims' lives. Once God and His Messenger decide a matter, a believer has no choice but to submit to that order and carry it out. This again demonstrates just how difficult it was to take an action that was contrary to tradition.

Background Cases

Whenever God and His Messenger have decided a matter, it is not for a believing man or a believing woman to claim freedom of choice in that matter. Whoever disobeys God and His Messenger strays far into error. (Verse 36)

Reports suggest that this verse was revealed in respect of Zaynab bint Jaḥsh when the Prophet wanted to remove all social considerations dividing people into different social classes. These strata were inherited by the Muslim community from their pre-Islamic days. The Prophet now, however, wanted to emphasize the full equality of all people, making the only factor that distinguishes between them their fear of God and good action. Up until this point, former slaves that had been freed were placed in a class lower than that of their masters. One such former slave was Zayd ibn Ḥārithah whom the Prophet had adopted.

The Prophet wanted to establish the full equality among people by giving Zayd a wife of noble birth, one from his own Hāshimite clan, and his own cousin, Zaynab bint Jahsh. In this way, the Prophet himself would remove class distinction within his own family. He had realized that class distinctions were so deeply entrenched in society that they could only be removed by his own practical example. His action would be the catalyst enabling humanity to follow in his footsteps.

In his discussion of this verse Ibn Kathīr quotes Ibn 'Abbās's report: "The Prophet wanted to choose a wife for Zayd ibn Ḥārithah, and he went into Zaynab bint Jahsh's home and proposed to her that she married him. She said: 'I do not wish to marry him.' The Prophet said: 'Do not say that. Marry him.' She said: 'Messenger of God! I will consider it.' As they were engaged in conversation God revealed this verse to His Messenger: *Whenever God and His Messenger have decided a matter, it is not for a believing man or a believing woman to claim freedom of choice in that matter.* (Verse 36) She asked the Prophet: 'Messenger of God! Are you happy for me to marry him?' He replied: 'Yes.' She said: 'Then I will not disobey God's Messenger. I will marry him.'"

Another report by Ibn 'Abbās mentions that Zaynab had a sharp element in her character and that when the Prophet proposed to her that she marry Zayd, she replied: 'I belong to a nobler family than his.' Then God revealed this verse in full. Other early scholars, for example, Mujāhid, Qatādah and Muqātil also confirm that this verse was revealed in connection with Zaynab's marriage to Zayd.

Ibn Kathīr includes in his commentary a different report attributed to 'Abd al-Raḥmān ibn Zayd ibn Aslam: "This verse was revealed in connection with the case of Umm Kulthūm bint 'Uqbah ibn Abī Mu'ayṭ who was the first woman to migrate to Madinah after the signing of the al-Ḥudaybiyah Peace Treaty. She offered herself to the Prophet as a gift. He said, 'I accept,' then he married her to Zayd ibn Ḥārithah [most probably after he had divorced Zaynab], but she and her brothers were displeased. Her brother said: 'We wanted her to be married to God's Messenger, but he married her to his former slave.' This verse was then revealed: *Whenever God and His Messenger have decided a matter, it is not for a believing man or a believing woman to claim freedom of choice in that matter.* (Verse 36) This is a specific order, but the *sūrah* includes one which is more general in its import: '*The Prophet has more claim on the believers than they have on their own selves.*' (Verse 6)

Imām Aḥmad mentions a third case reported by Anas: "The Prophet wanted to give Julaybīb, a former slave, a woman from the Anṣār as a wife and he proposed this to her father. The man said: 'I will consult her mother.' The Prophet said: 'That is fine.' The man went to his wife and told her what the Prophet proposed. She said: 'How come! The Prophet could not find us anyone better than Julaybīb when we have refused better men.' The girl was in her room and heard the conversation. As her father was about to go to tell the Prophet, the girl said to her parents: 'Do you want to refuse what the Prophet has suggested to you? If the Prophet is happy with the man, then accept him.' Her words came as a relief to her parents, and they agreed with her. Her father then went to the Prophet and said: 'If you are happy with him, we accept him.' The Prophet replied: 'I am certainly happy with him.' The Prophet then married the girl to Julaybīb. Some time later, Julaybīb joined a military expedition, but was killed in action, though around him were found several unbelievers whom he had killed during the fighting." Anas also reports: "I saw this woman later: she belongs to one of the most charitable families in Madinah."

These reports relate the revelation of the present verse to Zayd's marriage to Zaynab or to Umm Kulthūm bint 'Uqbah. We have added the third report about Julaybīb because it explains the sort of social environment Islam wanted to remove by assigning this task to the Prophet. This was part of his responsibility to reorganize the Muslim community on the basis of Islam, its constitution and value system.

Establishing a Principle

However, the import of the verse is much wider than just any one case. This because it also relates to the annulment of the effects of adoption, the permission to marry the divorcees of formerly adopted sons, and the Prophet's marriage to Zaynab after Zayd divorced her. This last situation attracted much talk at the time. In fact, some people who are hostile to Islam still use it to criticize the Prophet (peace be upon him) and to fabricate legends about him. Whether the verse was revealed in connection with the cases mentioned earlier or with the Prophet's own marriage to Zaynab, it nonetheless states a rule which is far more general than any specific case and one which has a profound effect on Muslims' lives.

This principle of the Islamic faith was, as a result, clearly established and deeply rooted in the hearts of the Muslim community, and it moulded their feelings. In essence, this rule is such that Muslims have no control over anything that belongs to them. They and all that they own belong to God, and He chooses for them whatever He pleases. Each and every individual is only a tiny part of the universe which follows the overall law God has set for it. The Creator of the universe who controls it determines their affairs and assigns to them their roles in the drama, stipulating all their actions on this universal stage. They cannot choose the role they play, because they do not know the full extent of the drama. Nor can they choose an action they prefer, because this may not fit in with the overall role assigned to them. They neither wrote the play nor do they own the stage. They are merely commissioned actors who earn their wages for their actions. The end result, however, is not their concern.

When this element of the Islamic faith had been established in the hearts of the first Muslim community, they surrendered themselves truly and completely to God, leaving nothing for themselves. This gave them harmony with the nature of the universe, and brought their actions into line with its course. Thus, they moved in their own orbits, just like stars and planets in theirs, never trying to move out, accelerate or slow down. They willingly accepted everything God willed for them, realizing deep down that it is God's will that determines every event and every situation. This acceptance gave them comfort and reassurance. Gradually they stopped being surprised or shocked when something happened to them by God's will. They neither felt panic which needs reassurance, nor pain which needs patience. They simply received God's will as something they expected, causing them neither astonishment nor taking them aback.

They no longer wished to hasten the turn of events so as to accomplish something they desired, not even when their desires focused on achieving victory for their faith. They simply accepted that God's will would take them wherever He willed, while they remained content and satisfied. They laid down their lives, strove hard and sacrificed their wealth, willingly, patiently, pressing no favours and feeling no sorrow, firmly believing that they were only doing what God willed them to do and that ultimately what took place was only what God willed, and further that everything occurs at the right time. Thus they submitted themselves completely to God, letting His hand lead them along the way, feeling safe, secure and trusting that whatever the outcome it would be the right one.

In all this, they only did what they could, withholding nothing, wasting neither time nor effort, and not overburdening themselves or trying to go beyond their human abilities. They neither claimed what they did not have nor did they profess what they could not do.

This balance between absolute submission to God's will, exerting all efforts and energies, and not trying to exceed abilities was the distinctive mark of that first Muslim community which enabled it to successfully fulfil the responsibility their faith assigned to them. This was a trust that is too heavy even for mountains to bear. In fact, when this basic element of Islamic faith found its root in the hearts of the first Muslim community, it was able to achieve the miraculous within its own lifespan and in the life of mankind in general. In short, its efforts yielded plentiful and sweet fruit in a very short period of time.

The great transformation that took place within their own souls was indeed the great miracle that no man can ever produce. It only happened by God's direct will. Numerous verses in the Qur'ān refer to this truth. God says: "*Indeed, you cannot guide aright everyone whom you love. It is God who guides whom He wills.*" (28: 56) "*It is not for you to make people follow the right guidance. It is God who guides whom He wills.*" (2: 272) "*All true guidance is God's guidance.*" (3: 73) This is the meaning of guidance both in its essence and in its broadest sense. It represents man's guidance about his place in this universe, one which gives his action harmony with what takes place elsewhere in the universe. Human efforts will not achieve their full results until people genuinely accept guidance in this sense, reassured that God's will controls everything.

Let us read again the verse that led to this long discussion: "*Whenever God and His Messenger have decided a matter, it is not for a believing man or a believing woman to claim freedom of choice in that matter. Whoever disobeys God and His Messenger strays far into error.*" (Verse 36) We see now that it has a far broader import than any particular event that might have led to its revelation. It establishes the most fundamental principle in the Islamic code.

Zaynab's Marriage

The *surah* then refers to the Prophet's marriage to Zaynab bint Jaḥsh and the rulings and directives that preceded or followed it:

> *You did say to the one to whom God had shown favour and you had shown favour, 'Hold on to your wife and have fear of God.' And thus you would hide in your heart that which God wanted to bring to light. You stood in awe of people, whereas it was God alone of whom you should have stood in awe. Then, when Zayd had come to the end of his union with her, We gave her to you in marriage, so that no blame should attach to the believers for marrying the spouses of their adopted sons when the latter have come to the end of their union with them. God's will must be fulfilled. No blame whatsoever attaches to the Prophet for doing what God has ordained for him. Such was God's way with those who went before him. God's will is always destiny absolute. Those are the ones who convey God's messages and stand in awe of Him, and hold none but God in awe. Sufficient is God to reckon all things. Muhammad is not the father of any one of your men, but is God's Messenger and the seal of all prophets. God has indeed full knowledge of everything.* (Verses 37–40)

Clear orders were given early in the *surah* prohibiting adoption and requiring that adopted children be called by their own fathers' names, returning family relations to their normal structure: "*He does not make your adopted sons truly your sons. These are only words you utter with your mouths, but God says the truth and He alone shows the right path. Call them by their fathers' names; that is more just in God's sight. If you do not know who their fathers are, then treat them as your brethren in faith and your protégés. You shall not be blamed if you make a mistake, but for what your hearts intend. God is indeed Much-Forgiving, Merciful."* (Verses 4–5) However, adoption had its effects in the practical life of the Arabian society, and the annulment of these practical effects was not going to be as easy as the prohibition of adoption. Social traditions have a strong hold on people. Hence why practical examples are needed to serve as precedents. Initially too such precedents meet with a hostile reception.

We have already stated that the Prophet married his formerly adopted son, Zayd ibn Ḥārithah, who used to be called Zayd ibn Muḥammad, to Zaynab bint Jaḥsh, whose mother was the Prophet's own paternal aunt. The Prophet wanted to achieve through this marriage the removal of class distinctions as also implementation of the Qur'ānic principle: *"Truly, the noblest of you in the sight of God is the one who is most genuinely God-fearing."* (49: 13) He wanted to give this new Islamic value practical endorsement.

God's will then dictated that the Prophet should undertake the annulment of the effects of adoption himself, by marrying Zayd's divorcee. He was to confront society with this action, which no man could undertake despite the earlier prohibition against adoption. Therefore, God informed His Messenger that Zayd would be divorcing Zaynab and that he would marry her, and all to fulfil God's purpose. By this time, relations between Zayd and Zaynab were troubled, the parties themselves aware that their marriage would not last long.

Time after time, Zayd complained to the Prophet that his life with Zaynab was not a happy one, saying that he could not carry on with her. Brave as he was in clearly and unhesitatingly confronting his people in matters of faith, the Prophet felt that the burden of Zaynab's situation was too heavy for him to carry. He was uneasy about confronting people with the practical destruction of their old adoption tradition. Zayd was also very close to the Prophet.[4] Therefore, he said

---

4. The verse mentions that Zayd was granted favours by God and His Messenger. God gave him the blessings of being a Muslim, and close to the Prophet who loved him better than any other man. Furthermore, the Prophet did him the favour of setting him free, and of bringing him up.

to Zayd: "*Hold on to your wife and have fear of God.*" (Verse 37) In so doing, he was delaying this serious challenge to social norms: "*And thus you would hide in your heart that which God wanted to bring to light. You stood in awe of people, whereas it was God alone of whom you should have stood in awe.*" (Verse 37) The Prophet knew that God would eventually bring it all to light, just as he knew through God's inspiration that it would take place. It was, thus, not a clear order from God. Had it been so, he would not have hesitated, not delayed for a moment. He would have declared it on the spot no matter what consequences he might have expected. Instead, it was simply an inspiration countered by the outcome he feared would take place. He thus waited until it was God's will for it to happen, for Zayd to divorce Zaynab with neither of them paying any thought to what would happen next. The prevailing tradition considered Zaynab as divorced by Muhammad's son, and as such she was permanently unlawful for Muhammad to marry. Up to this point, marriage between a man and the divorcee of his former adopted son was still unlawful. Changes to this rule had to wait until the Prophet's marriage to Zaynab, so that it could be practically established, despite people's reluctance.

These facts refute all contrary reports upheld by people hostile to Islam, in the past as well as in the present, and who have fabricated all sorts of legends around the situation.

The whole thing was exactly as God said: "*When Zayd had come to the end of his union with her, We gave her to you in marriage, so that no blame should attach to the believers for marrying the spouses of their adopted sons when the latter have come to the end of their union with them.*" (Verse 37) This was, then, one of the heavy burdens the Prophet had to bear in connection with his message. Extremely uneasy, he had to face society with it. Indeed he was reluctant to so confront people, even though he had no hesitation whatsoever in confronting them with the essence of faith based on God's oneness, or with his denunciation of false deities and alleged partners with God, or with criticizing their forefathers.

"*God's will must be fulfilled.*" (Verse 37) It cannot be overturned. It just comes about and nothing can stop it. Therefore, the Prophet's marriage to Zaynab took place after she had completed her waiting period. He then sent Zayd, her former husband and the person he loved most, to carry his proposal to her.

Anas reports: "When Zaynab finished her waiting period, the Prophet said to Zayd ibn Ḥārithah: 'Go and propose to her on my behalf.' He went to her home and saw her making her dough. He said: 'When I saw her I was in so much awe that I could not look at her, and say that God's Messenger wished to marry her. Therefore, I turned my back on her and, looking away, I said: Zaynab! I have happy news for you. God's Messenger has sent me to propose to you.' She said: 'I will do nothing until I have consulted my Lord.' She then went to pray. The Qur'ānic verse was revealed, and the Prophet came and entered her home without knocking." [Related by Muslim, Aḥmad and al-Nasā'ī.] Al-Bukhārī relates on the authority of Anas ibn Mālik that "Zaynab used to take pride among the Prophet's other wives, saying to them: 'It was your families that gave you in marriage while it was God Himself who, from over the seventh heaven, gave me in marriage.'"

To be expected, the matter did not pass easily. Rather, it came as a big surprise to the whole Muslim community, while the hypocrites were quick to circulate their allegations that the Prophet had 'married his son's wife'. The question, however, was that of establishing a new principle. Therefore, the Qur'ān emphasized this and removed its strange aspects: "*No blame whatsoever attaches to the Prophet for doing what God has ordained for him.*" (Verse 38) It was God who ordained that the Prophet should marry Zaynab and abolish the Arabian tradition that prohibited marriage to a former wife of an adopted son. Since God ordained this, no blame attaches to the Prophet. He was not the first prophet to find himself in such a position: "*Such was God's way with those who went before him.*" (Verse 38) This, then, comes to pass in accordance with God's consistent law which is not subject to people's ideas which in any case lack sound basis. "*God's will is always destiny absolute.*" It will always be done, unhindered by anything or anyone. It runs according to God's wisdom to achieve the goal He sets out.

This rule also applied to earlier messengers: "*Those are the ones who convey God's messages and stand in awe of Him, and hold none but God in awe.*" (Verse 39) When God commands them to do something, they are not swayed in some other direction by other people: indeed the latter are of no importance. They fear no one other than God who charged them with the task of delivering His message and putting it into action: *"Sufficient is God to reckon all things."* (Verse 39) It is He who holds them to account. They are accountable to no one else.

"Muhammad is not the father of any one of your men." (Verse 40) Zaynab was not his son's wife, and Zayd was not his son; he was Ḥārithah's son. Hence, when the matter is looked at from the angle of reality, it carries no blame whatsoever. Muhammad was in the same relation to all Muslims, including Zayd ibn Ḥārithah: it is a relation between a prophet and his community. He is *"God's Messenger and the seal of all prophets."* (Verse 40) He thus puts in place God's permanent law to be applied by all mankind for the rest of time. *"God has indeed full knowledge of everything."* (Verse 40) He knows what suits humanity and sets its life on the best course. He has ordained that the Prophet act in accordance with His wisdom and knowledge. Furthermore, He has set in motion the laws and regulations that best serve people's interests and bring them happiness.

From Darkness into Light

The *sūrah* goes on to establish this last meaning in the hearts of believers, keeping alive their relation with God who ordained whatever He willed for His Messenger and chose for the Muslim community what brought about their every good, replacing the darkness with light:

Believers! Remember God always, and glorify Him morning and evening. It is He who bestows His blessings upon you, with His angels, so that He might take you out of the depths of darkness into the light. He is truly merciful to the believers. On the day when they meet Him, they will be greeted with 'Peace', and He will have prepared for them a most generous reward. (Verses 41–44)

Remembering God means that one's heart is alive to God's remembrance, not the mere mention of His name. One should always be careful in whatever one does so as to remain within what God permits. To attend regularly to prayer is part of remembering God. In fact there are many *aḥādīth* and reports that almost equate God's remembrance with attending to prayer. The Prophet is quoted as saying: "If a man wakes his wife up at night and they offer two *rak'ahs* of night prayer, they will be considered that night as among those who remember God always." [Related by Abū Dāwūd, al-Nasā'ī and Ibn Mājah.]

God's remembrance though is broader than prayer. It includes every way in which a person is fully conscious of his Lord, whether his tongue moves to mention Him or not. What we are referring to here is a consciousness that motivates to action. A human heart remains lost or perplexed until it establishes its link with God, remembering Him and feeling secure in His care. It then knows the way to follow, the method to implement, and how to go about all this. It is for this reason that the Qur'ān and the *Sunnah* repeatedly urge people to remember God. The Qur'ān often links this to different times and situations in which man finds himself, so that these serve as reminders for him not to neglect this duty: *"Believers! Remember God always, and glorify Him morning and evening."* (Verses 41–42)

The early morning and the end of the day have much that urges human hearts to maintain their ties with God, who changes times and situations, without ever changing Himself. Yet everything else changes and disappears.

At the same time, people are reminded of God's grace and the care He takes of His creation and the favours He bestows on them. Yet He is in no need of them while they need His care and blessings: *"It is He who bestows His blessings upon you, with His angels, so that He might take you out of the depths of darkness into the light. He is truly merciful to the believers."* (Verse 43)

All glory to God who bestows great favours and doubles them over and over again. Yet He also remembers His weak servants who have no real power of their own and whose life is only transitory. He remembers them, taking care of them and blessing them together with His angels. When He mentions them in good terms among those on high, the entire universe echoes their mention, as the Prophet states: "God says: Whoever of My servants mentions Me to himself, I mention him to Myself; and whoever mentions Me in the presence of a group, I mention him in the presence of a better group." [Related by al-

Bukhārī.] This is indeed profound. One can hardly imagine it, when one knows that the whole earth with all the creatures living on and in it is no more than a tiny particle in relation to the great galaxies of the universe. Yet all these galaxies and what they contain of creatures are no more than a portion of the universe which God has willed to exist, saying to it, 'Be,' and it came into being.

"*It is He who bestows His blessings upon you, with His angels, so that He might take you out of the depths of darkness into the light.*" (Verse 43) God's light is one, comprehensive, continuous. What does not belong to it is darkness, which differs and has several depths. If people stray from God's light, they have only darkness to live in. Nothing can save them or bring them out of this darkness except God's light that enlightens hearts and minds, filling souls and guiding them to what suits their nature. The grace God bestows on them and the angels' blessings and prayers for them are what takes them out of the darkness into the light. This is what happens to them when their hearts open up to faith: "*He is truly merciful to the believers.*" (Verse 43)

Such is their situation in this life, when they need to work. As for their situation in the life to come, when reward is administered, God's grace continues to be with them. They are received there warmly, given honour and rich reward: "*On the day when they meet Him, they will be greeted with 'Peace', and He will have prepared for them a most generous reward.*" (Verse 44) They have a peace that contrasts with fear, tiring effort and hard work. It is a greeting from God, brought to them by the angels who enter from every door to deliver the message given to them from on high. This comes in addition to the noble reward God has in store for them. Such is their Lord who legislates and chooses what is best for them. Who would not prefer His choice?

The Prophet's Role

The Prophet who delivers to them what God has chosen, and shows them by practical example how to implement the laws God has enacted for them, is here given an outline of his own role. His position in relation to the believers is also explained.

Prophet! We have sent you as a witness, a bearer of good news and a warner; one who calls people to God by His leave and a light-giving beacon. Give to the believers the good news that a great bounty from God awaits them. Do not yield to the unbelievers and the hypocrites, and disregard their hurting actions. Place your trust in God; for God alone is worthy of all trust. (Verses 45–48)

The Prophet's position among them is that of a witness. They should, then, work to improve the testimony he gives, as it will state the facts, changing nothing and containing nothing that is false. He is also the *'bearer of good news'*, explaining what awaits those who work hard and well of God's grace, forgiveness of sins, honour and reward. Moreover, he is *'a warner'* to those who overlook their duties, telling them of what awaits the wrongdoers of punishment and suffering. Thus, they are not taken unawares. Furthermore, he is one who *'calls people to God'*, not to worldly glory, national pride, personal gain or position. He only calls to God in a consistent way that leads to Him *'by His leave'*. He does not invent anything, nor does he say anything of his own volition. He fulfils his task by God's leave, as He has commanded him. He is indeed *'a light-giving beacon'*. He dispels darkness, removes doubts and enlightens the way. He is a beacon that gives light to guide people aright, like a lamp that dispels darkness on the road.

Such was Muḥammad, God's Messenger, (peace be upon him), and such was the light he gave. He gave to people a clear and lucid concept of existence, of their relation with God and their position in relation to the universe and its Creator. He gave us a clear value system, one which is essential for the right existence of the universe and man's life therein. He also gave us a clear and decisive explanation of the origin of life and its end, the goal it serves and the course by which it is served. No ambiguity is found in anything he has given. His is a style that addresses human nature directly, using its wider gates and the most effective of ways.

The *sūrah* repeats once more the Prophet's task of giving good news to the believers, expressing this in more detail: "*Give to the believers the good news that a great bounty from God awaits them.*" (Verse 47) This gives flesh to something it mentioned in general a little earlier on: *"Prophet! We have sent you as a witness, a bearer of good news and a warner."* (Verse 45) Thus, the details serve to further explain God's favours bestowed on the believers.

This address to the Prophet concludes with an order to him not to pay any heed to the unbelievers and hypocrites, not to care about their actions or whether these may hurt him or his followers, and to always place his trust in God: *"Do not yield to the unbelievers and the hypocrites, and disregard their hurting actions. Place your trust in God; for God alone is worthy of all trust."* (Verse 48) It is the same address given at the outset of the *sūrah*, before it outlines any legislation for social reorganization. The Prophet is further instructed not to care for their hurting actions. He must not try to spare himself such hurt by relenting to them in anything, or relying on them in any way. God is sufficient for him to place his trust in Him alone.

We see how the situation of Zayd and Zaynab and the abrogation of the tradition that prohibited marriage with the divorcee of an adopted son was indeed difficult, requiring confirmation and explanation by God. This is why it was preceded by a long explanation and concluded with a long comment. All this emphasizes God's great care shown to the believers who must receive His orders with total acceptance and a willing submission.

5

Detailed Legal Provisions

Believers! If you marry believing women and then divorce them before the marriage is consummated, you have no reason to expect them to observe a waiting period. Hence, provide well for them and release them in a becoming manner. (49)

يَـٰٓأَيُّهَا ٱلَّذِينَ ءَامَنُوٓا إِذَا نَكَحْتُمُ ٱلْمُؤْمِنَـٰتِ ثُمَّ طَلَّقْتُمُوهُنَّ مِن قَبْلِ أَن تَمَسُّوهُنَّ فَمَا لَكُمْ عَلَيْهِنَّ مِنْ عِدَّةٍ تَعْتَدُّونَهَا فَمَتِّعُوهُنَّ وَسَرِّحُوهُنَّ سَرَاحًا جَمِيلًا ﴿٤٩﴾

Prophet! We have made lawful to you the wives whom you have paid their dowries, as well as those whom God has placed in your right hand through war, as also the daughters of your paternal uncles and aunts, and the daughters of your maternal uncles and aunts, who have migrated with you; and any believing woman who offers herself freely to the Prophet and whom the Prophet might be willing to wed: [this latter] applies to you alone and not to other believers. We well know

يَـٰٓأَيُّهَا ٱلنَّبِيُّ إِنَّآ أَحْلَلْنَا لَكَ أَزْوَٰجَكَ ٱلَّـٰتِىٓ ءَاتَيْتَ أُجُورَهُنَّ وَمَا مَلَكَتْ يَمِينُكَ مِمَّآ أَفَآءَ ٱللَّهُ عَلَيْكَ وَبَنَاتِ عَمِّكَ وَبَنَاتِ عَمَّـٰتِكَ وَبَنَاتِ خَالِكَ وَبَنَاتِ خَـٰلَـٰتِكَ ٱلَّـٰتِى هَاجَرْنَ مَعَكَ وَٱمْرَأَةً مُّؤْمِنَةً إِن وَهَبَتْ نَفْسَهَا لِلنَّبِىِّ إِنْ أَرَادَ ٱلنَّبِىُّ أَن يَسْتَنكِحَهَا خَالِصَةً لَّكَ مِن دُونِ ٱلْمُؤْمِنِينَ قَدْ عَلِمْنَا

what We have made obligatory to them in respect of their wives and other women their right hands possess; and thus no blame shall attach to you. God is Much-Forgiving, Merciful. (50)

مَا فَرَضْنَا عَلَيْهِمْ فِي أَزْوَٰجِهِمْ وَمَا مَلَكَتْ أَيْمَٰنُهُمْ لِكَيْلَا يَكُونَ عَلَيْكَ حَرَجٌ وَكَانَ ٱللَّهُ غَفُورًا رَّحِيمًا ۝

You may defer any of them you please, and take to yourself any of them you please. No blame will attach to you if you invite one whose turn you have previously set aside: this makes it more likely that they will be contented and not distressed, and that all of them will be satisfied with whatever you have to give them. God knows what is in your hearts. God is indeed All-Knowing, Forbearing. (51)

تُرْجِي مَن تَشَآءُ مِنْهُنَّ وَتُـْٔوِي إِلَيْكَ مَن تَشَآءُ وَمَنِ ٱبْتَغَيْتَ مِمَّنْ عَزَلْتَ فَلَا جُنَاحَ عَلَيْكَ ذَٰلِكَ أَدْنَىٰ أَن تَقَرَّ أَعْيُنُهُنَّ وَلَا يَحْزَنَّ وَيَرْضَيْنَ بِمَآ ءَاتَيْتَهُنَّ كُلُّهُنَّ وَٱللَّهُ يَعْلَمُ مَا فِي قُلُوبِكُمْ وَكَانَ ٱللَّهُ عَلِيمًا حَلِيمًا ۝

You [Muḥammad] are not permitted to take any further wives, nor to exchange these for other wives, even though you are attracted by their beauty, except for any that your right hand may possess. God keeps watch over all things. (52)

لَّا يَحِلُّ لَكَ ٱلنِّسَآءُ مِنۢ بَعْدُ وَلَآ أَن تَبَدَّلَ بِهِنَّ مِنْ أَزْوَٰجٍ وَلَوْ أَعْجَبَكَ حُسْنُهُنَّ إِلَّا مَا مَلَكَتْ يَمِينُكَ وَكَانَ ٱللَّهُ عَلَىٰ كُلِّ شَىْءٍ رَّقِيبًا ۝

Believers! Do not enter the Prophet's homes, unless you are given leave, for a meal without waiting for its proper time. But when you are invited, enter; and when you have eaten, disperse without lingering for the sake of mere talk. Such behaviour might give offence to the Prophet, and yet he might feel too shy to bid you go. God does not shy of stating what is right. When you ask the Prophet's wives for something, do so from behind a screen: this makes for greater purity for your hearts and theirs. Moreover, it does not behove you to give offence to God's Messenger, just as it would not behove you ever to marry his widows after he has passed away. That is certainly an enormity in God's sight. (53)

يَـٰٓأَيُّهَا ٱلَّذِينَ ءَامَنُوا۟ لَا تَدۡخُلُوا۟ بُيُوتَ ٱلنَّبِيِّ إِلَّآ أَن يُؤۡذَنَ لَكُمۡ إِلَىٰ طَعَامٍ غَيۡرَ نَـٰظِرِينَ إِنَىٰهُ وَلَـٰكِنۡ إِذَا دُعِيتُمۡ فَٱدۡخُلُوا۟ فَإِذَا طَعِمۡتُمۡ فَٱنتَشِرُوا۟ وَلَا مُسۡتَـٔۡنِسِينَ لِحَدِيثٍۚ إِنَّ ذَٰلِكُمۡ كَانَ يُؤۡذِى ٱلنَّبِيَّ فَيَسۡتَحۡىِۦ مِنكُمۡۖ وَٱللَّهُ لَا يَسۡتَحۡىِۦ مِنَ ٱلۡحَقِّۚ وَإِذَا سَأَلۡتُمُوهُنَّ مَتَـٰعًا فَسۡـَٔلُوهُنَّ مِن وَرَآءِ حِجَابٍۚ ذَٰلِكُمۡ أَطۡهَرُ لِقُلُوبِكُمۡ وَقُلُوبِهِنَّۚ وَمَا كَانَ لَكُمۡ أَن تُؤۡذُوا۟ رَسُولَ ٱللَّهِ وَلَآ أَن تَنكِحُوٓا۟ أَزۡوَٰجَهُۥ مِنۢ بَعۡدِهِۦٓ أَبَدًاۚ إِنَّ ذَٰلِكُمۡ كَانَ عِندَ ٱللَّهِ عَظِيمًا ٥٣

Whether you do anything openly or in secret, [remember that] God has full knowledge of everything. (54)

إِن تُبۡدُوا۟ شَيۡـًٔا أَوۡ تُخۡفُوهُ فَإِنَّ ٱللَّهَ كَانَ بِكُلِّ شَيۡءٍ عَلِيمًا ٥٤

It is no sin for them [to appear freely] before their fathers, their sons, their brothers, their brothers' sons, their sisters' sons,

لَّا جُنَاحَ عَلَيۡهِنَّ فِىٓ ءَابَآئِهِنَّ وَلَآ أَبۡنَآئِهِنَّ وَلَآ إِخۡوَٰنِهِنَّ وَلَآ أَبۡنَآءِ إِخۡوَٰنِهِنَّ وَلَآ أَبۡنَآءِ

their womenfolk, or such men slaves as their right hands possess. [Wives of the Prophet!] Always remain God-fearing; for God is witness to all things. (55)

أَخَوَٰتِهِنَّ وَلَا نِسَآبِهِنَّ وَلَا مَا مَلَكَتْ أَيْمَٰنُهُنَّ وَٱتَّقِينَ ٱللَّهَ إِنَّ ٱللَّهَ كَانَ عَلَىٰ كُلِّ شَىْءٍ شَهِيدًا ۝

God and His angels bless the Prophet. Believers! Bless him and give him greetings of peace. (56)

إِنَّ ٱللَّهَ وَمَلَٰٓئِكَتَهُۥ يُصَلُّونَ عَلَى ٱلنَّبِيِّ يَٰٓأَيُّهَا ٱلَّذِينَ ءَامَنُوا۟ صَلُّوا۟ عَلَيْهِ وَسَلِّمُوا۟ تَسْلِيمًا ۝

Those who affront God and His Messenger will be rejected by God in this world and in the life to come. He has prepared for them a humiliating suffering. (57)

إِنَّ ٱلَّذِينَ يُؤْذُونَ ٱللَّهَ وَرَسُولَهُۥ لَعَنَهُمُ ٱللَّهُ فِى ٱلدُّنْيَا وَٱلْءَاخِرَةِ وَأَعَدَّ لَهُمْ عَذَابًا مُّهِينًا ۝

And those who malign believing men and women for no wrong they might have done shall have burdened themselves with the guilt of calumny and with a blatant injustice. (58)

وَٱلَّذِينَ يُؤْذُونَ ٱلْمُؤْمِنِينَ وَٱلْمُؤْمِنَٰتِ بِغَيْرِ مَا ٱكْتَسَبُوا۟ فَقَدِ ٱحْتَمَلُوا۟ بُهْتَٰنًا وَإِثْمًا مُّبِينًا ۝

Prophet! Say to your wives, daughters and all believing women that they should draw over themselves some of their outer garments. This will be more conducive to their being recognized and not affronted. God is Much-Forgiving, Merciful. (59)

يَٰٓأَيُّهَا ٱلنَّبِيُّ قُل لِّأَزْوَٰجِكَ وَبَنَاتِكَ وَنِسَآءِ ٱلْمُؤْمِنِينَ يُدْنِينَ عَلَيْهِنَّ مِن جَلَٰبِيبِهِنَّ ذَٰلِكَ أَدْنَىٰٓ أَن يُعْرَفْنَ فَلَا يُؤْذَيْنَ وَكَانَ ٱللَّهُ غَفُورًا رَّحِيمًا ۝

If the hypocrites, those who are sick at heart and those who spread lies in the city do not desist, We will rouse you against them, and then they will not be your neighbours in this city except for a little while: (60)

لَّئِن لَّمْ يَنتَهِ ٱلْمُنَٰفِقُونَ وَٱلَّذِينَ فِى قُلُوبِهِم مَّرَضٌ وَٱلْمُرْجِفُونَ فِى ٱلْمَدِينَةِ لَنُغْرِيَنَّكَ بِهِمْ ثُمَّ لَا يُجَاوِرُونَكَ فِيهَآ إِلَّا قَلِيلًا ﴿٦٠﴾

bereft of God's grace, they shall be seized wherever they may be found, and will be slain. (61)

مَّلْعُونِينَ أَيْنَمَا ثُقِفُوٓاْ أُخِذُواْ وَقُتِّلُواْ تَقْتِيلًا ﴿٦١﴾

Such has been God's way with those who went before. Never will you find any change in God's way. (62)

سُنَّةَ ٱللَّهِ فِى ٱلَّذِينَ خَلَوْاْ مِن قَبْلُ وَلَن تَجِدَ لِسُنَّةِ ٱللَّهِ تَبْدِيلًا ﴿٦٢﴾

Overview

This passage begins with a general rule concerning women who are divorced before their marriage has been consummated. This is followed by a number of rules relating to the Prophet's own family life, including the relationship between his wives and men generally, how Muslims should approach the Prophet's home, and the honour God bestows on His Messenger's home and how it is viewed by the angels and those on high. It concludes with a general order that applies to the Prophet's wives, daughters and all Muslim women. They are ordered to draw their outer garments over their bodies when they go out, so that they are recognized as chaste women. Thus, men with bad characters, such as the hypocrites and other wicked people who used to tease and irritate women would not approach them. It concludes with a warning to the hypocrites and circulators of rumours that they would be expelled from Madinah unless they stopped disturbing and irritating the Muslim women.

101

These rules and directives form part of the reorganization of the Muslim community on the basis of the Islamic concept of life and society. As for matters that concern the Prophet's own private life, God has willed that life in the Prophet's home should remain a book open to all generations. Therefore, He incorporated these aspects into the Qur'ān, which will remain intact, and read in full, for the rest of time. At the same time, they are a sign of the honour God bestows on the Prophet's home, as He Himself undertakes to regulate its affairs and present it to mankind in His book, the Qur'ān.

Divorce Before Consummation

Believers! If you marry believing women and then divorce them before the marriage is consummated, you have no reason to expect them to observe a waiting period. Hence, provide well for them and release them in a becoming manner. (Verse 49)

The situation of women divorced before their marriages have been consummated is dealt with in specific provisions outlined in *Sūrah* 2, The Cow: "*You will incur no sin if you divorce women before having touched them or settled a dowry for them. Provide for them, the rich according to his means and the straitened according to his means. Such a provision, in an equitable manner, is an obligation binding on the righteous. If you divorce them before having touched them but after having settled a dowry for them, then give them half of that which you have settled, unless they forgo it or he in whose hand is the marriage tie forgoes it. To forgo what is due to you is closer to being righteous. Do not forget to act benevolently to one another. God sees all that you do.*" (2: 236–237)

This means that if a dowry has been agreed by the two parties in a marriage terminated before consummation, then the divorced woman is entitled to half the dowry. If the dowry has not been stated, then she is entitled to some provisions, in accordance with the means of the divorcing husband. Such a provision is binding on righteous people. The two verses in *Sūrah* 2 do not mention any waiting period for such a divorced woman. We now have here a rule concerning this aspect, making it clear that such a woman has no waiting period to observe.

The waiting period is primarily to establish whether or not there is a pregnancy, so that no child is attributed to anyone other than its father, and no father is deprived of his child who might still be in the early days of conception. If the marriage has not been consummated, then no pregnancy has taken place, and there is no need for a waiting period. *"You have no reason to expect them to observe a waiting period. Hence, provide well for them."* (Verse 49) This provision is according to what is mentioned in the other verses: half the agreed dowry or, if no dowry is agreed, a provision commensurate with the man's financial status. The other obligation is to *"release them in a becoming manner.* (Verse 49) There must never be any imposition of hardship. Divorced women should be released so that they can begin a new life with someone else. This rule applies generally to all Muslims, given here in the context of organizing the Muslim community's social life.

The Prophet's Wives

The Prophet is then told which women are lawful for him to marry, and the special dispensation for him after the limit of four wives was imposed in an earlier *sūrah*: *"You may marry of other women as may be agreeable to you, two or three or four."* (4: 3) At the time the Prophet had nine wives, each of whom he married for a specific reason. 'Ā'ishah and Ḥafṣah were the daughters of his two closest Companions, Abū Bakr and 'Umar. Umm Ḥabībah bint Abī Sufyān, Umm Salamah, Sawdah bint Zim'ah and Zaynab bint Khuzaymah[5] were women from the Muhājirīn who had lost their husbands and the Prophet wanted to honour them. None of them was young or very pretty. Marrying them was merely an honour the Prophet gave them. As for Zaynab bint Jaḥsh,

5. There is a little confusion here. Zaynab bint Khuzaymah lived only a very short period after her marriage to the Prophet. She was not one of the nine wives he had at the time when these rules were outlined. If we omit her name, eight remain. However, the ninth was Maymūnah, the last wife the Prophet married. Moreover, it is not exactly accurate to say that the four the author groups together were neither young nor pretty. While they were not young, they were not without beauty. There is no reason to try to justify the Prophet's marriages in this way. Some of the reasons the author mentions are certainly true, particularly in the cases of the last three he mentions, but the others need no justification. God gave His Messenger a dispensation and he made use of it. – Editor's note.

we have already discussed her marriage to the Prophet in detail. The other two were Juwayriyyah bint al-Ḥārith and Ṣafiyyah bint Ḥuyay. Both were taken captive in war, but the Prophet freed them from bondage and married them to strengthen relations with their tribes and communities. Moreover, their marriage to the Prophet was an honour. Both accepted Islam after their people suffered the hardship of defeat.

They had all become 'mothers of the believers' and had the honour of being so close to God's Messenger, choosing God, His Messenger and the life to come over the luxuries and comforts of this world, when that choice was offered to them. It would have been very hard for them to be divorced when the maximum number of wives a Muslim may have was fixed at four. God looked at their situation and exempted His Messenger from that rule, permitting him to retain all his wives. Then, the Qur'ān stipulated that he must not add to them or replace any of them. Thus, the Prophet's exemption from the maximum of four wives was given specifically to those whom he had already married, so that they would not be deprived of this honour. The following verses clearly indicate this:

Prophet! We have made lawful to you the wives whom you have paid their dowries, as well as those whom God has placed in your right hand through war, as also the daughters of your paternal uncles and aunts, and the daughters of your maternal uncles and aunts, who have migrated with you; and any believing woman who offers herself freely to the Prophet and whom the Prophet might be willing to wed: [this latter] applies to you alone and not to other believers. We well know what We have made obligatory to them in respect of their wives and other women their right hands possess; and thus no blame shall attach to you. God is Much-Forgiving, Merciful. You may defer any of them you please, and take to yourself any of them you please. No blame will attach to you if you invite one whose turn you have previously set aside: this makes it more likely that they will be contented and not distressed, and that all of them will be satisfied with whatever you have to give them. God knows what is in your hearts. God is indeed All-Knowing, Forbearing. You [Muḥammad] are not permitted to take any further wives, nor to exchange these for other wives, even though you are attracted by their beauty, except for any that your right hand may possess. God keeps watch over all things. (Verses 50–52)

These provisions make it lawful for the Prophet to marry any woman from the types mentioned, even though this might take the number of such wives above the maximum of four which applied to all other Muslims. These types included the women whom he had already married and paid their dowries; any slave he came to own; his paternal and maternal cousins who had migrated with him, but not those who had not already migrated, and any woman who presented herself as a gift to the Prophet without taking a dowry or having a guardian, if he wished to marry her.[6] God made this a special privilege for the Prophet since he was the guardian of all believers, men and women. All other men are subject to the rules God has imposed concerning their wives and women slaves. Thus the Prophet had no restrictions placed on his actions with regard to retaining the ones he had already married or to responding to the circumstances of his special position.

The Prophet is then given the choice to marry any woman who offered herself to him as a gift, or to so delay the same. If he so delayed, he could go back to her at any time. Moreover he was free to have sex with any of his wives he wished and to delay any: "*This makes it more likely that they will be contented and not distressed, and that all of them will be satisfied with whatever you have to give them.*" (Verse 51) It is clear that all these provisions take into account the Prophet's special circumstances and the fact that many were keen to be honoured by being close to him. God knew all this and, as we know, He determines all situations in accordance with His knowledge and compassion: "*God knows what is in your hearts. God is indeed All-Knowing, Forbearing.*" (Verse 51)

God then made it unlawful for the Prophet to marry anyone other than those to whom he was already married. This did not apply to numbers, but rather to those specific women married to the Prophet.

---

6. There are conflicting reports on whether the Prophet married any woman of this type or not. Perhaps it is more accurate to say that he gave all women who made themselves gifts to him to other men to marry.

Nor could he replace any of them. He had, however, not increased the number of his wives before this prohibition was made.

"*You [Muḥammad] are not permitted to take any further wives, nor to exchange these for other wives, even though you are attracted by their beauty, except for any that your right hand may possess.*" (Verse 52) This was the only exception, whereby he was allowed to have any number of slave women. "*God keeps watch over all things.*" (Verse 52) This is the best guarantee of observing the rules.

'Ā'ishah reports that this restriction prohibiting the Prophet from having any more wives was subsequently abrogated, and the Prophet was given the freedom to marry others as he pleased. He, however, did not marry others, making only these the ones honoured with the title 'mothers of the believers'.

Observing Good Manners

The *sūrah* moves on to delineate the position of Muslims *vis-à-vis* the Prophet's homes and his wives, both during his lifetime and after his death. It addresses the fact that some hypocrites and others with hearts full of sickness used to affront the Prophet by directing their annoying behaviour at his homes and wives. It issues a very strong warning to them, describing the enormity of their action in God's sight and reminding them that God is fully aware of their wickedness:

> Believers! Do not enter the Prophet's homes, unless you are given leave, for a meal without waiting for its proper time. But when you are invited, enter; and when you have eaten, disperse without lingering for the sake of mere talk. Such behaviour might give offence to the Prophet, and yet he might feel too shy to bid you go. God does not shy of stating what is right. When you ask the Prophet's wives for something, do so from behind a screen: this makes for greater purity for your hearts and theirs. Moreover, it does not behove you to give offence to God's Messenger, just as it would not behove you ever to marry his widows after he has passed away. That is certainly an enormity in God's sight. Whether you do anything openly or in secret, [remember that] God has full knowledge of everything. (Verses 53–54)

Al-Bukhārī relates on the authority of Anas ibn Mālik: "When the Prophet espoused Zaynab bint Jaḥsh, he served a meal of meat and bread. I was sent to invite people to come over, and they came in groups. They would eat and leave, then another group came in, ate, and left. I invited everyone until I could find none to invite. I said this to the Prophet, and he said to his family: 'Remove your food.' Three people remained in his home chatting. The Prophet went out to 'Ā'ishah's room and said: 'Peace be to you, members of this household, together with God's mercy and blessings.' She replied to his greeting in the same way and asked him: 'How have you found your wife, Messenger of God? May God bless you and yours.' He then went to the rooms of every one of his wives, and each one of them said to him the same as 'Ā'ishah. Then he went back, and found the three people still there chatting. The Prophet was very shy. He went out again, heading towards 'Ā'ishah's room. I am not sure whether it was she or someone else who told him that those people had left. He came back, and when he had one foot inside and one out, the door was closed. Then the Qur'ānic verse mentioning the screen was revealed."

The verse outlines certain manners with regard to entering people's homes that were unknown in pre-Islamic Arabia. People just came into a home without asking permission, as we explained in commenting on the relevant verses in *Sūrah* 24, The Light.[7] Perhaps this was more visible in the case of the Prophet's homes which were the source of knowledge and wisdom. Some people might come in, and if they saw food being prepared, they would wait to have a meal, without being invited. Some might stay on to chat after the meal was over, even though they had not been invited in the first place. They were totally oblivious to the inconvenience their behaviour caused the Prophet and his family. One report suggests that when those three people stayed on to chat on the night of the Prophet's wedding to Zaynab, she sat with her face to the wall. The Prophet was too shy to draw their attention to the inconvenience they caused. He could not say to his visitors something that might make them ashamed of themselves. Therefore, God stated this on his behalf, because: "*God does not shy of stating what is right.*" (Verse 53)

---

7. Volume 12, pp. 304–309.

It is also reported that 'Umar, who was endowed with refined sensitivity, suggested to the Prophet that he should put up a screen so that people would not enter his wives' rooms without leave. He hoped that God would order this and subsequently this verse was revealed endorsing his suggestion. Al-Bukhārī relates on Anas's authority: "'Umar said: 'Messenger of God! All sorts of people come into your home. You may wish to instruct the mothers of the believers to put up a screen.' God then revealed the verse requiring a screen to be put up."

This verse taught people that they must not enter the Prophet's homes without first seeking permission. Should they be invited to have a meal, they may go in. If they were not invited, they must not enter awaiting the food to be cooked. Then, when they had finished eating, they should leave. They should not stay on to chat. Muslims today badly need to stick to this standard of manners, which has been ignored by many. Guests often stay long after a meal, and in many cases they stay long at the table after they have finished eating. Their conversation may drag on, while the hosts, who hold on to some aspects of Islamic manners, find this terribly inconvenient. Islamic manners address all situations most appropriately. We would do well to revive these manners in our social dealings.

The verse then orders that the Prophet's wives be screened from men: "*When you ask the Prophet's wives for something, do so from behind a screen.*" In emphasizing that this is better for all, the *sūrah* states further: "*This makes for greater purity for your hearts and theirs.*" (Verse 53) It is not for anyone to say what is contrary to what God says. No one should say that easy mixing and chatting between the two sexes is more conducive to purity of hearts, and relief of suppressed instincts, giving both men and women a better approach to feelings and behaviour. We hear much talk in this vein, by unenlightened people. No one can say anything of this sort when God says: "*When you ask the Prophet's wives for something, do so from behind a screen: this makes for greater purity for your hearts and theirs.*" (Verse 53) We should remember that He says this while referring to the Prophet's wives, the mothers of the believers, who were all pure women, and to the Prophet's Companions who were exemplary in their morality. When God says something and some people say something different, it is God's statement that is right. Whatever is contrary to God's statements is wrong and can only be stated by one who dares to say that human beings have greater knowledge of man's psychology than his Creator.

The facts of life confirm the truth of what God says and the falsehood of what others say to the contrary. People's experience everywhere in the world confirms this. Countries where mixing has reached extreme limits give ample evidence in support of this.

The Qur'ānic verse has already mentioned that peoples' entry awaiting a meal to be cooked, without being invited, and their staying on for a chat, gave offence to the Prophet, but that he was too shy to hint that they should leave. Now the verse makes it clear that it does not behove any Muslim to give offence to the Prophet; nor does it behove them to marry his wives when he dies, considering that his wives are like mothers to them. Their special position in relation to the Prophet makes their marriage to anyone other than him prohibited. This gave the Prophet's home its special sanctity and unique position. "*It does not behove you to give offence to God's Messenger, just as it would not behove you ever to marry his widows after he has passed away.*" (Verse 53) Some reports mention that one of the hypocrites said that he was waiting to marry 'Ā'ishah! "*That is certainly an enormity in God's sight.*" (Verse 53) Terrible indeed is that which God describes as an enormity.

The *sūrah* does not, however, stop at this warning but goes on instead to deliver an even sterner one: "*Whether you do anything openly or in secret, [remember that] God has full knowledge of everything.*" (Verse 54) It is God, then, who will take care of this. He knows what remains on the surface and what is kept secret, and He is fully aware of every thought and plan. He has described such matters as an enormity. Let anyone who wishes try to do anything of the sort. He will soon discover that he is exposing himself to God's mighty punishment.

Having made this warning, the *sūrah* makes the exception of some close relatives with whom the Prophet's wives did not have to be so guarded: "*It is no sin for them [to appear freely] before their fathers, their sons, their brothers, their brothers' sons, their sisters' sons, their womenfolk, or such men slaves as their right hands possess. [Wives of the Prophet!] Always remain God-fearing; for God is witness to all things.*" (Verse 55)

These are the relatives a woman cannot marry, i.e. her *maḥram*. In fact it is lawful for all Muslim women to appear before these relatives in normal clothes, without covering their heads. I could not establish with any degree of certainty whether this verse addressing the Prophet's wives in particular or verse 31 of *Sūrah* 24, Light, addressing all Muslim women was revealed first. It is more likely, however, that the order was first issued to the Prophet's wives and then made applicable to others.

We should note here the instruction to always be conscious of God, and the reference to His awareness of everything. *"Always remain God-fearing; for God is witness to all things."* (Verse 55) This is indeed the best guarantee that people will pay heed.

Further Instructions and a Warning

The *sūrah* continues to warn those who give offence to the Prophet, either in person or with regard to his family, showing their action as an enormity. It does so in two ways: honouring the Prophet and describing his status with his Lord and on high, and stating that to give offence to the Prophet is to give offence to God Himself. Therefore, it earns the perpetrator expulsion from God's mercy both in the present life and in the life to come. Furthermore, the perpetrators stand to suffer a humiliating punishment:

> *God and His angels bless the Prophet. Believers! Bless him and give him greetings of peace. Those who affront God and His Messenger will be rejected by God in this world and in the life to come. He has prepared for them a humiliating suffering. (Verses 56–57)*

The Arabic text uses the word *ṣalāt* and its derivatives for what is rendered in English as 'bless'. *Ṣalāt* means prayer, but prayer by God for the Prophet means that God praises him to those on high, while when it refers to the angels it means that they pray to God for him. This gives the Prophet a sublime position: the whole universe echoes God's praise of His Prophet. No honour could be greater than this. How would a prayer and blessing by human beings compare with God's own blessing and honour bestowed on the Prophet, or with those of the angels among the community on high? There is certainly no comparison, but God wishes to bestow honour on the believers by putting their blessing of the Prophet together with His own, thus providing them with a tie with those on high.

When God so honours and praises the Prophet, it is exceedingly grotesque for humans to give offence to him: "*Those who affront God and His Messenger will be rejected by God in this world and in the life to come. He has prepared for them a humiliating suffering.*" (Verse 57) What makes this even more grotesque and ridiculous is that it is an affront to God by His creatures. They can never affront or offend God, but the expression here serves to show great sensitivity to any offence committed against the Prophet, in effect making it an offence against God Himself.

The *sūrah* then speaks of giving offence to believers generally, men and women, and falsely attributing to them what they do not have: "*And those who malign believing men and women for no wrong they might have done shall have burdened themselves with the guilt of calumny and with a blatant injustice.*" (Verse 58) This strong condemnation suggests that there was in Madinah at the time a group of people who schemed in this way against believers: they defamed them, conspired against them and circulated false allegations about them. This takes place in all communities at all times with believers in particular being so maligned. God therefore undertakes to reply to their accusers, describing them as hypocrites guilty of calumny and injustice. He certainly says only what is absolutely true.

God Almighty then instructs His Messenger to issue an order to his wives, daughters and Muslim women generally requiring them, when they leave their homes, to cover their bodies and heads with an outer garment. In this way, they would be recognized and be protected from the machinations of transgressors. Their modest appearance would distinguish them as chaste women, which embarrasses those who follow women to tease and malign them:

> *Prophet! Say to your wives, daughters and all believing women that they should draw over themselves some of their outer garments. This will be more conducive to their being recognized and not affronted. God is Much-Forgiving, Merciful.* (Verse 59)

Commenting on this verse, al-Suddī says: "Some wicked people in Madinah used to go out at nightfall to make indecent remarks to women. Houses in Madinah were small. Therefore, women went out at night to relieve themselves. However, they were maligned by such wicked remarks. When such people saw a woman wrapped in her outer cover, they refrained from maligning her as they recognized her as free and chaste. A woman who did not have such a cover was subjected to their affronts as they thought her to be a slave."

Mujāhid says: "When they put on their outer cover, they were recognized as free and chaste women. No one maligned them. As for the verse ending, '*God is Much-Forgiving, Merciful,*' it means that He forgave women what happened in the past, as they were not aware of what they should do.

We note the great care taken to purge all wicked behaviour from the Muslim society. These elements had to be pushed into a narrow corner, while new Islamic values and traditions took firm root in the Muslim community.

The passage concludes with a stern warning to the hypocrites and those who were sick at heart as well as those who circulated false rumours requiring that they stop all such wicked action, and refrain from affronting the believers and the Muslim community as a whole. Unless they stopped, God would empower His Messenger to drive them out of Madinah, so that they could be taken and killed wherever they were. This was the law applied, by God's leave, in past generations, and it could easily be revived:

> *If the hypocrites, those who are sick at heart and those who spread lies in the city do not desist, We will rouse you against them, and then they will not be your neighbours in this city except for a little while: bereft of God's grace, they shall be seized wherever they may be found, and will be slain. Such has been God's way with those who went before. Never will you find any change in God's way.* (Verses 60–62)

This powerful warning gives us a clear impression of the Muslims' strong position in Madinah after the Qurayẓah affair. Indeed, the Muslim state was now in full power. The hypocrites could only scheme in secret, unable to demonstrate their reality. Indeed, they remained always in fear.

6

Too Heavy for Mountains

People ask you about the Last Hour. Say: 'Knowledge of it rests with God alone.' Yet for all you know the Last Hour may well be near. (63)

يَسْـَٔلُكَ ٱلنَّاسُ عَنِ ٱلسَّاعَةِ قُلْ إِنَّمَا عِلْمُهَا عِندَ ٱللَّهِ وَمَا يُدْرِيكَ لَعَلَّ ٱلسَّاعَةَ تَكُونُ قَرِيبًا ٦٣

God has certainly rejected the unbelievers and prepared for them a blazing fire, (64)

إِنَّ ٱللَّهَ لَعَنَ ٱلْكَفِرِينَ وَأَعَدَّ لَهُمْ سَعِيرًا ٦٤

where they will permanently abide. They will find none to protect or support them. (65)

خَلِدِينَ فِيهَا أَبَدًا لَّا يَجِدُونَ وَلِيًّا وَلَا نَصِيرًا ٦٥

On the day when their faces shall be tossed about in the fire, they will say: 'Would that we had obeyed God and obeyed His Messenger.' (66)

يَوْمَ تُقَلَّبُ وُجُوهُهُمْ فِى ٱلنَّارِ يَقُولُونَ يَلَيْتَنَا أَطَعْنَا ٱللَّهَ وَأَطَعْنَا ٱلرَّسُولَا۠ ٦٦

And they shall say: 'Our Lord! We have paid heed to our masters and our leaders, but they have led us astray from the right path. (67)

وَقَالُوا رَبَّنَا إِنَّا أَطَعْنَا سَادَتَنَا وَكُبَرَآءَنَا فَأَضَلُّونَا ٱلسَّبِيلَا۠ ٦٧

113

Our Lord! Give them double suffering, and banish them utterly from Your grace.' (68)

رَبَّنَآءَاتِهِمْ ضِعْفَيْنِ مِنَ ٱلْعَذَابِ وَٱلْعَنْهُمْ لَعْنًا كَبِيرًا ۝

Believers! Do not be like those who gave offence to Moses. God showed him to be innocent of whatever they alleged against him. Indeed, he was highly honoured in God's sight. (69)

يَٰٓأَيُّهَا ٱلَّذِينَ ءَامَنُوا۟ لَا تَكُونُوا۟ كَٱلَّذِينَ ءَاذَوْا۟ مُوسَىٰ فَبَرَّأَهُ ٱللَّهُ مِمَّا قَالُوا۟ وَكَانَ عِندَ ٱللَّهِ وَجِيهًا ۝

Believers! Have fear of God and say only what is just and true (70)

يَٰٓأَيُّهَا ٱلَّذِينَ ءَامَنُوا۟ ٱتَّقُوا۟ ٱللَّهَ وَقُولُوا۟ قَوْلًا سَدِيدًا ۝

for then He will cause your deeds to be good and sound, and He will forgive you your sins. Whoever obeys God and His Messenger will certainly achieve a great triumph. (71)

يُصْلِحْ لَكُمْ أَعْمَٰلَكُمْ وَيَغْفِرْ لَكُمْ ذُنُوبَكُمْ وَمَن يُطِعِ ٱللَّهَ وَرَسُولَهُۥ فَقَدْ فَازَ فَوْزًا عَظِيمًا ۝

We offered the trust to the heavens and the earth and the mountains, but they refused to bear it and were afraid to receive it. Yet man took it up. He has always been prone to be wicked, foolish. (72)

إِنَّا عَرَضْنَا ٱلْأَمَانَةَ عَلَى ٱلسَّمَٰوَٰتِ وَٱلْأَرْضِ وَٱلْجِبَالِ فَأَبَيْنَ أَن يَحْمِلْنَهَا وَأَشْفَقْنَ مِنْهَا وَحَمَلَهَا ٱلْإِنسَٰنُ إِنَّهُۥ كَانَ ظَلُومًا جَهُولًا ۝

So it is that God will punish the hypocrites, men and women, as well as the men and women who associate partners with Him; and He will turn in mercy to the believers, both men and women. God is Much-Forgiving, Merciful. (73)

لِيُعَذِّبَ ٱللَّهُ ٱلْمُنَٰفِقِينَ وَٱلْمُنَٰفِقَٰتِ وَٱلْمُشْرِكِينَ وَٱلْمُشْرِكَٰتِ وَيَتُوبَ ٱللَّهُ عَلَى ٱلْمُؤْمِنِينَ وَٱلْمُؤْمِنَٰتِ وَكَانَ ٱللَّهُ غَفُورًا رَّحِيمًۢا ۝

Overview

This final passage of the *surah* mentions people's questions about the Last Hour, when the Day of Judgement arrives. People have often asked for the Last Hour to be hastened, expressing doubt about it. The answer to this question always leaves its timing to God Almighty, warning people that it is close at hand, and that it could take them unawares at any time. The *surah* then portrays an image of the Last Hour that certainly does not please those who hasten it. It is an image of their own faces as they are turned over in the fire, expressing profound regret for not obeying God and His Messenger, and praying that their masters and chiefs be given double punishment. It is a scene of catastrophe that no one likes to consider. The *surah* then turns again to the present world, warning the believers against following in the footsteps of those who gave offence to Moses and levelled accusations against him, but God confirmed his innocence. This appears to be in answer to something that actually took place. It might have been referring to the fact that some of them spoke about the Prophet's marriage to Zaynab, which was contrary to Arab tradition. The believers are invited to say only what is right, refrain from slander, so that God will accept their deeds and forgive them their sins. It makes obeying God and His Messenger more appealing to them, promising them great reward for this.

The final verses refer to the trust which the heavens, the earth and the mountains would not agree to shoulder, fearing that it was too heavy for them. Nevertheless, man undertook to bear it, so that God's purpose is accomplished: reward then is commensurate with action, and man will have to account for his choices.

The Timing of the Last Hour

People ask you about the Last Hour. Say: 'Knowledge of it rests with God alone.' Yet for all you know the Last Hour may well be near. (Verse 63)

Those people continued to ask the Prophet about the Last Hour, which he has long warned them against, while the Qur'ān gave vivid descriptions of some of its scenes, which they could almost see before their eyes. They ask the Prophet about its timing, and demand that it should be hastened. This implied doubt, rejection or ridicule of the whole question, according to the nature of the person asking and how close or far removed they were from faith.

The Last Hour is part of what lies beyond our perception. God is the only one who knows all about it. It is His will that no one among His creatures should know its timing, not even His messengers and favoured angels. A *hadīth* summing up Islamic faith is reported by 'Umar ibn al-Khaṭṭāb, who reports:

One day as we were sitting with God's Messenger (peace be upon him), there appeared before us a man whose clothes were exceedingly white and whose hair was exceedingly black; no sign of travelling was to be seen on him but none of us knew him. He walked up to the Prophet and sat down by him. Resting his knees against the Prophet's knees and placing his hands on his thighs, he said: 'Muḥammad, tell me about Islam.' The Prophet said: 'Islam is to testify that there is no deity other than God and Muḥammad is God's Messenger, to attend regularly to prayer, to pay *zakāt*, to fast in Ramaḍān and to make the pilgrimage to the House if you are able to do so.' The man said: 'You have spoken rightly.' We were amazed at him asking the question and then confirming that the answer was right.

He then said: 'Tell me about faith, or *īmān*.' The Prophet said: 'Faith is to believe in God, His angels, His books, His messengers and the Last Day, and to believe in divine destiny, both its good and evil manifestations. He said: 'You have spoken rightly. Then tell me about attaining to perfection, or *iḥsān*.' The Prophet answered: 'It is to worship God as though you are seeing Him,

knowing that while you cannot see Him, yet He sees you.' He
said: 'Then tell me about the Last Hour.' The Prophet said: 'The
one questioned about it knows no better than the questioner.' ...
The Prophet then told us: 'The man was Gabriel who came here
to teach you your religion.' [Related by Muslim, Abū Dāwūd, al-
Tirmidhī and al-Nasā'ī.]

It is exactly as the Prophet said: the one questioned about the Last
Hour, i.e. the Prophet himself, and the questioner, i.e. the Angel
Gabriel, have no knowledge of it. This is because 'Knowledge of it rests
with God alone,' and He imparts that knowledge to none of His
creatures.

God has willed this for a purpose, of which we can see a part: people
are warned that they should expect it at any time, ready to receive it as
it comes all of a sudden. This is the attitude of the believers who remain
God-fearing. By contrast, those who are oblivious of the Last Hour,
and do not expect its arrival at any time, are the ones who deceive
themselves and do not protect themselves against God's punishment.
God has warned them, making the Last Hour a secret that could come
upon them at any moment of the night or day: 'Yet for all you know
the Last Hour may well be near.' (Verse 63)

God has certainly rejected the unbelievers and prepared for them a
blazing fire, where they will permanently abide. They will find none to
protect or support them. On the day when their faces shall be tossed
about in the fire, they will say: 'Would that we had obeyed God and
obeyed His Messenger.' And they shall say: 'Our Lord! We have paid
heed to our masters and our leaders, but they have led us astray from the
right path. Our Lord! Give them double suffering, and banish them
utterly from Your grace.' (Verses 64–68)

As they are questioning the Prophet about the Last Hour, they are
given a scene from it: "God has certainly rejected the unbelievers and
prepared for them a blazing fire.' (Verse 64) He has rejected them, expelling
them from His grace. And He has prepared for them a raging fire which
is kept ready for them: "where they will permanently abide." (Verse 65)
They abide there for an extended term, the length of which is known
only to God. Its end is known only to Him and is dependent on His

will. They are deprived of all help and support. They cannot hope to escape: "*They will find none to protect or support them.*" (Verse 65)

In the midst of all this suffering, they appear very miserable: "*On the day when their faces shall be tossed about in the fire.*" The fire surrounds them from every corner. Yet the description here is intended to exaggerate the movement so as to feel that the fire touches every spot on their faces. "*They will say: Would that we had obeyed God and obeyed His Messenger.*" (Verse 66) It is a useless wish that can in no way be accepted. It is now too late for anything. They can only express regret and feel remorse.

At this point, they express unreserved anger with their masters and leaders who led them astray: "*And they shall say: 'Our Lord! We have paid heed to our masters and our leaders, but they have led us astray from the right path. Our Lord! Give double suffering, and banish them utterly from Your grace.'*" (Verses 67–68) Such is the Last Hour: what need is there to ask about its timing? The only way to ensure salvation on that day is to work hard in earning God's pleasure.

Baseless Accusations

It seems that the Prophet's marriage to Zaynab bint Jaḥsh, which was intended to replace the norms prevailing in pre-Islamic days, did not pass so easily. Many of the hypocrites and the sick at heart began to speak ill of it. So did some of those who had not yet ascertained the Islamic concept of social relations. All such people cast remarks and innuendoes, sometimes in a whisper, sometimes openly: they all expressed monstrous thoughts. The hypocrites and those who spread lies were not going to keep quiet. They sought every opportunity to inject their poison into the new Muslim society, just as we saw them do during the attack by the confederate forces, the story of falsehood, the division of booty, etc. They were always on the look out for something which they could use to cause the Prophet pain.

By this time, when the Qurayẓah were expelled, preceded by other Jewish tribes, no one was left in Madinah who was openly an unbeliever. All its inhabitants were now Muslims, even though some of them only put up appearances while in actuality they were hypocrites. It was these hypocrites who circulated rumours and fabricated lies. Some believers unwittingly fell prey to them, repeating some of what they had heard. Now, the *sūrah* warns them against giving offence to the Prophet, in the same way as the Children of Israel gave offence to Moses. It directs them to say only what is right, correct and proper, telling them that only through obedience to God and His Messenger could they hope to achieve the great success:

> *Believers! Do not be like those who gave offence to Moses. God showed him to be innocent of whatever they alleged against him. Indeed, he was highly honoured in God's sight. Believers! Have fear of God and say only what is just and true for then He will cause your deeds to be good and sound, and He will forgive you your sins. Whoever obeys God and His Messenger will certainly achieve a great triumph.* (Verses 69–71)

The Qur'ān does not specify the sort of offence the Israelites directed at Moses, but some reports mention it specifically. However, we feel that there is no need to give details of something the Qur'ān alluded to in general terms. The aim here is to warn the believers against everything that could give offence to the Prophet. The Israelites are cited as an example of deviation from the right course on many occasions in the Qur'ān. Therefore, it is sufficient here to refer only to the fact that they gave offence to their prophet, warning the Muslims against following in their footsteps. This makes every believer refrain from doing what would place him among such deviant people.

God established Moses' innocence of whatever his people alleged against him. He was in a position of honour with God: "*He was highly honoured in God's sight.*" (Verse 69) God makes it clear that His messengers are innocent of all that is fabricated and falsely alleged against them. Muḥammad, the most noble of God's messengers, has the first claim to be proven innocent by God Himself.

The *sūrah* directs the believers to say only what is just, true and accurate. They should make sure of what they say and its effects, before they accept what the hypocrites and spreaders of lies say, and before they pay attention to any wild accusation or evil fabrication against the Prophet, their leader and guide. It directs them to say right words leading to right action. God takes care of those who make sure of saying what is right, proper and accurate, guiding their footsteps and making their deeds sound, producing good results. God also forgives the sins of those who say what is right and do righteous deeds, for even they are not immune to slips and errors. They are all human, and by nature humans err and need God's forgiveness.

"*Whoever obeys God and His Messenger will certainly achieve a great triumph.*" (Verse 71) To obey God and His Messenger is, in itself, a great triumph, because it means consciously following the way God has marked out. It gives comfort and reassurance. To be sure that one is following the right way gives happiness, even if it does not earn any reward. A person who follows a direct, easy way that is full of light and who finds that all God's creatures respond to him and help him has totally different prospects from one who follows a blocked, rough way that is covered in darkness with all God's creatures emitting hostility towards him. Obedience to God and His Messenger brings its own immediate reward. Moreover, it achieves a great triumph now, before the Day of Judgement and entry into heaven. Enjoying bliss in the life to come is an act of grace which is over and above the reward for such obedience. It is a grace bestowed by God freely, without anything being asked in return.

Man's Weakness

In this act of grace, God considers man's weakness, the great burden he shoulders and the trust he has been bearing alone when the heavens, the earth and the mountains refused, fearing that they could not cope with its requirements. Yet man is not only weak; he suffers from pressures created by his desires and inclinations, lack of knowledge, short life span as also barriers of time and place. All this makes him lacking in proper knowledge, unable to see what is beyond barriers or to look far ahead:

We offered the trust to the heavens and the earth and the mountains, but they refused to bear it and were afraid to receive it. Yet man took it up. He has always been prone to be wicked, foolish. (Verse 72)

The heavens, the earth and the mountains, great and magnificent beings as they are, are chosen for discussion by the Qur'ān. Compared to these, man who lives in or beside them appears small and insignificant. These creatures, however, know their Lord without having to make an effort. They follow His law by their very nature and the system applicable to them, without need for an intermediary, reflection or choice. They run their respective courses without fail, fulfilling their tasks by virtue of their nature and constitution. The sun moves in its orbit in absolute accuracy, sending its rays and thus fulfilling the role God has assigned to it. It unconsciously holds its satellite planets and other celestial bodies in a set measure of gravity, thus fulfilling its role in the universe. The earth also runs its cycle, yielding its plants and feeding its population, burying the dead and sending up its water in springs, all in accordance with God's law, and without having to make a choice. The moon, stars, planets, the wind, the clouds, air and water, mountains and valleys – all fulfil their functions, by their Lord's leave. They know their Lord and are subject to His will without having to make an effort. What is this trust which they all dreaded to receive? It is the trust of responsibility, will power, personal knowledge and choice.

"*Yet man took it up.*" (Verse 72) Man took it up because he is able to know God through his faculties and feelings. He can recognize God's law by reflection and consideration, and apply this law by his endeavour, obeying God willingly and by choice, resisting desires that lead to deviation and disobedience. In every step along this way man is acting by his own will, using his own knowledge, choosing his way fully aware of the end to which it leads.

It is a huge burden that this small creature, with little power and a short life, and with pressurizing desires and inclinations, has undertaken. In so doing, he runs great risks. Hence, man is '*prone to be wicked,*' putting himself in the wrong, and '*foolish,*' not knowing his ability. This is true in relation to the great responsibility he has shouldered. However, when he fulfils this trust, acquires the knowledge leading him to his Lord, knows His law and obeys Him fully, he becomes equipped with the knowledge, the guidance and the obedience which bring him to the level of ease and perfection enjoyed by creatures like the heavens, earth and mountains, which obey God and follow His law naturally and directly. When man attains this level, while aware, conscious and exercising free choice, he attains a noble standard and is given a unique position among God's creation.

The acquisition of knowledge, the ability to choose and the willingness to be accountable constitute the quality that distinguishes man among God's creatures. This is the quality that earns man his position of honour, declared by God to those on high as He ordered the angels to prostrate themselves before Adam. In addition, He announced this honour in His revealed book, the Qur'ān: "*We have indeed honoured the children of Adam.*" (17: 70) It behoves man to know why he has been honoured and to live up to the trust he has accepted, while stronger creatures refused it dreading the responsibility.

All this has a definite purpose:

> *So it is that God will punish the hypocrites, men and women, as well as the men and women who associate partners with Him; and He will turn in mercy to the believers, both men and women. God is Much-Forgiving, Merciful.* (Verse 73)

For man to take the trust upon himself means that he has to accept the consequences of his choice, and to make his reward dependent on action. This means that punishment is earned by the hypocrites and the unbelievers, while the believers are given help, which ensures that God forgives them their errors which they are bound to make, considering their weakness, the pressures on them and the barriers standing in their way. This help comes by an act of divine grace, for God is always Much-Forgiving, Merciful.

On this powerful note ends the *sūrah* that began with a directive to the Prophet to obey God, not yield to the unbelievers and the hypocrites, follow God's revelations and place his trust in God alone. The *sūrah* also included numerous directives and pieces of legislation for the Muslim community. This powerful and final note describes man's huge responsibility and great trust, indicating what makes it so heavy. With this conclusion, the beginning and end of the *sūrah* are in full harmony with its subject matter. This, in itself, is evidence pointing to the Author of the Qur'ān.

SŪRAH 34

Saba'

(Sheba)

Prologue

This *sūrah*, a Makkan revelation, tackles the main themes of faith: belief in God's oneness, the revelation of the Qur'ān and the truth of resurrection. The *sūrah* also provides the correct view of a number of essential values related to these themes. It makes clear that faith and good action, rather than wealth and offspring, form the basis of the ultimate judgement by God. It clearly states that no power can protect anyone against God's punishment and no intercession is of any use unless He approves it.

The main emphasis in the *sūrah* is on the question of resurrection and reward, as well as God's limitless, comprehensive and accurate knowledge. These two closely intertwined topics are raised time after time, in a variety of styles and approaches, and are diffused through the *sūrah* from start to finish. Thus on resurrection we have: *"The unbelievers say: 'Never shall the Last Hour come upon us!' Say: 'Yes, by my Lord, it shall most certainly come to you.'"* (Verse 3) And on reward the *sūrah* makes this early statement: *"He may reward those who believe and do righteous deeds. It is they who shall have forgiveness and generous provisions."* (Verse 4)

This same theme is raised again a little later on: *"The unbelievers say: 'Shall we point out to you a man who will tell you that, when you have been utterly torn into pieces, you shall be restored to life in a new act of*

123

creation? Has he invented a lie about God, or is he a madman?' No! It is those who do not believe in the life to come who shall be suffering torment as they have gone far in error." (Verses 7–8)

The *sūrah* also portrays a number of scenes from the Day of Judgement, showing how unbelievers are rebuked for their rejection of the truth as well as images of the punishment they used to deny or express strong doubts about: *"If only you could see how the wrongdoers shall be made to stand before their Lord, hurling reproaches at one another. Those of them who were weak on earth will say to those who had deemed themselves mighty: 'Had it not been for you, we would certainly have been believers.' The ones who deemed themselves mighty will say to those who were weak: 'Was it we who prevented you from following right guidance after it had been given you? No. It was you who were guilty.' Those who were weak will reply to those who deemed themselves mighty: 'No. It was your scheming, night and day, ordering us to disbelieve in God and to set up equals to Him.' When they see the punishment awaiting them, they will all harbour utter and unmitigated remorse. We shall put chains round the necks of the unbelievers. Are they to be requited for anything other than what they did?"* (Verses 31–33)

Again such scenes are portrayed at various places in the *sūrah*, including its conclusion: *"If you could but see when they are seized by terror, with nowhere to escape; for they will have been seized from a place nearby. They will say: 'We do believe in it,' but how could they attain it from so far away, seeing that they had at first denied it all. They used to cast scorn from far away on what is imperceptible. A barrier will be set between them and all that they desire, just as was done with their kind before. They were lost in perplexing doubt."* (Verses 51–54)

On the theme of God's knowledge and its extent and fullness, we read at the outset: *"He knows all that goes into the earth and all that comes out of it; all that descends from the skies and all that ascends to them."* (Verse 2) And in a comment on those who deny the Day of Judgement, the *sūrah* says: *"Say: 'Yes, by my Lord, it shall most certainly come to you. It is He who knows all that lies beyond the reach of human perception. Not an atom's weight in the heavens or the earth escapes Him; nor is there anything smaller or larger but is recorded in a clear book."* (Verse 3) This is further confirmed towards the *sūrah*'s end where it states: *"Say: My Lord hurls forth the truth. He has full knowledge of all that is beyond the reach of people's perception."* (Verse 48)

On the theme of God's oneness, the *sūrah* begins with praising God *"to whom belongs all that is in the heavens and the earth; and to Him will be due all praise in the life to come. He is truly wise, All-Aware."* (Verse 1) The *sūrah* again challenges them with regard to the deities they allege to be God's partners: *"Say: Call upon those whom you imagine to be partners with God. They do not have even an atom's weight of authority either in the heavens or the earth, nor have they any share in either, nor does He have any helper from among them."* (Verse 22)

In one of the scenes it portrays of the Day of Judgement, the *sūrah* refers to their worship of angels and *jinn*: *"On the day He gathers them all together, He will say to the angels: 'Was it you that these people worshipped?' They will answer: 'Limitless are You in Your glory! You alone are our patron, not they. In fact they worshipped the* jinn *and most of them believed in them.'"* (Verses 40–41) It refutes their ideas about intercession by the angels on their behalf: *"Before Him, intercession is of no avail, except by one to whom He may have granted permission. When the terror is lifted from their hearts, they will ask [one another]: 'What has your Lord ordained?' They will answer: 'The truth. He is the Most High, the Supreme.'"* (Verse 23) In connection with their worship of the *jinn* mention is made of Solomon and how the *jinn* were placed in his service. It highlights the fact that they were unable to realize that he was dead: *"When We decreed his death, nothing showed them that he was dead except an earthworm that gnawed away at his staff. And when he fell to the ground, the* jinn *saw clearly that, had they understood the reality which was beyond [their] perception, they would not have remained in humiliating servitude."* (Verse 14)

On the theme of the revelation of God's message, the *sūrah* reports: *"The unbelievers say: We will never believe in this Qur'ān, nor in any earlier revelations."* (Verse 31) *"When Our revelations are recited to them in all their clarity, they say: 'This is but a man who wants to turn you away from what your forefathers worshipped.' They also say: 'This is nothing but an invented falsehood.' Furthermore, when the truth comes to them, the unbelievers will say: 'This is just plain sorcery.'"* (Verse 43) The *sūrah* issues a decisive reply: *"Those who are endowed with knowledge are well aware that what has been revealed to you by your Lord is indeed the truth, and*

125

that it guides to the way that leads to the Almighty, the One to whom all praise is due." (Verse 6) *"We have sent you to all mankind so that you bring them good news and give them warning; but most people do not understand."* (Verse 28)

On the question of the values to be applied, the *sūrah* proffers the following verses: *"Whenever We sent a warner to any community, those of them who lived in luxury said: 'We do not believe in the message with which you have been sent.' They also say: 'Richer than you are we in wealth, and we have more children. We certainly are not going to be made to suffer.' Say: 'My Lord gives in abundance, or gives in scant measure, to whomever He wills; but most people do not understand.' It is neither your riches nor your children that can bring you nearer to Us: only he who believes and does what is right [comes near to Us]. To these multiple reward will be given for all that they have done. They will dwell in safety in the mansions of paradise; whereas all who strive against Our revelations, seeking to defeat their purpose, shall be given over to suffering."* (Verses 34–38) The *sūrah* gives some historical examples, citing David and his household who demonstrated their gratitude for God's favours and contrasting this with the people of Sheba who were totally ungrateful. What happened to both communities was well known, confirming God's promises and warnings.

All Makkan *sūrahs* tackle these topics, but in each *sūrah* they are portrayed against a special cosmic background. Indeed, this theme is accompanied by diverse influences that we feel to be new each time. The background in the present *sūrah* is the wide space of the heaven and earth, the awesome, unfathomable realm that lies beyond the reach of our perception, the limitless plateau where the gathering takes place on the Day of Judgement, the inner depths of the human soul, and a number of amazing historical scenes. Each has its clear message for our hearts, ensuring we remain alert. At the very beginning of the *sūrah* we are introduced to this broad universal expanse and God's limitless knowledge: *"He knows all that goes into the earth and all that comes out of it; all that descends from the skies and all that ascends to them... The unbelievers say: 'Never shall the Last Hour come upon us!' Say: 'Yes, by my Lord, it shall most certainly come to you. It is He who knows all that lies beyond the reach of human perception. Not an atom's weight in the heavens or the earth escapes Him; nor is there anything smaller or larger but is recorded in a clear book."* (Verses 2–3)

Those who deny resurrection and the hereafter are warned against great celestial catastrophes: *"Do they not consider how much of the sky and the earth lies open before them and how much lies hidden from them? If We so willed, We could cause the earth to swallow them, or cause fragments of the sky to fall upon them. In all this, there is a sign for every servant of God turning to Him in repentance."* (Verse 9) On the other hand, those who worship angels or *jinn* are faced with an awesome scene: *"Before Him, intercession is of no avail, except by one to whom He may have granted permission. When the terror is lifted from their hearts, they will ask [one another]: 'What has your Lord ordained?' They will answer: 'The truth. He is the Most High, the Supreme.'"* (Verse 23) Alternatively, they are placed face to face with the angel on the Day of Resurrection when no argument or ambiguity is allowed: *"On the day He gathers them all together, He will say to the angels: Was it you that these people worshipped?"* (Verse 40)

Those who denied the Prophet Muḥammad, accusing him of fabricating lies or alleging that he was mad are put before their own nature when it is free of alien influences: *"Say: I counsel you one thing: stand before God, in pairs or singly, and think: there is no madness in your Companion [Muḥammad]. He is only a warner to you of awesome suffering to come."* (Verse 46)

Thus the *sūrah* takes our hearts to such horizons and brings into play some inspiring influences. Finally, it concludes with a powerful scene of the Day of Judgement.

Praise of God forms the beginning of the *sūrah*, identifying some of His attributes, such as having dominion in the heavens and earth, receiving praise in the hereafter, wisdom and full knowledge of all that takes place in the universe. It also mentions the unbelievers' denial of the Last Hour and God's emphatic reply that it will certainly come. Again the *sūrah* states that not an atom's weight in the whole universe escapes God's knowledge, which will ensure that God's requital to all, believers and unbelievers, will be based on accurate and full knowledge of all situations and circumstances. In this early part, the *sūrah* states that those who are endowed with wisdom confirm that what God has revealed to His

Messenger is the truth. It states that the unbelievers find the idea of resurrection strange, refuting their arguments and telling them that they suffer as a result of being far in error. It warns them that they could be swallowed up by the earth or that the skies could fall apart on them. On this note, the first part of the *sūrah* ends.

The second part highlights some aspects of the history of David and his household, who were all very grateful for God's favours. God placed at the command of David and Solomon numerous powers, and they acknowledged God's favours, taking no personal pride in them. One of these powers was the *Jinn* who are worshipped by some idolaters. They often consulted such *Jinn* over questions relating to the realm beyond our perception, but the *Jinn* know nothing of this realm. In Solomon's story, as related in this *sūrah*, the *Jinn* continued to do some hard and menial jobs for him even after his death, of which they continued to be unaware. Contrasted with this gratitude for God's favours, is that of total ingratitude as represented by the people of Sheba. Therefore, *"We caused them to become a tale, and scattered them throughout the land."* (Verse 19) They deserved this end because they did Satan's bidding, even though he had no power over them. In other words, they willingly allowed him to lead them astray.

The third part challenges the idolaters to invoke their alleged deities, and tells them that these *"do not have even an atom's weight of authority either in the heavens or the earth, nor have they any share in either, nor does He have any helper from among them."* (Verse 22) None of these false deities can intercede with God on anyone's behalf, not even if they were angels, for angels stand in awe of God, do His bidding and do not talk until they are reassured. As instructed, the Prophet asks them who provides their sustenance out of the heavens and the earth, when it is God who has dominion over both? He, and no one else, provides for them and for all other creatures. The Prophet then leaves the matter between himself and them to God for judgement. This part of the *sūrah* ends with a similar challenge to that with which it began: *"Say: 'Show me those whom you allege to be partners with Him. Nay! He alone is God, the Almighty, the Wise.'"* (Verse 27)

Together the fourth and fifth parts tackle the question of the revelation of God's message and the unbelievers' attitude towards it. They speak about how the affluent view every call to faith, and how they show pride in their wealth and children. These two parts establish the fact that faith and good actions are the basic criteria for reward. Several scenes are shown here of the different fates of the believers and unbelievers, in which we see the leaders disowning their followers and the angels disassociating themselves from those who worshipped them. In between these scenes, the *sūrah* calls on the unbelievers to resort to their own nature, seeking its answers free from all the fuss they create about God's Messenger. It reminds them that they have no evidence for the accusations they level at him, when he asks them for no reward and tells them no lie. Each of these two parts is concluded with a scene from the Day of Resurrection. Then, finally, the *sūrah* ends with a run of short verses that are characterized by a powerful, fast rhythm: *"Say: 'My Lord hurls forth the truth. He has full knowledge of all that is beyond the reach of people's perception.' Say: 'The truth has now come. Falsehood neither creates anything new, nor restores anything.' Say: 'Were I to go astray, I would but go astray to the loss of myself. But if I am on the right path, it is through what my Lord reveals to me. He is All-Hearing, ever-near.' If you could but see when they are seized by terror, with nowhere to escape; for they will have been seized from a place nearby."* (Verses 48–51)

I

Infinite and Accurate Knowledge

Saba' (Sheba)

In the Name of God, the Lord of Grace, the Ever Merciful

All praise is due to God, to whom belongs all that is in the heavens and the earth; and to Him will be due all praise in the life to come. He is truly Wise, All-Aware. (1)

He knows all that goes into the earth and all that comes out of it; all that descends from the skies and all that ascends to them. He is the Merciful, the truly Forgiving. (2)

The unbelievers say: 'Never shall the Last Hour come upon us!' Say: 'Yes, by my Lord, it shall most certainly come to you. It is He who knows all that lies beyond the

131

reach of human perception. Not an atom's weight in the heavens or the earth escapes Him; nor is there anything smaller or larger but is recorded in a clear book, (3)

لَا يَعْزُبُ عَنْهُ مِثْقَالُ ذَرَّةٍ فِي السَّمَوَاتِ وَلَا فِي الْأَرْضِ وَلَا أَصْغَرُ مِن ذَلِكَ وَلَا أَكْبَرُ إِلَّا فِي كِتَبٍ مُّبِينٍ ۝

so that He may reward those who believe and do righteous deeds. It is they who shall have forgiveness and generous provisions.' (4)

لِّيَجْزِيَ الَّذِينَ ءَامَنُوا وَعَمِلُوا الصَّلِحَتِ أُوْلَئِكَ لَهُم مَّغْفِرَةٌ وَرِزْقٌ كَرِيمٌ ۝

As for those who strive against Our revelations, seeking to defeat their purpose, these shall have a most painful suffering. (5)

وَالَّذِينَ سَعَوْ فِي ءَايَتِنَا مُعَجِزِينَ أُوْلَئِكَ لَهُمْ عَذَابٌ مِّن رِّجْزٍ أَلِيمٌ ۝

Those who are endowed with knowledge are well aware that what has been revealed to you by your Lord is indeed the truth, and that it guides to the way that leads to the Almighty, to whom all praise is due. (6)

وَيَرَى الَّذِينَ أُوتُوا الْعِلْمَ الَّذِي أُنزِلَ إِلَيْكَ مِن رَّبِّكَ هُوَ الْحَقَّ وَيَهْدِي إِلَى صِرَطِ الْعَزِيزِ الْحَمِيدِ ۝

The unbelievers say: 'Shall we point out to you a man who will tell you that, when you have been utterly torn into pieces, you shall be restored to life in a new act of creation? (7)

وَقَالَ الَّذِينَ كَفَرُوا هَلْ نَدُلُّكُمْ عَلَى رَجُلٍ يُنَبِّئُكُمْ إِذَا مُزِّقْتُمْ كُلَّ مُمَزَّقٍ إِنَّكُمْ لَفِي خَلْقٍ جَدِيدٍ ۝

Has he invented a lie about God, or is he a madman?' No! It is those who do not believe in the life to come who are suffering torment as they have gone far in error. (8)

أَفْتَرَىٰ عَلَى ٱللَّهِ كَذِبًا أَم بِهِۦ جِنَّةُۢ بَلِ ٱلَّذِينَ لَا يُؤْمِنُونَ بِٱلْأَخِرَةِ فِي ٱلْعَذَابِ وَٱلضَّلَٰلِ ٱلْبَعِيدِ ٨

Do they not consider how much of the sky and the earth lies open before them and how much lies hidden from them? If We so willed, We could cause the earth to swallow them, or cause fragments of the sky to fall upon them. In all this, there is a sign for every servant of God turning to Him in repentance. (9)

أَفَلَمْ يَرَوْا۟ إِلَىٰ مَا بَيْنَ أَيْدِيهِمْ وَمَا خَلْفَهُم مِّنَ ٱلسَّمَآءِ وَٱلْأَرْضِ إِن نَّشَأْ نَخْسِفْ بِهِمُ ٱلْأَرْضَ أَوْ نُسْقِطْ عَلَيْهِمْ كِسَفًا مِّنَ ٱلسَّمَآءِ إِنَّ فِي ذَٰلِكَ لَءَايَةً لِّكُلِّ عَبْدٍ مُّنِيبٍ ٩

Where Praise is Due

This *surah*, which speaks at length about the idolaters who associated partners with God, denied His Messenger, doubted the hereafter and dismissed the idea of resurrection, begins with praising God. All praise is due to Him for being God, even though no human being utters a word of praise addressed to Him. He is praised by the universe and all creation, even though some human beings take a different attitude.

Coupled with this is God's attribute of being the Sovereign of the universe. No one has any portion of heaven or earth: He alone owns all there is. This is the central issue of faith: God's oneness.

"To Him will be due all praise in the life to come." (Verse 1) All the praise offered by all His servants, including those who disbelieved in Him in this life or associated partners with Him as a result of being led astray, will converge in the life to come and be addressed totally and purely to Him. *"He is truly Wise, All-Aware."* (Verse 1) Whatever He does is based on wisdom. Indeed, He conducts the affairs of this life and

133

the Next, and the affairs of the entire universe in perfect wisdom. Moreover, He is aware of everything that takes place, and His knowledge is full, accurate and absolute.

The *sūrah* gives us a notion of God's knowledge, portrayed against the background of heaven and earth: "*He knows all that goes into the earth and all that comes out of it; all that descends from the skies and all that ascends to them.*" (Verse 2) This is a vast image drawn in a few simple words, painting an amazing multitude of things, motions, sizes, shapes, forms and meanings that go beyond any imagination. Should all the people on earth spend their entire lives monitoring and recording what takes place in just one moment of the things mentioned in the verse, they would not be able to do so. How many things go into the earth in such a moment? How many leave it? And how many come down from the sky or go up into it?

Consider what goes into the earth: the seeds that are buried in the ground, the worms, insects, crawling creatures, drops of rain, gases, electrical rays... all poured into every corner of this vast earth, yet God's eye watches them all. Then look at what comes out of it: plants shooting out, springs gushing forth, erupting volcanoes, emanating gases, crawlers and insects leaving their underground homes. How many countless things do we see and know about that come out of the earth and how many countless others we do not see or know about?

Reflect also on what comes down from the skies: drops of rain, comets, meteors, rays that burn or give light, divine orders, acts of grace that favour certain creatures while benefiting the whole universe, and also provisions God grants to His servants in plentiful or measured quantities. Then turn over in your mind what goes up into the sky: the breathing of humans, animals and plants, as well as other creatures only known to God, and supplications, uttered aloud or in secret, heard only by God. How many a soul of creatures known or unknown to us is gathered and rises to God; how many an angel ascends to carry out God's order; how many drops of seawater evaporate and rise into the atmosphere; how many molecules of gas emanate from all type of creatures?

How much of all this takes place in one moment? How much can human knowledge record of what happens of all this even should they devote all their lives to monitoring and recording it all? Yet God's knowledge reckons all this up, in all places and at all times, as well as all human thoughts, feelings, actions and movements. But God nevertheless gives us our privacy and forgives us our shortcomings: *"He is the Merciful, the truly Forgiving."* (Verse 2) Just one Qur'ānic verse like the present one is sufficient to prove that this Qur'ān could not have been written by a human being. By nature, such descriptions do not occur to any person, nor does human nature contemplate matters in this way. That such a comprehensive vision is provided in one simple touch reflects the superiority of God's style.

The *sūrah* then mentions the unbelievers' denial of the inevitability of the Last Hour, even though they are totally unaware what tomorrow will bring. That it will come is certain; it is necessary so that both those who do good and those who do evil should receive their fair reward:

> *The unbelievers say: 'Never shall the Last Hour come upon us!' Say: 'Yes, by my Lord, it shall most certainly come to you. It is He who knows all that lies beyond the reach of human perception. Not an atom's weight in the heavens or the earth escapes Him; nor is there anything smaller or larger but is recorded in a clear book, so that He may reward those who believe and do righteous deeds. It is they who shall have forgiveness and generous provisions.' As for those who strive against Our revelations, seeking to defeat their purpose, these shall have a most painful suffering.* (Verses 3–5)

The unbelievers deny the life to come because they do not understand God's wisdom. In His infinite wisdom, He does not let people do what they please, whether good or evil, and then leave them at that, without giving reward to the doers of good and requiting those who do otherwise. He has informed us, through His messengers, that He leaves the reward in full or in part to the Day of Judgement. Therefore, all those who understand His wisdom with regard to His creation realize that the life to come is essential for the fulfilment of God's promise. The unbelievers, however, are oblivious of divine wisdom. Hence, they impolitely say: *"Never shall the Last Hour come upon us."* (Verse 3) Hence the emphatic retort: *"Yes, by my Lord, it shall most certainly come to you."* They have no knowledge of what is beyond their world, but they nevertheless are quick to assert something of which they have no knowledge. Yet the one confirming this is the One *"who knows all that lies beyond the reach of human perception."* (Verse 3) What He states is the truth. Furthermore, this truth is simple, complete and based on sound and true knowledge.

Once more God's knowledge is portrayed against a similarly universal background testifying once more to the Originator of the Qur'ān. Such thoughts simply do not occur to human minds: *"Not an atom's weight in the heavens or the earth escapes Him; nor is there anything smaller or larger but is recorded in a clear book."* (Verse 3) Such images do not occur in ordinary prose or poetry. When people describe knowledge as complete, comprehensive and accurate, they do not paint such a captivating universal image, *'Not an atom's weight in the heavens or the earth escapes Him; nor is there anything smaller or larger…'* I have never seen in human language any attempt to draw such a picture. This is a description by God of His own knowledge, using human language in a way humans do not use it. Thus the Muslims' own concept of God is set on a nobler level. The nearest meaning of the phrase, *'recorded in a clear book,'* is that God's knowledge takes note of everything, including the tiniest of atoms and what is even smaller.

It is useful to reflect a little on the point raised by use of the wording: *"Not an atom's weight… nor is there anything smaller."* Until recently, it was universally accepted that the atom is the smallest thing. Now that it has been possible to cause atomic diffusion, man has learnt that the atom is comprised of a number of other elements. All glory to God who teaches His human servants, at a time of His choosing, what He wishes them to learn of His inner attributes and the secrets of His creation.

Why a Judgement Day?

The inevitable arrival of the Last Hour and God's knowledge that does not exclude anything small or large have a definite purpose: *"so that He may reward those who believe and do righteous deeds. It is they who shall have forgiveness and generous provisions. As for those who strive against Our revelations, seeking to defeat their purpose, these shall have a most painful suffering."* (Verses 4–5) Everything is based on God's wisdom who has created everything according to a set measure so as to administer the right reward or punishment for the believers or those who exert all efforts to turn people away from the truth. Those who give credence to their faith by good actions earn God's forgiveness of any errors they make or sins they commit. They also have *generous provisions*. We note that the *sūrah* frequently mentions the provisions and sustenance God grants. Hence, it is fitting that the happiness they are assured to have in the life to come is described here as *provisions*, which in fact it is. The others, who strive hard to turn people away from God and His message will receive some of the worst type of punishment which fits their wicked efforts. Thus is God's purpose fulfilled.

Within the overall context of God's knowledge and His purpose the next statement makes clear that those endowed with knowledge realize that what the Prophet Muḥammad receives from God is the truth, providing sound guidance: "*Those who are endowed with knowledge are well aware that what has been revealed to you by your Lord is indeed the truth, and that it guides to the way that leads to the Almighty, to whom all praise is due.*" (Verse 6)

Some reports suggest that the phrase, *'those who are endowed with knowledge',* refers to the people of earlier revelations who are told in their scriptures about the Qur'ān and its provision of true guidance. However, the Qur'ānic verse has a wider scope. All those endowed with proper knowledge, at all times and wherever they happen to be, will realize this on the basis of their knowledge, if it is truly sound. The Qur'ān is open for all people throughout all generations. It includes enough truth to reveal itself to everyone who has sound knowledge. It also states the truth inherent in the very existence of the universe.

Moreover, the Qur'ān "*guides to the way that leads to the Almighty, to whom all praise is due.*" (Verse 6) The way leading to the Almighty is the system He has placed in the universe and chosen for mankind so that their lives may be in harmony with the universe they live in. It is the law that applies to absolutely everything that takes place in the universe.

The Qur'ān provides such guidance through the concept it gives believers of the universe: its values, relations, man's place and role in it, the cooperation of all its parts in the fulfilment of God's will and purpose and the harmony common to them. It also provides a sound basis for human thinking so as to make it consistent with the interaction between human nature and the universe. This enables man to understand the nature of the universe and its laws so as to use these in a positive way. The Qur'ān also lays down a system of education for humanity, empowering the individual to interact harmoniously with the rest of mankind, and empowering mankind to do the same with the rest of God's creation in the universe, comfortably benefiting by its nature. The legislation it lays down is consistent with man's circumstances as well as with the universal laws that apply to all creation. Thus, man does not become the odd one out among the countless communities of creatures in the universe. It is the Qur'ān that leads to that way: it is the guide provided by the Creator of man and the system that suits him. Consider the traveller who is guided on his journey by the engineer who built the road he is travelling on: how fortunate he would feel for having such expertise! How, then, about a guide provided by the One who originated the way and the person travelling on it?

The *sūrah* again mentions their reception to news of a Day of Judgement, expressing their total amazement at such a subject. They, in fact, suggest that to claim that resurrection takes place on a day when all humanity will be individually judged by God can only be attributed to a madman or someone who invents lies and attributes them to God. "*The unbelievers say: 'Shall we point out to you a man who will tell you that, when you have been utterly torn into pieces, you shall be restored to life in a new act of creation? Has he invented a lie about God, or is he a madman?' No! It is those who do not believe in the life to come who are suffering torment as they have gone far in error.*" (Verses 7–8)

Their amazement at the thought of resurrection is such that they invite people to join them in wondering at the condition of the person claiming it, using an especially derisive style: "*Shall we point out to you a man who will tell you that, when you have been utterly torn into pieces, you shall be restored to life in a new act of creation?*" (Verse 7) Do you want to see such a strange man uttering wild claims of a new creation after you have been long dead and your bodies have decomposed? Such derision then turns to defamation: "*Has he invented a lie about God, or is he a madman?*" According to them, such claims can only be made by a liar, by someone who fabricates ideas and claims that they are God's, or by a madman affected by the *jinn* to such an extent that he says what is incomprehensible.

What justifies their attitude? Is it simply because he says that they will be resurrected? Why is this so amazing when they have already gone through the process of being created? They do not even reflect on this amazing event, which they know to have taken place, i.e. their creation in the first instance. Had they reflected on this, they would not have marvelled at a second creation. They have already gone astray. Hence, the *sūrah* comments: "*No! It is those who do not believe in the life to come who are suffering torment as they have gone far in error.*" (Verse 8)

That they are in torment may refer to their punishment in the life to come. Since it will inevitably overtake them, then it is as if they are already in it, just like they have gone irremediably into error. But the statement may be understood in a different way, which suggests that those who do not believe in the life to come live in torment just as they live in error. This is a profound statement. A person who spends his life without belief in a second life suffers mental torment, as he lives without hope of justice, fair reward or compensation for what happens in his life. Indeed human life is full of situations and trials which man cannot face properly unless he looks up with hope for justice and reward for good action and punishment for those who do evil. There are things that one cannot do or bear without looking up to God, hoping to earn His pleasure in the life to come, when nothing large or small is overlooked. Whoever is deprived of this window of hope, which brings comfort and satisfaction, undoubtedly lives in torment as well as in error. Such a person suffers all this in the present life, before suffering punishment in the hereafter for his misdeeds which brought about his present life's suffering.

Belief in the hereafter brings the grace and blessings God grants to whoever of His servants deserves them through his desire to be guided to the truth and his diligent pursuit of it. My own feeling is that this second meaning is the one the present verse implies, as it describes those who do not believe in the hereafter as suffering torment and as being in deep error.

These people, who disbelieve in the life to come, are jerked from their slumber and presented with a fearful scene which could happen to them, if God so wills. Should they continue to go far into error, they will face terrible consequences: "*Do they not consider how much of the sky and the earth lies open before them and how much lies hidden from them? If We so*

139

willed, We could cause the earth to swallow them, or cause fragments of the sky to fall upon them. In all this, there is a sign for every servant of God turning to Him in repentance." (Verse 9) Here we have an image of terrible world events which they could see or perceive. Avalanches and landslides occur, and people see or hear of them, and fragments fall from the sky, such as meteors and thunderbolts. Again they have heard of such falls. The mention of such events here serves as a wake-up call to those who are heedless and those who discount the possibility of the arrival of the Last Hour. God's punishment is closer to them than all this. It only requires that God wills to inflict it upon them in this life, before the Last Hour. It could come to them in the form of the earth or the sky which surrounds them from all directions. Both are around them, unlike the Last Hour which belongs to God's own knowledge. Only the wrongdoers remain oblivious to what God may do.

What they see in the heavens and earth, and what may befall them at any time, should God wish it, present clear signs for anyone who reflects and turns to God with submission: *"there is a sign for every servant of God turning to Him in repentance."* (Verse 9)

2

Contrasting Attitudes

We graced David with Our favour. We said: "You mountains, sing with him God's praises! And likewise you birds!" We caused iron to become soft for him, (10)

ولَقَدْ ءَاتَيْنَا دَاوُدَ مِنَّا فَضْلاً يَٰجِبَالُ أَوِّبِى مَعَهُۥ وَالطَّيْرَ وَأَلَنَّا لَهُ الْحَدِيدَ ١٠

saying: "Make coats of mail and measure their links with care. Do good, all of you. I certainly see all that you do." (11)

أَنِ اعْمَلْ سَٰبِغَٰتٍ وَقَدِّرْ فِى السَّرْدِ وَاعْمَلُوا صَٰلِحًا إِنِّى بِمَا تَعْمَلُونَ بَصِيرٌ ١١

To Solomon [We made subservient] the wind: its morning course [covered the distance of] a month's journey, and its evening course a month's journey. We caused a fountain of molten brass to flow for him, and some of the *jinn* worked under his control by permission of his Lord. Whoever of them deviated from Our command We shall make him taste suffering through a blazing flame.(12)

وَلِسُلَيْمَٰنَ الرِّيحَ غُدُوُّهَا شَهْرٌ وَرَوَاحُهَا شَهْرٌ وَأَسَلْنَا لَهُۥ عَيْنَ الْقِطْرِ وَمِنَ الْجِنِّ مَن يَعْمَلُ بَيْنَ يَدَيْهِ بِإِذْنِ رَبِّهِۦ وَمَن يَزِغْ مِنْهُمْ عَنْ أَمْرِنَا نُذِقْهُ مِنْ عَذَابِ السَّعِيرِ ١٢

They made for him whatever he
pleased: shrines and statues, basins
as large as watering troughs, and
firmly anchored cauldrons. We
said: 'Work thankfully, family of
David, for few of My servants are
truly thankful.' (13)

يَعْمَلُونَ لَهُۥ مَا يَشَآءُ مِن مَّحَٰرِيبَ
وَتَمَٰثِيلَ وَجِفَانٍ كَٱلْجَوَابِ وَقُدُورٍ
رَّاسِيَٰتٍ ٱعْمَلُوٓا۟ءَالَ دَاوُۥدَ شُكْرًا
وَقَلِيلٌ مِّنْ عِبَادِىَ ٱلشَّكُورُ ۝

When We decreed his death,
nothing showed them that he was
dead except an earthworm that
gnawed away at his staff. And
when he fell to the ground, the
jinn saw clearly that, had they
understood the reality which was
beyond [their] perception, they
would not have remained in
humiliating servitude. (14)

فَلَمَّا قَضَيْنَا عَلَيْهِ ٱلْمَوْتَ مَا دَلَّهُمْ
عَلَىٰ مَوْتِهِۦٓ إِلَّا دَآبَّةُ ٱلْأَرْضِ تَأْكُلُ
مِنسَأَتَهُۥ فَلَمَّا خَرَّ تَبَيَّنَتِ ٱلْجِنُّ أَن
لَّوْ كَانُوا۟ يَعْلَمُونَ ٱلْغَيْبَ مَا لَبِثُوا۟
فِى ٱلْعَذَابِ ٱلْمُهِينِ ۝

There was a sign for the people of
Sheba in their dwelling place: two
gardens, one to the right and one
to the left: 'Eat of what your Lord
has provided for you, and give
thanks to Him: a land most goodly
and a Lord Much-Forgiving.' (15)

لَقَدْ كَانَ لِسَبَإٍ فِى مَسْكَنِهِمْ ءَايَةٌ
جَنَّتَانِ عَن يَمِينٍ وَشِمَالٍ كُلُوا۟ مِن
رِّزْقِ رَبِّكُمْ وَٱشْكُرُوا۟ لَهُۥ بَلْدَةٌ
طَيِّبَةٌ وَرَبٌّ غَفُورٌ ۝

But they paid no heed, and so We
let loose upon them a raging
torrent and replaced their two
gardens with others yielding bitter
fruit, tamarisks, and a few lote
trees. (16)

فَأَعْرَضُوا۟ فَأَرْسَلْنَا عَلَيْهِمْ سَيْلَ
ٱلْعَرِمِ وَبَدَّلْنَٰهُم بِجَنَّتَيْهِمْ جَنَّتَيْنِ
ذَوَاتَىْ أُكُلٍ خَمْطٍ وَأَثْلٍ وَشَىْءٍ
مِّن سِدْرٍ قَلِيلٍ ۝

Thus We requited them for their ingratitude: would We thus requite any but the totally ungrateful? (17)

ذَٰلِكَ جَزَيۡنَٰهُم بِمَا كَفَرُواْ وَهَلۡ نُجَٰزِىٓ إِلَّا ٱلۡكَفُورَ ۝

We had placed between them and the cities which We had blessed towns within sight of one another so that they could travel in measured stages: 'Travel through them by night and day in safety.' (18)

وَجَعَلۡنَا بَيۡنَهُمۡ وَبَيۡنَ ٱلۡقُرَى ٱلَّتِى بَٰرَكۡنَا فِيهَا قُرًى ظَٰهِرَةً وَقَدَّرۡنَا فِيهَا ٱلسَّيۡرَ سِيرُواْ فِيهَا لَيَالِىَ وَأَيَّامًا ءَامِنِينَ ۝

But they said: 'Our Lord! Make our journeys longer.' They sinned against their souls; so We caused them to become a tale, and scattered them throughout the land. Surely, there are signs in all this for anyone who is patient in adversity, deeply grateful. (19)

فَقَالُواْ رَبَّنَا بَٰعِدۡ بَيۡنَ أَسۡفَارِنَا وَظَلَمُوٓاْ أَنفُسَهُمۡ فَجَعَلۡنَٰهُمۡ أَحَادِيثَ وَمَزَّقۡنَٰهُمۡ كُلَّ مُمَزَّقٍ إِنَّ فِى ذَٰلِكَ لَءَايَٰتٍ لِّكُلِّ صَبَّارٍ شَكُورٍ ۝

Indeed *Iblīs* proved that his opinion of them was right: they all followed him, except for a group of believers. (20)

وَلَقَدۡ صَدَّقَ عَلَيۡهِمۡ إِبۡلِيسُ ظَنَّهُۥ فَٱتَّبَعُوهُ إِلَّا فَرِيقًا مِّنَ ٱلۡمُؤۡمِنِينَ ۝

Yet he had no power at all over them; it is only for the end that We might make a clear distinction between those who truly believe in the life to come and those who are in doubt about it. Your Lord watches over all things. (21)

وَمَا كَانَ لَهُۥ عَلَيۡهِم مِّن سُلۡطَٰنٍ إِلَّا لِنَعۡلَمَ مَن يُؤۡمِنُ بِٱلۡءَاخِرَةِ مِمَّنۡ هُوَ مِنۡهَا فِى شَكٍّ وَرَبُّكَ عَلَىٰ كُلِّ شَىۡءٍ حَفِيظٌ ۝

143

Overview

This passage contains contrasting images of gratitude and a lack of it, as well as making some powers and creatures subservient, by God's will, to certain people even though they are not normally subordinate to any human being. God's will and power are not limited to what is normal or familiar to humans. Through these images we learn certain things about the *jinn* whom some idolaters worshipped. Others tried to learn through them news from the world beyond perception, but they themselves know nothing about that realm. We also have additional information about how Satan can prevail over man, despite the fact that Satan has no power over man except in as much as man gives him this by his own choice. Other clear elements within the passage concern the means by which God reveals some secret human actions so that they appear before us in real terms. He will then give those responsible for them reward in the life to come. This passage concludes, like the first one, with a reference to the life to come.

Special Favours for David

"*We graced David with Our favour. We said: 'You mountains, sing with him God's praises! And likewise you birds!' We caused iron to become soft for him, saying: 'Make coats of mail and measure their links with care. Do good, all of you. I certainly see all that you do.'*" (Verses 10–11) David was the type of servant described at the end of the first part of the *sūrah*: "*In all this, there is a sign for every servant of God turning to Him in repentance.*" (Verse 9) The *sūrah* follows this reference by recounting some of his history, preambled by details of the grace God bestowed on him: "*You mountains, sing with him God's praises! And likewise you birds!*" (Verse 10) Reports suggest that David had an unusually beautiful voice, and he used to sing his Psalms, which are praises of God mentioned in the Old Testament, but God knows which of them were truly David's. An authentic *ḥadīth* tells us that the Prophet overheard Abū Mūsā al-Ash'arī reciting the Qur'ān deep at night. He stopped to listen to him, and then commented: 'This man has been given one of David's Psalms.'

The Qur'ānic description shows that David (peace be upon him) attained such a sublime standard of devotion and transparency in his praises that barriers between him and other creatures disappeared. Thus the truth between them became interrelated as they all praise God. Hence the mountains and the birds echoed his praises of God. When all of them had direct links with God, whatever separates species and creatures was removed. They felt that their bond with God overcame all barriers between them. Hence, they echoed one another in praising God, attaining an extraordinary level of transparency which can only be attained through God's grace.

When David raised his voice singing God's praises and glorifying Him, the mountains and the birds echoed him. The universe returned their songs as these were presented to God, the One. This is a remarkably splendid point in time which cannot be appreciated except by one who so experiences it, and even then only momentarily.

"*We caused iron to become soft for him.*" (Verse 10) This is another aspect of the grace God bestowed on David. Within the context wherein it occurs, this seems to be a miracle going beyond what is familiar to us. The *sūrah* is not speaking here of heating iron until it becomes soft and moulding it into the required shape. Rather, it appears that the iron was softened in a different way from what normally occurs, yet God knows best. Although guiding man to the softening of iron by heating is in itself an aspect of God's grace, our assumption here rests on the fact that the overall atmosphere is one of miracles and unfamiliar phenomena.

"*Make coats of mail and measure their links with care.*" (Verse 11) Reports suggest that prior to David's time, armour was plated, each coat being made up of one plate or sheet, which was very heavy for soldiers making them stiff and rigid. God instructed David in how to make armour from fine links which could be easily moulded so as to move in accordance with the body. David was also ordered to make these links narrow so that they could give complete protection against spears, preventing them from penetrating through. This is the reference in the verse to measuring the links with care. All this was taught to David through divine inspiration.

David and his household were told: "*Do good, all of you. I certainly see all that you do.*" (Verse 11) This does not apply to their making coats of mail. Instead it is clear that they must be on their guard in all that they do because God sees all and rewards everyone in accordance with what they deserve. Nothing escapes Him.

More Favours for Solomon

All this grace was given to David. Solomon was also given the ability to perform extraordinary feats, as a manifestation of God's grace: "*To Solomon [We made subservient] the wind: its morning course [covered the distance of] a month's journey, and its evening course a month's journey. We caused a fountain of molten brass to flow for him, and some of the jinn worked under his control by permission of his Lord. Whoever of them deviated from Our command We shall make him taste suffering through a blazing flame. They made for him whatever he pleased: shrines and statues, basins as large as watering troughs, and firmly anchored cauldrons. We said: 'Work thankfully, family of David, for few of My servants are truly thankful.'*" (Verses 12–13)

There are plenty of reports about the wind being subservient to Solomon, but many appear to have an Israelite origin even though the original Jewish texts do not mention anything about this. It is, therefore, much better to refrain from discussing these reports and to confine ourselves to the Qur'ānic text, going no further than its surface meaning. Thus we can say that God placed the wind at Solomon's command, making it travel forward to a specific place [which according to *Sūrah* 21, The Prophets, is the Holy Land] for a month, and then making its return journey over a period of a month. Certain objectives were achieved by these two journeys. These were known to Solomon and he accomplished them by God's command. We prefer not to say any more on this point so as not to indulge in unsubstantiated legends.

"*We caused a fountain of molten brass to flow for him.*" (Verse 12) The general context of these verses again suggests that this was also a miracle, like the softening of iron for David. This might have taken place in the form of a volcanic fountain pouring forth brass that had been molten underground. Likewise, God might have instructed Solomon on how to get brass to become fluid and mould it into different shapes. Regardless of how all this took place, it was nonetheless an act of God's abundant grace.

146

"*Some of the* jinn *worked under his control by permission of his Lord.*" (Verse 12) God also gave him *jinn* to work under His command. Linguistically speaking, the word *jinn* refers to anything that people cannot see. There is also a type of creature God gave the name *jinn* to and about whom we know nothing except what God states. He mentions here that He placed a group of them under Solomon's command. Whoever disobeys will be punished by God. "*Whoever of them deviated from Our command We shall make him taste suffering through a blazing flame.*" (Verse 12) That this comment occurs here, before completing the aspects of their subservience to Solomon, highlights the fact that the *jinn* are also subject to God, even though some idolaters worshipped them. Like mankind, the *jinn* are liable to God's punishment should they deviate from His orders.

They were placed under Solomon's command: "*They made for him whatever he pleased: shrines and statues, basins as large as watering troughs, and firmly anchored cauldrons.*" (Verse 13) All these articles are examples of what the *jinn* used to make, by God's leave, whenever Solomon bid them. Again all these are miraculous things, and we cannot imagine them to be anything but. This is the only interpretation we can give to this statement.

The verse concludes with an address to David's household: "*We said: 'Work thankfully, family of David.'*" (Verse 13) All this was given you by God's grace, through David and Solomon. You must not take false pride in it, but instead give proper thanks. Good action is an important form of thanksgiving.

However, "*few of My servants are truly thankful.*" (Verse 13) This comment also serves as a directive. It tells us on the one hand that the grace and favours God bestows on His servants are so great that few of them are able to express due thanks for them, and on the other that people often neglect their thanksgiving duty. In fact, however much people try to express their gratitude, they cannot give due thanks for what God bestows on them. What is their status, then, if they slacken and overlook this duty?

Yet the question is: how can a human being, with limited ability, be sufficiently grateful for God's unlimited favours? God tells us in the Qur'ān: "*Should you try to count God's blessings, you will never be able to compute them.*" (14: 34) These blessings are constantly around man no matter where he looks. They are both within him and within his surroundings. Indeed, he himself is one major blessing in this world. For example, at one time we were a group of people chatting about a wide variety of subjects when our little cat came over and started walking around us as if looking for something. It was clear that the cat needed something in particular, but it could not tell us what it was, and we could not understand his purpose. Then it occurred to us that he might be looking for water, and we were right. When we put the water before him we realized that he was very thirsty but could not express himself. We realized then just how much God has favoured us with the gift of communication. We expressed our gratitude to God for this blessing, but what thanks, heartfelt as they may be, can be enough for such a blessing!

On a prolonged occasion we were deprived of sunshine. At times, however, a ray of sunlight as small as a little coin would creep in, and we would take turns to stand in it, moving ourselves so as to let it fall on our faces, hands, chests, backs, abdomens and legs. I cannot forget the time when all this was over and we were allowed out: one of us was beaming with delight as he said: 'Oh God! How lovely to see the sun again! It still rises every day! All praise to God for this blessing!"[1]

How much of this light, which is necessary for life, do we waste every day as we enjoy the sun and its warmth? Indeed we always bathe in this blessing granted to us freely by God. We neither pay for it, nor do we exert any effort to come by it.

When we reflect on God's blessings in this way, we can spend all our lives and energy covering but a little. Therefore, we only make this brief reference, following the Qur'ānic method of giving a hint or a pointer. It is up to everyone to reflect on it and try to express gratitude to God as they can. Indeed to be thankful to God is itself a blessing enjoyed by those who are sincere in their devotion.

Let us move now to the last scene in the story which shows Solomon's death while the *Jinn* continue to work hard as he had bid them, unaware

---

1. It is clear that both these situations refer to the author's time in prison. Some of us may wonder that cats are in prison, but accounts by different prisoners confirm that stray cats frequently came to them and they found them a source of solace. – Editor's note.

of the fact of his death, until a worm had gnawed at his staff sufficiently for him to fall down: "*When We decreed his death, nothing showed them that he was dead except an earthworm that gnawed away at his staff. And when he fell to the ground, the* jinn *saw clearly that, had they understood the reality which was beyond [their] perception, they would not have remained in humiliating servitude.*" (Verse 14)

It is reported that in the position he was in at the moment of his death, he was leaning over his stick and that he remained in that position while the *jinn* continued performing the task he assigned them. Then a worm that eats wood came upon his stick. This type of worm gnaws persistently at wood ruining roofs, doors and buildings foundations. In parts of Upper Egypt, some villages do not use a single piece of wood in their homes for fear of woodworm. When the woodworm had gnawed at Solomon's staff, it could no longer support him, and he fell down. Only then did the *jinn* realize that he was dead: "*the* jinn *saw clearly that, had they understood the reality which was beyond [their] perception, they would not have remained in humiliating servitude.*" (Verse 14)

Such, then, are the *jinn* whom some people worship. We see them here subservient to one of God's servants. They are totally unable to fathom something which is hidden from them, yet is very close: how then can they gratify people's appeals to learn the secrets of what is beyond the reach of perception!

No Gratitude for God's Favours

David and his family were full of gratitude to God for all His blessings and used such favours for good purpose. The people of Sheba, however, are to be contrasted with such role models. In *Sūrah* 27, The Ants, we have a report of what took place between their queen and Solomon. Here, the story gives an account of what happened to them after Solomon, which suggests that the events included here date back to a period after the queen's exchanges with Solomon. What makes this more likely is that the story here speaks of Sheba's people becoming ungrateful for God's blessings, which were then withdrawn and the people scattered. Under the queen mentioned in *Sūrah* 27, they enjoyed a plentiful period and were very powerful. The first report received by Solomon about them was from a hoopoe who told him: "*I found there a woman ruling over them; and she has been given of all good things, and hers is a magnificent throne. I found her and her people prostrating themselves to the sun instead of God; and Satan has made their deeds seem goodly to them, thus turning them away from the path [of God], so that they cannot find the right way.*" (27: 23–24)

This was subsequently followed by the queen's submission to God, as she embraced the divine faith. The story here, then, is certainly of a subsequent period. It tells of what happened to them after they turned away from God and refused to thank Him for His favours.

The story opens with a description of the great blessings they enjoyed and the provisions they were granted, as well as the requirement that they should demonstrate their gratitude as they could: "*There was a sign for the people of Sheba in their dwelling place: two gardens, one to the right and one to the left: 'Eat of what your Lord has provided for you, and give thanks to Him: a land most goodly and a Lord Much-Forgiving.'*" (Verse 15)

Sheba is the name of a community living in southern Yemen, in a fertile land some of which remains so today. They were highly civilized and were able to make good use of their water resources, as they were blessed with much rainfall, occupying territory close to the sea in the south and east. They were thus able to build a natural dam between two mountains, erecting a great wall down the valley, with controlled openings. In this way they were able to retain water in great quantities which they used as they needed. This great dam was known as the Ma'rib Dam.

The gardens to the right and left symbolize the splendid fertility of their land which gave them beauty and affluence. Therefore, they were signs reminding them of God who gives every good thing. They were commanded to make full use of what was granted to them and to thank the Giver: "*Eat of what your Lord has provided for you, and give thanks to Him.*" (Verse 15) They were also reminded of the nature of their blessings: the productive land and the forgiveness of their sins: "*a land most goodly and a Lord Much-Forgiving.*" (Verse 15) When such priceless blessings are given in plenty, why were they unwilling to give thanks? "*But they paid no heed, and so We let loose upon them a raging torrent and replaced their two gardens with others yielding bitter fruit, tamarisks, and a few lote trees."* (Verse 16)

When they failed to show their gratitude to God and use what God favoured them with in a goodly and beneficial way, He took away their source of affluence and let loose raging, stone-carrying torrents which destroyed their dam and its water flooded the whole area. With the dam no longer functioning, the land dried up. Instead of beautiful gardens they now had only a desert in which only a few wild trees were to grow, bearing no good fruit. The verse says that their gardens were *"replaced ...with others yielding bitter fruit, tamarisks, and a few lote trees."* (Verse 16) This was the best that their land could subsequently produce and even then it was only in small quantities.

"Thus We requited them for their ingratitude: would We thus requite any but the totally ungrateful." (Verse 17) Until then they had remained in their villages and homes. God stinted their provisions and replaced their riches with austerity, but He had not yet scattered them over a wider area. They had easy contacts with the cities blessed by God: Makkah and Jerusalem. To the north of Sheba, Yemen was well inhabited and its land routes to other areas were safe and comfortable: *"We had placed between them and the cities which We had blessed towns within sight of one another so that they could travel in measured stages: 'Travel through them by night and day in safety.'"* (Verse 18) It is reported that a traveller would leave one township in the morning and arrive at the next before dark. This meant that journey times were short, making travel easy, safe and comfortable.

Yet Sheba's people paid no heed to the first warning. Nor did the change in their circumstances make them turn to God and appeal to Him to give back their comfortable lives. On the contrary, their prayer betrayed stupidity and ignorance: *"But they said: 'Our Lord! Make our journeys longer."* They wanted long distance travel, which is undertaken only infrequently. In so doing, they demonstrated nothing but arrogance: *"They sinned against their souls."* Their prayer was answered, but only as such a prayer should be answered: *"So We caused them to become a tale, and scattered them throughout the land."* (Verse 19) They became like refugees scattered throughout Arabia. They also became the subject of discussions in others' gatherings. In other words, they were no longer a recognized community, but a tale people told. "*Surely, there are signs in all this for anyone who is patient in adversity, deeply grateful.*" (Verse 19) We note that patience and steadfastness are mentioned alongside thanksgiving in times of plenty. The history of Sheba gives signs on both counts.

This is one way of understanding the last two verses. However, they may also be understood in a different way, which would then render the first statement as: "*We had placed between them and the cities which We had blessed towns that have dominance.*" As these places had power and dominance, the people of Sheba became poor, living like desert dwellers, and having to travel time after time to find pasture and water. They could not withstand the test that this entailed. Therefore, they prayed to God, and in this case their supplication would be rendered as: '*Our Lord! Lengthen the time between our journeys,*' or make them less frequent, as travel has become too tiring for us. They did not couple this prayer with turning to God with repentance and seeking His forgiveness, so that He would grant them what they prayed for. Since they behaved arrogantly when they had God's blessings, and did not persevere when they faced adversity, God punished them by scattering them and so they disappeared, featuring only in people's tales. This makes the comment at the end of these verses fitting for their lack of gratitude for God's favour and lack of patience in adversity: "*Surely, there are signs in all this for anyone who is patient in adversity, deeply grateful.*" (Verse 19) I feel this understanding of the verses to be also acceptable. God, however, knows His own purpose best.

As the story concludes, the *sūrah* mentions the overall divine planning and the rules God operates in life generally. It tells us what lessons we should draw from this and what lies behind it: "*Indeed* Iblīs *proved that his opinion of them was right: they all followed him, except for a group of believers. Yet he had no power at all over them; it is only for the end that We might make a clear distinction between those who truly believe in the life to come and those who are in doubt about it. Your Lord watches over all things.*" (Verses 20–21)

The people of Sheba went the way that leads to a miserable end: *Iblīs* felt that he could lead them astray, and they let him do so. Thus, except for a group of believers, they all followed him. This is what normally happens in all communities. It is rare that a community is totally bereft of believers who will not give in to Satan and his machinations. They thus prove that the truth remains, even in the worst of conditions, available to everyone who seeks it and wants to hold to it. *Iblīs* never had an overpowering authority over them from which they could not be free. He can only approach them in order that they be tested, and everyone who wishes to stick to the truth could do so, while everyone else will go astray. Thus, in life, a type of person emerges who '*truly believe in the life to come*', and thus his beliefs keep him on the right path. This type are distinct from the other '*who are in doubt*' about the life to come. It is the latter who succumb to *Iblīs*'s temptations, heedless of the Day of Judgement. God certainly knows what happens before it actually takes place. However, He makes His reward dependent upon the thing actually taking place.

When we look at the story of Sheba's people from a broader angle, we see that its moral can apply to all communities at all times. The story can then be seen as demonstrating what happens when communities follow divine guidance or stray away from it. It also shows the reasons that make people take the direction they do. "*Your Lord watches over all things.*" (Verse 21) Nothing is lost or overlooked.

Thus the second passage of the *sūrah* concludes, speaking of the life to come, just as did the first passage. It also emphasizes the limitless nature of God's knowledge and His awareness of all things. Both subjects are given much emphasis in this *sūrah*.

3

Distinct Ways, Different Ends

Say: 'Call upon those whom you imagine to be partners with God. They do not have even an atom's weight of authority either in the heavens or the earth, nor have they any share in either, nor does He have any helper from among them. (22)

قُلِ ٱدْعُوا۟ ٱلَّذِينَ زَعَمْتُم مِّن دُونِ ٱللَّهِ لَا يَمْلِكُونَ مِثْقَالَ ذَرَّةٍ فِي ٱلسَّمَٰوَٰتِ وَلَا فِي ٱلْأَرْضِ وَمَا لَهُمْ فِيهِمَا مِن شِرْكٍ وَمَا لَهُۥ مِنْهُم مِّن ظَهِيرٍ ۝

Before Him, intercession is of no avail, except by one to whom He may have granted permission. When the terror is lifted from their hearts, they will ask [one another]: 'What has your Lord ordained?' They will answer: 'The truth. He is the Most High, the Supreme.' (23)

وَلَا تَنفَعُ ٱلشَّفَٰعَةُ عِندَهُۥ إِلَّا لِمَنْ أَذِنَ لَهُۥ حَتَّىٰ إِذَا فُزِّعَ عَن قُلُوبِهِمْ قَالُوا۟ مَاذَا قَالَ رَبُّكُمْ قَالُوا۟ ٱلْحَقَّ وَهُوَ ٱلْعَلِيُّ ٱلْكَبِيرُ ۝

Say: 'Who is it that gives you sustenance out of the heavens and the earth?' Say: 'It is God; and either we or you are on the right path or have clearly gone astray!' (24)

قُلْ مَن يَرْزُقُكُم مِّنَ ٱلسَّمَٰوَٰتِ وَٱلْأَرْضِ قُلِ ٱللَّهُ وَإِنَّا أَوْ إِيَّاكُمْ لَعَلَىٰ هُدًى أَوْ فِي ضَلَٰلٍ مُّبِينٍ ۝

Say: 'Neither shall you be called to account for whatever we have become guilty of, nor shall we be called to account for whatever you are doing.' (25)

قُل لَّا تُسْـَٔلُونَ عَمَّآ أَجْرَمْنَا وَلَا نُسْـَٔلُ عَمَّا تَعْمَلُونَ ﴿٢٥﴾

Say: 'Our Lord will bring us all together, and then He will lay open the truth between us, in justice. He alone is the One who opens all truth, the All-Knowing.' (26)

قُلْ يَجْمَعُ بَيْنَنَا رَبُّنَا ثُمَّ يَفْتَحُ بَيْنَنَا بِٱلْحَقِّ وَهُوَ ٱلْفَتَّاحُ ٱلْعَلِيمُ ﴿٢٦﴾

Say: 'Show me those whom you allege to be partners with Him. Nay! He alone is God, the Almighty, the Wise.' (27)

قُلْ أَرُونِيَ ٱلَّذِينَ أَلْحَقْتُم بِهِۦ شُرَكَآءَ كَلَّا بَلْ هُوَ ٱللَّهُ ٱلْعَزِيزُ ٱلْحَكِيمُ ﴿٢٧﴾

Overview

This short passage tackles the issue of God's oneness in contrast to attributing partners to Him. Yet it takes us on a round of the universe, with both its apparent realm and that which is hidden from us, its present and past, heavens and earth, this life and the life to come. Our hearts shudder with awe at the mere mention of some of these majestic aspects. The passage also refers to man's sustenance, actions and reward. It looks at how people are grouped together and then separated into two distinct parties. All this is delivered in a quick rhythm with strong accompanying beats. The word, 'say,' is repeatedly used for added emphasis. After each such usage, a new proof is given which is both irrefutable and overpowering.

The Truth Will Out

"Say: 'Call upon those whom you imagine to be partners with God. They do not have even an atom's weight of authority either in the heavens or the

earth, nor have they any share in either, nor does He have any helper from among them." (Verse 22) The verse begins with a challenge that applies to the entire universe, without exception: "Say: 'Call upon those whom you imagine to be partners with God.'" Call on them to come and stand before all the world. Let them then say, or you can say yourselves, if they own anything in the heavens or on earth, large or small. "They do not have even an atom's weight of authority either in the heavens or the earth." (Verse 22) They cannot even claim to own anything in the heavens or the earth. An owner of something has full authority over it: he can do or dispense with it as he likes. What, then, do those alleged deities own in this vast universe?

They do not own an atom's weight either as their own private property or as something in which they have a share: "nor have they any share in either." (Verse 22) Moreover, God does not seek their help in anything. He is in no need of help: "nor does He have any helper from among them." (Verse 22)

The verse appears to refer to a particular type of alleged partner with God. These are the angels whom the Arabs claimed to be God's daughters, alleging that they could intercede with God on people's behalf. Perhaps they were among those partners about whom the Arabs said: "We worship them for no reason other than that they would bring us nearer to God." (39: 3) Therefore, in the next verse the *surah* denies that they have any means of intercession while drawing a scene that fills hearts with fear: "Before Him, intercession is of no avail, except by one to whom He may have granted permission." (Verse 23) Intercession, then, is dependent on God's permission. Needless to say, God will not permit intercession on behalf of people who do not believe in Him and deserve His grace. Those who associate partners with Him do not deserve that He grant permission to angels or anyone else to intercede on their behalf.

The *surah* then describes the fearful scene when intercession is needed: "When the terror is lifted from their hearts, they will ask [one another]: 'What has your Lord ordained?' They will answer: 'The truth. He is the Most High, the Supreme.'" (Verse 23) The day is exceedingly hard: people stand awaiting developments, and those who can intercede and the ones who hope for intercession in their favour wait for a signal from the Almighty permitting such intercession. The wait continues, faces look down, sounds die out and hearts go quiet as all await a signal from the Lord, full of majesty and glory.

The word of permission is then given and all prospective intercessors and the ones they are interceding for are overwhelmed with awe. They are unable to comprehend. Then, *"when the terror is lifted from their hearts,'* and they recover their senses and faculties, they begin to ask one another: *"What has your Lord ordained?"* They wonder whether they have understood what God said. The answer is given in one word: *'The truth.'* It may be that the angels of the highest order are the ones who give this perfect answer. Your Lord has stated the truth, complete and perfect; the truth that comes from Him who is truth absolute. For whatever God says is absolutely true. *"He is the Most High, the Supreme."* (Verse 23) It is a most fitting description.

This short answer, in one word, imparts the awesomeness of the situation when intercession is permitted. It describes how the angels stand before their Lord. Can anyone who looks at it pretend to be a partner with God, interceding in favour of those who attribute partners to Him?

Either One or the Other

That was the first note of this splendid and awe-inspiring scene. The second note refers to the provisions granted to them. Although they are oblivious to the source that gives them their provisions, the fact that they have them proves His oneness and that no one else has any control over what He decides to give or deny. *"Say: 'Who is it that gives you sustenance out of the heavens and the earth?' Say: 'It is God; and either we or you are on the right path or have clearly gone astray!'"* (Verse 24) Providing sustenance is something people know about as it happens in their lives. It comes from heaven in the form of rain, heat and light, which were known to the people addressed first by the Qur'ān, but also in other forms and shapes which man discovers at one time or another. Other sustenance comes from the earth in the form of plants, animals, water, oils, metals and treasure. Much of these were known to the people of olden days and much is discovered as time passes on.

The question is: *"Who is it that gives you sustenance out of the heavens and the earth?"* The answer is not awaited. In fact, the Prophet is told to say: "*It is God.*" They cannot argue about this or make any contrary claim. What the Prophet is also instructed to do is to leave matters entirely to God concerning the fates of both parties. One party is inevitably right and the other wrong; one is guided aright and the other is in error. The two cannot be together either on the track of proper guidance or of going astray: "*Either we or you are on the right path or have clearly gone astray!*" (Verse 24)

This is the ultimate in fairness and politeness when arguing one's case. For God's Messenger to say to the idolaters that either party could be following right guidance leaves the question open as to who is on which side: this, thus, calls for cool reflection and reasonable deliberation. There is no room for futile argument or an illogical hardening of attitude. The Prophet is given instructions to say this to them as his role is that of a guide and a teacher hoping that they will see the truth of the guidance he brings them. He is not out to score a point or win an argument.

Arguments made in such a polite and inspiring manner are more likely to have a positive effect on those whose position in society prompts them to take a hard line to the message of truth. They may even show a willingness to consider and reflect at ease. It is exactly the approach that should be adopted by advocates of Islam everywhere.

The third note puts everyone before their actions and responsibilities, but again using the most polite and fair approach: "*Say: Neither shall you be called to account for whatever we have become guilty of, nor shall we be called to account for whatever you are doing.*" (Verse 25)

This might have been in answer to the repeated accusations of the idolaters branding the Prophet and his Companions as guilty and in the wrong. They had in this respect berated them for renouncing their forefathers' religion. This happens all the time, when the followers of falsehood accuse the followers of truth of being in error. Hence, the Prophet is instructed to tell them in exemplary politeness that everyone is responsible for his or her own deeds: "*Say: Neither shall you be called to account for whatever we have become guilty of, nor shall we be called to account for whatever you are doing.*" (Verse 25) Everyone must reflect and determine whether their attitude will lead them to success or bring about their ruin. This is the first step towards recognizing the truth before attaining conviction.

The fourth note is given in the verse that says: "*Say: Our Lord will bring us all together, and then He will lay open the truth between us, in justice. He alone is the One who opens all truth, the All-Knowing.*" (26) At first, God gathers both the followers of truth and those who follow falsehood together, so that both truth and falsehood meet face to face. Then, the advocates of truth will call on others to join them. At this stage, issues become confused, and a battle ensues between truth and falsehood. Doubts may blur evidence, and falsehood may appear to gain the upper hand, but all this will be for a limited duration. Then, God will judge between the two parties in fairness and state the truth clearly, without any ambiguity or confusion. "*He alone is the One who opens all truth, the All-Knowing.*" (Verse 26)

This gives reassurance since God is certain to make His judgement clear, laying the truth open before all. He does not allow matters to remain confused except for a limited period. He does not put the advocates of truth together with those who follow falsehood except to give the former a chance to carry on with their advocacy, exerting their best efforts. Then God will issue His verdict on both sides. It is He who knows best when the appropriate time for judgement comes. No one else should decide its timing, or hasten it. It is all left to Him.

The final note in this passage sounds similar to the first one, throwing out a challenge to those who associated partners with him: "*Say: Show me those whom you allege to be partners with Him. Nay! He alone is God, the Almighty, the Wise.*" (Verse 27) The very request is sarcastic: demanding that they reveal the subject of their claims: who are they; what is their status, position and role; how did they merit such a position? All these questions betray an element of derision. This is followed by strong censure: "*Nay!*" They are not, and cannot be, God's partners. "*He alone is God, the Almighty, the Wise.*" (Verse 27) The One who has such attributes has no partners of any sort.

4

Futile Argument

We have sent you to all mankind so that you bring them good news and give them warning; but most people do not understand. (28)

وَمَآ أَرْسَلْنَاكَ إِلَّا كَآفَّةً لِّلنَّاسِ بَشِيرًا وَنَذِيرًا وَلَـٰكِنَّ أَكْثَرَ ٱلنَّاسِ لَا يَعْلَمُونَ ۝

They ask: 'When is this promise to be fulfilled, if what you say be true?' (29)

وَيَقُولُونَ مَتَىٰ هَـٰذَا ٱلْوَعْدُ إِن كُنتُمْ صَـٰدِقِينَ ۝

Say: 'There has been appointed for you a day which you can neither delay nor advance by a single moment.' (30)

قُل لَّكُم مِّيعَادُ يَوْمٍ لَّا تَسْتَـٔخِرُونَ عَنْهُ سَاعَةً وَلَا تَسْتَقْدِمُونَ ۝

The unbelievers say: 'We will never believe in this Qur'ān, nor in any earlier revelations.' If only you could see how the wrongdoers shall be made to stand before their Lord, hurling reproaches at one another. Those of them who were weak on earth will say to those who had deemed themselves mighty: 'Had it not been for you, we would certainly have been believers.' (31)

وَقَالَ ٱلَّذِينَ كَفَرُوا لَن نُّؤْمِنَ بِهَـٰذَا ٱلْقُرْءَانِ وَلَا بِٱلَّذِي بَيْنَ يَدَيْهِ وَلَوْ تَرَىٰ إِذِ ٱلظَّـٰلِمُونَ مَوْقُوفُونَ عِندَ رَبِّهِمْ يَرْجِعُ بَعْضُهُمْ إِلَىٰ بَعْضٍ ٱلْقَوْلَ يَقُولُ ٱلَّذِينَ ٱسْتُضْعِفُوا لِلَّذِينَ ٱسْتَكْبَرُوا لَوْلَآ أَنتُمْ لَكُنَّا مُؤْمِنِينَ ۝

The ones who deemed themselves mighty will say to those who were weak: 'Was it we who prevented you from following right guidance after it had been given you? Certainly not! It was you who were guilty.' (32)

قَالَ ٱلَّذِينَ ٱسْتَكْبَرُواْ لِلَّذِينَ ٱسْتُضْعِفُوٓاْ أَنَحْنُ صَدَدْنَـٰكُمْ عَنِ ٱلْهُدَىٰ بَعْدَ إِذْ جَآءَكُم بَلْ كُنتُم مُّجْرِمِينَ ۝

Those who were weak will reply to those who deemed themselves mighty: 'Not so! It was your scheming, night and day, ordering us to disbelieve in God and to set up equals to Him.' When they see the punishment awaiting them, they will all harbour utter and unmitigated remorse. We shall put chains round the necks of the unbelievers. Are they to be requited for anything other than what they did? (33)

وَقَالَ ٱلَّذِينَ ٱسْتُضْعِفُواْ لِلَّذِينَ ٱسْتَكْبَرُواْ بَلْ مَكْرُ ٱلَّيْلِ وَٱلنَّهَارِ إِذْ تَأْمُرُونَنَآ أَن نَّكْفُرَ بِٱللَّهِ وَنَجْعَلَ لَهُۥٓ أَندَادًا وَأَسَرُّواْ ٱلنَّدَامَةَ لَمَّا رَأَوُاْ ٱلْعَذَابَ وَجَعَلْنَا ٱلْأَغْلَـٰلَ فِىٓ أَعْنَاقِ ٱلَّذِينَ كَفَرُواْ هَلْ يُجْزَوْنَ إِلَّا مَا كَانُواْ يَعْمَلُونَ ۝

Whenever We sent a warner to any community, those of them who lived in luxury said: 'We do not believe in the message with which you have been sent.' (34)

وَمَآ أَرْسَلْنَا فِى قَرْيَةٍ مِّن نَّذِيرٍ إِلَّا قَالَ مُتْرَفُوهَآ إِنَّا بِمَآ أُرْسِلْتُم بِهِۦ كَـٰفِرُونَ ۝

They also say: 'Richer than you are we in wealth, and we have more children. We certainly are not going to be made to suffer.' (35)

وَقَالُواْ نَحْنُ أَكْثَرُ أَمْوَٰلًا وَأَوْلَـٰدًا وَمَا نَحْنُ بِمُعَذَّبِينَ ۝

Say: 'My Lord gives in abundance, or gives in scant measure, to whomever He wills; but most people do not understand.' (36)

قُلْ إِنَّ رَبِّي يَبْسُطُ الرِّزْقَ لِمَن يَشَآءُ وَيَقْدِرُ وَلَٰكِنَّ أَكْثَرَ ٱلنَّاسِ لَا يَعْلَمُونَ ﴿٣٦﴾

It is neither your riches nor your children that can bring you nearer to Us: only he who believes and does what is right [comes near to Us]. To these multiple reward will be given for all that they have done. They will dwell in safety in the mansions of paradise; (37)

وَمَآ أَمْوَٰلُكُمْ وَلَآ أَوْلَٰدُكُم بِٱلَّتِي تُقَرِّبُكُمْ عِندَنَا زُلْفَىٰٓ إِلَّا مَنْ ءَامَنَ وَعَمِلَ صَٰلِحًا فَأُوْلَٰٓئِكَ لَهُمْ جَزَآءُ ٱلضِّعْفِ بِمَا عَمِلُوا۟ وَهُمْ فِى ٱلْغُرُفَٰتِ ءَامِنُونَ ﴿٣٧﴾

whereas all who strive against Our revelations, seeking to defeat their purpose, shall be given over to suffering. (38)

وَٱلَّذِينَ يَسْعَوْنَ فِىٓ ءَايَٰتِنَا مُعَٰجِزِينَ أُوْلَٰٓئِكَ فِى ٱلْعَذَابِ مُحْضَرُونَ ﴿٣٨﴾

Say: 'My Lord gives in abundance, or gives in scant measure, to whomever He wills of His servants; whatever you give for His sake He will replace it for you, for He is the best of providers.' (39)

قُلْ إِنَّ رَبِّي يَبْسُطُ ٱلرِّزْقَ لِمَن يَشَآءُ مِنْ عِبَادِهِۦ وَيَقْدِرُ لَهُۥ وَمَآ أَنفَقْتُم مِّن شَىْءٍ فَهُوَ يُخْلِفُهُۥ وَهُوَ خَيْرُ ٱلرَّٰزِقِينَ ﴿٣٩﴾

On the day He gathers them all together, He will say to the angels: 'Was it you that these people worshipped?' (40)

وَيَوْمَ يَحْشُرُهُمْ جَمِيعًا ثُمَّ يَقُولُ لِلْمَلَٰٓئِكَةِ أَهَٰٓؤُلَآءِ إِيَّاكُمْ كَانُوا۟ يَعْبُدُونَ ﴿٤٠﴾

They will answer: 'Limitless are You in Your glory! You alone are our patron, not they. In fact they worshipped the *jinn* and most of them believed in them.' (41)

قَالُواْ سُبْحَٰنَكَ أَنتَ وَلِيُّنَا مِن دُونِهِم بَلْ كَانُواْ يَعْبُدُونَ ٱلْجِنَّ أَكْثَرُهُم بِهِم مُّؤْمِنُونَ ﴿٤١﴾

Today none of you has any power to benefit or harm another. We will say to the wrongdoers: 'Taste now the suffering through fire which you persistently denied.' (42)

فَٱلْيَوْمَ لَا يَمْلِكُ بَعْضُكُمْ لِبَعْضٍ نَّفْعًا وَلَا ضَرًّا وَنَقُولُ لِلَّذِينَ ظَلَمُوٓاْ ذُوقُواْ عَذَابَ ٱلنَّارِ ٱلَّتِي كُنتُم بِهَا تُكَذِّبُونَ ﴿٤٢﴾

Overview

This passage tackles the unbelievers' attitude of the Prophet Muḥammad's message. Indeed their attitude echoes that of the affluent to every divine message. Such people are normally deluded by their riches and their offspring, and the fact that they command much of what this life can offer, thinking that this indicates they are favoured by God, and that such favours will ensure they do not suffer punishment in the hereafter. Therefore, the *sūrah* shows them their situation in the life to come, as though it is happening now before their very eyes. This so that they will know whether anything of what they have can benefit or protect them on the Day of Judgement. These scenes show clearly that neither the angels nor the *jinn* they worshipped in this life, and from whom they sought help, can give them anything whatsoever in the life to come. As the argument progresses the *sūrah* explains what carries real weight in God's measure. Thus the false values they have in this world are seen for what they are. It becomes clear that granting wealth in abundance or otherwise in this present life depends on God's will. It should not be taken as evidence of anyone's position with Him. It is all a means of testing people.

The Prophet's Responsibility

We have sent you to all mankind so that you bring them good news and give them warning; but most people do not understand. They ask: 'When is this promise to be fulfilled, if what you say be true?' Say: 'There has been appointed for you a day which you can neither delay nor advance by a single moment.' (Verses 28–30)

This clarifies what was stated in the previous passage about each individual's accountability to God, and that the role of the advocates of truth does not go beyond delivering God's message and presenting it clearly before the rest of mankind. The current passage starts with explaining the mission assigned to the Prophet. It is clear that they are unaware of its nature. Hence they try to hasten what he promises or threatens them with. It makes clear that this comes at the time God has determined for it, which is unknown to anyone other than Him: "*We have sent you to all mankind so that you bring them good news and give them warning.*" (Verse 28) Such is the remit of the message addressed to all mankind: to bring good news and to give warning. When this is done, the messenger's role has ended. As for the fulfilment of promise and warning, this is all left to God to determine: "*but most people do not understand.*" (Verse 28)

"*They ask: When is this promise to be fulfilled, if what you say be true?*" (Verse 29) The very question implies that they do not understand the messenger's role or the limits of the message. The Qur'ān wants the question of God's oneness to be absolutely clear: Muḥammad is His Messenger with a clearly defined remit. He fulfils his task but does not go beyond this. All authority belongs to God: it is He who has given him the message to deliver, clearly defining his role. It is not part of his role to decide, or even to know, when the promise and the warning are to be fulfilled. This all belongs to God. The Prophet knows his limits. Therefore, he does not even question anything God has not chosen to inform him of, or has not assigned to him. Here, God instructs him to give them this particular reply: "*Say: There has been appointed for you a day which you can neither delay nor advance by a single moment.*" (Verse 30)

Everything occurs at its particular time which God has determined. It is neither hastened nor delayed for anyone. Nothing occurs by coincidence. On the contrary, everything is created according to a particular plan, in which things are interrelated. God's will determines events and timings according to His own wisdom, of which we only understand what God chooses to impart to us. When people try to hasten His promise or warning, they betray their ignorance of this fundamental fact. Hence, since most people do not understand, this leads them to questioning and hastening things.

Stubborn to the Hilt

The next verse speaks about a determined attitude to reject all divine guidance: "*The unbelievers say: We will never believe in this Qur'ān, nor in any earlier revelations.*" (Verse 31) They make it clear that they will never believe, neither in the Qur'ān nor in any divine book that preceded the Qur'ān, which in fact confirms its truth. They are not prepared to believe in any of this at any time in the future either. They are determined to disbelieve, deliberately refusing even to consider anything that points to faith. It is all, then, a well considered stance. Therefore, the *sūrah* puts before their eyes what happens to them on the Day of Judgement as a result of their stubborn rejection:

If only you could see how the wrongdoers shall be made to stand before their Lord, hurling reproaches at one another. Those of them who were weak on earth will say to those who had deemed themselves mighty: 'Had it not been for you, we would certainly have been believers.' The ones who deemed themselves mighty will say to those who were weak: 'Was it we who prevented you from following right guidance after it had been given you? Certainly not! It was you who were guilty.' Those who were weak will reply to those who deemed themselves mighty: 'Not so! It was your scheming, night and day, ordering us to disbelieve in God and to set up equals to Him.' When they see the punishment awaiting them, they will all harbour utter and unmitigated remorse. We shall put chains round the necks of the unbelievers. Are they to be requited for anything other than what they did? (Verses 31–33)

Their assertion that they will never believe in any revealed book is made in this life. So, what will they say in a totally different situation? If only we could see these wrongdoers when they are 'made to stand', i.e. forced into it against their will or better judgement. They are guilty, made to stand and await a decision by their Lord, in whose words and scriptures they profess they will never believe. Yet now they stand before Him. If you could watch them, you would see how they reproach one another, exchanging accusations and trying to blame each other. So, what is it that they say?

"*Those of them who were weak on earth will say to those who had deemed themselves mighty: 'Had it not been for you, we would certainly have been believers.*" (Verse 31) They blame their leaders, accusing them of being responsible for this humiliation and what will come next of great suffering. They state this now but were totally unable to confront them in this way during their life on earth, prevented as they were by their weakness and submission. They had sold out the freedom and dignity God had granted them, as well as the reasoning He had blessed them with. Now that all false values have been discarded, and they are put face to face with a long-lasting suffering, they can express themselves without fear: "*Had it not been for you, we would certainly have been believers.*" (Verse 31)

Those who used to think much of their power base are fed up with those whom they treated with humiliation. Both face the same punishment, but the weaker elements want them to bear responsibility for leading them astray, which is what has brought them to this suffering. Therefore, their reply is haughty, disowning any responsibility. They also tell them rudely what they think of them: "*The ones who deemed themselves mighty will say to those who were weak: Was it we who prevented you from following right guidance after it had been given you? Certainly not! It was you who were guilty.*" (Verse 32)

It is not only that they deny responsibility for others, but they acknowledge that the message they received was one of guidance. In their first life, they paid little heed to the weak or their views. In fact, they treated them as if they did not exist, accepting neither argument nor opposition from them. Now that they are facing the punishment of the hereafter, they reproachfully ask them: "*Was it we who prevented you from following right guidance after it had been given you?"* (Verse 32) With this denial comes an accusation: *"It was you who were guilty."* (Verse 32) You refused the guidance that was given you because you yourselves were guilty.

Had this exchange taken place in this life, the weak would have sat quietly, unable to utter a word. But on the Day of Judgement, when false airs are seen for what they are, and when the facts that were hidden are brought into the open, the weak do not accept this accusation. Instead, they speak out telling the others that it was they who consistently schemed to turn them away from God's guidance, it was they who established false beliefs, created confusion around the truth, and who used power and influence to keep people astray: *"Those who were weak will reply to those who deemed themselves mighty: Not so! It was your scheming, night and day, ordering us to disbelieve in God and to set up equals to Him."* (Verse 33)

Both groups will then realize that such a depressing dialogue benefits neither. It will not spare either the punishment they deserve. Each party is guilty of their own sins: the ones who claimed power have to account for their own sins, as well as for leading others astray; and similarly the weak are responsible for their own sins and for following tyrants. They cannot be exempt on account of the fact that they were weak. God favoured them with reason and freedom, but they chose not to use their reason and sold their freedom, accepting humiliation and servility. Thus, they all deserve to be punished. When they see the suffering they have to endure, they are in deep sorrow, regretting all that they have done: *"When they see the punishment awaiting them, they will all harbour utter and unmitigated remorse."* (Verse 33) This is a description of a state of total regret that leaves the person unable to utter a word. Hearts are buried and lips are sealed.

They are then taken to where their punishment, hard and painful, is meted out: *"We shall put chains round the necks of the unbelievers."* (Verse 33) As they are being so driven, the *sūrah* addresses the onlookers, saying: *"Are they to be requited for anything other than what they did?"* (Verse 33)

The curtains are drawn leaving behind both those who enjoyed power and those who were servile. Both are wrongdoers. One group does wrong by tyrannizing, distorting the truth and exceeding their limits, while the other does wrong by surrendering their human dignity, reason and freedom, and accepting tyranny. Both groups are equally punished; both are requited only for what they did.

The scene shows the wrongdoers what they will face, bringing it alive before their very eyes. They see themselves in the hereafter while they are still in this life. Not only so, but others also see their end. All this is done when there is still time for all to make amends and correct their attitudes.

An Ever Repeated Story

The wealthy Qurayshī people behaved in exactly the same way as others of affluence when they received a divine message: "*Whenever We sent a warner to any community, those of them who lived in luxury said: 'We do not believe in the message with which you have been sent.'*" (Verse 34) Thus, it is the same story repeated again and again throughout the generations. Luxurious life hardens hearts, blunts sensitivity, and corrupts nature so that it no longer sees the pointers divine guidance provides. It thus lures people into arrogance, darkness and falsehood.

People who live in luxury are often deceived by false values and transient affluence. They are deluded by the power and wealth they enjoy, thinking that it will spare them God's punishment or that it is evidence of God's being pleased with them, or that in their position they are above accountability for their deeds: "*They also say: Richer than you are we in wealth, and we have more children. We certainly are not going to be made to suffer.*" (Verse 35)

The Qur'ān puts in front of them the standard of values God wants. It explains to them that whether God grants provisions in plenty or makes them scanty is no indication of God's being pleased or displeased with a person. It has nothing to do with the correct standard of values; it neither prevents punishment nor induces it. It is totally separate from the question of accountability, reckoning, requital and God's pleasure. It is subject to a totally different divine rule: "*Say: My Lord gives in abundance, or gives in scant measure, to whomever He wills; but most people do not understand.*" (Verse 36)

This question of wealth and property, and how much someone has of the means of luxury and pleasure, is one that makes many people wonder.

They are troubled when they see that the wicked, the corrupt and the perpetrators of evil have whatever they wish for of wealth and power, while those who are virtuous, good and honest are deprived of it all. Some tend to think that God only gives in abundance to someone who enjoys a privileged position with Him. Others may even doubt whether goodness, honesty and virtue have any real value, since they often go hand in hand with poverty and deprivation. Therefore, the Qur'ān separates the riches and luxuries of this world from the values which God approves of. It states that God grants sustenance in abundance or scant measure to whomever He wills, and this has nothing to do with Him being pleased or displeased with anyone. God may indeed give riches in abundance to someone with whom He is displeased as well as to one who has earned His pleasure. Likewise, He may stint the provisions of anyone, good or evil. Most certainly the actions they do will not lead to the same result.

God may give in plenty to the perpetrators of evil, giving them the chance to delve further into evil, compound their corruption and increase their record of sin and crime. He will then punish them for their evil in this life or in the life to come as He, in His infinite wisdom, may determine. On the other hand, He may give them sustenance in a tight and scanty measure, and as a result they may go further on the loose, adding to their crimes and sins, despairing of ever receiving God's grace. Again their record of sin and evil will mount.

By contrast, God may bestow His favours in abundance on good and virtuous people so as to enable them to do many more good things that they would not have been able to do without having plentiful provisions. Thus, they will show their gratitude to Him by feeling, word and action. Their record of good things will then grow in accordance with their actions and with the goodness of their hearts, which is known to God. Alternatively, He may grant them sustenance only in small measure to test their perseverance, trust in their Lord, reassurance and acceptance of whatever lot is assigned to them. Again, if they prove themselves, there will be a manifold increase in their record of goodness.

Whatever the reasons for giving people in plenty or in limited measure are, the whole question is entirely separate from people's respective positions with God. A person's wealth, position or offspring in this life bear no indication of that person's standing with God. Such standing is determined on the basis of how people behave. If God grants someone wealth and children, and he uses both in a good way, God may give him double reward for this good action in connection with the blessings received from Him. It is their conduct that gives them double reward, not the wealth, power or offspring.

It is neither your riches nor your children that can bring you nearer to Us: only he who believes and does what is right [comes near to Us]. To these multiple reward will be given for all that they have done. They will dwell in safety in the mansions of paradise; whereas all who strive against Our revelations, seeking to defeat their purpose, shall be given over to suffering. (Verses 37–38)

The rule concerning people's provisions and whether they are given in abundance or small measure is restated, making it clear that it is subject to God's wisdom. It tells us that whatever of our provision is spent for God's sake is the portion that remains and grows. We need to keep this fact clear in our minds:

Say: My Lord gives in abundance, or gives in scant measure, to whomever He wills of His servants; whatever you give for His sake He will replace it for you, for He is the best of providers. (Verse 39)

Who Benefits Whom

The passage concludes with a scene from the Day of Judgement, where we see them gathered, and God confronts them with the angels they used to worship instead of Him. It ends with them suffering the torment they used to hasten, as the *sūrah* has already mentioned:

On the day He gathers them all together, He will say to the angels: 'Was it you that these people worshipped?' They will answer: 'Limitless are You in Your glory! You alone are our patron, not they. In fact they worshipped the jinn *and most of them believed in them.' Today none of you has any power to benefit or harm another. We will say to the wrongdoers: 'Taste now the suffering through fire which you persistently denied.'* (Verses 40–42)

These are the angels they used to worship, or hope would intercede for them with God: they are brought face to face with them, but the angels glorify God, stating that He is exalted above all that these people allege. They disassociate themselves from such false worship, as though it had not taken place. They are indeed in Satan's service, either worshipping him and appealing to him for help, or obeying him by associating partners with God. In fact, when they worshipped angels, they were actually worshipping Satan. Indeed worship of the *jinn* was practised by some Arabs. Some of them actually addressed their worship to the *jinn*, while others sought their help. Hence, the *sūrah* says: "*They worshipped the* jinn *and most of them believed in them.*" (Verse 41) This explains the relevance of Solomon's story with the *jinn* to the major issues discussed in this *sūrah*.

As this scene concludes, the mode of expression changes from narrative to address. The blame is squarely put on them, and they are severely reproached: "*Today none of you has any power to benefit or harm another.*" (Verse 42) Neither can the angels benefit people, nor can those unbelievers benefit one another. The fire the wrongdoers used to deny is now in front of them. It is an undoubted reality: "*We will say to the wrongdoers: 'Taste now the suffering through fire which you persistently denied.'* (Verse 42)

Like all previous passages, this one concludes with further emphasis on the question of resurrection, accountability, reckoning and reward.

5

Final Warning

When Our revelations are recited to them in all their clarity, they say: 'This is but a man who wants to turn you away from what your forefathers worshipped.' They also say: 'This is nothing but an invented falsehood.' Furthermore, when the truth comes to them, the unbelievers will say: 'This is just plain sorcery.' (43)

وَإِذَا تُتۡلَىٰ عَلَيۡهِمۡ ءَايَٰتُنَا بَيِّنَٰتٖ قَالُواْ مَا هَٰذَآ إِلَّا رَجُلٞ يُرِيدُ أَن يَصُدَّكُمۡ عَمَّا كَانَ يَعۡبُدُ ءَابَآؤُكُمۡ وَقَالُواْ مَا هَٰذَآ إِلَّآ إِفۡكٞ مُّفۡتَرٗىۚ وَقَالَ ٱلَّذِينَ كَفَرُواْ لِلۡحَقِّ لَمَّا جَآءَهُمۡ إِنۡ هَٰذَآ إِلَّا سِحۡرٞ مُّبِينٞ ٤٣

Yet never have We given them any books to study, nor have We sent them any warner before you. (44)

وَمَآ ءَاتَيۡنَٰهُم مِّن كُتُبٖ يَدۡرُسُونَهَاۖ وَمَآ أَرۡسَلۡنَآ إِلَيۡهِمۡ قَبۡلَكَ مِن نَّذِيرٖ ٤٤

Those who have gone before them likewise denied the truth. These people have not attained even one tenth of what We gave their predecessors, yet when they denied My messengers, how terrible was My condemnation. (45)

وَكَذَّبَ ٱلَّذِينَ مِن قَبۡلِهِمۡ وَمَا بَلَغُواْ مِعۡشَارَ مَآ ءَاتَيۡنَٰهُمۡ فَكَذَّبُواْ رُسُلِيۖ فَكَيۡفَ كَانَ نَكِيرِ ٤٥

Say: 'I counsel you one thing: stand before God, in pairs or singly, and think: there is no madness in your Companion [Muḥammad]. He is only a warner to you of awesome suffering to come.' (46)

قُلْ إِنَّمَآ أَعِظُكُم بِوَٰحِدَةٍۖ أَن تَقُومُواْ لِلَّهِ مَثْنَىٰ وَفُرَٰدَىٰ ثُمَّ تَتَفَكَّرُواْۚ مَا بِصَاحِبِكُم مِّن جِنَّةٍۚ إِنْ هُوَ إِلَّا نَذِيرٌ لَّكُم بَيْنَ يَدَيْ عَذَابٍ شَدِيدٍ ٤٦

Say: 'If I have ever asked you for any reward, you can keep it. My reward rests with none other than God. He is witness to everything.' (47)

قُلْ مَا سَأَلْتُكُم مِّنْ أَجْرٍ فَهُوَ لَكُمْۖ إِنْ أَجْرِيَ إِلَّا عَلَى اللَّهِۖ وَهُوَ عَلَىٰ كُلِّ شَيْءٍ شَهِيدٌ ٤٧

Say: 'My Lord hurls forth the truth. He has full knowledge of all that is beyond the reach of people's perception.' (48)

قُلْ إِنَّ رَبِّي يَقْذِفُ بِالْحَقِّ عَلَّٰمُ الْغُيُوبِ ٤٨

Say: 'The truth has now come. Falsehood neither creates anything new, nor restores anything.' (49)

قُلْ جَآءَ الْحَقُّ وَمَا يُبْدِئُ الْبَٰطِلُ وَمَا يُعِيدُ ٤٩

Say: 'Were I to go astray, I would but go astray to the loss of myself. But if I am on the right path, it is through what my Lord reveals to me. He is All-Hearing, ever-near.' (50)

قُلْ إِن ضَلَلْتُ فَإِنَّمَآ أَضِلُّ عَلَىٰ نَفْسِيۖ وَإِنِ اهْتَدَيْتُ فَبِمَا يُوحِي إِلَيَّ رَبِّيٓۚ إِنَّهُ سَمِيعٌ قَرِيبٌ ٥٠

If you could but see when they are seized by terror, with nowhere to escape; for they will have been seized from a place nearby. (51)

وَلَوْ تَرَىٰ إِذْ فَزِعُوا۟ فَلَا فَوْتَ وَأُخِذُوا۟ مِن مَّكَانٍ قَرِيبٍ ﴿٥١﴾

They will say: 'We do believe in it,' but how could they attain it from so far away, (52)

وَقَالُوٓا۟ ءَامَنَّا بِهِۦ وَأَنَّىٰ لَهُمُ ٱلتَّنَاوُشُ مِن مَّكَانٍ بَعِيدٍ ﴿٥٢﴾

seeing that they had at first denied it all. They used to cast scorn from far away on what is imperceptible. (53)

وَقَدْ كَفَرُوا۟ بِهِۦ مِن قَبْلُ وَيَقْذِفُونَ بِٱلْغَيْبِ مِن مَّكَانٍ بَعِيدٍ ﴿٥٣﴾

A barrier will be set between them and all that they desire, just as was done with their kind before. They were lost in perplexing doubt. (54)

وَحِيلَ بَيْنَهُمْ وَبَيْنَ مَا يَشْتَهُونَ كَمَا فُعِلَ بِأَشْيَاعِهِم مِّن قَبْلُ إِنَّهُمْ كَانُوا۟ فِى شَكٍّ مُّرِيبٍ ﴿٥٤﴾

Overview

This last passage in the *sūrah* speaks about the idolaters and what they said against the Prophet and the Qur'ān that was revealed to him. It reminds them of what happened to others like them who denied God's revelations and how His punishment overwhelmed them even though they were stronger, wealthier and more knowledgeable than the Arab unbelievers.

This is followed by several hard notes, each resounding like a hammer. The first one calls on them to stand before God after shedding all influences that prevent them from objectively assessing the call that is addressed to them. The second note invites them to reflect on the real motives of God's Messenger when he repeatedly calls on them to accept God's message and believe in Him, when he has nothing to gain from this. Since he does not ask them for any wages in return, why should they doubt his sincerity and turn away? Further notes follow, each violently shaking people's hearts.

The *sūrah* concludes with a scene from the Day of Judgement that is full of violent movement and which fits perfectly with the preceding strong tones.

A Man Like You

> When Our revelations are recited to them in all their clarity, they say: 'This is but a man who wants to turn you away from what your forefathers worshipped.' They also say: 'This is nothing but an invented falsehood.' Furthermore, when the truth comes to them, the unbelievers will say: 'This is just plain sorcery.' Yet never have We given them any books to study, nor have We sent them any warner before you. Those who have gone before them likewise denied the truth. These people have not attained even one tenth of what We gave their predecessors, yet when they denied My messengers, how terrible was My condemnation. (Verses 43–45)

They met the clear truth the Prophet recited to them with a confused legacy of past traditions that had neither a clear basis nor solid foundation. They realized that the simple, clear and consistent truth that was the Qur'ān represented a serious threat to their confused medley of inherited beliefs and traditions. Hence they claimed: "*This is but a man who wants to turn you away from what your forefathers worshipped.*" (Verse 43) They realized, however, that this was not enough. That it contradicted their forefathers' beliefs was not enough to convince everyone. Hence, they also questioned the honesty of the Messenger who delivered God's message: "*They also say: This is nothing but an invented falsehood.*" (Verse 43) Needless to say, what is 'false' must be fabricated, but they wanted to give it stronger emphasis by saying "*This is nothing but an invented falsehood.*" (Verse 43) In other words, they sought to undermine it, raising doubts about its divine source.

Then they moved on to describe the Qur'ān itself: "*When the truth comes to them, the unbelievers will say: 'This is just plain sorcery.'*" (Verse 43) They realized that the Qur'ān is powerful and shakes people's hearts.

Hence, it was not enough to say that it was fabricated. They had to explain its power and so alleged that it was 'plain sorcery.'

With such allegations, one following the other, they sought to divert people's attention from the clear and powerful verses of the Qur'ān. They knew they could not back up their claims, and indeed many of those who made such allegations, i.e. tribal chiefs and those who were influential in society, were certain that the Qur'ān was God's revelation as no human being could have produced anything like it. References have been made earlier in this book to what some of the elders of the Quraysh said in private conversations about Muḥammad (peace be upon him) and the Qur'ān, and what they schemed in order to turn people away from listening to the Qur'ān which captivates people's hearts.

The Qur'ān exposes them as it states that they were not given books in the past so as to evaluate new ones and judge revelations. How can they, then, say that what they now received was neither revelation nor a divine book? How can they say that it was not from God, when they did not have any messengers in the past? Their claims are devoid of substance: "*Yet never have We given them any books to study, nor have We sent them any warner before you.*" (Verse 44)

The *sūrah* then touches their hearts by reminding them of the destruction of earlier communities. Those Arabs had not been given one tenth of what those earlier people had of knowledge, wealth and power. When they denied God's messengers, punishment overwhelmed them: "*Those who have gone before them likewise denied the truth. These people have not attained even one tenth of what We gave their predecessors, yet when they denied My messengers, how terrible was My condemnation.*" (Verse 45) This condemnation destroyed them all. The Quraysh knew of some of these old communities who suffered God's punishment. Therefore, this brief reminder is sufficient. It comes in the form of a sarcastic question: '*how terrible was My condemnation.*' It is a question put to those who knew the extent of that condemnation.

A Search for the Truth

At this point the Prophet is instructed to call on them in all sincerity to search for the truth, to distinguish between what is false and what is

177

true, and to assess the situation they are in, free of distortion and fabrication:

> *Say: I counsel you one thing: stand before God, in pairs or singly, and think: there is no madness in your Companion [Muḥammad]. He is only a warner to you of awesome suffering to come.* (Verse 46)

This is an invitation to stand before God, in all sincerity, removing from one's mind all personal prejudices, interests, motivations, desires, environmental and social influences. It is an invitation to look at the facts, plain and simple. This invitation seeks to put before their eyes the plain argument of human nature, away from everything that blurs or obscures what is clear and simple. At the same time, it is a simple means to search for truth, discarding all outside influences and being mindful only of God.

There is only '*one thing*', that ensures that the way is the right one and the method sound. This is to stand before God in all sincerity, looking to satisfy no prejudice, or ensure any personal gain or interest; and to be free of all influences and pressures; and then to think and reflect in complete sincerity. What, then, is this one thing? "*Stand before God, in pairs or singly:*" '*in pairs*' so that one can speak frankly to another and argue with him, without being influenced by the masses and their spontaneous reactions, and '*singly*' so that you can face the facts in a cool and reflective way.

"*And think: there is no madness in your Companion [Muḥammad]*." (Verse 46) You have known him for a long time, and everything you have seen from him points to his wisdom and logic. He does not say anything that could cause anyone to suspect the soundness of his mind. He only says powerful words of wisdom that are plainly stated.

"*He is only a warner to you of awesome suffering to come*." (Verse 46) This statement shows the suffering to be close at hand, and the warning precedes it by only by one step, hoping to save anyone who listens. It is like an alarm warning of a fire that threatens lives. It urges immediate action to escape inevitable suffering.

Quoting one of the Prophet's Companions, Imām Aḥmad relates the following *ḥadīth*: "The Prophet came out one day and called us three times, then said: 'Do you realize what my position is in relation to you?' People said: 'God and His Messenger know best.' He rejoined: 'My position in relation to you is like that of a community who feared that an enemy might be heading towards them, so they sent one of them to gather intelligence. As he went about his mission, he saw the enemy drawing near, and he moved fast to warn his people. However, he feared that he might be caught by the enemy before he could warn his people. So he waved his robe and shouted: the enemy is nigh; the enemy is nigh.'" In another *ḥadīth*, the Prophet is quoted as saying: "I was sent with my message at the approach of the Last Hour: it could have almost been ahead of me."

That was the first note: powerful and inspiring. It is closely followed by another note: "*Say: If I have ever asked you for any reward, you can keep it. My reward rests with none other than God. He is witness to everything.*" (Verse 47) At first the *sūrah* called on them to think carefully about the man delivering the message and the fact that he is of sound mind, without the faintest trace of madness. Now they are asked to think about the reasons that motivate him to warn them against the painful suffering that may befall them: what is his interest in all this? How can he benefit by it? The Qur'ān orders the Prophet to put this to them in a way that fits with their logic and touches their consciences: "*If I have ever asked you for any reward, you can keep it.*" Take it all! Whatever I asked you, you keep for yourselves. This combines sarcasm with guidance and instruction: "*My reward rests with none other than God.*" (Verse 47) It is He who has charged me with this message and He gives me my reward for it. It is to Him alone that I look for reward. If a person expects to be rewarded by God, all that others can offer is trifling. "*He is witness to everything.*" (Verse 47) He sees and knows everything. Nothing is hidden from Him. He is my witness in whatever I intend, say or do.

The third note is stronger and faster: "*Say: My Lord hurls forth the truth. He has full knowledge of all that is beyond the reach of people's perception.*" (Verse 48) What I have given you is the truth, which is powerful in its own right. However, it is God who hurls it forth: who can stand up to His truth? It is like a missile whose trajectory penetrates what otherwise would not be possible to penetrate. The one who hurls it is God, who *'has full knowledge of all that is beyond the reach of people's perception.'* When He hurls it, He is fully aware of what takes place. No goal is hidden from Him and no shield or fortification can stop what He hurls.

The fourth note is just as fast and strong: *"Say: The truth has now come. Falsehood neither creates anything new, nor restores anything."* (Verse 49) This truth has now come, in one of its forms, in the message embodied in the Qur'ān and its straight path. The Prophet is ordered here to declare the coming of the truth, strong, overpowering, rising high and imposing its authority: *"Falsehood neither creates anything new, nor restores anything."* (Verse 49) Falsehood is done for: it has no life of its own and nowhere to function. It is destined for a miserable end. As we listen, we feel as if the end has already been sealed.

This is indeed the case. Ever since the Qur'ān was revealed, the truth has been established on solid foundations. Compared with its clarity and power, falsehood is nothing more than a futile argument which is known to be so. Falsehood may appear to triumph in certain situations, but this is not a victory over the truth, but rather over the people who claim loyalty to it; it's a triumph of people, not principles. Such a victory is temporary, not permanent. The truth remains the same: clear and simple.

The final note says: *"Say: Were I to go astray, I would but go astray to the loss of myself. But if I am on the right path, it is through what my Lord reveals to me. He is All-Hearing, ever-near."* (Verse 50) You will lose nothing if I go astray, because I will be the one accountable for it. If I am following guidance, it is because God has guided me aright when He gave me His revelation. I can produce nothing of that. I only remain subject to God's will, receiving His bounty.

"He is All-Hearing, ever-near." (Verse 50) This is how those who responded to the Prophet's call and believed in his message felt God's presence. They felt His interaction with them. They felt Him near to them, listening to what they said, taking direct care of their affairs. Their complaints and appeals went directly to Him, and He did not overlook them or give them to someone else to deal with. This made them aware that they lived under God's supervision, close to Him and receiving His

care and kindness. This they felt in reality, not as an abstract notion or a representation of an idea. It was real fact: "*He is All-Hearing, ever-near.*" (Verse 50)

The Final Scene

The *sūrah* concludes with a fast and powerful scene from the Day of Judgement, full of strong movement that goes to and fro between this life and the life to come, as if both are within the same domain:

If you could but see when they are seized by terror, with nowhere to escape; for they will have been seized from a place nearby. They will say: 'We do believe in it,' but how could they attain it from so far away, seeing that they had at first denied it all. They used to cast scorn from far away on what is imperceptible. A barrier will be set between them and all that they desire, just as was done with their kind before. They were lost in perplexing doubt. (Verses 51–54)

"*If you could but see.*" The scene is there to look at. "*When they are seized by terror*" because of the terrible situation they find themselves in. It appears they may try to find a way out, but there is "*nowhere to escape.*" They have nowhere to turn: "*they will have been seized from a place nearby.*" They could not go far with their miserable attempt.

"*They will say: We do believe in it,*" but it is now too late. For, "*how could they attain it from so far away?*" How can they regain it in their new position when the place to believe is now so far away? It was available to them in their life in this world, but they let the chance go unheeded.

"*They had at first denied it all.*" The matter is over and they cannot try again. "*They used to cast scorn from far away on what is imperceptible.*" They did this when the Day of Judgement was beyond their perception. They denied it without a shred of evidence to support their denial. They did so from afar but are now trying to attain faith from a distant place.

"*A barrier will be set between them and all that they desire.*" This is a reference to the faith they wish to have now when it is too late. It cannot spare them the punishment or save them from the danger they see looming. They are in the same position as earlier communities: *"just as was done with their kind before."* Those earlier communities also tried to escape God's punishment when no escape was possible. *"They were lost in perplexing doubt."* Now they see it for certain after they had been in doubt of it ever happening.

The *sūrah* concludes on this fast, powerful note, with a scene from the Day of Judgement confirming the main issue. This issue is stated at the outset and re-stated here at the end.

SŪRAH 35

Fāṭir
(The Originator)

Prologue

This Makkan *sūrah* possesses a special character both in its subject and style. It perhaps best compares with *Sūrah* 13, Thunder, in the way in which it addresses the human heart, using, from start to finish, a fascinating rhythm employing various beats. It moves us into contemplation of the great universe and the numerous signs to be found in every nook and cranny. Man thus remembers God's blessings and appreciates the grace and favour He bestows on all His creatures. He also visualizes the end suffered by earlier communities and their fate on the Day of Judgement. He thus feels humility as he looks at the countless marvels that constitute God's work. He also recognizes that there is only one truth and one law running through all existence, and that this is controlled by God's hand. The *sūrah* imparts all this in a style and rhythm that leaves a profound and powerful effect on our minds.

The *sūrah* is a complete unit with interlinked rings, making it hard to divide into parts addressing separate subjects. In fact it has only one subject, but it plays its rhythm on the strings of the human heart so as to fill our souls, calling us to believe and submit ourselves to God.

The most distinctive feature of the *sūrah* is that its puts all these strings in God's hand, showing how they work, being pulled or stretched, separated or combined, without restriction or influence. We note this distinctive feature at the outset, and it runs through the *sūrah* to its very end.

The great universe, with its limitless expanse, has been brought into existence by God, according to His design: "*All praise is due to God, the Originator of the heavens and the earth, who assigns angels to be messengers, endowed with wings, two, or three, or four. He adds to His creation what He pleases. Indeed God has power over all things.*" (Verse 1)

This strong hand of God opens up to send us flowing mercy without restriction, and then clinches to stop it at source. No one can alter this: "*Whatever grace God opens up to man, none can withhold it; and whatever He withholds, none other than Him can release. He alone is Almighty, Wise.*" (Verse 2)

To follow guidance and to be in error are two opposite ends of the mercy spectrum: the first is flowing, the other withheld: "*God lets go astray him that wills [to go astray], just as He guides him that wills [to be guided].*" (Verse 8) "*God can make hear whoever He wills, whereas you cannot make those who are in their graves hear you. You are only a warner.*" (Verses 22–23)

It is this very able hand that makes life in the first place, and then brings the dead back to life in the hereafter: "*It is God who sends forth the winds, so that they raise clouds, and We drive them to a dead land and thereby give life to the earth after it had been lifeless. Thus shall resurrection be.*" (Verse 9)

Power and glory belong to Him alone. Whoever wants any of this must derive it from Him alone: "*Whoever desires might and glory should know that all might and glory belong to God alone.*" (Verse 10)

Creation and giving shape and form to creatures, giving them offspring and determining their life duration are all within God's grasp, never let loose: "*It is God who creates you all out of dust, then out of a gamete. He then makes you into two sexes. No female conceives or gives birth without His knowledge. No one attains to old age or has his life cut short unless it be thus laid down in [God's] decree. All this is easy for God.*" (Verse 11)

Also in His grasp are all the controls to the heavens, the earth, and other celestial bodies: "*He causes the night to pass into the day, and the day to pass into the night; and He has made the sun and the moon subservient [to His laws], each running its course for an appointed term. Thus is God, your Lord: to Him belongs all dominion, while those whom you invoke instead of Him do not own even the skin of a date-stone."* (Verse 13)

God's able hand works in this universe according to its own inspiring fashion, adding colour to man, animals, plants and inanimate objects: *"Are you not aware that God sends down water from the skies, with which We bring forth fruits of different colours? In the mountains there are streaks of white and red of various shades, as well as others jet-black. Similarly, human beings, beasts and cattle have various colours. (Verses 27–28)*

The same hand puts human beings on the move, making one generation succeed another: *"We have given this Book to such of Our servants as We chose."* (Verse 32) *"It is He who made you inherit the earth."* (Verse 39) It holds this universe, protecting it lest it deviate: *"It is God alone who holds the celestial bodies and the earth, lest they deviate [from their courses]. If they should ever deviate, no one else could uphold them after Him."* (Verse 41) He holds everything in control, nothing stands in defiance of His will: *"God can never be foiled by anything whatever in the heavens and the earth."* (Verse 44)

Throughout the *sūrah* God's different attributes are emphasized. He is the One who has power over all things; the Almighty; the Wise; to whom all things return; who knows all that they do; to whom all dominion belongs; who is free of all wants, worthy of all praise; with whom all journeys end; much-forgiving; most appreciative; all-aware; all-seeing; who knows all that is hidden in the heavens and earth; fully aware of what is in people's hearts; ever-forbearing; infinite in His power and who has all His servants in His sight.

These verses and the comments at the end of each create the special ambience of the *sūrah* and the overall effect it has on our hearts. Despite its being a single whole, with continuous beats, we have chosen to divide it into six sections to enable easier discussion.

I

Giving All Grace

Fāṭir (The Originator)

In the Name of God, the Lord of Grace, the Ever Merciful

All praise is due to God, the Originator of the heavens and the earth, who assigns angels to be messengers, endowed with wings, two, or three, or four. He adds to His creation what He pleases. Indeed God has power over all things. (1)

Whatever grace God opens up to man, none can withhold it; and whatever He withholds, none other than Him can release. He alone is Almighty, Wise. (2)

187

People! Remember the blessings God has bestowed upon you. Is there any creator other than God who can give you sustenance from heaven and earth? There is no deity other than Him. How can you turn away? (3)

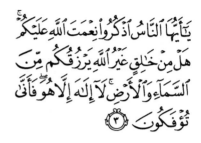

The Originator

All praise is due to God, the Originator of the heavens and the earth, who assigns angels to be messengers, endowed with wings, two, or three, or four. He adds to His creation what He pleases. Indeed God has power over all things. (Verse 1)

The *sūrah* begins by offering all praise to God, as its whole purpose is to make our hearts turn to Him, contemplate His signs, appreciate His mercy, and look at the wonders of His creation. We are made to fully appreciate these wonders so that our hearts overflow with His praise and glorification: *"All praise is due to God."*

Next comes God's attribute indicating creation and His bringing it into being: *"the Originator of the heavens and the earth."* It is He who has originated all these great bodies, some of which we see around us. We know only a little about the smallest and nearest to us of all these bodies, i.e. our mother earth. Yet they are all subject to one law of nature that keeps them in harmony, despite the huge distances separating them, which we can only imagine with great difficulty. Despite their great sizes and endless spaces separating their orbits, there exists certain relations between them which, if disturbed even by just a little, could lead to a major catastrophe.

We often pay little attention to Qur'ānic references to the creation of the heavens and the earth, or to its scenic descriptions of the universe. This is because our senses have been blunted by familiarity. Therefore, these scenes do not elevate us to the same level of inspiration that they give a heart that remembers God always, and thus remains sensitive to what His able hand produces. Only such a heart feels the awe these scenes impart.

An alert heart which maintains its bond with God does not need accurate information about the exact positions of stars, their sizes, relations to each other in position or movement, the thickness of the atmosphere around each, or the orbits they follow in order to appreciate the awesomeness of this great, wonderful and beautiful creation. It is enough for such a heart that these scenes play their precisely stringed music. It is enough for it to look at the stars shining across the dark night sky; or the light reflected by a full moon; or the dawn breaking through the darkness giving a feeling of new life; or the sunset heralding the darkness that brings a feeling of farewell; or the earth with its endless vistas; or indeed a single flower with its colour and shape that takes us long to contemplate.

The Qur'ān gives us inspiring directives so that we contemplate these creatures, large and small. Looking at only one of them is enough evidence of the greatness of its Creator and makes us address our glorification, praise and prayer to Him alone.

"All praise is due to God, the Originator of the heavens and the earth, who assigns angels to be messengers, endowed with wings, two, or three, or four." (Verse 1) This *sūrah* dwells long on God's messengers, revelation and the truth it contains. The angels are God's messengers to His chosen servants on earth. The message they bring is the greatest thing in life. Hence God follows the reference to His creation of the heavens and the earth by mentioning the role of the angels whereby it is they who make contact between heaven and earth, fulfilling the greatest task of all as they deliver His message. It is a message from the Originator of the heavens and the earth to His prophets whom He sends as guides to mankind.

For the first time in the Qur'ān we have a physical description of the angels. Previously we were given descriptions of their nature and role, such as *"Those that are with Him are never too proud to worship Him and never grow weary of that. They extol His limitless glory by night and day, tirelessly."* (21: 19–20) *"Those who are near to your Lord are never too proud to worship Him. They extol His limitless glory, and before Him alone prostrate themselves."* (7: 206) Here, however, we have a reference to

189

their physical appearance. They are '*endowed with wings, two, or three, or four.*' This description does not, however, help us imagine how they look, because we do not know anything about their physique or about the form their wings take. We can do no more than take this description as it is, without adding anything from our imagination, for anything we may imagine could be wrong. We do not have any definite description of how the angels look from a reliable source. What we do have though in the Qur'ān is this description and a reference to the angels in charge of hell: "*Over it are appointed angels who are stern and severe: they do not disobey God in whatever He has commanded them, but always do what they are bidden to do.*" (66: 6) Again this description does not give any physical delineation. It is reported in a *ḥadīth* that 'the Prophet saw Gabriel in his natural form twice.' One report mentions that Gabriel 'has 600 wings'. [Related by al-Bukhārī and Muslim.] Again we do not have here a physical description, so we must leave it at the level God has imparted to us, accepting that all knowledge belongs to Him.

Wings are specified as being in twos, threes and fours, but man knows only a two-winged form in all birds. Therefore, the opening verse states that God '*adds to His creation what He pleases,*' thus making it clear that God's will is free, unlimited to any one form of creation. We know and see countless forms of creation, but the ones we do not know about are far more numerous. "*Indeed God has power over all things.*" This comment is broader and more comprehensive than the statement before it. Its import applies to all forms of creation, origination, transformation and alteration.

Unrestricted Grace

Whatever grace God opens up to man, none can withhold it; and whatever He withholds, none other than Him can release. He alone is Almighty, Wise. (Verse 2)

What we have in this second verse of the *sūrah* is an aspect of God's power mentioned at the end of the first verse. When this aspect is instilled in a person's heart and mind, he undergoes a complete transformation in his concepts, feelings, values, standards and life generally. It invalidates any thought of any other power having any control over the heavens and earth, and puts him in touch with God's own power. It makes him abandon any thought of receiving grace from anyone else and links all to God's grace. It closes before him every door and way in the universe yet opens for him the door and the way leading to God.

God's grace can be reflected in countless aspects. Indeed man cannot even begin to record these. They are within him and the way he is created; the position of honour he is given; the blessings that are all around him from every side and from above and beneath him. It is also to be found in the favours showered on him.

God's grace is reflected in what man has been denied just as much as it is reflected in what he has been granted. When God opens it up to anyone, that person finds it in every situation, thing, condition and place. He even finds it within himself, his feelings, all around him, wherever and however he happens to be, even though he may be deprived of everything people consider to be important. Conversely, should God withhold His grace from anyone, that person will miss it in every thing, situation, place and condition, even though he may have at his disposal everything people associate with wealth and happiness.

Whatever favour a person is granted becomes a hardship if it is associated with the withholding of God's grace; and whatever hardship or trial he undergoes becomes a favour once it is coupled with His grace. A man may lie on a bed of thorns, but, with God's grace, he finds it very comfortable; while silk mattresses and cushions feel like hard nails if that grace is denied him. With divine grace the most difficult problem becomes easy and danger becomes safety, but without it, what is normally easy becomes insoluble and safe roads and ways lead to ruin.

Should you be granted God's grace, you will not feel miserable even though you may be in solitary confinement, enduring torture or facing danger; while misery will be your lot if it is withheld, even though you are in the most luxurious and splendid of surroundings. It is from deep inside that happiness, contentment and reassurance flow by God's grace, and deep inside you feel misery, worry and affliction when it is denied.

If the door of God's grace is open, you will not care if all doors and windows are locked: you will find ease, comfort and happiness; and if it is closed, you will benefit nothing if all other doors and windows are left wide open.

God may give anyone plentiful wealth, and that person will find it a source of enjoyment, comfort and a means to a good position in the life to come, provided that it is coupled with God's grace. If that grace is withheld, his wealth becomes a source of worry, envy and hatred. It may also mean deprivation, if the wealthy person is stingy or ill; and it may bring ruin if he is wasteful and careless.

The same can be said about children, health and high position. With God's grace, any of these can be a source of goodness, enjoyment, delight, happiness and joy, as also a means to increase one's reward in the life to come. Should God's grace be denied, any of these will bring misery, distress, sleepless nights, or expose their owner to other people's envy, hatred and hostility. Likewise, knowledge, long life and comforts can be associated with either situation of happiness or misery. Yet little knowledge could bring about beneficial effects; a short period of life could enjoy much blessing; and little comfort may mean happiness and delight. In all these respects, communities are like individuals, in all conditions, situations and circumstances.

One aspect of God's grace is to feel it. God's grace abounds for every one of us, but it is your feeling that it is bestowed on you, your expectation, hope and trust that it is coming that is mercy and grace. By contrast, to doubt or despair of it is pure misery, but this is something that a believer will not suffer: "*None but unbelievers can ever despair of God's mercy.*" (12: 87)

God's grace will not be denied anyone who seeks it at any place and in any condition. Abraham found it when he was thrown in the fire; Joseph found it in the well where his brothers threw him and later in prison; Jonah found it in the whale's belly, under three covers of darkness; Moses found it in the river when he was a helpless infant, as also in Pharaoh's palace when Pharaoh sought to kill him. The young men who retreated to a cave, as told in *Sūrah* 18, found it there in the cave when it was not to be found in homes and palaces. They said to one another: "*Now that you have withdrawn from them and all that they worship instead of God, take refuge in the cave. God may well spread His grace over you and make fitting arrangements for you in your affairs.*" (18: 16) The Prophet Muḥammad and his Companion, Abū Bakr found it in the cave of Mount Thawr, where they hid from their pursuers. Indeed no one who sought it to the exclusion of everything else, aware that only God grants strength, power and mercy, has been left lacking.

It is also important to realize that when God opens the gates of His grace to anyone, nothing can withhold it; and when He withholds it, nothing can release it. Therefore, no one and nothing should be feared, while hope should never be pinned on anyone or anything. We should never fear to miss out on something, and never trust to any means. It all depends on God and what He wills. Whatever He determines will be done. It is He who is 'Almighty, Wise'. Nothing He determines is without clear purpose.

"*Whatever grace God opens up to man, none can withhold it.*" (Verse 2) All that people need to be assured of God's mercy is to request it from Him directly, without intermediaries: "*And whatever He withholds, none other than Him can release.*" (Verse 2)

This single verse paints a totally different picture of life. It gives a new set of values and standards that are unaffected by any consideration or pressure, be it light or heavy. When this vision is firmly settled in a person's heart, that person can stand firmly in the face of all events, people, situations, powers and considerations. Even if all people on earth as well as the *jinn* were to range themselves against him, he would be able to resist them all knowing that they cannot control God's grace.

It was with verses and images like this that the Qur'ān produced that unique community of believers in the early days of Islam. It was a community moulded under God's own care, and through the Qur'ān, so as to function as a means of God's will and establish on earth the faith, values and systems He wanted to establish. In that first community we have a unique example of human life that seems to us today to belong to the realm of legends and dreams. That community did not deal with the Qur'ān as words, sentences and verses with superb meanings, but dealt with the truth those verses represented. Furthermore, they practised it in real life. Yet, still today, the Qur'ān is able to produce, by means of its verses, individuals and communities that can achieve, by God's leave, whatever God wills them to achieve. All of us can read the Qur'ān seriously, implement it fully and live its meanings as though they are a tangible reality.

A Personal Experience

It behoves me personally to praise God and record here my gratitude to Him for the grace He bestowed on me in relation to this verse of the Qur'ān. This verse was present with me at a time when I was in great, compounded difficulty, experiencing spiritual dryness, psychological hardship and much affliction. It was this verse that came to my support, for God facilitated for me that I should see its truth, which poured into my spirit like a cool drink passing through the limbs of an extremely thirsty person. That was not a meaning I understood; rather, it was a reality I experienced. Thus, it was in itself an act of grace. It presented itself to me as a real interpretation of the verse, opening up to me like flower buds on a spring day. I had read and heard it many times before, but at that moment, it delivered its meaning as a sweet reality, showing me its inner self and saying: 'I am here, a sample of God's grace when He opens it.'

Nothing changed around me, but everything underwent a fundamental change in my appreciation. It is a great blessing that our hearts should open to receive a great truth of existence, such as the one the present verse states. It is a blessing one can experience and appreciate, but can seldom impart to others. I lived that moment and went through the experience. It was perhaps the hardest time of my life. Yet suddenly I found all difficulty disappear, and I was released of all trouble and hardship. I was experiencing a spiritual thrill, while I was still in the same place. That is God's grace which He opens to anyone He chooses and makes it overflow in just one verse of the Qur'ān. One verse opens up a window of light, lets a spring of divine grace gush through, charts a way to contentment and reassurance and all in a split second. My

Lord, You have bestowed this Qur'ān from on high to provide guidance and grace to believers. My Lord, I praise You with my tongue and heart, and my gratitude to You is without limit.[1]

Who Else?

The third verse in this short passage confirms the import of the first two, reminding people of God's blessings, emphasizing that God is the only One who creates and provides sustenance for His creation, and wondering at how people lose sight of this truth when it is so clear and obvious:

> *People! Remember the blessings God has bestowed upon you. Is there any creator other than God who can give you sustenance from heaven and earth? There is no deity other than Him. How can you turn away?* (Verse 3)

Nothing is needed more than the mention of God's blessings for people to see, feel and recognize them. Nevertheless, they do forget them. The earth around them and the skies above them give them abundant blessings and unlimited sustenance, in every step and at every moment. It is God the Creator who gives all this. They are asked here whether there is a different creator who provides them with all the good things in their hands. Obviously, they cannot say this. Indeed, they did not even claim this during their worst period of idolatry, associating all sorts of partners with God. Since there is none other than God to create and provide, why do they not remember and express gratitude? Why do they not address their gratitude to Him alone and express their thanks by praises and prayers? Indeed *"There is no deity*

---

1. Although the author does not specify the time and the occasion that he is describing here as the most difficult in his life, he is most probably referring to a specific experience during his second imprisonment (1954–64). I believe what caused him most difficulty was to see a great number of men of all ages being severely tortured, and many dying under torture, for no crime any of them had committed, with no end to their plight in sight. This was bound to weigh heavily on a man with a sensitive and compassionate nature like the author. – Editor's note.

195

other than Him." How is it that they turn away from this indisputable truth? *"How can you turn away?"* (Verse 3) It is most singular that anyone should turn away from this clear truth, evidenced by the constant sustenance they are provided with from heaven and earth. Even more singular is for a person to turn away from it all while admitting that all sustenance comes from God alone.

Just these three verses constitute the first section of the *sūrah*. In each we have an image that gives man rebirth. All that is needed is for him to firmly establish God's truth in his heart and conscience.

2

The Lurking Enemy

If they accuse you of lying, other messengers, who had gone before you, were similarly accused. It is to God that all things return. (4)

وَإِن يُكَذِّبُوكَ فَقَدْ كُذِّبَتْ رُسُلٌ مِّن قَبْلِكَ وَإِلَى ٱللَّهِ تُرْجَعُ ٱلْأُمُورُ ۝

People! God's promise is true indeed. So do not let the life of the present world delude you, and do not let deceptive thoughts about God delude you. (5)

يَـٰٓأَيُّهَا ٱلنَّاسُ إِنَّ وَعْدَ ٱللَّهِ حَقٌّ فَلَا تَغُرَّنَّكُمُ ٱلْحَيَوٰةُ ٱلدُّنْيَا وَلَا يَغُرَّنَّكُم بِٱللَّهِ ٱلْغَرُورُ ۝

Satan is your enemy, so treat him as an enemy. He only calls on his followers so that they will be among those destined for the blazing fire. (6)

إِنَّ ٱلشَّيْطَـٰنَ لَكُمْ عَدُوٌّ فَٱتَّخِذُوهُ عَدُوًّا إِنَّمَا يَدْعُوا۟ حِزْبَهُۥ لِيَكُونُوا۟ مِنْ أَصْحَـٰبِ ٱلسَّعِيرِ ۝

For the unbelievers there is severe suffering in store; while for those who believe and do righteous deeds there is forgiveness of sins and a great reward. (7)

ٱلَّذِينَ كَفَرُوا۟ لَهُمْ عَذَابٌ شَدِيدٌ وَٱلَّذِينَ ءَامَنُوا۟ وَعَمِلُوا۟ ٱلصَّـٰلِحَـٰتِ لَهُم مَّغْفِرَةٌ وَأَجْرٌ كَبِيرٌ ۝

How about the one whose evil deeds seem alluring to him so as to regard them as good? God lets go astray him that wills [to go astray], just as He guides him that wills [to be guided]. Therefore, do not waste yourself sorrowing for them. God has full knowledge of all that they do. (8)

أَفَمَن زُيِّنَ لَهُۥ سُوٓءُ عَمَلِهِۦ فَرَءَاهُ حَسَنًا فَإِنَّ ٱللَّهَ يُضِلُّ مَن يَشَآءُ وَيَهْدِى مَن يَشَآءُ فَلَا تَذْهَبْ نَفْسُكَ عَلَيْهِمْ حَسَرَٰتٍ إِنَّ ٱللَّهَ عَلِيمٌۢ بِمَا يَصْنَعُونَ ﴿٨﴾

Overview

The first section highlighted three major truths of the Islamic faith: the oneness of God, the Creator of all; the grace that He alone bestows; and that He is the only One who provides sustenance for all His creation. In this second section, the *sūrah* addresses the Prophet, comforting him because his people's rejection of his message and their false accusations of his lying caused him much pain. It stresses that all matters are in God's hand. It also addresses us all, confirming that God's promise is a true promise and warning us against Satan's schemes which aim to divert us from recognizing the major truths already outlined. What Satan, our avowed enemy, wants is to lead us to hell and its torment. It shows us the types of requital that await the believers and unbelievers in the life to come. Finally it enjoins the Prophet not to worry about what might happen to them. Both belief and rejection are in God's hand, and He knows all that people do.

The True Promise

The first address is aimed at the Prophet: *"If they accuse you of lying, other messengers, who had gone before you, were similarly accused. It is to God that all things return."* (Verse 4) With all these truths easily and clearly recognizable, you need not worry that they accuse you of lying. The same thing happened to earlier messengers. All matters eventually return to God who determines every end the way He pleases.

Then the address is made general, to all people:

People! God's promise is true indeed. So do not let the life of the present world delude you, and do not let deceptive thoughts about God delude you. Satan is your enemy, so treat him as an enemy. He only calls on his followers so that they will be among those destined for the blazing fire. (Verses 5–6)

God's promise is true: there is no doubt that it will come; it is a reality that will not fail; it is the truth. Nothing can cause it to disappear, lose its way or change. Nevertheless this present life can delude people, as can Satan. Therefore, do not let anything get the better of you: *"do not let the life of the present world delude you, and do not let deceptive thoughts about God delude you."* (Verse 5) Satan has declared his hostility to you and that he will never be anything but an enemy to you. Therefore, *"treat him as an enemy."* (Verse 6) Do not befriend him, listen to his advice, follow in his footsteps, for no rational person would follow in his enemy's footsteps. Moreover, you should realize that he does not call you to anything good, nor does he want you to be safe: *"He only calls on his followers so that they will be among those destined for the blazing fire."* (Verse 6) Can anyone with reason and clear thinking answer a call that would put him in the fire?

This is a sincere, heartfelt address. When man remembers the eternal battle he has to fight against his avowed enemy, Satan, he will muster all his strength, defending himself and ensuring his own safety. He will do his utmost not to fall to any temptation, keep himself on guard, evaluate every thought by the scales God has given him. He is alert to the fact that any seemingly innocent thought may involve clever deception by his old enemy.

This is the sort of sensitivity Islam wants its followers to have. They need to be on the alert so as to reject any temptation Satan presents. This entails the mobilization of all one's responses against evil, both its inner appeal and surface attraction. Thus, one is always on red alert, prepared to engage in this battle which rages persistently throughout this present life.

Such single-mindedness demanded from believers is followed by an outline of the fate of those who responded to Satan's call. To reinforce the contrast, the situation of the believers who reject him and drive him away is reiterated: *"For the unbelievers there is severe suffering in store; while for those who believe and do righteous deeds there is forgiveness of sins and a great reward."* (Verse 7)

The Key to Evil

This is followed by an explanation of what makes people go astray, the nature of Satan's work, the door through which all evil flows. It shows the route that takes people astray and why, when a person goes far along it, he cannot turn back:

> *How about the one whose evil deeds seem alluring to him so as to regard them as good? God lets go astray him that wills [to go astray], just as He guides him that wills [to be guided]. Therefore, do not waste yourself sorrowing for them. God has full knowledge of all that they do.* (Verse 8)

"How about the one whose evil deeds seem alluring to him so as to regard them as good?" This is the key to all evil: Satan makes evil deeds seem fair to people, and they will then admire themselves for what they do. Such a person will not review his work to identify what is right or where he has gone wrong, because he feels he cannot go wrong. He is so preoccupied with self-admiration that he does not give a thought to self-criticism. Needless to say, he likes accountability to others much less. He does not permit anyone to question him about anything he does, because he feels it is good and, therefore, above criticism. This is the worst curse Satan invokes on man, and can be likened to a yoke he puts around his neck taking him far into error and its inevitable results.

A person who follows God's guidance is one who is careful, wary and alert. He knows that feelings change, that weakness may creep into one's heart, and that a short fall may occur. He is, therefore, always looking at his own work, wary of yielding to Satan's temptation and

200

praying for God's help. This is indeed the point of difference between right and wrong, success and failure. It is a fine psychological point which the Qur'ān describes in a few succinct words: *"How about the one whose evil deeds seem alluring to him so as to regard them as good?"* (Verse 8)

No answer is given in the *sūrah*, so as to allow every answer, such as: His is a hopeless case; How can such a person be on the same level as one who is always taking stock of his actions to ensure that he is on the right track; Can he be compared with a humble, God-fearing person. This sort of style is often used in the Qur'ān.

The Qur'ānic verse adds a statement that can be taken as implying a reply: *"God lets go astray him that wills [to go astray], just as He guides him that wills [to be guided]. Therefore, do not waste yourself sorrowing for them."* (Verse 8) It is as if we are told that such a person is doomed to be in error as a result of Satan making his evil deeds seem fair to him. It is in the nature of error and guidance that the former makes an evil action seem fair and that the latter keeps a person on the alert ensuring good work.

Therefore, *"do not waste yourself sorrowing for them. God has full knowledge of all that they do."* (Verse 8) This question of going astray or following guidance does not belong to any human being, not even God's Messenger. It belongs to God alone. It is He who changes hearts as He pleases. As He states this fact, God comforts His Messenger so that his tender heart does not sorrow too much for the unbelievers. The Prophet always grieved when he saw his people's persistence in going astray, knowing where that would lead them. Therefore, God tells him not to let his desire to make them follow guidance and recognize the truth overburden him with sorrow. God wanted him to know that this is none of his concern.

The same desire is felt by advocates of Islam. The more sincere they are in their advocacy, and the more they appreciate the goodness and beauty of their way, the keener they are that other people should see the truth for what it is and follow it. These advocates, however, would be better advised to understand what God says here to His Messenger and to act on the same. They should do their best to present their message, but they must not grieve for those who remain blind to it.

201

"*God has full knowledge of all that they do.*" (Verse 8) He sets them on the road to His guidance or lets them go astray according to what He knows of their work. He knows the truth about all their deeds and what they involve even before they do them. He determines their lot in accordance with His absolute knowledge, but he does not hold people to account until they have actually done their deeds.

3

Fashioning All Creation

It is God who sends forth the winds, so that they raise clouds, and We drive them to a dead land and thereby give life to the earth after it had been lifeless. Thus shall resurrection be. (9)

Whoever desires might and glory should know that all might and glory belong to God alone. To Him ascends all good words, and He exalts the good deed. For those who plot evil there is severe suffering in store. All their plotting will come to nothing. (10)

It is God who creates you all out of dust, then out of a gamete. He then makes you into pairs (males and females). No female conceives or gives birth without His knowledge. No one attains to old age or has his life cut short unless it be thus laid down in [God's] decree. All this is easy for God. (11)

وَٱللَّهُ ٱلَّذِىٓ أَرْسَلَ ٱلرِّيَٰحَ فَتُثِيرُ سَحَابًا فَسُقْنَٰهُ إِلَىٰ بَلَدٍ مَّيِّتٍ فَأَحْيَيْنَا بِهِ ٱلْأَرْضَ بَعْدَ مَوْتِهَا كَذَٰلِكَ ٱلنُّشُورُ ۝

مَن كَانَ يُرِيدُ ٱلْعِزَّةَ فَلِلَّهِ ٱلْعِزَّةُ جَمِيعًا إِلَيْهِ يَصْعَدُ ٱلْكَلِمُ ٱلطَّيِّبُ وَٱلْعَمَلُ ٱلصَّٰلِحُ يَرْفَعُهُۥ وَٱلَّذِينَ يَمْكُرُونَ ٱلسَّيِّئَاتِ لَهُمْ عَذَابٌ شَدِيدٌ وَمَكْرُ أُوْلَٰٓئِكَ هُوَ يَبُورُ ۝

وَٱللَّهُ خَلَقَكُم مِّن تُرَابٍ ثُمَّ مِن نُّطْفَةٍ ثُمَّ جَعَلَكُمْ أَزْوَٰجًا وَمَا تَحْمِلُ مِنْ أُنثَىٰ وَلَا تَضَعُ إِلَّا بِعِلْمِهِۦ وَمَا يُعَمَّرُ مِن مُّعَمَّرٍ وَلَا يُنقَصُ مِنْ عُمُرِهِۦٓ إِلَّا فِى كِتَٰبٍ إِنَّ ذَٰلِكَ عَلَى ٱللَّهِ يَسِيرٌ ۝

The two great bodies of water on earth are not alike: one is palatable, sweet and pleasant to drink, and the other is salty and bitter. Yet from each you eat fresh meat and extract ornaments to wear. You also see there ships that plough their course through them so that you may go in quest of some of His bounty and be grateful. (12)

وَمَا يَسْتَوِي ٱلْبَحْرَانِ هَٰذَا عَذْبٌ فُرَاتٌ سَآئِغٌ شَرَابُهُۥ وَهَٰذَا مِلْحٌ أُجَاجٌ وَمِن كُلٍّ تَأْكُلُونَ لَحْمًا طَرِيًّا وَتَسْتَخْرِجُونَ حِلْيَةً تَلْبَسُونَهَا وَتَرَى ٱلْفُلْكَ فِيهِ مَوَاخِرَ لِتَبْتَغُوا۟ مِن فَضْلِهِۦ وَلَعَلَّكُمْ تَشْكُرُونَ ﴿١٢﴾

He causes the night to pass into the day, and the day to pass into the night; and He has made the sun and the moon subservient [to His laws], each running its course for an appointed term. Thus is God, your Lord: to Him belongs all dominion, while those whom you invoke instead of Him do not own even the skin of a date-stone. (13)

يُولِجُ ٱلَّيْلَ فِي ٱلنَّهَارِ وَيُولِجُ ٱلنَّهَارَ فِي ٱلَّيْلِ وَسَخَّرَ ٱلشَّمْسَ وَٱلْقَمَرَ كُلٌّ يَجْرِي لِأَجَلٍ مُّسَمًّى ذَٰلِكُمُ ٱللَّهُ رَبُّكُمْ لَهُ ٱلْمُلْكُ وَٱلَّذِينَ تَدْعُونَ مِن دُونِهِۦ مَا يَمْلِكُونَ مِن قِطْمِيرٍ ﴿١٣﴾

If you invoke them they cannot hear your call. Even if they could hear, they would not respond to you. On the Day of Resurrection they will utterly disown your having associated them with God. None can give you information like the One who is all-aware. (14)

إِن تَدْعُوهُمْ لَا يَسْمَعُوا۟ دُعَآءَكُمْ وَلَوْ سَمِعُوا۟ مَا ٱسْتَجَابُوا۟ لَكُمْ وَيَوْمَ ٱلْقِيَٰمَةِ يَكْفُرُونَ بِشِرْكِكُمْ وَلَا يُنَبِّئُكَ مِثْلُ خَبِيرٍ ﴿١٤﴾

Overview

This third section takes us on several rounds in the great universe where the Qur'ān depicts a variety of phenomena and imagery which all confirm faith and provide irrefutable proof in support of it. This follows from the earlier discussion about guidance and going astray, and comforting the Prophet so he would not grieve over the unbelievers' constant rejection. Whoever wants to look for the truth, its evidence is available with glorious clarity everywhere in the universe. Anyone who chooses to go astray does so against such irrefutable evidence.

The image of life springing up from a dead land is clear evidence that also serves to confirm resurrection. Similar evidence can be deduced from man's creation from dust and his progression to the highly sophisticated form we know. Every stage of his creation and life goes according to predetermined measures. We see the image of the two great bodies of water, clearly distinct, yet they provide man with endless blessings for which he should show gratitude. The night and day move in a cycle that always brings one into the other, and they get longer or shorter as time moves round. The sun and the moon are also controlled within the same accurate system. All these images provide evidence about the great universal stage. All are created and controlled by God. He owns it all. The false deities that unbelievers worship own nothing whatsoever. They neither hear nor respond. On the Day of Judgement they even disown the very people who worshipped them.

The Source of All Power

It is God who sends forth the winds, so that they raise clouds, and We drive them to a dead land and thereby give life to the earth after it had been lifeless. Thus shall resurrection be. (Verse 9)

This phenomenon is frequently mentioned within the context of evidence to the truth derived from the universe. It shows the wind raising clouds. In fact hot winds make sea water evaporate, then cold winds in the atmosphere condense the vapour making clouds which are then driven in different directions by winds in the upper strata of the atmosphere. Then they arrive at the destination God has determined for them, which may be a dead land which He wants to quicken by means of the rain carried by these clouds. Indeed, water is the source of all life on this planet. *"We thereby give life to the earth after it was lifeless."* Thus the miracle occurs. It happens at every moment, but people are oblivious to its significance. Yet despite this miracle of life springing up at every moment, they continue to deny resurrection which they see happening in their world all about them. Simply and without argument, the Qur'ān says: *"Thus shall be the resurrection."*

This scene is used frequently in the Qur'ān for two reasons: first it provides tangible, undeniable evidence and secondly it has a strong influence on people's hearts and minds when they contemplate it without hindrance. Moreover, it is a beautiful image, particularly in the desert, which looks barren and lifeless today, and then gushes with life the next. In this way the Qur'ān uses the inspiration of things people see all around them. They may ignore them because of familiarity, but when they contemplate them with an alert mind and heart, they appreciate just how miraculous they are.

There is here a sudden jolt as the *sūrah* moves on to speak of might, power and dignity, linking this with good words that are welcome by God and good action that is blessed by Him. The opposite is also shown, whereby wicked scheming leads to ruin:

> *Whoever desires might and glory should know that all might and glory belong to God alone. To Him ascends all good words, and He exalts the good deed. For those who plot evil there is severe suffering in store. All their plotting will come to nothing.* (Verse 10)

Perhaps the link between life starting in what is lifeless and a good word and action is the fact that there is good life in all. There is certainly a strong relation between life and the universe. Allusion to this relation is stated in *Sūrah* 14, Abraham: *"Do you not see how God compares a good word to a good tree? Its roots are firm and its branches reach to the sky. It yields its fruits at all times by its Lord's leave. Thus does God set parables for people so that they may reflect. And an evil word is like a corrupt tree, torn up onto the face of the earth. It cannot have a stable position.*" (14: 24–26) The relation is almost real in the nature of both the word and the tree: both live and grow.

The idolaters used their idolatry to retain their religious position in Makkah, one which gave them leadership of the Arabian tribes, and which facilitated various privileges. Needless to say, the most important of these were power and glory. Hence they used to say to the Prophet: "*If we were to follow the guidance along with you, we would be torn away from our land.*" (28: 57) Therefore, God tells them: "*Whoever desires might and glory should know that all might and glory belong to God alone.*" (Verse 10)

When this fact is well established in people's hearts and minds, it ensures that values, standards, as well as means and methods undergo a complete change. The truth is that might and glory belong totally to God. No one else possesses a shred of either. Therefore, if anyone wants them, and they are incidentally expressed in one Arabic word, *ʿizzah*, which combines both and adds connotations of dignity, then they should seek them from their only source: God Almighty. They cannot be found with anyone else.

The Quraysh sought to enjoy might and glory among the Arabs through idolatrous beliefs that lacked real substance. They feared to follow divine guidance, even though they acknowledged that it was guidance, because they feared for their own status. Yet those people, the Arabian tribes and clans, were not a source of might and glory. They could not give or deny these to anyone: "*all might and glory belong to God alone.*" (Verse 10) If they enjoyed any measure of power and might, it was only because God gave them this. Therefore, anyone who wishes to have these should go to the original source, not to a recipient of that source. Recipients can only give what they have in excess. Besides, recipients are also weak and in need.

This is an essential truth of Islamic faith which establishes values, standards, judgement, behaviour, ways and means. When this truth is firmly rooted in one's heart, one does not hesitate to stand up in dignity and glory to the rest of the world, knowing from whom one derives might and glory. Such a person does not bow before any despot, storm, calamity, state, or worldly force whatsoever. Why would they when all might and glory belong to God alone, and when no one receives any portion of it without His leave?

This is the reason good words and right actions are mentioned here: "*To Him ascends all good words, and He exalts the good deed.*" (Verse 10) This is mentioned here for a purpose: it is a reference to the means by which might and glory are assured for those who seek it from God. Good words and good deeds which are allowed to ascend to God where they are received with honour that reflects on the speaker who says the good word and does the good work.

True *'izzah*, combining all connotations of dignity and glory, is first established in one's heart before it takes any form in the outside world. When it is so established, the person concerned rises above all considerations that cause humiliation and prostration before anyone other than God. He rises first of all above his own fears, desires and ambitions that may be gratified by others. When he has done this, no one will ever be able to humiliate or subjugate him. People are only humbled by their desires, fears and ambitions. Should these be held in check, that person will retain his glory and dignity in all situations and with all people. This is indeed true might, glory and dignity.

True *'izzah* is not stubbornness that seeks strength through falsehood, or tyranny that uses brutal force to silence others, or an overwhelming upsurge motivated by desire, or a blind force that pays no heed to right and justice. It is none of this. It is the ability to rise above one's own desires, rejecting fetters and humiliations, and refusing to submit to any other than God. It also means submitting only to God, fearing Him alone and obeying Him in all situations. It is through submission to God alone that our heads are raised high, and through fearing Him that we can stand up to whatever He disapproves of. Our watching Him also means that we care nothing for anything other than earning His pleasure. This then explains the relation between the good word and deed on the one hand and might, glory and dignity on the other.

The opposite picture is then given: "*For those who plot evil there is severe suffering in store. All their plotting will come to nothing.*" (Verse 10) Such people will see that their plots and schemes yield no fruit and end in failure, and that they will endure severe suffering as a result. We note here the contrasting image which brings life to a lifeless land.

These people plot evil because they are after false power and imagined glory. They may appear to have power at their command, but it is the good word and deed that ascend to God and through which we receive *'izzah* in its full sense. Evil schemes and plots cannot achieve this, even though they may occasionally be coupled with physical power. Their assured end, however, is ruin and severe suffering. This is God's promise that never fails.

Man's Creation

Having referred to the fact that all life starts with water, the *sūrah* now refers to the start of man's own life, beginning with pregnancy and followed by a term in this world, which can be long or short as God determines:

> *It is God who creates you all out of dust, then out of a gamete. He then makes you into a couple. No female conceives or gives birth without His knowledge. No one attains to old age or has his life cut short unless it be thus laid down in [God's] decree. All this is easy for God.* (Verse 11)

Reference to man's origin as a creature made from dust in the first place is often mentioned in the Qur'ān, as is the first element in producing a pregnancy, namely the gamete. While a gamete is something that carries the potential of life, dust has no trace of life. The first miracle is 'life' itself, and no one knows where it came from or how it was mixed with the first element. This remains a closed book as far as humanity is concerned. Yet it is a fact we all see and have no option but to accept and recognize. The evidence it provides, pointing to the Creator who gives life, is irrefutable.

The transformation that gives life to what is lifeless represents a bridge over a gap that is far greater than any distance in time and place. Contemplating such transformation will never tire a mind that looks at the great secrets of the universe. Again, the gap separating the stage of one cell, a gamete, from that of a fully formed embryo, when a male is distinguished from a female, is again too wide to imagine. It is to this latter stage that the Qur'ān refers in the sentence, "*He makes you into pairs (males and females),*" whether this is a reference to a couple, male and female, in the embryo stage, or to married couples after they have become adults. How far removed is the one-cell gamete from the greatly complex human constitution which includes numerous systems and functions, and also from a human being with its many characteristics?

Look at the senseless fertilized egg as it divides and multiplies, and then each group of cells it produces joining together to form a particular organ with a specific nature and function. Look how all these organs fit together and group to make a single creature which is remarkably distinct from all other creatures of the human race, including those who are most closely related to him. Thus, no two human beings are exactly and completely identical. Yet all of them come from gametes that carry no distinctive mark of any sort, or at least that we can make out. Then look at these cells and follow their way until they become couples able to restart the cycle once more, with new gametes that follow the same line and the same stages, without deviation. All this is amazing, truly wonderful. This is the reason for the repeated references in the Qur'ān to this miraculous process, or indeed processes, involving unknown secrets. People should listen to these references and set their minds thinking about this process of creation. It may awaken their spirits to its message.

Next comes an image of God's absolute knowledge, which is akin to the images given in the preceding *sūrah*, Sheba: "*No female conceives or gives birth without His knowledge.*" (Verse 11) The reference here is not merely to women, but to all females, including animals, birds, fish, reptiles, insects and others which we may or may not know about. All of them conceive and give birth, including those which lay eggs. An egg is an embryo which does not fully develop inside its mother's body. It is laid in the form of an egg, and is then incubated, either by its mother or in an incubator, until it completes its development, and breaks its shell to continue its growth. God's knowledge includes every conception, of every form, and every birth throughout the universe.

Describing God's absolute knowledge in this way is not something a human mind normally follows, neither in conception nor expression.

By itself it is proof that the Qur'ān is revelation from God: it confirms its divine source thereby.

The same applies to the reference to age in the same verse: "*No one attains to old age or has his life cut short unless it be thus laid down in [God's] decree. All this is easy for God.* (Verse 11) Let our imagination follow every living thing in the universe, including trees, birds, animals, humans and others, with their different shapes, sizes, kinds, races, abodes and times. No one can imagine the total number of all these. Yet imagine that every single one of them may be allowed to attain to old age, or may have its life cut short, and that whatever happens is according to specific knowledge concerning this individual, and indeed concerning every part of every individual. A leaf in a tree may be allowed to remain green, extending its life span, or it may dry up and fall. A bird's feather may remain in its wing or fall and be blown by the wind. A horn may remain in an animal or get broken in a quarrel. A human eye, or a hair, may stay or be removed. Yet all this occurs in accordance with specific knowledge which is '*laid down in God's decree*' that is part of His comprehensive knowledge. It neither requires an effort nor constitutes a burden: "*All this is easy for God.*" (Verse 11)

If we let our imagination follow this line and look at what it entails, our amazement is endless. It is a line that human imagination does not normally follow, nor does it normally try to understand or describe facts in this way.

The Arabic verb *nuʿammir*, which is translated as '*attain to old age*', also connotes blessing someone's life so as to use one's days and years in what is useful and beneficial, as well as filling it with feelings, actions and lasting benefits. Likewise, cutting one's life short may mean giving that person a shorter number of years to live or making his life devoid of blessing so as to spend his days producing nothing of real value. A blessed hour that is full of useful action, ideas and feelings may be equal to a complete lifetime, while a whole year may be spent without recording anything of value either in human life's measure or in God's scales. Yet everything any human being thinks or does anywhere in the universe is recorded by God.

Nations and communities are the same as individuals: they may live long or have their lives cut short. Hence, the Qur'ānic statement includes them, as indeed it includes inanimate objects, such as rocks, caves and rivers which could have a long or short life span. Likewise, man-made things, such as buildings, machines and appliances, clothes, etc., may all live long or short lives. Every life duration, of every creature and every thing, is recorded in God's book. This belongs to His absolute and infinite knowledge.

When we look at things in this light, we feel we want to contemplate the universe in a new way. Anyone who feels that God's hand and eye controls everything in such a meticulous manner will hardly ever forget or go astray. He will see God's hand, power and care in everything around him. This is the effect the Qur'ān has on people's hearts and minds.

Different Waters

The *surah* then focuses on a different phenomenon we all see, which is water and its varieties. One type of water is sweet and palatable while the other is bitter and salty. They go their separate ways, or meet together, by God's will, serving man's needs:

> The two great bodies of water on earth are not alike: one is palatable, sweet and pleasant to drink, and the other is salty and bitter. Yet from each you eat fresh meat and extract ornaments to wear. You also see there ships that plough their course through them so that you may go in quest of some of His bounty and be grateful. (Verse 12)

That God wanted water to be of different types is clear. That such variety serves a definite purpose is also something we should be clear about. We know some aspects of the wisdom behind providing sweet, palatable water, since we use it for different purposes. It is indeed essential for life. As for the other type of water, which is bitter and salty, filling seas and oceans, we may quote a few lines from a famous scientist explaining this immaculate design:

In spite of all the gaseous emanations from the earth of all the ages, most of them poisonous, the atmosphere remains practically uncontaminated and unchanging in its balanced relationship necessary to man's very existence.

The great balance wheel is that vast mass of water, the sea, from which have come life, food, rain, temperate climate, plants, animals, and ultimately man himself. Let him who comprehends this stand in awe before its majesty and gratefully acknowledge his obligations.[2]

This is some of what we have been able to understand of the purpose behind the diversity of creation. It is clear that it is all done for a specific reason aiming to achieve harmony and balance, which allows the overall system of the universe to function. This can only be done by the Creator of the universe and everything that lives in it. Such a meticulously accurate system cannot come about by sheer coincidence. The reference to the difference in the two great bodies of water suggests that, like every other variation, it is done deliberately. Later on, the *sūrah* refers to some aspects of this variety in the realm of feelings, values and standards.

The two different bodies of water are shown as united in being subjected to man: "*Yet from each you eat fresh meat and extract ornaments to wear. You also see there ships that plough their course through them.*" (Verse 12) The fresh meat refers to fish and the great variety of marine animals, while the ornaments refer to pearls and corals. Pearls are found in the body of certain bivalve molluscs. It is a hard smooth round iridescent mass, formed of layers of calcium carbonate deposited around a foreign body in the shell of these molluscs. After a while it solidifies in the form of a pearl, which is valued as a gem for its lustre. Coral is a sort of plant made by marine polyps which can become extensive reefs stretching over an area of several miles. It can also present a hazard to shipping and to any foreign creature that falls within it. It can be cut by special methods and is often used in jewellery and ornamentation.

Ships plough their way through rivers and seas, benefiting by what God has given every creature of characteristics and qualities. The density of the water and the substances used in shipbuilding is a factor in

2. A. Cressy Morrison, *Man Does Not Stand Alone*, London, Fleming H. Revell Co., 1944, p. 28.

making ships float and move. Another factor is wind. Other forces may be used to achieve this useful condition, such as electric and steam power. All are subjected to man's will by God.

"*So that you may go in quest of some of His bounty and be grateful.*" (Verse 12) Thus you may use both bodies of water to travel and do business, as also find food and nourishment. It behoves you to be grateful to God for all this bounty, which is made available to you.

This part concludes on another universal beat that mentions the alternation of day and night, and the subjection of the sun and the moon to the divine system until their appointed time: "*He causes the night to pass into the day, and the day to pass into the night; and He has made the sun and the moon subservient [to His laws], each running its course for an appointed term.*" (Verse 13) The passing of the day and the night into each other may be a reference to the two spectacular scenes when the night creeps into the day, with its light gradually diminishing and the darkness increasing until the sun has disappeared followed by the darkness moving in and slowly spreading its wings. The other scene witnesses the start of the day creeping into the night, with the first breath of dawn. The light then begins to gradually spread while the darkness bit by bit disappears. Then the sun rises and the day is resplendent with brightness. Alternatively, the Qur'ānic expression may refer to the night as it takes a bite out of the day, as if it is going into the day, and also the day getting longer as it takes one bite after another off the night. It could also mean both situations at the same time, describing them together. All these scenes have a profound effect on our hearts, spreading a feeling of awe and even fear as we see God's hand pulling one line here and relaxing one there in a fine, accurate and balanced system that does not miss a tick day after day, century after century.

Again making the sun and the moon subservient to God's law and setting them on their courses until the appointed term, known only to God, is another phenomenon that everyone of us sees. They appear and disappear, rise and set before everyone. Their unfailing movements do not require any knowledge or calculation to contemplate. They serve as signs for all generations to contemplate. We may know about them more than what the first people addressed by the Qur'ān knew, but this is not the point. What is important is that these phenomena give us the same inspiration as they gave them. They certainly motivate us to contemplate the work of God's hand in the universe.

Thus is God

Concluding these inspiring scenes, the *surah* states the truth of God's Lordship over the universe. It also states the falsehood of every claim of partnership with God, and its ultimate and miserable result on the Day of Judgement:

> *Thus is God, your Lord: to Him belongs all dominion, while those whom you invoke instead of Him do not own even the skin of a date-stone. If you invoke them they cannot hear your call. Even if they could hear, they would not respond to you. On the Day of Resurrection they will utterly disown your having associated them with God. None can give you information like the One who is all-aware.* (Verses 13–14)

The One who sends the wind driving the clouds, makes the dead land quicken, creates you out of dust, makes you in pairs, knows what each female bears and gives birth to, what gets a long life or a short one, has created the two great bodies of water, causes the day and night to pass into each other and makes the sun and the moon subservient to His law: that One is *"your Lord: to Him belongs all dominion, while those whom you invoke instead of Him do not own even the skin of a date-stone."* (Verse 13) They do not even own such a trifling thing as a date-stone.

The *surah* goes further in drawing a true image of them: *"If you invoke them they cannot hear your call."* (Verse 14) They are statues, idols, trees, stars, angels or *jinn*; and none of them actually owns the skin of a date-stone. None of them can respond to those who worship them, but, *"Even if they could hear, they would not respond to you."* (Verse 14) This applies, for example, to the *jinn* and the angels. The *jinn* cannot respond, while the angels do not respond to those who have gone astray. All this is relevant to this present life, but on the Day of Judgement they disassociate themselves from error and those who follow it: "*On the Day of Resurrection they will utterly disown your having associated them with God.*" (Verse 14) This is stated by the One who knows everything in this life and beyond it, who overlooks nothing in the universe now or in the life to come: "*None can give you information like the One who is all-aware.*" (Verse 14)

So does this passage conclude. It only remains to be said that it gives any human mind enough to last a lifetime. Indeed, it is sufficient for any human heart to listen carefully to a single passage of any *sūrah* if he is seeking proof and searching for guidance.

4

Individual Responsibility

People! It is you who stand in need of God, whereas He alone is free of all wants, worthy of all praise. (15)

يَـٰٓأَيُّهَا ٱلنَّاسُ أَنتُمُ ٱلۡفُقَرَآءُ إِلَى ٱللَّهِ ۖ وَٱللَّهُ هُوَ ٱلۡغَنِيُّ ٱلۡحَمِيدُ ﴿١٥﴾

If He so wishes, He can do away with you and bring in your place a new creation; (16)

إِن يَشَأۡ يُذۡهِبۡكُمۡ وَيَأۡتِ بِخَلۡقٍ جَدِيدٍ ﴿١٦﴾

this is not difficult for God. (17)

وَمَا ذَٰلِكَ عَلَى ٱللَّهِ بِعَزِيزٍ ﴿١٧﴾

No soul will bear the burden of another. If a heavily laden soul should call upon others for help, nothing of its load shall be carried by anyone, not even by a close relative. Hence, you can truly warn only those who stand in awe of their Lord, even though He is beyond the reach of their perception, and attend regularly to prayers. Whoever purifies himself does so for his own benefit. With God is all journeys' end. (18)

وَلَا تَزِرُ وَازِرَةٌ وِزۡرَ أُخۡرَىٰ ۚ وَإِن تَدۡعُ مُثۡقَلَةٌ إِلَىٰ حِمۡلِهَا لَا يُحۡمَلۡ مِنۡهُ شَيۡءٌ وَلَوۡ كَانَ ذَا قُرۡبَىٰٓ ۗ إِنَّمَا تُنذِرُ ٱلَّذِينَ يَخۡشَوۡنَ رَبَّهُم بِٱلۡغَيۡبِ وَأَقَامُواْ ٱلصَّلَوٰةَ ۚ وَمَن تَزَكَّىٰ فَإِنَّمَا يَتَزَكَّىٰ لِنَفۡسِهِۦ ۚ وَإِلَى ٱللَّهِ ٱلۡمَصِيرُ ﴿١٨﴾

217

The blind and the seeing are not equal; (19)

وَمَا يَسْتَوِى ٱلْأَعْمَىٰ وَٱلْبَصِيرُ ﴿١٩﴾

nor are darkness and light; (20)

وَلَا ٱلظُّلُمَٰتُ وَلَا ٱلنُّورُ ﴿٢٠﴾

nor the [cooling] shade and the scorching heat; (21)

وَلَا ٱلظِّلُّ وَلَا ٱلْحَرُورُ ﴿٢١﴾

and neither are equal the living and the dead. God can make hear whoever He wills, whereas you cannot make those who are in their graves hear you. (22)

وَمَا يَسْتَوِى ٱلْأَحْيَآءُ وَلَا ٱلْأَمْوَٰتُ إِنَّ ٱللَّهَ يُسْمِعُ مَن يَشَآءُ وَمَآ أَنتَ بِمُسْمِعٍ مَّن فِى ٱلْقُبُورِ ﴿٢٢﴾

You are only a warner. (23)

إِنْ أَنتَ إِلَّا نَذِيرٌ ﴿٢٣﴾

We have sent you with the truth, as a bearer of happy news and a warner. There was never a community that has not had a warner. (24)

إِنَّآ أَرْسَلْنَٰكَ بِٱلْحَقِّ بَشِيرًا وَنَذِيرًا وَإِن مِّنْ أُمَّةٍ إِلَّا خَلَا فِيهَا نَذِيرٌ ﴿٢٤﴾

If they accuse you of lying, other communities before them made similar accusations when there came to them messengers with all evidence of the truth, and with books of divine wisdom, and with light-giving revelations; (25)

وَإِن يُكَذِّبُوكَ فَقَدْ كَذَّبَ ٱلَّذِينَ مِن قَبْلِهِمْ جَآءَتْهُمْ رُسُلُهُم بِٱلْبَيِّنَٰتِ وَبِٱلزُّبُرِ وَبِٱلْكِتَٰبِ ٱلْمُنِيرِ ﴿٢٥﴾

but in the end I took the unbelievers to task: how terrible was My condemnation. (26)

Overview

Once more the *sūrah* urges people to look at their relation with God and at themselves. It also comforts the Prophet, seeking to alleviate his distress at their rejection of his message. This is in fact a continuation of the previous passage, but the *sūrah* adds here a reference to the nature of following divine guidance and the nature of going astray. It makes it clear that the difference between them is as profound as the difference between blindness and sight, light and darkness, coolness and scorching heat, life and death. It asserts that following divine guidance, having eyesight, light, cooling shade and being alive are similar, interlinked. Likewise, blindness, darkness, excessive heat and death are similar, interlinked. The passage ends with a reference to the fate met by earlier communities, serving as a warning.

Replaceable Creation

People! It is you who stand in need of God, whereas He alone is free of all wants, worthy of all praise. If He so wishes, He can do away with you and bring in your place a new creation; this is not difficult for God. (Verses 15–17)

People need to be reminded of this truth within the context of God's message, inviting them to accept and follow it, and urging them to abandon the darkness they are in to emerge into the light of His guidance. They need to be reminded that they are in need of God, while He has no need of them or of anyone else. When they are invited to believe in God, worship Him and praise Him for His bounty and favours, they must remember that He has no need for such worship and praise, because He is the Praised One. They are not immune to whatever God wishes of them. Should He wish, He can take them away and replace them by a new creation, either of their own type or of a totally different type. It is all so easy for Him.

People need to be reminded of this so that they do not give themselves airs. They need to be reminded that God in His limitless glory takes care of them and sends them messengers who strive hard to bring them out of the darkness into the light. They should not feel themselves too important for God, or that their worship or their following His message will increase His kingdom in any way. God is indeed free of all wants and worthy of all praise. God Almighty bestows such great care and mercy on His servants, and adds to this by sending them His messengers who suffer much hardship from those who reject His divine message. It is all part of His essential attributes to give in abundance and without reckoning. The recipients, mere humans, do not contribute anything to God's kingdom by following His guidance, nor do they decrease it in any way when they turn blindly away from it. They are not irreplaceable.

What man receives of God's grace is amazing, considering how man is so small, ignorant and weak a creature. Man is then but a small creature on earth which, in turn, is a small satellite of the sun, which is one of countless stars. Gigantic as they are, stars are no more than small dots scattered in open space, the limits of which are known only to God. Yet this great space in which the stars are thus scattered is merely a small portion of God's creation. Yet man receives all this care from God: He creates him, puts him in charge of the earth, equips him with all he needs to discharge his task, be these in his own constitution or in the things of the universe available to him. Yet this creature goes astray and becomes arrogant to the extent that he denies his Lord, but God nevertheless sends him one messenger after another, giving each books of guidance as well as miracles. God's favours continue and He sends them His final message, in which He gives them accounts of what happened to earlier communities, and speaks to them about themselves, their abilities and potentials, as well as their frailties and weaknesses. He even speaks to particular individuals, saying to one, 'you did this, and you omitted that,' and saying to another, 'here is the solution to your problem, and this is how you relieve your distress.'

Man should remember his position in the universe and reflect upon the fact that he has been given all this care by God. It is He who created this universe, with all that it contains, by merely willing it to be, and He can replace it all in the same way. People should consider this so they appreciate the extent of God's care and grace. They will then feel ashamed if they turn away from God and deny Him and His grace. Thus we see that these verses represent a confirmed truth in addition to their inspirational effect. The Qur'ān touches people's hearts with hard facts, because fact and truth have a greater effect. Moreover, the Qur'ān is the word of truth, and it was bestowed from on high to lay down this truth. In short, it states nothing but the truth.

Everyone on Their Own

The *sūrah* then emphasizes individual responsibility, which means that everyone will have what they deserve. No one benefits anyone else in any way. The Prophet has no personal interest in guiding people to the truth. Everyone bears his or her own burden, alone, without help. Therefore a person who seeks to be pure will be the only one to benefit from this endeavour. The matter is ultimately left to God to determine:

> No soul will bear the burden of another. If a heavily laden soul should call upon others for help, nothing of its load shall be carried by anyone, not even by a close relative... Whoever purifies himself does so for his own benefit. With God is all journeys' end. (Verse 18)

The fact of individual responsibility and reward has a decisive effect on morality and behaviour. When people are fully aware that they are rewarded according to their own deeds, that none will be responsible for anyone else, and that none can escape responsibility, they realize the need to take stock of their actions before they have to answer for them. At the same time, this is reassuring, because no individual needs to worry about answering for the actions of his community. As long as he has done his duty, giving advice to his community to follow divine guidance, no further responsibility is laid on him. God Almighty does not hold mankind to account for their collective actions. They account to Him individually, each for their own work. It is the duty of the individual to advise others and try hard to bring them into line. Once he has done this, however, he bears no responsibility for their wickedness or corruption. He will be credited for his own good work. Similarly, if he lives in a good community, its goodness will not benefit him if he himself is wicked.

We see, then, an image of a multitude, each person carrying his or her own burden, with none able to help others. Even if someone requests help from the closest of relatives, none will oblige. It is thus a long queue, with people carrying loads and moving towards the check-point where the load will be weighed. Everyone is tired, preoccupied with the heaviness of their load, unable to think of others, even their own kin.

At this point, the *sūrah's* address is directed to the Prophet: "*Hence, you can truly warn only those who stand in awe of their Lord, even though He is beyond the reach of their perception, and attend regularly to prayers.*" (Verse 18) It is such people that can really appreciate the warning: they are the ones who fear God even though they have not seen Him, and who attend to their worship so as to maintain relations with Him. The Prophet is told that these are the ones to benefit by admonition. Others, who have no fear of God, need not worry him.

"*Whoever purifies himself does so for his own benefit.*" No one receives the benefit of purification except the one who does it. Moreover, purification has pleasant and transparent connotations that apply to one's heart, thoughts, feelings, behaviour and attitudes. "*With God is all journeys' end.*" (Verse 18) He is the one who reckons people's actions and rewards them accordingly. Nothing good or evil is overlooked.

Needless to say, with God belief and unbelief, good and evil, guidance and error cannot be treated on an equal basis. In the same way, blindness and sight, darkness and light, coolness and heat, life and death are unequal. All have essentially different qualities:

> *The blind and the seeing are not equal; nor are darkness and light; nor the [cooling] shade and the scorching heat; and neither are equal the living and the dead.* (Verses 19–22)

There is a close link between the nature of unbelief and the nature of blindness, darkness, scorching heat and death, just as there is a contrasting link between the nature of belief and that of clear sight, light, cool shade and life.

Faith is a light that penetrates into the heart, the senses and perceptions so as to give a true assessment of things, values, events and how they interact. A believer looks at things in this light, which is God's light, and determines how to approach and deal with them in an assured, confident way. Faith also provides a believer with a quality of sight that gives a clear picture of things that is neither hazy nor blurred. Furthermore, it provides a cooling shade in which a believer can take refuge from the burning heat of anxiety, doubt and worry. Faith is a light that touches hearts, feelings and purposes, and it is constructive action that never stops to build, allowing no waste.

By contrast, unbelief is blindness. It prevents people from seeing the evidence in support of faith and recognizing the true nature of the universe, its relations, values, and events. It is also a darkness: when people move away from the light of faith, they fall into different types of darkness making it difficult for them to see things with any degree of accuracy. Furthermore, unbelief is a hot desert where burning doubts and worry over one's origin and destiny compound to eventually lead the unbeliever to the fire of hell. Finally, unbelief is death because it separates the unbeliever from the true source of life, making him unable to interact in any way that promotes life. Each type has its distinctive nature, and its special reward. The two cannot be equal in God's sight.

At this point the *surah* addresses the Prophet, comforting him and outlining his terms of reference. He is to do what has been assigned to him and leave matters to God. It is He who will do whatever He determines.

God can make hear whoever He wills, whereas you cannot make those who are in their graves hear you. You are only a warner. We have sent you with the truth, as a bearer of happy news and a warner. There was never a community that has not had a warner. If they accuse you of lying, other communities before them made similar accusations when there came to them messengers with all evidence of the truth, and with books of divine wisdom, and with light-giving revelations; but in the end I took the unbelievers to task: how terrible was My condemnation. (Verses 22–26)

Differences between opposites, whether in the universe or within the human soul, are clear and deeply rooted. Similarly genuine and firm are the differences between people and the way they receive God's message. It all refers to God's will, purpose, wisdom and power. God's Messenger, then, is no more than a warner. His human task is limited to this. He cannot make grave dwellers hear him. Those who live with dead hearts are in the same position: cold and gravelike. It is God alone who can make hear whomever He wills, in the way He chooses. Why should the Prophet, then, worry about who chooses to go astray, about who turns away from divine guidance. All he has to do is to discharge the duties assigned to him to the best of his abilities. Once he has delivered his message, let people choose whether to respond or not.

Earlier in the *sūrah*, God says to the Prophet: "*do not waste yourself sorrowing for them.*" (Verse 8) God sent him, like his brothers the earlier messengers, with the truth. They were many, because: "*There was never a community that has not had a warner.*" (Verse 24) If he is met with rejection and people accuse him of lying, this is all in the nature of things, and earlier messengers met the same type of reception, through no fault of theirs, or lack of supporting evidence: "*If they accuse you of lying, other communities before them made similar accusations when there came to them messengers with all evidence of the truth, and with books of divine wisdom, and with light-giving revelations.*" (Verse 25) Such evidence could be of various types, including the miracles they demanded or were given to God's messengers in support of their messages. The books refer to whatever different prophets were given of wisdom, directives and admonition. The *'light-giving revelations'* refer most probably to the Torah. Yet such communities denied it all.

There was thus nothing new in how the Prophet Muḥammad (peace be upon him) was received. Therefore, the *sūrah* mentions the fate of earlier communities to warn the new unbelievers: "*But in the end I took the unbelievers to task.*" (Verse 26) This is followed by a question that gives a sense of gravity and intimates the most horrible of ends: "*How terrible was My condemnation.*" (Verse 26) The condemnation was final, one whereby the unbelievers met their total destruction. Those latter day unbelievers should therefore take the warning seriously and make sure that they do not meet the same fate.

224

5

Reciters of God's Revelations

Are you not aware that God sends down water from the skies, with which We bring forth fruits of different colours? In the mountains there are streaks of white and red of various shades, as well as others jet-black. (27)

أَلَمْ تَرَ أَنَّ ٱللَّهَ أَنزَلَ مِنَ ٱلسَّمَآءِ مَآءً فَأَخْرَجْنَا بِهِۦ ثَمَرَٰتٍ مُّخْتَلِفًا أَلْوَٰنُهَا وَمِنَ ٱلْجِبَالِ جُدَدٌۢ بِيضٌ وَحُمْرٌ مُّخْتَلِفٌ أَلْوَٰنُهَا وَغَرَابِيبُ سُودٌ ۝

Similarly, human beings, beasts and cattle have various colours. It is those who are endowed with knowledge that stand truly in awe of God. Indeed God is Almighty, Much-Forgiving. (28)

وَمِنَ ٱلنَّاسِ وَٱلدَّوَآبِّ وَٱلْأَنْعَٰمِ مُخْتَلِفٌ أَلْوَٰنُهُۥ كَذَٰلِكَ إِنَّمَا يَخْشَى ٱللَّهَ مِنْ عِبَادِهِ ٱلْعُلَمَٰٓؤُاْ إِنَّ ٱللَّهَ عَزِيزٌ غَفُورٌ ۝

Those who recite God's book, attend regularly to prayer, and give in charity, secretly and openly, from what We have provided for them, look forward to a bargain that can never fail, (29)

إِنَّ ٱلَّذِينَ يَتْلُونَ كِتَٰبَ ٱللَّهِ وَأَقَامُواْ ٱلصَّلَوٰةَ وَأَنفَقُواْ مِمَّا رَزَقْنَٰهُمْ سِرًّا وَعَلَانِيَةً يَرْجُونَ تِجَٰرَةً لَّن تَبُورَ ۝

for He will grant them their just rewards, and give them yet more out of His bounty. He is indeed Much-Forgiving, most thankful. (30)

وَٱلَّذِىٓ أَوۡحَيۡنَآ إِلَيۡكَ مِنَ ٱلۡكِتَٰبِ هُوَ ٱلۡحَقُّ مُصَدِّقٗا لِّمَا بَيۡنَ يَدَيۡهِۚ إِنَّ ٱللَّهَ بِعِبَادِهِۦ لَخَبِيرُۢ بَصِيرٞ ﴿٣١﴾

The book that We have revealed to you is the truth confirming previous scriptures. Of His servants God is well-aware, all-seeing. (31)

ثُمَّ أَوۡرَثۡنَا ٱلۡكِتَٰبَ ٱلَّذِينَ ٱصۡطَفَيۡنَا مِنۡ عِبَادِنَاۖ فَمِنۡهُمۡ ظَالِمٞ لِّنَفۡسِهِۦ وَمِنۡهُم مُّقۡتَصِدٞ وَمِنۡهُمۡ سَابِقُۢ بِٱلۡخَيۡرَٰتِ بِإِذۡنِ ٱللَّهِۚ ذَٰلِكَ هُوَ ٱلۡفَضۡلُ ٱلۡكَبِيرُ ﴿٣٢﴾

We have given this Book to such of Our servants as We choose: among them are some who wrong their own souls, some follow a middle course; and some who, by God's leave, are foremost in deeds of goodness. That is the greatest favour. (32)

جَنَّٰتُ عَدۡنٖ يَدۡخُلُونَهَا يُحَلَّوۡنَ فِيهَا مِنۡ أَسَاوِرَ مِن ذَهَبٖ وَلُؤۡلُؤٗاۖ وَلِبَاسُهُمۡ فِيهَا حَرِيرٞ ﴿٣٣﴾

Gardens of bliss will they enter, where they will be adorned with bracelets of gold and pearls, and where they will be clad in silk garments. (33)

وَقَالُواْ ٱلۡحَمۡدُ لِلَّهِ ٱلَّذِىٓ أَذۡهَبَ عَنَّا ٱلۡحَزَنَۖ إِنَّ رَبَّنَا لَغَفُورٞ شَكُورٌ ﴿٣٤﴾

They will say: 'All praise is due to God, who has removed all sorrow from us. Our Lord is certainly Much-Forgiving, most appreciative. (34)

It is He who, out of His bounty, has settled us in this abode of permanent life, where we shall endure neither toil nor fatigue.' (35)

ٱلَّذِىٓ أَحَلَّنَا دَارَ ٱلْمُقَامَةِ مِن فَضْلِهِۦ لَا يَمَسُّنَا فِيهَا نَصَبٌ وَلَا يَمَسُّنَا فِيهَا لُغُوبٌ ﴿٣٥﴾

As for the unbelievers, the fire of hell awaits them. No term shall be determined for them so that they could die, nor shall its suffering be reduced for them. Thus shall We requite all unbelievers. (36)

وَٱلَّذِينَ كَفَرُوا۟ لَهُمْ نَارُ جَهَنَّمَ لَا يُقْضَىٰ عَلَيْهِمْ فَيَمُوتُوا۟ وَلَا يُخَفَّفُ عَنْهُم مِّنْ عَذَابِهَا كَذَٰلِكَ نَجْزِى كُلَّ كَفُورٍ ﴿٣٦﴾

There they will cry aloud: 'Our Lord! Let us out and we will do good, not like what we did before.' 'Have We not given you lives long enough for anyone who would be warned to take warning? And a warner had come to you. Taste it, then. Wrong-doers shall have none to support them.' (37)

وَهُمْ يَصْطَرِخُونَ فِيهَا رَبَّنَآ أَخْرِجْنَا نَعْمَلْ صَٰلِحًا غَيْرَ ٱلَّذِى كُنَّا نَعْمَلُ أَوَلَمْ نُعَمِّرْكُم مَّا يَتَذَكَّرُ فِيهِ مَن تَذَكَّرَ وَجَآءَكُمُ ٱلنَّذِيرُ فَذُوقُوا۟ فَمَا لِلظَّٰلِمِينَ مِن نَّصِيرٍ ﴿٣٧﴾

God knows all that is hidden in the heavens and earth; He fully knows what is in people's hearts. (38)

إِنَّ ٱللَّهَ عَٰلِمُ غَيْبِ ٱلسَّمَٰوَٰتِ وَٱلْأَرْضِ إِنَّهُۥ عَلِيمٌۢ بِذَاتِ ٱلصُّدُورِ ﴿٣٨﴾

Overview

This new passage is composed of readings from the book of the universe and the revealed book. We look at the wonderful pages of this book: its great variety of colours, species and kinds; fruits of every colour; mountains with colourful passages, as also people, animals and cattle of different hues. It is a highly effective touch, drawing our attention to the wonderful and natural world of colour that we tend to overlook.

The passage adds readings from God's revealed book, confirming the truth it contains and an endorsement of what had gone before it of revelations. It speaks about how this book has been granted to the Muslim community as its rightful legacy, making it clear that the heirs are of different classes, but that they all expect to receive God's pardon and forgiveness of sins. An image of their enjoyment of God's favours in the life to come is painted to contrast with an image of what awaits the unbelievers of punishment. This round, rich in colour, is concluded by a statement that all takes place in accordance with God's knowledge.

Colour in All Creation

Are you not aware that God sends down water from the skies, with which We bring forth fruits of different colours? In the mountains there are streaks of white and red of various shades, as well as others jet-black. Similarly, human beings, beasts and cattle have various colours. It is those who are endowed with knowledge that stand truly in awe of God. Indeed God is Almighty, Much-Forgiving.
(Verses 27–28)

This is a remarkable touch confirming the source of the Qur'ān. It looks at the entire world with a special focus on colour, pointing out its great variety in fruits, mountains, people, animals and cattle. It only takes a few words to group together animate and inanimate objects throughout the earth, leaving us in full amazement at this wonderful exhibition.

It all begins with water being sent down from the skies, and the fruits that it brings forth with their rich variety of hue. Because the exhibition intended here concentrates on visual imagery, the only quality given to the fruits is their colour: "*We bring forth fruits of different colours.*" (Verse 27) The colours of these fruits combine a grading that cannot be reproduced, even partially, by any painter. No two types of fruits are of the same colour. In fact, no two pieces of the same type of fruit are identical in colour. Good scrutiny will reveal variation even on such a scale.

The *sūrah* then switches, almost suddenly, to refer to the colours of mountains. A close palette study, however, shows that this is a perfectly natural switch. There is a close similarity between the richness of colour in fruits and its richness in mountain rocks. Some rocks may even resemble fruit both in shape and in size, so that they can sometimes be mistaken for fruit. "*In the mountains there are streaks of white and red of various shades, as well as others jet-black.*" (Verse 27) The 'streaks' refer to lines and courses in mountains. The text here refers to a fine point: the white lines contain different shades of whiteness, while the red ones contain different red shades, and both differ in the richness of colour and in the mix of other colours that give them their special appeal. There are other streaks of very black colour.

The switch to this colour diversity in rocks, after having highlighted such diversity in fruits has a profound effect. It alerts in us a refined sense of the aesthetic which sees beauty in a rock just as it appreciates it in a fruit, despite the great difference between the two in nature and function. In this way we are reminded to better appreciate our surroundings, not least their aesthetic beauty.

The *sūrah* also mentions people's colours, which are not limited to the major categories that distinguish different racial groups. Indeed every human being has a distinctive colour separating him or her from the rest of their race. Indeed, it distinguishes each twin from the other. The same applies to animals and cattle. Cattle, which include camels, cows, sheep and goats, are mentioned as a separate category of fauna because they are much closer to man. They also demonstrate a similarly great diversity of colour.

The universe is thus shown as a splendidly colourful book which the Qur'ān opens and looks through. It then says that scholars who read, appreciate and comprehend this book are the ones who have a true God-fearing sense: *"It is those who are endowed with knowledge that stand truly in awe of God."* (Verse 28) The universe is a superb book of which the *sūrah* has shown but a few pages. It takes a good measure of knowledge to appreciate this wonderful book and to get to truly know God through His creation and power. People who do so realize the measure of His greatness by appreciating His work. Therefore, they are truly God-fearing, and they worship Him in true submission. This is not the result of a mysterious feeling that we sometimes experience when we look at a splendid natural scene; rather, it is the product of true and direct knowledge. The pages of this universal book that the *sūrah* has shown are only a sample. The great diversity of colour it has mentioned serves only as an indicator of the great variety and meticulous harmony available everywhere in the universe. It can however only be appreciated by people endowed with knowledge and by those who feel the value of their knowledge deep in their hearts, and who do not leave it in a cold, dry academic corner.

The aesthetic element is intentionally added into the design of the universe. Its beauty, however, is raised to perfection by the fact that different things discharge their functions through that very beauty. The splendid colours of flowers, along with their scents, attract bees and butterflies which, as far as the flower is concerned, are the means of inoculation, so as to ensure fruition. Thus the flower completes its own function through its very beauty. In sex, beauty is the main attraction which leads to the couple fulfilling their task of reproduction. Because beauty is intended, the Qur'ān draws our attentions to it in these various ways.

"Indeed God is Almighty, Much-Forgiving." (Verse 28) He is certainly able to create all sorts of fine and beautiful creatures, as also to requite people for their actions. At the same time, He forgives much, overlooking the mistakes of those who fall short of appreciating His beautiful work.

The Revealed Book

Having looked at these pages of the book of the universe, the *sūrah* turns to the revealed book and those who recite it, their hopes and expected rewards:

> *Those who recite God's book, attend regularly to prayer, and give in charity, secretly and openly, from what We have provided for them, look forward to a bargain that can never fail, for He will grant them their just rewards, and give them yet more out of His bounty. He is indeed Much-Forgiving, most thankful.* (Verses 29–30)

Reciting God's book means something other than going through its words, vocalizing them or not; it means reading with reflection that leads to understanding, action and behaviour. This also entails attending regularly to prayer, giving secretly and openly in charity, as well as entertaining the hope that what is so offered will never be a failed bargain. Those who do all this know that what God has in store is far more valuable than what they give away. As they give only for God's sake, dealing with Him directly, their bargain is especially profitable. Ultimately, they will receive their reward in full, coupled with an increase of God's bounty. For, "*He is indeed Much-Forgiving, most thankful.*" (Verse 30) He forgives shortfalls and appreciates good action. His being thankful refers to what is normally associated with gratitude for pleasure and fine reward. Yet the verse inspires us to be grateful to Him who bestows His favours on us. If He appreciates what His servants do and thanks them for it, should they not then show their gratitude for all He gives them?

This is followed by a reference to the nature of God's revealed book and the truth it contains, as a prelude to speaking about those who are the heirs to this book:

> *The book that We have revealed to you is the truth confirming previous scriptures. Of His servants God is well-aware, all-seeing.* (Verse 31)

The evidence of the truth in this book is clear in its make up. The Qur'ān is an accurate translation of the universe in its true nature, or we can say that it is the spoken page while the universe is the silent page. Moreover, it confirms the books revealed earlier from the same source. The truth is one; it cannot be multiple. The One who revealed it to mankind knows them well, knows what suits them and improves their lot: "*Of His servants God is well-aware, all-seeing.*" (Verse 31)

Such is this book, and God has given it to the Muslim community as its heritage. He has chosen this community to be its heir, as He states in His book: "*We have given this Book to such of Our servants as We choose.*" (Verse 32) The Muslim community should know from these words that it has been given a position of honour by God. It should also realize that the responsibility it shoulders as a result is of great importance. It is a responsibility which assigns duties that have to be fulfilled. Will the Muslim community listen and respond?

God has honoured the Muslim community. He has chosen it to be the heir to His message, and He has graced it with a favourable reward, even for those who do not perform well:

> *We have given this Book to such of Our servants as We choose: among them are some who wrong their own souls, some follow a middle course; and some who, by God's leave, are foremost in deeds of goodness.* (Verse 32)

The group mentioned first, probably because it is the majority, are the ones who '*wrong their own souls,*' by doing more bad things than good, and the second have a balance between the two, following '*a middle course,*' while the third are '*foremost in deeds of goodness,*' having a preponderance of these. However, God's grace is bestowed on all three, leading them all to heaven where they experience the bliss described in the verses that follow. We will not go into any further detail here, preferring to leave the discussion with the idea conveyed by the verse, making it clear that the Muslim community head to this end in its entirety by God's grace:

> *That is the greatest favour. Gardens of bliss will they enter, where they will be adorned with bracelets of gold and pearls, and where they will be clad in silk garments. They will say: 'All praise is due to God, who has removed all sorrow from us. Our Lord is certainly*

Much-Forgiving, most appreciative. It is He who, out of His bounty, has settled us in this abode of permanent life, where we shall endure neither toil nor fatigue. (Verses 32–35)

These verses give us an image of material comfort and psychological bliss. They are '*adorned with bracelets of gold and pearls, and they will be clad in silk garments,*' which are aspects of the material comfort that satisfies some of what people desire. Coupled with this are feelings of security, reassurance and gratification: "*They will say: All praise is due to God, who has removed all sorrow from us.*" (Verse 34) This present life, with all that it involves of worry about the future and all its struggles, counts as sorrow when it is compared to the enduring bliss in heaven. Moreover, the worry each individual experiences on the Day of Judgement concerning their fate is also a source of great sorrow. "*Our Lord is certainly Much-Forgiving, most appreciative.*" (Verse 34) He has forgiven us our sins and appreciated our work, rewarding us well for it. "*It is He who has settled us in this abode of permanent life,*" where we shall permanently reside. It is all '*out of His bounty*'. We have no right to claim. It is He who gives it all by His grace. "*Where we shall endure neither toil nor fatigue.*" (Verse 35) There we have all we need: comfort, bliss and reassurance.

The ambience generated here is one of ease, comfort and bliss. The words are chosen for their sound so as to enhance such feelings. Heaven is described as the '*abode of permanent life*' while toil and fatigue do not come near them. In this way the music of these verses is slow and soft.

On the other side we see the unbelievers wracked with worry, lacking confidence, and unable to see an end to their troubles: "*As for the unbelievers, the fire of hell awaits them. No term shall be determined for them so that they could die, nor shall its suffering be reduced for them.*" (Verse 36) Not even the comfort of death is granted them. "*Thus shall We requite all unbelievers.*" (Verse 36) Then we begin to hear loud, harsh voices. The echoes are mixed, the wailing confused, and it comes from those who have been thrown into hell: "*There they will cry aloud.*" What are these harsh voices saying, then? They say: "*Our Lord! Let us out and we will do good, not like what we did before.*"

(Verse 37) This is an expression of regret for what they did in the past, but it is all too late. Hence, the reply carries a strong reproach: "*Have We not given you lives long enough for anyone who would be warned to take warning?*" (Verse 37) You did not benefit from the duration of your lives on earth, which was enough for anyone who wished to heed the warnings. "*And a warner had come to you.*" This was in addition to the warnings. Yet you paid no heed. "*Taste it, then. Wrongdoers shall have none to support them.*" (Verse 37)

These are two contrasting images: one of peace, comfort and security and the other full of worry and insecurity. The melodious sound of gratitude to God and of praying to Him is contrasted with screams and cries for help. The image of care and honour shown to the believers is the opposite of the neglect and reproach the unbelievers experience. The soft and quiet rhythm contrasts with the violent rhythm. Thus the comparison is complete, and overall harmony is maintained both in detail and in general atmosphere.

We then have a comment on all these scenes and images, as well as what has preceded them of choosing the Muslim community for its task: "*God knows all that is hidden in the heavens and earth; He fully knows what is in people's hearts.*" (Verse 38)

It is God who knows everything in the universe and what is in people's hearts. On the basis of His knowledge, He judges all matters.

6

The Fate of Evil Design

It is He who made you inherit the earth. Hence, anyone who denies the truth will bear the consequences of his unbelief. In denying Him the unbelievers will have nothing but an increase of their loathsomeness in God's sight; and in denying Him the unbelievers will only add to their loss. (39)

هُوَ ٱلَّذِى جَعَلَكُمْ خَلَٰٓئِفَ فِى ٱلْأَرْضِ فَمَن كَفَرَ فَعَلَيْهِ كُفْرُهُۥ وَلَا يَزِيدُ ٱلْكَٰفِرِينَ كُفْرُهُمْ عِندَ رَبِّهِمْ إِلَّا مَقْتًا وَلَا يَزِيدُ ٱلْكَٰفِرِينَ كُفْرُهُمْ إِلَّا خَسَارًا ۝

Say: 'Have you considered those beings whom you claim to be partners with God and whom you call upon beside Him? Show me what it is that they have created on earth! Or do they have a share in the heavens?' Have We ever vouchsafed them a book on which they could rely as evidence? No. What the unbelievers promise one another is nothing but delusion. (40)

قُلْ أَرَءَيْتُمْ شُرَكَآءَكُمُ ٱلَّذِينَ تَدْعُونَ مِن دُونِ ٱللَّهِ أَرُونِى مَاذَا خَلَقُوا۟ مِنَ ٱلْأَرْضِ أَمْ لَهُمْ شِرْكٌ فِى ٱلسَّمَٰوَٰتِ أَمْ ءَاتَيْنَٰهُمْ كِتَٰبًا فَهُمْ عَلَىٰ بَيِّنَتٍ مِّنْهُ بَلْ إِن يَعِدُ ٱلظَّٰلِمُونَ بَعْضُهُم بَعْضًا إِلَّا غُرُورًا ۝

It is God alone who holds the celestial bodies and the earth, lest they deviate [from their courses]. If they should ever deviate, no one else could uphold them after Him. He is indeed Ever-Forbearing, Much-Forgiving. (41)

إِنَّ ٱللَّهَ يُمْسِكُ ٱلسَّمَوَٰتِ وَٱلْأَرْضَ أَن تَزُولَا ۚ وَلَئِن زَالَتَا إِنْ أَمْسَكَهُمَا مِنْ أَحَدٍ مِّنۢ بَعْدِهِۦٓ ۚ إِنَّهُۥ كَانَ حَلِيمًا غَفُورًا ﴿٤١﴾

They swear by God with their most solemn oaths that if a warner should ever come to them, they would follow his guidance better than some other community, but when a warner did come to them, they turned away with increased aversion, (42)

وَأَقْسَمُوا۟ بِٱللَّهِ جَهْدَ أَيْمَٰنِهِمْ لَئِن جَآءَهُمْ نَذِيرٌ لَّيَكُونُنَّ أَهْدَىٰ مِنْ إِحْدَى ٱلْأُمَمِ ۖ فَلَمَّا جَآءَهُمْ نَذِيرٌ مَّا زَادَهُمْ إِلَّا نُفُورًا ﴿٤٢﴾

behaving arrogantly in the land and plotting evil. Yet such evil scheming will engulf none but its authors. Can they expect anything but the way of those unbelievers of old times? No change will you ever find in God's ways; no deviation will you ever find there. (43)

ٱسْتِكْبَارًا فِى ٱلْأَرْضِ وَمَكْرَ ٱلسَّيِّئِ ۚ وَلَا يَحِيقُ ٱلْمَكْرُ ٱلسَّيِّئُ إِلَّا بِأَهْلِهِۦ ۚ فَهَلْ يَنظُرُونَ إِلَّا سُنَّتَ ٱلْأَوَّلِينَ ۚ فَلَن تَجِدَ لِسُنَّتِ ٱللَّهِ تَبْدِيلًا ۖ وَلَن تَجِدَ لِسُنَّتِ ٱللَّهِ تَحْوِيلًا ﴿٤٣﴾

Have they not travelled in the land and seen what happened in the end to those before them, even though they were much mightier than them? God can never be foiled by anything whatever in the heavens and the earth. He is All-Knowing, infinite in His power. (44)

أَوَلَمْ يَسِيرُوا۟ فِى ٱلْأَرْضِ فَيَنظُرُوا۟ كَيْفَ كَانَ عَٰقِبَةُ ٱلَّذِينَ مِن قَبْلِهِمْ وَكَانُوٓا۟ أَشَدَّ مِنْهُمْ قُوَّةً ۚ وَمَا كَانَ ٱللَّهُ لِيُعْجِزَهُۥ مِن شَىْءٍ فِى ٱلسَّمَٰوَٰتِ وَلَا فِى ٱلْأَرْضِ ۚ إِنَّهُۥ كَانَ عَلِيمًا قَدِيرًا ﴿٤٤﴾

If God were to punish people [at once] for the wrongs they do, He would not leave a single living creature on the surface of the earth. However, He grants them respite for a term set [by Him]. When their term comes to an end, [they realize that] God has all His servants in His sight. (45)

وَلَوْ يُؤَاخِذُ ٱللَّهُ ٱلنَّاسَ بِمَا كَسَبُواْ مَا تَرَكَ عَلَىٰ ظَهْرِهَا مِن دَآبَّةٍ وَلَٰكِن يُؤَخِّرُهُمْ إِلَىٰٓ أَجَلٍ مُّسَمًّى فَإِذَا جَآءَ أَجَلُهُمْ فَإِنَّ ٱللَّهَ كَانَ بِعِبَادِهِۦ بَصِيرًۢا ٤٥

Overview

This last passage of the *sūrah* includes several rounds that go far and wide, inspiring our hearts and minds. One round looks at humanity and how one generation succeeds another. Another takes us across the heavens and earth in search of any trace of those whom the unbelievers allege to be God's partners. Then we go across the heavens and earth again to contemplate God's power as He holds the celestial bodies and the earth keeping them on their respective courses. The unbelievers are then made to face their broken promises and oaths. They swore that should they have a messenger to warn them, they would do better than past communities, but when a messenger came to them, this only increased their deviation from the truth. A look at the fates of earlier unbelieving communities follows. This is to demonstrate to those who denied the message of Islam that they should know that God's laws are constantly in operation. Although they were aware of what happened to earlier unbelievers, they still did not take on board that the same fate could just as easily befall them. The *sūrah* concludes with a warning that should strike fear in people's hearts. It tells them that if God were to punish people immediately for what they incur, no one would remain on the face of the earth. It behoves us then, to acknowledge God's grace in allowing us time to reflect and consider our position.

Lessons to Reflect Upon

It is He who made you inherit the earth. Hence, anyone who denies the truth will bear the consequences of his unbelief. In denying Him the unbelievers will have nothing but an increase of their loathsomeness in God's sight; and in denying Him the unbelievers will only add to their loss. (Verse 39)

One generation of humanity inherits another; one state disappears to allow another to rise in its place; one flame is extinguished and one is lit: it is all the same continuous, progressive movement. If we contemplate this endless round, lessons clearly present themselves. Indeed, we feel that soon we ourselves will belong to the past and that future generations will look at the traces we leave behind in the same way as we read about those who passed before us. We then realize that age determination belongs to the One who allows the heirs to inherit those that have served their term. Thus everything goes its way and disappears. It is God alone who is everlasting, unaffected by the passage of time.

The person who knows that he stays for a while and goes, like a tourist on holiday, leaving those who succeed him to look at what he has done, should endeavour to make his short stay worthwhile. He should leave behind what earns for him good remembrance and do what benefits him in his ultimate destination for all return to the One who holds everyone accountable for whatever they say and do. Such too is how mankind moves from one generation to another: *"It is He who made you inherit the earth."* (Verse 39)

Then follows a reminder of individual responsibility. None will be made to bear any part of another person's burden; none will protect another in any way. This verse also refers to their persistent denial of the truth and its ultimate results: *"Hence, anyone who denies the truth will bear the consequences of his unbelief. In denying Him the unbelievers will have nothing but an increase of their loathsomeness in God's sight; and in denying Him the unbelievers will only add to their loss."* (Verse 39) The Arabic word, *maqt*, which is translated here as 'loathsomeness', indicates the highest degree of hate. If a person incurs God's hate, his loss exceeds all that we can imagine.

238

The second round takes us across the heavens and the earth to look for evidence of those whom they allege to be God's partners. However, neither the heavens nor the earth bare any trace of them:

> *Say: 'Have you considered those beings whom you claim to be partners with God and whom you call upon beside Him? Show me what it is that they have created on earth! Or do they have a share in the heavens?' Have We ever vouchsafed them a book on which they could rely as evidence? No. What the unbelievers promise one another is nothing but delusion.* (Verse 40)

The argument is strong and the evidence is clear. This is the earth, stretched before us in all directions. Which part of it, and which creature on it, can anyone claim to have been created by other than God? Should anyone dare to make such a claim, everything on earth will rebut it loud and clear. Indeed, everything tells the same thing: all have been created by God Almighty. Everything bears the mark of the inimitable work of the Maker.

"*Or do they have a share in the heavens?*" (Verse 40) This is even more evident. No one claims that such alleged deities have any part in the creation or ownership of the heavens. Not a single one makes such a claim, not even for the *jinn* or the angels. All that they can claim is that they sought the *jinn's* help to bring them news from on high. All they hope for is that the angels will intercede with God on their behalf. Yet at no time did they claim that their alleged deities had a portion of the heavens.

"*Have We ever vouchsafed them a book on which they could rely as evidence?*" (Verse 40) Their alleged partners cannot even reach this stage of having a book given them by God and of which they are certain to be true. The question, however, admits another possibility whereby it is addressed to the idolaters themselves. Their persistence with false claims that God has partners may suggest that their faith is based on solid proof in the form of a book given to them by God. Again this is untrue, and they cannot claim it. If we take the question in this second sense, it implies that faith can only be based on a book given by God: this is the only reliable source. Again, they can make no such claim.

The Prophet, on the other hand, has a book given him by God which he presents to them. Why, then, are they turning away from it when it is the only source of true faith?

"*No. What the unbelievers promise one another is nothing but delusion.*" (Verse 40) The wrongdoers are quick to promise each other that their methods are the correct ones and that they will eventually prevail. They are indeed deluded. Moreover, they live in worthless delusion.

Sustaining the Universe

The third round reveals the limitless nature of God's power as He is the One who holds the heavens and the earth and sustains them in place. No one else has any say or role in all this:

> *It is God alone who holds the celestial bodies and the earth, lest they deviate [from their courses]. If they should ever deviate, no one else could uphold them after Him. He is indeed Ever-Forbearing, Much-Forgiving.* (Verse 41)

A glance at the heavens and the earth, and the celestial bodies moving in their orbits, without error or deviation, maintaining their speeds without the slightest increase or decrease, should open our minds to the mighty hand that holds them all in position. Should these celestial bodies or the heavens or the earth deviate from their courses and scatter no one would ever be able to hold them back. This is indeed the time frequently mentioned in the Qur'ān as signalling the end of the world: a point when the system holding all celestial bodies in position is broken, and destruction ensues. It is the time God has appointed for reckoning and reward for whatever takes place in this present life. This signals a transfer to the next world which is totally different from the world we currently live in.

Hence the statement that God holds the universe in place ends with the comment: "*He is indeed Ever-Forbearing, Much-Forgiving.*" (Verse 41) He forbears allowing people time. He does not put an end to their world or hold them to account before the term He has appointed. He gives them chances to repent, begin the good work and prepare for their future lives. Nor does He make people account for everything they do. On the contrary, He forgives much of their wrongdoing when they show any inclination to do well. This statement, then, should make people seize the opportunity provided before it is too late.

The next round speaks about the Arab idolaters and the pledges they made to God, which they then breached, spreading corruption on earth. They are warned that God's laws will always operate, never fail:

They swear by God with their most solemn oaths that if a warner should ever come to them, they would follow his guidance better than some other community, but when a warner did come to them, they turned away with increased aversion, behaving arrogantly in the land and plotting evil. Yet such evil scheming will engulf none but its authors. Can they expect anything but the way of those unbelievers of old times? No change will you ever find in God's ways; no deviation will you ever find there. (Verses 42–43)

The Arabs had Jewish neighbours in the Arabian Peninsula and they realized how far the Jews had deviated from the right path. They had heard much of their history and how they had killed their prophets, turning away from the truth these prophets advocated. The Arabs used to blame the Jews, and to swear most earnestly that *"if a warner should ever come to them, they would follow his guidance better than some other community."* (Verse 42) They deliberately made their oaths in this way, not mentioning the Jews although clearly referring to them.

Thus were their oaths, which the Qur'ān presents to everyone so as to make them witnesses to what the Arabs used to say in pre-Islamic days. The *sūrah* then reveals what they did when God gave them what they wished for, sending them a messenger to warn them: *"but when a warner did come to them, they turned away with increased aversion, behaving arrogantly in the land and plotting evil."* (Verses 42–43)

Needless to say, only a foul people would swear so strongly and then behave with such arrogance and evil. The *sūrah* exposes them, recording their behaviour, before adding to their disgrace a warning to all who emulate such actions: *"Yet such evil scheming will engulf none but its authors."* (Verse 43) Thus, their evil will harm none but themselves. It will engulf and ruin them.

This being the case, what are they waiting for? They cannot wait for anything other than the fate that engulfed those who rejected the truth in the past. They are well aware of that fate. Hence, they can await for nothing other than the operation of God's law which will never change: *"Can they expect anything but the way of those unbelievers of old times? No change will you ever find in God's ways; no deviation will you ever find there."* (Verse 43)

If Only...

Things never move haphazardly and life does not move aimlessly. There are constant laws that allow no change. The Qur'ān states this truth and wants people to learn it so that they do not look at any event in isolation, overlooking the operation of God's law. It draws their attention to the links and relations in life and the laws of existence, making it clear that these will always remain true. This present round gives an example of how the Qur'ān draws people's attention to this fact, after having confirmed that God's laws remain constant:

> Have they not travelled in the land and seen what happened in the end to those before them, even though they were much mightier than them? God can never be foiled by anything whatever in the heavens and the earth. He is All-Knowing, infinite in His power. (Verse 44)

When we travel with open eyes and alert minds, looking at the fates of earlier communities and how they perished after having commanded strength and power, this should give us clear inspiration and awaken our God-fearing sense. It is for this reason that the Qur'ān often directs people to travel, look around and reflect. Unless people do so, they will remain oblivious of the truth, and they will not draw lessons from the fates of past communities. Nor will they link such events to the universal laws that apply to them. Yet this is the quality that distinguishes man from animals. By contrast, the whole of the human race is one unit *vis-à-vis* the unity of the system and the universal law that applies to all.

While they are made to contemplate the fates of earlier communities, whose greater power availed them of nothing, they are reminded of God's might. It is He who sealed the fate of those communities, for nothing can withstand His power: "*God can never be foiled by anything whatever in the heavens and the earth.*" (Verse 44) This is a truism which is supported by clear explanation: "*He is All-Knowing, infinite in His power.*" (Verse 44) His knowledge encompasses everything in the heavens and on earth. When His power is added to His perfect and absolute knowledge, nothing escapes Him or stands up to Him. Hence, nothing in the universe can foil His purpose. There is no way that anyone can escape His power or hide from His knowledge.

The last verse in the *sūrah* speaks of God's forbearance and compassion, juxtaposing these with His power and knowledge. It emphasizes that people are given a chance, not punished immediately, but that this does not affect the eventual accurate reckoning of their deeds or the fairness of the results at the end. All this is an aspect of His grace:

> If God were to punish people [at once] for the wrongs they do, He would not leave a single living creature on the surface of the earth. However, He grants them respite for a term set [by Him]. When their term comes to an end, [they realize that] God has all His servants in His sight. (Verse 45)

People commit all sorts of bad actions, showing ingratitude for God's favours, spreading evil and corruption on earth, committing all manner of injustices and excesses. Were God to mete out fair punishment to people for their actions, His punishment would have gone beyond them to include every living thing on the face of the earth. The whole planet would then be unsuitable for any type of life, not merely human life.

This highlights the terrible nature of what people perpetrate as a destructive force that could end life in its entirety. However, God does

243

not take people to task straightaway; He forbears and gives them chances: "*However, He grants them respite for a term set [by Him].*" (Verse 45) He grants respite to individuals until the end of their lives on earth, and gives communities respite to fulfil their responsibility in performing the task He has assigned mankind to build human life on earth, until they hand over to the next generation. He also grants respite to the human race until the end of human life in this world when the Last Hour arrives. He provides us with all these chances so that we mend our ways and improve our actions.

"*When their term comes to an end…*" when the time for work and earning reward is over; when it is time for reckoning and administering reward; God will not begrudge them anything of their reward. On the contrary, He will be fair to all: "*God has all His servants in His sight.*" (Verse 45) The fact that He has them all in His sight ensures that they will be fairly requited for whatever they have done in their lives. Nothing serious or trivial will be discounted for or against them.

Thus ends this *sūrah* which started with praising God, the Originator of the heavens and the earth, "*who assigns angels to be messengers, endowed with wings,*" delivering His message, with its warnings and happy news to people on earth.

Yā Sīn

Prologue

This Makkan *sūrah* is characterized by short verses and a fast rhythm. Composed of 83 verses, it is slightly shorter in overall length than the preceding *sūrah* which contained only 45 verses. Such short verses together with the fast rhythm give the *sūrah* a special outlook. Its rhythm sounds successive beats, the effect of which is increased by the numerous images it draws, all leaving a profound impression.

It shares the same main themes of all Makkan *sūrahs*, aiming to lay the foundation of faith. At the very outset it dwells on the nature of revelation and the truth of the message: *"Yā Sīn. By the Qur'ān, full of wisdom, you are indeed one of God's messengers, pursuing a straight way. It is a revelation by the Almighty, the Ever Merciful."* (Verses 1–5) It relates the story of the people of the township to which messengers were sent, using the story to warn against rejection of the message and denial of the revelation. It shows the end that befell the people of the township to emphasize the message the *sūrah* wants to deliver. Towards the end, the *sūrah* picks up this point again: *"We have not taught the Prophet poetry; nor is it fitting for him [to be a poet]. This is but a reminder and a Qur'ān making all things clear, to warn everyone who is alive, and that the word of God be proved against the unbelievers."* (Verses 69–70)

245

The *sūrah* also discusses the oneness of the Godhead, giving the voice of denunciation of polytheism to the man who came from the farthest end of town. It is he who argues with his people about their denial of God's messengers: "*Why should I not worship the One who has brought me into being? It is to Him that you will all return. Should I worship other deities beside Him? If the Lord of Grace should will that harm befall me, their intercession will avail me nothing, nor will they save me. Indeed, I should clearly be in error.*" (Verses 22–24) The same point is emphasized again towards the end of the *sūrah*: "*Yet they have taken to worship deities other than God, hoping for [their] support. They are unable to support them; yet their worshippers stand like warriors to defend them.*" (Verses 74–75)

The issue that is most strongly emphasized in the *sūrah* is that of resurrection. Mention of this is first made at the very outset: "*It is We who will bring the dead back to life. We record whatever [deeds] they send ahead, as well as the traces they leave behind. We keep an account of all things in a clear record.*" (Verse 12) Resurrection is further alluded to in the story of the township as it mentions the reward given to the man arguing the case of faith: "*He was told: Enter paradise. He said: Would that my people knew how my Lord has forgiven me my sins, and has placed me among the highly honoured!*" (Verses 26–27) In the middle of the *sūrah* resurrection is once again referred to: "*They also ask: 'When will this promise be fulfilled, if what you say be true?' All they are waiting for is a single blast that will overtake them while they are still disputing. No time will they have to make bequests, nor will they return to their own people.*" (Verses 48–50) And at the end of the *sūrah*, it is stated in the form of dialogue: "*He comes up with arguments against Us, forgetting how he himself was created. He asks: 'Who could give life to bones that have crumbled to dust?' Say: 'He who brought them into being in the first instance will give them life again. He has full knowledge of every act of creation.*" (Verses 78–79)

These fundamental issues of faith are repeatedly discussed in Makkan *sūrahs*. Each time though they are tackled from a different angle, brought under new focus, and given effects that fit the overall ambience of the *sūrah*, maintaining harmony with its rhythm, images and impressions.

These effects vary in this *surah*. Some derive from the scenes of the Day of Judgement, the scenes in the story and the positions taken in it and the dialogue it includes as also the end suffered by earlier communities. Other effects are derived from the numerous images given of the universe, each of which imparts its own message. The dead land as life begins to emerge in it; the night stripped out of the day to spread total darkness; the sun running its course up to its point of destination; the moon moving from one phase to another until it becomes like an old date stalk; the boats laden with the offspring of old human generations; the cattle made subservient to man; the gamete being transformed into a human being who argues and quarrels; and the green tree made into a fire from which they light their own fires. It is by using all these scenes and images that the *surah* emphasizes its message.

Alongside these there are other effects made to touch our hearts and alert our minds. One of these is the image of those who deny the truth when God's judgement befalls them. No longer can they derive any benefit from the signs and the warnings given them: *"Around their necks We have put chains, reaching up to their chins, so that their heads are forced up. And We have set a barrier before them and a barrier behind them, and We enshrouded them in veils so that they cannot see."* (Verses 8–9) Another is the fact that whatever they harbour inside their hearts and whatever they leave open are known to God; nothing is hidden from Him. A third effect is the description of the mechanism of creation as involving nothing but one short word: *"When He intends something to be, He only says to it, 'Be,' and it is."* (Verse 82)

The *surah* can be divided into three parts. The first begins with an oath God makes by the expression of two separate letters, *Yā Sīn*, and by the Qur'ān, which is full of wisdom, to emphasize the truth of the Prophet's message and that he follows a straight path. This is followed by describing the miserable end of those who pay no heed to the message and deny its truth. They will never find a way to guidance because this is God's judgement. It explains that the warning only benefits those who follow the revelations given by God and who fear Him despite the fact that their faculties of perception cannot reach Him. Such people open their hearts to receive the evidence of divine guidance and the pointers to the path of faith. In this part, the Prophet is asked to cite the example of the people of the township who denied God's messengers and the end they suffered. It also shows the nature of faith and how it affects the heart of the man arguing its case.

The second part begins with a call of sorrow for those people who continue to deny every messenger God sends them, ridiculing them and their message, paying no heed to what happened to earlier communities who denied the truth, or to the great many signs God has placed all around them. This part includes the universal images we have already mentioned as well as a long and detailed scene from the Day of Judgement.

The third and final part sums up all the themes of the *sūrah*, starting with a denial that what Muḥammad recited was poetry, and emphasizing the fact that the Prophet never had anything to do with poetry. It portrays a number of images confirming God's oneness. It decries the unbelievers' practice of having deities to which they pray to give them victory over their enemies, when in fact they themselves have to protect those alleged deities. It discusses the issue of resurrection, reminding them of their origin and how their creation starts with a gamete. This should enable them to understand that giving life to bones that have crumbled into dust is barely different from their first creation from a gamete. It reminds them of the green trees and how they become fire fuel, although the two concepts seem to be far apart. The creation of the heavens and the earth is also mentioned as a reminder that God is able to create them in both stages of their life. Finally, the last beat that concludes the *sūrah* is: "*When He intends something to be, He only says to it, 'Be,' and it is. Limitless, then, in His glory is He in whose hand rests the mighty dominion over all things, and to Him you all will be brought back.*" (Verses 82–83)

I

Appeal to Reason

Yā Sīn

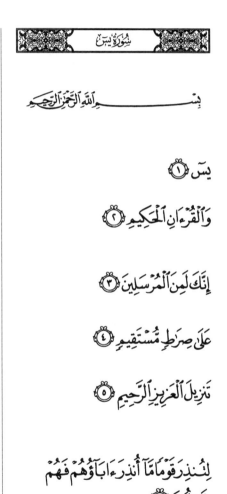

In the Name of God, the Lord of Grace, the Ever Merciful

Yā Sīn. (1)

By the Qur'ān, full of wisdom, (2)

you are indeed one of God's messengers, (3)

pursuing a straight way. (4)

It is a revelation by the Almighty, the Ever Merciful, (5)

so that you may warn people whose forefathers had not been warned, and who therefore are unaware [of the truth]. (6)

The verdict has been passed against most of them, for they will not believe. (7)

لَقَدْ حَقَّ ٱلْقَوْلُ عَلَىٰٓ أَكْثَرِهِمْ فَهُمْ لَا يُؤْمِنُونَ ٧

Around their necks We have put chains, reaching up to their chins, so that their heads are forced up. (8)

إِنَّا جَعَلْنَا فِىٓ أَعْنَٰقِهِمْ أَغْلَٰلًا فَهِىَ إِلَى ٱلْأَذْقَانِ فَهُم مُّقْمَحُونَ ٨

And We have set a barrier before them and a barrier behind them, and We enshrouded them in veils so that they cannot see. (9)

وَجَعَلْنَا مِنۢ بَيْنِ أَيْدِيهِمْ سَدًّا وَمِنْ خَلْفِهِمْ سَدًّا فَأَغْشَيْنَٰهُمْ فَهُمْ لَا يُبْصِرُونَ ٩

It is all the same to them whether you warn them or you do not warn them: they will not believe. (10)

وَسَوَآءٌ عَلَيْهِمْ ءَأَنذَرْتَهُمْ أَمْ لَمْ تُنذِرْهُمْ لَا يُؤْمِنُونَ ١٠

You can truly warn only such a one as follows this reminder and who stands in awe of the Lord of Grace although He is beyond the reach of human perception. To such, then, give the happy news of God's forthcoming forgiveness and a generous reward. (11)

إِنَّمَا تُنذِرُ مَنِ ٱتَّبَعَ ٱلذِّكْرَ وَخَشِىَ ٱلرَّحْمَٰنَ بِٱلْغَيْبِ فَبَشِّرْهُ بِمَغْفِرَةٍ وَأَجْرٍ كَرِيمٍ ١١

It is We who will bring the dead back to life. We record whatever [deeds] they send ahead, as well as the traces they leave behind. We keep an account of all things in a clear record. (12)

إِنَّا نَحْنُ نُحْىِ ٱلْمَوْتَىٰ وَنَكْتُبُ مَا قَدَّمُوا۟ وَءَاثَٰرَهُمْ وَكُلَّ شَىْءٍ أَحْصَيْنَٰهُ فِىٓ إِمَامٍ مُّبِينٍ ١٢

Cite for them, as a case in point, the people of a township to which messengers came. (13)

وَٱضْرِبْ لَهُم مَّثَلًا أَصْحَـٰبَ ٱلْقَرْيَةِ إِذْ جَآءَهَا ٱلْمُرْسَلُونَ ﴿١٣﴾

We sent them two messengers, but they rejected them; so We reinforced them with a third, and they said: 'We are messengers who have been sent to you.' (14)

إِذْ أَرْسَلْنَآ إِلَيْهِمُ ٱثْنَيْنِ فَكَذَّبُوهُمَا فَعَزَّزْنَا بِثَالِثٍ فَقَالُوٓا۟ إِنَّآ إِلَيْكُم مُّرْسَلُونَ ﴿١٤﴾

They replied: 'You are nothing but mortals like ourselves. Moreover, the Lord of Grace has never revealed anything; you do nothing but lie.' (15)

قَالُوا۟ مَآ أَنتُمْ إِلَّا بَشَرٌ مِّثْلُنَا وَمَآ أَنزَلَ ٱلرَّحْمَـٰنُ مِن شَىْءٍ إِنْ أَنتُمْ إِلَّا تَكْذِبُونَ ﴿١٥﴾

They said: 'Our Lord knows that we have indeed been sent to you. (16)

قَالُوا۟ رَبُّنَا يَعْلَمُ إِنَّآ إِلَيْكُمْ لَمُرْسَلُونَ ﴿١٦﴾

Our only duty is to clearly deliver the message [entrusted to us]. (17)

وَمَا عَلَيْنَآ إِلَّا ٱلْبَلَـٰغُ ٱلْمُبِينُ ﴿١٧﴾

Said [the others]: 'We augur evil from you. Unless you desist, we will surely stone you and inflict on you a painful suffering.' (18)

قَالُوٓا۟ إِنَّا تَطَيَّرْنَا بِكُمْ لَئِن لَّمْ تَنتَهُوا۟ لَنَرْجُمَنَّكُمْ وَلَيَمَسَّنَّكُم مِّنَّا عَذَابٌ أَلِيمٌ ﴿١٨﴾

[The messengers] replied: 'The evil you forebode is within yourselves. [Why do you take this as an evil omen] when you are only being reminded of the truth? Truly, you are going too far.' (19)

قَالُواْ طَـٰٓئِرُكُم مَّعَكُمْ أَئِن ذُكِّرْتُم بَلْ أَنتُمْ قَوْمٌ مُّسْرِفُونَ ﴿١٩﴾

Then a man came from the farthest end of the city at speed. He said: 'My people! Follow these messengers. (20)

وَجَآءَ مِنْ أَقْصَا ٱلْمَدِينَةِ رَجُلٌ يَسْعَىٰ قَالَ يَـٰقَوْمِ ٱتَّبِعُواْ ٱلْمُرْسَلِينَ ﴿٢٠﴾

Follow those who ask you for no reward, and are themselves rightly guided. (21)

ٱتَّبِعُواْ مَن لَّا يَسْـَٔلُكُمْ أَجْرًا وَهُم مُّهْتَدُونَ ﴿٢١﴾

Why should I not worship the One who has brought me into being? It is to Him that you will all return. (22)

وَمَا لِىَ لَآ أَعْبُدُ ٱلَّذِى فَطَرَنِى وَإِلَيْهِ تُرْجَعُونَ ﴿٢٢﴾

Should I worship other deities beside Him? If the Lord of Grace should will that harm befall me, their intercession will avail me nothing, nor will they save me. (23)

ءَأَتَّخِذُ مِن دُونِهِۦٓ ءَالِهَةً إِن يُرِدْنِ ٱلرَّحْمَـٰنُ بِضُرٍّ لَّا تُغْنِ عَنِّى شَفَـٰعَتُهُمْ شَيْـًٔا وَلَا يُنقِذُونِ ﴿٢٣﴾

Indeed, I should clearly be in error. (24)

إِنِّىٓ إِذًا لَّفِى ضَلَـٰلٍ مُّبِينٍ ﴿٢٤﴾

I do believe in the Lord of you all; so listen to me.' (25)

إِنِّىٓ ءَامَنتُ بِرَبِّكُمْ فَٱسْمَعُونِ ﴿٢٥﴾

He was told: 'Enter paradise.' He said: 'Would that my people knew (26)

قِيلَ ٱدۡخُلِ ٱلۡجَنَّةَ قَالَ يَٰلَيۡتَ قَوۡمِي يَعۡلَمُونَ ٢٦

how my Lord has forgiven me my sins, and has placed me among the highly honoured!' (27)

بِمَا غَفَرَ لِي رَبِّي وَجَعَلَنِي مِنَ ٱلۡمُكۡرَمِينَ ٢٧

After that, We did not send an army from heaven against his people; nor do We send any. (28)

وَمَآ أَنزَلۡنَا عَلَىٰ قَوۡمِهِۦ مِنۢ بَعۡدِهِۦ مِن جُندٖ مِّنَ ٱلسَّمَآءِ وَمَا كُنَّا مُنزِلِينَ ٢٨

Nothing was needed but one single blast, and they fell down lifeless. (29)

إِن كَانَتۡ إِلَّا صَيۡحَةٗ وَٰحِدَةٗ فَإِذَا هُمۡ خَٰمِدُونَ ٢٩

A Book Full of Wisdom

"*Yā Sīn. By the Qur'ān, full of wisdom.*" (Verses 1–2) God says an oath by these two letters and by the Qur'ān. This combination endorses the view we have expressed elsewhere about the mention of separate letters at the beginning of many *sūrahs*, and the relation between mentioning these letters and the Qur'ān. The proof that God is the source of the Qur'ān is obvious from these letters which are available to all Arabs to use yet they are incapable of producing with them anything like the thoughts and modes of expression contained in the Qur'ān. Yet seldom do they consider such confirmation.

As He swears by the Qur'ān, God Almighty describes it as being full of wisdom. In fact, a literal translation should be 'By the wise Qur'ān.' Wisdom is a quality of rational beings, which suggests that the oath is phrased in this way to impart to the Qur'ān the qualities of life, having a purpose and a will, which are essential for a wise being.

253

Although this is allegorical, nonetheless it describes a fact, bringing it closer to our minds' eye. This Qur'ān has a soul of its own, giving it qualities similar to those of a living person with whom you have mutual responses and feelings. This takes place when you pay full attention to it and listen to it with your heart and soul. Whenever you open your faculties up to it, the Qur'ān reveals to you more of its secrets. When you have lived for a while in the company of the Qur'ān, you will long for its distinctive features, just as you long for the features of a close friend. God's Messenger used to love to listen to the Qur'ān being recited by other people. He would even stop by people's doors if he overheard someone inside reciting the Qur'ān, just like a lover listens to a conversation about the one he loves.

The Qur'ān is certainly wise. It addresses everyone according to their ability; touching heart strings, speaking in a measured way, and using a wisdom that suits each person. Furthermore, the Qur'ān is full of wisdom. It educates people wisely, according to a straight logical and psychological system that releases all human potential and directs people to what is good and beneficial. It establishes a code of living that allows every human activity within the limits of its wise system.

God Almighty swears by the two letters, *Yā* and *Sīn*, and by the Qur'ān to confirm the truth of revelation and the message delivered by the Prophet: *"You are indeed one of God's messengers, pursuing a straight way."* (Verses 3–4) Limitless in His glory, God does not need to express an oath, but this oath by the Qur'ān and its letters gives the subject of the oath added greatness. God would not swear by anything unless it were great indeed, worthy of being sworn by.

"You are indeed one of God's messengers." (Verse 3) The way this verse is phrased imparts a feeling that sending messengers is a well recognized fact, with many past cases. This is not what is being proved here. Instead, what is being emphasized is that Muḥammad (peace be upon him) is one of these messengers. The oath is addressed to Muḥammad himself, not to those who deny his message, so as to place the oath, the Messenger and the message above argument or discussion. It is a fact being stated by God about His Messenger.

"You are indeed one of God's messengers, pursuing a straight way." (Verses 3–4) This explains the nature of the message after the truth

about the Messenger has been stated. By nature, this message is straightforward. It is as straight as the edge of a sword. It admits no crookedness, deviation, or prejudice. The truth it contains is clear, free of ambiguity, and does not bend to serve any interest or to satisfy any desire. Whoever wants this truth will find it pure, simple and accurate.

Because it is straight, this truth is simple, free of complexity and problems that beset controversial issues. It states the truth in the simplest and most direct way that needs the least amount of explanation and interpretation. It does not give words and sentences any special colour or overtone. As such, it is readily understood by people of all standards of education and civilization: each finds in it what they need for their lives to take an easy course, being also properly organized and well regulated.

Moreover, the Qur'ānic message is consistent with the nature of the universe and its system, as well as the nature of all that is around man. Hence, it neither conflicts with any thing in existence nor requires man to be in conflict. It follows its own way benefiting from, and cooperating with the laws that govern the universe and all creatures living in it.

As such, the Islamic message pursues its straight way to God, sure to reach Him. Its adherents do not fear that they may lose their way to Him, or take a path away from Him. They know that they are on a straight path leading to His pleasure. The Qur'ān is the guide along this way. As long as man takes up the Qur'ān, he will find a consistent concept of the truth, outlining detailed values, each having a clear and well defined role.

"*It is a revelation by the Almighty, the Ever Merciful.*" (Verse 5) We note how God identifies Himself in such situations so that people will understand the true nature of what has been revealed to them. God is the Almighty who does what He pleases, yet He is Merciful to His servants. Whatever He does to them is born out of His mercy.

The purpose of this revelation is to warn people and give them God's message: "*so that you may warn people whose forefathers had not been warned, and who therefore are unaware [of the truth].*" (Verse 6) To be unaware is the worst form of corruption. Unawareness makes a heart unable to respond or interact. It sees the pointers to the truth yet is unable to respond, unable to feel their presence. Therefore, a warning is the best thing that can be given to such people who remain unaware, having gone for generations without anyone to alert them to the truth. They were the descendants of Ishmael, and they had had no messenger from God since his time. A strong warning may, then, alert people who have long been unaware.

The *sūrah* then speaks of the fate of these people, and the judgement that is certain to befall them, considering that God knows all there is in their hearts and minds, and all that they did in the past or will do in the future: "*The verdict has been passed against most of them, for they will not believe.*" (Verse 7) Judgement has been passed, as God knows that they will not believe. Hence, this is the fate of the majority of them because they will not see divine guidance for what it is nor will they interact with it.

At this point, the *sūrah* draws an image of their psychological condition, and we see them with chains around their necks, barriers separating them from divine guidance, and with a cover over their eyes depriving them of the ability to see: "*Around their necks We have put chains, reaching up to their chins, so that their heads are forced up. And We have set a barrier before them and a barrier behind them, and We enshrouded them in veils so that they cannot see.*" (Verses 8–9) Their hands are fastened with chains to their necks, placed under their chins, which has the effect of lifting up their heads such that they cannot see what is in front of them. Moreover, there are walls and barriers both in front of and behind them, which means that even if they were released from these chains, they still could not see through the barriers. Furthermore, the covers placed over their eyes makes it even more impossible for them to see.

Although this image is fierce and sharp, we actually do encounter people of this ilk. When you see them overlooking the plain truth that is in front of them, you feel as if there is a wall separating them from it. Although their hands are not chained and nor are their heads forced up, you nonetheless feel that their souls and minds are turned away from the truth, unable to see guidance. It is as if there are barriers preventing them from approaching it. Such were the people who turned deaf ears to the Qur'ān and who received it with irrational denial as it put before them its argument and proof. This is when the Qur'ān is itself irrefutable proof.

"It is all the same to them whether you warn them or you do not warn them: they will not believe." (Verse 10) Their case is settled. God knows that faith will not penetrate their hearts. No warning will ever benefit a heart that has steeled itself against divine guidance, and barracked its approach. Warnings do not create hearts; it only alerts a heart that is alive, ready to receive guidance: *"You can truly warn only such a one as follows this reminder and who stands in awe of the Lord of Grace although He is beyond the reach of human perception. To such, then, give the happy news of God's forthcoming forgiveness and a generous reward."* (Verse 11)

Most probably, the *'reminder'* in this instance refers to the Qur'ān. A person who follows the Qur'ān and fears God despite not seeing Him is the one who benefits by the warning. It is as if the warning has been given to such people only and the Prophet directed it to them alone, even though he addressed it to all people. Since the others are prevented from receiving the warning, it looks as if it is given only to those who follow the Qur'ān and fear God. Such people deserve to be given good news. Hence the Prophet is told to give them *'the happy news of God's forthcoming forgiveness and a generous reward.'* (Verse 11) They need the forgiveness of any sin they commit providing they do not persist in doing it, and they deserve the generous reward for fearing God and following what He has revealed. These two aspects go hand in hand: when a person truly fears God, he or she is certain to follow His guidance and implement the system He has laid down.

At this point, the truth of resurrection is emphasized, together with the reckoning that ignores nothing: *"It is We who will bring the dead back to life. We record whatever [deeds] they send ahead, as well as the traces they leave behind. We keep an account of all things in a clear record."* (Verse 12) Bringing the dead back to life has always been an issue fraught with argument, of which we will see several types in this *sūrah.* They are warned here that whatever they do and whatever effects their deeds cause are written down, and nothing is forgotten. It is God Almighty who brings the dead back to life, records their actions and reckons everything. All this, then, is done in the perfect way that fits anything done by God. As for the 'clear record' and similar descriptions such as 'the imperishable tablet', these are most probably references to God's perfect knowledge that transcends time and place.

A Historical Case

Having presented the issues of revelation and resurrection in the form of a factual statement, the *sūrah* now presents them again in narrative form so as to touch hearts with a story about the fate of those who persist in denying the truth:

> *Cite for them, as a case in point, the people of a township to which messengers came. We sent them two messengers, but they rejected them; so We reinforced them with a third, and they said: 'We are messengers who have been sent to you.' They replied: 'You are nothing but mortals like ourselves. Moreover, the Lord of Grace has never revealed anything; you do nothing but lie.' They said: 'Our Lord knows that we have indeed been sent to you. Our only duty is to clearly deliver the message [entrusted to us]. Said [the others]: 'We augur evil from you. Unless you desist, we will surely stone you and inflict on you a painful suffering.' [The messengers] replied: 'The evil you forebode is within yourselves. [Why do you take this as an evil omen] when you are only being reminded of the truth? Truly, you are going too far.'* (Verses 13–19)

The Qur'ān does not mention which township this was or who were its people. Different reports suggest different towns and cities, but there is no real benefit in trying to establish its identity. The fact that the Qur'ān neither identifies it nor mentions its location does not detract from the import of the story. It is a city to which God sent two messengers, just as He sent Moses and his brother Aaron to Pharaoh and his nobles. The people of the city rejected their message, accusing them of lying. God supported His two messengers with a third, confirming that they were truly His messengers. All three of them again presented their message, saying to the people: "*We are messengers who have been sent to you.*" (Verse 14)

At this point, the people of the city aired the same objections that were given to God's messengers throughout history: "*They replied: You are nothing but mortals like ourselves. Moreover, the Lord of Grace has never revealed anything; you do nothing but lie.*" (Verse 15) This oft-repeated objection to the fact that God sends human messengers to human communities betrays a naïve understanding and ignorance of the nature of the messenger's role. People expected that both the personality and the life of the messenger should entail some deep secret which could feed their imaginations. In other words, they expected the unusual in such a way as attracted legend. Was he not a messenger sent from the heavens to the earth? How come, then, that he is just a simple ordinary person with no puzzling secrets surrounding him? He is no different from anyone else, no different from the multitude to be found everywhere.

Such thinking is certainly naïve. Secrets and enigmas are not essential qualities for prophethood and divine messages; not in this childish way of thinking. There is indeed a great secret involved, but it is epitomized in the plain fact that an ordinary person is given the ability to receive revelations from on high once God has chosen him for that task. This is something of far greater wonder than sending an angel as God's messenger, as unbelievers suggest.

The divine message is a code of living for a human community. The messenger's life represents a practical example of how this code is implemented. It is given as a model for people to follow. Since they are human, the messenger showing them this example must be human like them so that he sets the sort of example they can emulate.

Therefore, the Prophet's life was held open before his followers. The Qur'ān records the main features of his life in their minute detail, so as to make it clear and available for future generations. These details include aspects of his home and personal life, and even, at times, his thoughts and feelings. In this way, even future generations would recognize the man behind the Prophet's personality.

Yet it was this simple and clear fact that invited people's objections. In this *sūrah*, those who lived in the city said to their three messengers: "*You are nothing but mortals like ourselves,*" which meant that they were not truly messengers from God. They also said: "*The Lord of*

Grace has never revealed anything," of what you claim. They further added: "*You do nothing but lie,*" when you claim to be messengers from God.

Certain that they said nothing but the truth, and knowing the remit of the mission assigned to them, the messengers replied: "*Our Lord knows that we have indeed been sent to you. Our only duty is to clearly deliver the message [entrusted to us].*" (Verses 16–17) It is sufficient that God knows. The task assigned to God's messengers is to deliver their message, and they did just that. People are then free to choose what they wish for themselves, and what burden their choices represent. Once the messengers have delivered their message, the matter is left to God to determine.

However, those who persist in denying the truth do not take matters in such a simple and easy way. They cannot tolerate the advocates of faith's presence. They resort to rough tactics in rejecting sound argument. The point is that falsehood is impatient, aggressive: "*Said [the others]: We augur evil from you. Unless you desist, we will surely stone you and inflict on you a painful suffering.*" (Verse 18) We view your call with gloom, expecting it to bring evil upon us. Unless you stop, we will no longer tolerate you: '*we will surely stone you and inflict on you a painful suffering.*' Thus falsehood declares its intentions, threatening those advocating divine guidance and resorting to heavy handed tactics in answering the quiet word of truth.

However, the task assigned to God's messengers requires them to proceed along their way: "*[The messengers] replied: The evil you forebode is within yourselves.*" (Verse 19) Forebodings of evil as a result of a message being delivered or a face being encountered is nothing but ignorant superstition. The messengers tell them so, and make clear to them that their share of good or evil comes from within themselves. In other words it relates to their actions and intentions. It is up to them to increase their share of goodness or evil. What God wills for people comes from within themselves and from their own choices and actions. This is the truth based on a firm foundation. To associate bad omens with faces, places or words is superstitious nonsense.

The messengers also said to them: "*[Why do you take this as an evil omen] when you are only being reminded of the truth?*" (Verse 19) Would you stone us and torture us only because we remind you of the truth? Is this how you reward reminders? *"Truly, you are going too far."* (Verse 19) You certainly exceed the limits of judgement if you reward a mere reminder with threats and punishment, and requite advocacy of the truth with stoning and torture.

Welcome Support

Such was the response of hearts that would not open to God's message. It is such people that were mentioned at the outset of the *sūrah*. The other type, who follow the reminder and fear God despite their inability to see Him, also have here a behavioural example to emulate:

> *Then a man came from the farthest end of the city at speed. He said: 'My people! Follow these messengers. Follow those who ask you for no reward, and are themselves rightly guided. Why should I not worship the One who has brought me into being? It is to Him that you will all return. Should I worship other deities beside Him? If the Lord of Grace should will that harm befall me, their intercession will avail me nothing, nor will they save me. Indeed, I should clearly be in error. I do believe in the Lord of you all; so listen to me.'* (Verses 20–25)

This is the response of sound human nature to the straightforward message of the truth: it reflects sincerity, simplicity, warmth and correct understanding. It shows us a man giving a positive response to the message, once he has recognized the elements of truth and sound logic in it. He points out these elements to his people as he addresses them. When he felt the truth of faith in his heart, he could not stay quiet or sit at home caring nothing while the truth was being rebuffed and falsehood upheld all around him. Instead he actively advocated the truth among his people, among those who were threatening the messengers with severe punishment. He travelled from the furthest end of the city to fulfil his duty, to call on his people to espouse the truth and to stop their opposition to it and aggression against God's messengers.

It is apparent that the man did not command a position of honour, power or influence among his people. He was an ordinary person motivated by faith to travel from one end of the city to the other to make his stand clear. "*He said: 'My people! Follow these messengers. Follow those who ask you for no reward, and are themselves rightly guided.*" (Verses 20–21) Anyone who advocates such a message, seeking no gain or reward, must be honest and sincere. What else could motivate him to undertake such trouble, enduring such opposition, unless he was required to do so by God? Why would he bear such a burden, confronting people with a faith that is unfamiliar to them, exposing himself in the process to threats, ridicule and persecution when he stood to make no gain nor earn any benefit?

"*Follow those who ask you for no reward, and are themselves rightly guided.*" (Verse 21) That they are guided aright is obvious: they advocate belief in the One God, following a clear system, and a faith that is free of ambiguity and superstition. Their way is clearly straight.

The man then speaks about himself, outlining the reasons that motivated him to believe, and appealing to sound human nature: "*Why should I not worship the One who has brought me into being? It is to Him that you will all return. Should I worship other deities beside Him? If the Lord of Grace should will that harm befall me, their intercession will avail me nothing, nor will they save me. Indeed, I should clearly be in error.*" (Verses 22–24) The question is posed by sound human nature which feels the presence of its Creator and the source of its existence: "*Why should I not worship the One who has brought me into being?*" Why would I deviate from this natural way which is the first to present itself to human nature? Needless to say, man is by nature attracted to his Creator and only deviates from Him under the pressure of some outside element. To turn to the Creator is the right and appropriate course, requiring no alien element or a pull from outside. The man here strongly feels this and states it clearly and simply.

The man also feels by nature that a created being must in the end return to its Creator, in the same natural law that brings everything homing to its originator: "*It is to Him that you will all return.*" He wonders why he should not worship his Creator when he is bound to return to Him, as will we all. It is He who creates, and it is He who should be worshipped.

The man then looks at the opposite way, which is contrary to sound nature, only to find that it is nothing but manifest error: "*Should I worship other deities beside Him? If the Lord of Grace should will that harm befall me, their intercession will avail me nothing, nor will they save me.*" (Verse 23) Can anyone be in greater error than the one who abandons the way of sound nature which requires that a created being worship its Creator? Why would anyone choose to worship someone or something else unnecessarily? Indeed, the one who turns his back on the Creator, resorting instead to weak deities that cannot protect him, has gone far into error: "*Indeed, I should clearly be in error.*" (Verse 24)

Now that the man has stated his case, speaking for sound human nature that is aware of the truth, he declares his own final decision, confronting his people who had threatened God's messengers. The voice of sound nature in his heart was clearer and stronger than any threat: "*I do believe in the Lord of you all; so listen to me.*" (Verse 25) He wants them to witness his stand on the side of truth, implying that they too should follow his suit and declare themselves believers.

Killing an Innocent Man

The drift of the story suggests that the unbelievers then killed the man. The *sūrah*, however, does not mention this clearly. Instead, it lets the curtain drop to cover this city, its people and their preoccupations. When the curtain rises again we see the martyr who spoke out clearly and loudly for the truth, confronting those in power. We see him in the next world and see the honour granted him by God, as fits a brave believer who does not hesitate to stand up for the truth: "*He was told: Enter paradise. He said: Would that my people knew how my Lord has forgiven me my sins, and has placed me among the highly honoured!*" (Verses 26–27)

Thus this present life is connected to the life to come: death is merely a transfer from this transitory world to the one that is everlasting. It is but a step that takes a believer from the narrowness of the earth to the expanse of heavens, from the tyranny of falsehood to the security of the truth, and from the darkness of ignorance to the light of certainty. When the man sees what God has in store for him in heaven, he good-naturedly remembers his people, wishing that they could see the happiness and honour God has granted him so that they would know and accept the truth.

Such is the reward of faith. As for tyranny, it is too weak to require that God should send angels to destroy it: *"After that, We did not send an army from heaven against his people; nor do We send any. Nothing was needed but one single blast, and they fell down lifeless."* (Verses 28–29) The *sūrah* does not speak in detail about how these people were destroyed. They are too insignificant to deserve such mention. They needed no more than one blast and no further trace of life was to be seen from them.

2

Signs Galore

Alas for mankind! Whenever a messenger comes to them, they level ridicule on him. (30)

يَـٰحَسْرَةً عَلَى ٱلْعِبَادِ مَا يَأْتِيهِم مِّن رَّسُولٍ إِلَّا كَانُوا بِهِ يَسْتَهْزِءُونَ ﴿٣٠﴾

Are they not aware of how many a generation We have destroyed before them, and that they [who have perished] will never return to them? (31)

أَلَمْ يَرَوْا كَمْ أَهْلَكْنَا قَبْلَهُم مِّنَ ٱلْقُرُونِ أَنَّهُمْ إِلَيْهِمْ لَا يَرْجِعُونَ ﴿٣١﴾

Yet, they all will be brought before Us. (32)

وَإِن كُلٌّ لَّمَّا جَمِيعٌ لَّدَيْنَا مُحْضَرُونَ ﴿٣٢﴾

There is a sign for them in the lifeless earth: We give it life and produce out of it grain for them to eat. (33)

وَءَايَةٌ لَّهُمُ ٱلْأَرْضُ ٱلْمَيْتَةُ أَحْيَيْنَـٰهَا وَأَخْرَجْنَا مِنْهَا حَبًّا فَمِنْهُ يَأْكُلُونَ ﴿٣٣﴾

We place in it gardens of date palms and grapes, and cause springs to gush out of it, (34)

وَجَعَلْنَا فِيهَا جَنَّـٰتٍ مِّن نَّخِيلٍ وَأَعْنَـٰبٍ وَفَجَّرْنَا فِيهَا مِنَ ٱلْعُيُونِ ﴿٣٤﴾

so that they may eat of its fruit. It was not their own hands that made all this. Will they, then, not give thanks? (35)

لِيَأْكُلُوا مِن ثَمَرِهِ وَمَا عَمِلَتْهُ أَيْدِيهِمْ أَفَلَا يَشْكُرُونَ ﴿٣٥﴾

Limitless in His glory is He who created all things in pairs: whatever the earth produces, their own human kind and other creatures of which they have no knowledge. (36)

سُبْحَنَ ٱلَّذِي خَلَقَ ٱلْأَزْوَجَ كُلَّهَا مِمَّا تُنْبِتُ ٱلْأَرْضُ وَمِنْ أَنفُسِهِمْ وَمِمَّا لَا يَعْلَمُونَ ۝

Another sign for them is the night: We strip the daylight from it, and they are plunged in darkness. (37)

وَءَايَةٌ لَّهُمُ ٱلَّيْلُ نَسْلَخُ مِنْهُ ٱلنَّهَارَ فَإِذَا هُم مُّظْلِمُونَ ۝

The sun also runs its set course: that is laid down by the will of the Almighty, the All-Knowing. (38)

وَٱلشَّمْسُ تَجْرِي لِمُسْتَقَرٍّ لَّهَا ذَٰلِكَ تَقْدِيرُ ٱلْعَزِيزِ ٱلْعَلِيمِ ۝

And for the moon We have determined phases until it finally becomes like an old date stalk. (39)

وَٱلْقَمَرَ قَدَّرْنَهُ مَنَازِلَ حَتَّىٰ عَادَ كَٱلْعُرْجُونِ ٱلْقَدِيمِ ۝

Neither the sun can overtake the moon, nor can the night outrun the day. Each floats in its own orbit. (40)

لَا ٱلشَّمْسُ يَنۢبَغِي لَهَآ أَن تُدْرِكَ ٱلْقَمَرَ وَلَا ٱلَّيْلُ سَابِقُ ٱلنَّهَارِ وَكُلٌّ فِي فَلَكٍ يَسْبَحُونَ ۝

And yet another sign for them is that We carry their offspring in laden ships, (41)

وَءَايَةٌ لَّهُمْ أَنَّا حَمَلْنَا ذُرِّيَّتَهُمْ فِي ٱلْفُلْكِ ٱلْمَشْحُونِ ۝

and that We create things of similar kind for them to ride in. (42)

وَخَلَقْنَا لَهُم مِّن مِّثْلِهِۦ مَا يَرْكَبُونَ ۝

If such be Our will, We may cause them to drown, with none to respond to their cries for help, and then they cannot be saved, (43)

وَإِن نَّشَأْ نُغْرِقْهُمْ فَلَا صَرِيخَ لَهُمْ وَلَا هُمْ يُنقَذُونَ ﴿٤٣﴾

unless it be by an act of mercy from Us, leaving them to enjoy life for a while. (44)

إِلَّا رَحْمَةً مِّنَّا وَمَتَاعًا إِلَىٰ حِينٍ ﴿٤٤﴾

When they are told: 'Beware of that which lies before you and behind you, so that you may be graced with His mercy,' [they pay no heed]. (45)

وَإِذَا قِيلَ لَهُمُ ٱتَّقُوا مَا بَيْنَ أَيْدِيكُمْ وَمَا خَلْفَكُمْ لَعَلَّكُمْ تُرْحَمُونَ ﴿٤٥﴾

Every single sign that comes to them from their Lord do they ignore. (46)

وَمَا تَأْتِيهِم مِّنْ ءَايَةٍ مِّنْ ءَايَٰتِ رَبِّهِمْ إِلَّا كَانُوا عَنْهَا مُعْرِضِينَ ﴿٤٦﴾

And when they are told: 'Give [in charity] out of what God has provided for you,' the unbelievers say to those who believe: 'Are we to feed those whom God could have fed, had He so willed? Clearly, you are lost in error.' (47)

وَإِذَا قِيلَ لَهُمْ أَنفِقُوا مِمَّا رَزَقَكُمُ ٱللَّهُ قَالَ ٱلَّذِينَ كَفَرُوا لِلَّذِينَ ءَامَنُوا أَنُطْعِمُ مَن لَّوْ يَشَاءُ ٱللَّهُ أَطْعَمَهُ إِنْ أَنتُمْ إِلَّا فِي ضَلَٰلٍ مُّبِينٍ ﴿٤٧﴾

They also ask: 'When will this promise be fulfilled, if what you say be true?' (48)

وَيَقُولُونَ مَتَىٰ هَٰذَا ٱلْوَعْدُ إِن كُنتُمْ صَٰدِقِينَ ﴿٤٨﴾

All they are waiting for is a single blast that will overtake them while they are still disputing. (49)

مَا يَنظُرُونَ إِلَّا صَيْحَةً وَاحِدَةً تَأْخُذُهُمْ وَهُمْ يَخِصِّمُونَ ﴿٤٩﴾

No time will they have to make bequests, nor will they return to their own people. (50)

فَلَا يَسْتَطِيعُونَ تَوْصِيَةً وَلَا إِلَىٰٓ أَهْلِهِمْ يَرْجِعُونَ ﴿٥٠﴾

The Trumpet will be sounded, and out of their graves they will rise and hasten to their Lord. (51)

وَنُفِخَ فِي الصُّورِ فَإِذَا هُم مِّنَ الْأَجْدَاثِ إِلَىٰ رَبِّهِمْ يَنسِلُونَ ﴿٥١﴾

They will say: 'Woe betide us! Who has roused us from our resting place? This is what the Lord of Grace had promised. The messengers told the truth.' (52)

قَالُوا يَٰوَيْلَنَا مَنۢ بَعَثَنَا مِن مَّرْقَدِنَا ۗ هَٰذَا مَا وَعَدَ الرَّحْمَٰنُ وَصَدَقَ الْمُرْسَلُونَ ﴿٥٢﴾

It takes nothing but one single blast, and they will all have been brought before Us. (53)

إِن كَانَتْ إِلَّا صَيْحَةً وَاحِدَةً فَإِذَا هُمْ جَمِيعٌ لَّدَيْنَا مُحْضَرُونَ ﴿٥٣﴾

Today, no one shall be wronged in the least: you will be requited for nothing other than that which you did in life. (54)

فَالْيَوْمَ لَا تُظْلَمُ نَفْسٌ شَيْئًا وَلَا تُجْزَوْنَ إِلَّا مَا كُنتُمْ تَعْمَلُونَ ﴿٥٤﴾

Those who are destined for paradise are today happily occupied. (55)

إِنَّ أَصْحَٰبَ الْجَنَّةِ الْيَوْمَ فِي شُغُلٍ فَٰكِهُونَ ﴿٥٥﴾

Together with their spouses, they will be in shady groves seated on soft couches. (56)

هُمْ وَأَزْوَٰجُهُمْ فِى ظِلَٰلٍ عَلَى ٱلْأَرَآئِكِ مُتَّكِـُٔونَ ۝

There they have fruit and whatever they ask for: (57)

لَهُمْ فِيهَا فَٰكِهَةٌ وَلَهُم مَّا يَدَّعُونَ ۝

peace and fulfilment through the word of the Lord of mercy. (58)

سَلَٰمٌ قَوْلًا مِّن رَّبٍّ رَّحِيمٍ ۝

But stand aside today, you guilty ones! (59)

وَٱمْتَٰزُوا۟ ٱلْيَوْمَ أَيُّهَا ٱلْمُجْرِمُونَ ۝

Children of Adam! Did I not enjoin on you that you should not worship Satan, as he is your open foe, (60)

أَلَمْ أَعْهَدْ إِلَيْكُمْ يَٰبَنِىٓ ءَادَمَ أَن لَّا تَعْبُدُوا۟ ٱلشَّيْطَٰنَ إِنَّهُۥ لَكُمْ عَدُوٌّ مُّبِينٌ ۝

and that you should worship Me alone? This is the straight path. (61)

وَأَنِ ٱعْبُدُونِى هَٰذَا صِرَٰطٌ مُّسْتَقِيمٌ ۝

He had already led astray a great many of you. Could you not, then, use your reason? (62)

وَلَقَدْ أَضَلَّ مِنكُمْ جِبِلًّا كَثِيرًا أَفَلَمْ تَكُونُوا۟ تَعْقِلُونَ ۝

This, then, is the hell that you were repeatedly warned against: (63)

هَٰذِهِۦ جَهَنَّمُ ٱلَّتِى كُنتُمْ تُوعَدُونَ ۝

endure it today for your persistent rejection [of the truth].' (64)

أَصْلَوْهَا ٱلْيَوْمَ بِمَا كُنتُمْ تَكْفُرُونَ ﴿٦٤﴾

On that day We shall set a seal on their mouths, but their hands will speak to Us, and their feet will bear witness to whatever they have done. (65)

ٱلْيَوْمَ نَخْتِمُ عَلَىٰ أَفْوَٰهِهِمْ وَتُكَلِّمُنَآ أَيْدِيهِمْ وَتَشْهَدُ أَرْجُلُهُم بِمَا كَانُواْ يَكْسِبُونَ ﴿٦٥﴾

Had it been Our will, We could have blotted their eyes. They would have striven to find the way, but how could they have seen it? (66)

وَلَوْ نَشَآءُ لَطَمَسْنَا عَلَىٰٓ أَعْيُنِهِمْ فَٱسْتَبَقُواْ ٱلصِّرَٰطَ فَأَنَّىٰ يُبْصِرُونَ ﴿٦٦﴾

And had it been Our will, We could have paralysed them, right in their places, so that they could not move forward or backward. (67)

وَلَوْ نَشَآءُ لَمَسَخْنَٰهُمْ عَلَىٰ مَكَانَتِهِمْ فَمَا ٱسْتَطَٰعُواْ مُضِيًّا وَلَا يَرْجِعُونَ ﴿٦٧﴾

If We grant long life to a human being, We also cause him to decline in his powers. Will they not use their reason? (68)

وَمَن نُّعَمِّرْهُ نُنَكِّسْهُ فِي ٱلْخَلْقِ أَفَلَا يَعْقِلُونَ ﴿٦٨﴾

Overview

The first passage spoke about the idolaters who opposed the message of Islam and cited the case of the people of the township who rejected their three messengers and how it took no more than one blast for them to fall down lifeless. In the present passage the *sūrah* speaks generally of all people who oppose every divine religion. It shows mankind straying in error across the generations. It calls with sorrow on all people to take heed of what happened to earlier communities who passed before them and who will not return until the Day of Resurrection, when *"they all will be brought before Us."* (Verse 32)

The *sūrah* then presents a number of universal signs which people see constantly without paying any attention to the message they impart. These signs are within themselves and all around them, while others have passed into history, yet still they pay no heed, and when they are reminded, they choose not to remember: *"Every single sign that comes to them from their Lord do they ignore."* (Verse 46) Indeed, they hasten their own punishment, believing that it will never happen: *"They also ask: When will this promise be fulfilled, if what you say be true?"* (Verse 48)

The passage also presents a long scene from the Day of Judgement, showing the fate that they hasten. This is done in such a way that it appears to happen before their very eyes.

A Sorrowful Condition

> *Alas for mankind! Whenever a messenger comes to them, they level ridicule on him. Are they not aware of how many a generation We have destroyed before them, and that they [who have perished] will never return to them? Yet, they all will be brought before Us.* (Verses 30–32)

The first phrase expresses reaction to a sorrowful situation. This situation cannot be changed though sorrow and pain about it can be expressed. God Almighty does not experience such a feeling Himself, but He states that the situation these people are in deserves such reaction by others. Theirs is a depressing condition that leads to great misery.

"Alas for mankind!" They are offered a chance to save themselves but they turn away. This even though they see how earlier communities perished, yet they benefit nothing by the lessons they present. God opens wide the doors of His mercy to them, time after time, as He sends them messengers, but they ignore His mercy and behave with insolence and ill manners: *"Whenever a messenger comes to them, they level ridicule on him. Are they not aware of how many a generation We*

have destroyed before them, and that they [who have perished] will never return to them?" (Verses 30–31) The fact that earlier communities, over countless generations, perished should provide a clear lesson to anyone who reflects. People, however, do not pay heed, even though they realize that they are going to meet the same end. What could invite greater sorrow? An animal shudders to see its fellow animal perish, and it will inevitably try to avoid the same fate. How come that man sees so many communities suffering and meeting the same end, and yet he continues to follow in their footsteps? Arrogance blinds him to the result which he will inevitably reach.

While those who had already gone will not return to their successors, they will not be ignored or left without reckoning. They will all face that at the proper time: *"Yet, they all will be brought before Us."* (Verse 32)

Only Look Around

> *There is a sign for them in the lifeless earth: We give it life and produce out of it grain for them to eat. We place in it gardens of date palms and grapes, and cause springs to gush out of it, so that they may eat of its fruit. It was not their own hands that made all this. Will they, then, not give thanks? Limitless in His glory is He who created all things in pairs: whatever the earth produces, their own human kind and other creatures of which they have no knowledge.* (Verses 33–36)

Everything around them in the universe speaks to them about God, giving evidence of His presence. They only need to look at the land in front of them and how they see it dead, lifeless, lacking a drop of water. Then they see it quicken, producing grain and adorned with gardens replete with dates and grapes. Springs of water gush through it; and in no time, it is full of life.

Life is a miracle which no man can produce. It is God's hand that produces miracles, initiating life in what has been dead. The sight of growing plants, flowering gardens and ripening fruit should open people's eyes and hearts to appreciate the wonderful work engendered by God's hand. It splits the earth to allow the shoot to appear, longing for freedom and light, gives vigour to the stem which is eager to enjoy sunlight, loads the branches with leaves and fruit, opens up flowers and gets the fruit ready for picking, "*so that they may eat of its fruit. It was not their own hands that made all this.*" (Verse 35) It was God's dextrous hand that enabled them to achieve all this; it was He who made the plants grow and yield their harvest: "*Will they, then, not give thanks?*" (Verse 35)

Having given them this gentle and inspiring touch, the *sūrah* then turns away from them a little to glorify God who gave them the flourishing gardens, making all plants in pairs, male and female, like men and women and countless other species known only to God: "*Limitless in His glory is He who created all things in pairs: whatever the earth produces, their own human kind and other creatures of which they have no knowledge.*" (Verse 36)

With this glorification of God, voiced at exactly the right place and time, a great fact of the universe is brought to the fore; that is, the oneness of creation, the rule that applies to it and the way it is made. God has created all living things in pairs, and this applies to plants in the same way as it applies to man, and everything else: '*and other creatures of which they have no knowledge.*' This unity points to the fact that the Creator is one. It is He who put in place the oneness of creation, despite the great varieties of shape, size, kind, race, features, etc. in all these creatures which are known only to Him. This rule of creating things in pairs may apply to everything in the universe, including inanimate objects, but this is knowledge that rests with God alone. It has now, for example, been established that the atom, which is the smallest unit of matter we know includes a pair of electric charges, positive and negative. Moreover, thousands of pairs of stars have been observed: each pair of stars move together in the same orbit, as if they are playing the same tune.

That was the sign given by the dead land quickening to produce life. We now look at the sign presented by the skies and the phenomena people see with their own eyes as God's hand produces miracles:

> *Another sign for them is the night: We strip the daylight from it, and they are plunged in darkness. The sun also runs its set course:*

that is laid down by the will of the Almighty, the All-Knowing. And for the moon We have determined phases until it finally becomes like an old date stalk. Neither the sun can overtake the moon, nor can the night outrun the day. Each floats in its own orbit. (Verses 37–40)

When the night comes, light disappears and darkness spreads: this is something everyone sees every day in every corner of the world, except for polar areas. Despite its daily occurrence, it is a remarkable sign that deserves contemplation. The Qur'ānic description here is unique as it shows the day intertwined with the night and then God strips the day off the night to let darkness spread. We may perhaps further appreciate the unique way the Qur'ān uses to express this image when we remember how it actually happens. As the earth rotates facing the sun, every spot of it actually comes face to face with the sun when the day spreads over it. When the rotation of the earth changes and that spot no longer faces the sun, the day is stripped off it so as to plunge it into darkness. The same thing happens over every little part of the earth in progression, as if the light of day is pulled away or stripped to allow darkness to replace it. Thus the wording here accurately describes the reality.

"*The sun also runs its set course.*" (Verse 38) It was generally believed that the sun stays in its position but turns around its axis, but it has recently been confirmed that it moves in a single direction in the great universal space, and astronomers have calculated the speed of its movement as being 12 miles per second. God Almighty, who knows its movement and destination, says that it moves along its course to a particular destination which is known only to Him. He alone knows when and what this is.

When we remember that the sun is around a million times bigger than the earth we live on and imagine this great mass running its set course in space, unsupported, we appreciate what power controls and conducts the affairs of the universe and the sort of might and knowledge that power commands: "*that is laid down by the will of the Almighty, the All-Knowing.*" (Verse 38)

"*And for the moon We have determined phases until it finally becomes like an old date stalk.*" (Verse 39) People see the moon in these phases,

274

as it is born a thin crescent then grows every day until it takes its shape as a full moon before it begins to decrease until it looks like an old date stalk. If you observe the moon night after night, you will appreciate this remarkable way of expression, particularly the use of the word 'old'. In the early and final nights of its cycle, the moon has a crescent shape, but whereas it reflects freshness and vigour in the early days, it rises in the latter part of its cycle as if it is weighed down by a heavy burden and looks worried and pale; the same paleness as an old date stalk. Hence, the inspiring Qur'ānic description.

Observing the moon night after night gives us fresh, rich and profound feelings. Furthermore, we perceive that it is all the work of the able hand that combines beauty with majesty while operating an accurate celestial system. We feel all this whether we know why the moon has such phases or not: it is sufficient to observe the moon for our hearts to overflow with feelings and for our minds to be deep in reflection.

The *sūrah* then makes it clear that the system regulating all these great celestial bodies is most accurate, and that this controls its resulting phenomena: "*Neither the sun can overtake the moon, nor can the night outrun the day. Each floats in its own orbit.*" (Verse 40) Indeed every planet and star has its own orbit which it follows accurately. Stars and planets are so far apart that the distances separating them are huge. Our planet earth is approximately 93 million miles away from the sun, while the moon is around 240,000 miles away from us. Hardly imaginable as these distances are, they are nothing compared to the distance between our solar system and the nearest star to us outside it, which is estimated to be four light years. We should remember that light travels at a speed of 186,000 miles per second.

God, the Creator, willed that such distances should separate the orbits of stars and planets, and He planned the universe according to this design in order to prevent any collision, until a time He has set and that is known only to Him. Therefore, the sun will not overtake the moon, and the night cannot outrun the day, because the cycle of day and night never fails.

"*Each floats in its own orbit.*" (Verse 40) The movement of all these great bodies in space is similar to the movement of ships and boats in

275

the sea. Huge as these bodies are, they are no more than little spots floating on the surface of the sea. Compare man to all this, and think of the millions of millions of stars and planets floating in space!

> *And yet another sign for them is that We carry their offspring in laden ships, and that We create things of similar kind for them to ride in. If such be Our will, We may cause them to drown, with none to respond to their cries for help, and then they cannot be saved, unless it be by an act of mercy from Us, leaving them to enjoy life for a while.* (Verses 41–44)

There is a clear analogy between the stars and planets floating in their orbits and ships floating on water carrying human passengers. The two types are not dissimilar in appearance or movement. Moreover, it is only through God's will and design that these two types of floating take place while He controls the entire universe ensuring the safety of all. At the same time, both are signs that we see but hardly ever contemplate. The floating of laden ships is closer to us and easier to reflect upon, if only we would open our hearts.

In the original Arabic text, the term '*laden ships*' could be read to mean 'the laden ark', which makes it a reference to Noah's ark in which Adam's offspring was carried. God then enabled mankind to make ships. In both cases, the floating was made possible by God's will, power and the laws He has set in operation and the nature of boats, water, wind, steam, and other types of energy, which combine to allow ships to float on water. All these are parts of God's creation.

"*If such be Our will, We may cause them to drown, with none to respond to their cries for help, and then they cannot be saved, unless it be by an act of mercy from Us, leaving them to enjoy life for a while.*" (Verses 43–44) Large, heavy and carefully built as it may be, a ship in water is like a feather in the air: it can disappear and perish in a moment, unless it is protected by God's grace. People who have crossed oceans, whether in a boat with sails or in a large vessel, appreciate the danger represented by the sea and the little protection there is, should a storm ensue. They recognize that only God's grace provides protection in the midst of storms and currents that run over the sea, which is after all a creature controlled only by God's caring hand. But all this applies *'for a while,'* only until the time God has set arrives.

What Opens Sealed Hearts

Clear and inspiring as these signs are, people continue to pay little heed. Their hearts remain closed and they persist in ridicule and denial, hastening the end against which God's messengers have warned them:

> *When they are told: 'Beware of that which lies before you and behind you, so that you may be graced with His mercy,' [they pay no heed]. Every single sign that comes to them from their Lord do they ignore. And when they are told: 'Give [in charity] out of what God has provided for you,' the unbelievers say to those who believe: 'Are we to feed those whom God could have fed, had He so willed? Clearly, you are lost in error.' They also ask: 'When will this promise be fulfilled, if what you say be true?'* (Verses 45–48)

Although all these signs are enough to cause an open heart to shudder and bring it in line with the universe, the unbelievers will not see them for what they are, and even if they do see them, they still do not reflect on them. Because His grace is endless, God does not leave them to themselves. He sends them messengers to warn them and to call them to their Lord, the Creator of the universe. The messengers' role is to alert people's hearts so that they can see why they should be God-fearing, and to warn them against incurring God's displeasure, pointing out its causes and teaching them how to avoid it. Signs are constantly given them in their lives, time after time, in addition to the signs that are available in the universe around them, but they choose to remain blind: "*When they are told: Beware of that which lies before you and behind you, so that you may be graced with His mercy, [they pay no heed]. Every single sign that comes to them from their Lord do they ignore.*" (Verses 45–46) If they are urged to be charitable and to give to the poor a portion of what God has provided for them, they say in ridicule: "*Are we to feed those whom God could have fed, had He so willed?*" (Verse 47) They would even be impolite in their reply to those calling on them to be charitable, saying: "*Clearly, you are lost in error.*" (Verse 47)

Viewing the matter in such a mechanical way betrays their ignorance of the law God has set for human life. It is God who feeds and provides for all. All the provisions that people receive on earth are created by Him. They cannot create any of that; indeed, they cannot create anything whatsoever. It is God's will that people should have needs which they cannot attain to without hard work, such as planting the earth, extracting its raw material to manufacture things, transporting its produce from place to place, offering such produce in return for other products or for money, etc. It is also His will that people differ in their talents and abilities to ensure that everything needed to fulfil man's task of building human life on earth is available. The accomplishment of this task not only needs talents and abilities that earn money and produce wealth; it also requires others that can meet different human needs, without earning money. This makes for a complex human society, in which people have different lots in a bustling world, and across generations. However, the resulting differences of the means available to different people does not lead to the ruination of life and society. In fact it is a by-product of life's movement.

Therefore, Islam addresses the individual, requiring those who have plenty to relinquish a portion of their money, which is given to the poor to provide for their food and other needs. By doing so, Islam reforms a great many people, rich and poor alike. This portion is *zakāt*, which, by definition, implies purification. Islam makes it one of its acts of worship, and uses it to establish cordial and caring relations between the rich and the poor in the unique society it establishes.

Therefore, when those people, unable to see God's wisdom, say, "*are we to feed those whom God could have fed, had He so willed?*" and when they speak arrogantly to those who ask them to be charitable, saying, "*clearly, you are lost in error,*" they betray their own ignorance. They are blind to the nature of God's law, life's movement and the reasons why God gave different talents and abilities to different people, with the result that they have different means.

Islam puts in place a system that ensures fair opportunities for everyone. It then allows varied human activities, which are necessary for the fulfilment of man's role on earth, to run their course. Furthermore, it deals with any negative side effects.

Finally the *sūrah* mentions their expressed doubts about God's promise and their ridicule of the warnings given them: "*They also ask: When will this promise be fulfilled, if what you say be true?*" (Verse 48) God's promise is not brought forward or delayed because of people's pleas. With God everything has its definite measure; everything takes place at its appointed time and place, in accordance with His infinite wisdom. It is He who conducts the universe and all that happens in it according to a perfect system. The answer to this rude question is given in the form of a scene from the Day of Judgement, showing them what happens then, but not its timing.

Mercy: the Essential Quality

All they are waiting for is a single blast that will overtake them while they are still disputing. No time will they have to make bequests, nor will they return to their own people. The Trumpet will be sounded, and out of their graves they will rise and hasten to their Lord. They will say: 'Woe betide us! Who has roused us from our resting place? This is what the Lord of Grace had promised. The messengers told the truth.' It takes nothing but one single blast, and they will all have been brought before Us. (Verses 49–53)

Here we see the answer to the question about the time of resurrection: it comes in the form of a quick image, a single blast that ends all life. "*All they are waiting for is a single blast that will overtake them while they are still disputing. No time will they have to make bequests, nor will they return to their own people.*" (Verses 49– 50) It takes them suddenly, in a moment, as they argue and dispute going about their day-to-day lives, expecting nothing of the sort. Then it is all over. All perish in the situation and the condition they are in. They have no chance to make a will or to arrange something for loved ones who may stay behind. No one can return to his family to say a word to them. In fact every single person faces the same end, with all life finished.

The Trumpet is then sounded and they all rise from their graves, moving hurriedly, shocked, in fear. The question on everyone's lips is: "*Who has roused us from our resting place?*" (Verse 52) As the shock begins to wear off, it is replaced by a growing realization: "*This is what the Lord of Grace had promised. The messengers told the truth.*" (Verse 52) Then comes the final blast and all those bewildered individuals, moving hurriedly and aimlessly, take their positions: "*It takes nothing but one single blast, and they will all have been brought before Us.*" (Verse 53) Only a short moment and all are stationed in place, ranged in rows as if they were in a parade. The supreme decree explaining the nature of the moment as well as the forthcoming reckoning and reward is announced to all: "*Today, no one shall be wronged in the least: you will be requited for nothing other than that which you did in life.*" (Verse 54) The quick succession of these three images forms a complete and coherent answer to those who have been voicing doubts about the Day of Resurrection.

The *sūrah* does not dwell on how the believers face the reckoning. Instead, it moves quickly on to show their happy end:

> *Those who are destined for paradise are today happily occupied. Together with their spouses, they will be in shady groves seated on soft couches. There they have fruit and whatever they ask for: peace and fulfilment through the word of the Lord of mercy.* (Verses 55–58)

They are occupied with the comforts available to them, happy, relaxed, enjoying the fruits served to them and the shady groves providing a cool breeze. They are joined by their spouses in perfect enjoyment. Whatever they need is immediately made available to them. Above all this, they are honoured with a greeting of peace from none other than their merciful Lord.

By contrast the *sūrah* dwells on the scene of reckoning faced by the others. It is shown with all that it involves of reproach and blame:

> *But stand aside today, you guilty ones! Children of Adam! Did I not enjoin on you that you should not worship Satan, as he is your open foe, and that you should worship Me alone? This is the straight path. He had already led astray a great many of you. Could you*

not, then, use your reason? This, then, is the hell that you were repeatedly warned against: endure it today for your persistent rejection [of the truth]. (Verses 59–64)

Contempt marks the treatment they receive. They are first told to stand aside, away from the believers. They are then addressed as '*Children of Adam,*' which is an address implying reproach: "*Children of Adam! Did I not enjoin on you that you should not worship Satan, as he is your open foe.*" (Verse 60) It was Satan who caused the expulsion of their father, Adam, from heaven. He has declared his permanent hostility to them, yet they continue to worship him.

They were also enjoined to do something that was certain to set them on a straight path, leading to God's pleasure and a happy end in the life to come: "*You should worship Me alone. This is the straight path.*" (Verse 61) They are reminded that this enemy led astray many generations. Hence the rhetorical question: "*Could you not, then, use your reason?*" (Verse 62) At the end of this very hard and humiliating position, the dreaded sentence is passed, given in overtones of reproach and derision: "*This, then, is the hell that you were repeatedly warned against: endure it today for your persistent rejection [of the truth].*" (Verses 63–64)

However, the scene does not end here. It moves on to provide a most singular image: "*On that day We shall set a seal on their mouths, but their hands will speak to Us, and their feet will bear witness to whatever they have done.*" (Verse 65) Thus, they let each other down; their own bodies give witness against them; their personalities are torn apart with each part claiming that the other is lying. Each organ in their bodies returns to their Lord separately, in full submission to Him. This is a terrible scene, one that we can hardly contemplate.

The scene ends with the unbelievers in that state of tied tongues, speaking hands and legs giving witness. This is totally different from what they knew of their nature, and different from what they were expecting. Had God willed, He could have put them in a totally different situation, making them endure whatever hardship He wished to impose on them. The *sūrah* gives us here two examples of such hardships, making it clear that God could impose the same on anyone:

*Had it been Our will, We could have blotted their eyes. They
would have striven to find the way, but how could they have seen
it? And had it been Our will, We could have paralysed them,
right in their places, so that they could not move forward or
backward.* (Verses 66–67)

These two examples combine ridicule with contempt: the former
answers those who used to pour ridicule on the believers and the divine
message, and the latter answers those who were contemptuous when
addressed by the message. It was they who used to ask about the time
when the promise of the hereafter would be fulfilled, implying that
they did not believe it would ever come about. In the first example we
see them blind, yet despite their blindness, they rush to find a way,
pushing one another aside and in their haste many of them fall down.
How could they see? In the second example, they are frozen like statues
unable to move an inch. In both examples they appear like toys, inviting
ridicule after they were the ones to pour ridicule on the believers and
their faith.

All this takes place when the promise they used to hasten becomes
due. Should they be left to live long on earth, they will end up in a
miserable situation, when they will prefer for the promise to be
hastened. They attain to old age with all its weaknesses, and they suffer
dementia and retardation in feeling and thought. "*If We grant long life
to a human being, We also cause him to decline in his powers. Will they
not use their reason?*" (Verse 68)

Old age is a second childhood, but without a child's sweet innocence.
An aged person moves backward, forgetting what he has learnt, losing
physical and mental powers, unable to endure much, until he is no
more than a child. However, a child is always met with a smile when it
does something silly. An aged person receives no support, unless it
comes from a sense of pity and duty. He is also ridiculed whenever he
betrays an element of childishness or stupidity.

Both fates await those who persist in rejecting the truth. They are
the ones that deprive themselves of the blessings of faith.

3

What Prevents Resurrection?

We have not taught the Prophet poetry; nor is it fitting for him [to be a poet]. This is but a reminder and a Qur'ān making all things clear, (69)

وَمَا عَلَّمْنَٰهُ ٱلشِّعْرَ وَمَا يَنۢبَغِى لَهُۥٓ إِنْ هُوَ إِلَّا ذِكْرٌ وَقُرْءَانٌ مُّبِينٌ ٦٩

to warn everyone who is alive, and that the word of God be proved against the unbelievers. (70)

لِّيُنذِرَ مَن كَانَ حَيًّا وَيَحِقَّ ٱلْقَوْلُ عَلَى ٱلْكَٰفِرِينَ ٧٠

Are they not aware that, among all the things Our hands have made, We have created for them cattle which they control? (71)

أَوَلَمْ يَرَوْا۟ أَنَّا خَلَقْنَا لَهُم مِّمَّا عَمِلَتْ أَيْدِينَآ أَنْعَٰمًا فَهُمْ لَهَا مَٰلِكُونَ ٧١

We have subjected these to them, so that some of them they use for riding and of some they may eat, (72)

وَذَلَّلْنَٰهَا لَهُمْ فَمِنْهَا رَكُوبُهُمْ وَمِنْهَا يَأْكُلُونَ ٧٢

and they have other benefits from them, and [milk] to drink. Will they not give thanks? (73)

وَلَهُمْ فِيهَا مَنَٰفِعُ وَمَشَارِبُ أَفَلَا يَشْكُرُونَ ٧٣

Yet they have taken to worship deities other than God, hoping for [their] support. (74)

وَٱتَّخَذُواْ مِن دُونِ ٱللَّهِ ءَالِهَةً لَّعَلَّهُمْ يُنصَرُونَ ﴿٧٤﴾

They are unable to support them; yet their worshippers stand like warriors to defend them. (75)

لَا يَسْتَطِيعُونَ نَصْرَهُمْ وَهُمْ لَهُمْ جُندٌ مُّحْضَرُونَ ﴿٧٥﴾

Let not their words grieve you. We know all that they keep secret as well as all that they bring into the open. (76)

فَلَا يَحْزُنكَ قَوْلُهُمْ إِنَّا نَعْلَمُ مَا يُسِرُّونَ وَمَا يُعْلِنُونَ ﴿٧٦﴾

Is man, then, not aware that it is We who create him out of a gamete; and then he becomes flagrantly contentious? (77)

أَوَلَمْ يَرَ ٱلْإِنسَٰنُ أَنَّا خَلَقْنَٰهُ مِن نُّطْفَةٍ فَإِذَا هُوَ خَصِيمٌ مُّبِينٌ ﴿٧٧﴾

He comes up with arguments against Us, forgetting how he himself was created. He asks: 'Who could give life to bones that have crumbled to dust?' (78)

وَضَرَبَ لَنَا مَثَلًا وَنَسِيَ خَلْقَهُۥ قَالَ مَن يُحْيِ ٱلْعِظَٰمَ وَهِيَ رَمِيمٌ ﴿٧٨﴾

Say: 'He who brought them into being in the first instance will give them life again. He has full knowledge of every act of creation; (79)

قُلْ يُحْيِيهَا ٱلَّذِىٓ أَنشَأَهَآ أَوَّلَ مَرَّةٍ وَهُوَ بِكُلِّ خَلْقٍ عَلِيمٌ ﴿٧٩﴾

He who produces for you fire out of the green tree, and from this you kindle your fires.' (80)

ٱلَّذِى جَعَلَ لَكُم مِّنَ ٱلشَّجَرِ ٱلْأَخْضَرِ نَارًا فَإِذَآ أَنتُم مِّنْهُ تُوقِدُونَ ﴿٨٠﴾

Is, then, He who has created the heavens and the earth unable to create their like? Of course He can. He alone is the supreme Creator, the All-Knowing. (81)

أَوَلَيْسَ ٱلَّذِى خَلَقَ ٱلسَّمَٰوَٰتِ وَٱلْأَرْضَ بِقَٰدِرٍ عَلَىٰٓ أَن يَخْلُقَ مِثْلَهُم بَلَىٰ وَهُوَ ٱلْخَلَّٰقُ ٱلْعَلِيمُ ﴿٨١﴾

When He intends something to be, He only says to it, 'Be,' and it is. (82)

إِنَّمَآ أَمْرُهُۥٓ إِذَآ أَرَادَ شَيْـًٔا أَن يَقُولَ لَهُۥ كُن فَيَكُونُ ﴿٨٢﴾

Limitless, then, in His glory is He in whose hand rests the mighty dominion over all things, and to Him you all will be brought back. (83)

فَسُبْحَٰنَ ٱلَّذِى بِيَدِهِۦ مَلَكُوتُ كُلِّ شَىْءٍ وَإِلَيْهِ تُرْجَعُونَ ﴿٨٣﴾

Overview

In this final part, the *surah* reviews all the issues it tackled earlier: the nature of revelation; Godhead and its oneness, and resurrection. These are reviewed in separate sections and shown with strong effects coupled with a clear rhythm. The overall aim is to show how God's hand controls everything in the universe. This concept is summed up in the last verse of the *surah*: "*Limitless, then, in His glory is He in whose hand rests the mighty dominion over all things, and to Him you all will be brought back.*" (Verse 83) His hand, strong and innovative, has created cattle and subjected them to man, and created man from a mere gamete. The same hand can also give life to bones that had broken into dust, just like it originated them in the first instance. It was this hand that produced fire from the green tree and brought the heavens and the earth into being. In the end, it has control of everything in the universe. This, then, is the gist of this final part of the *surah*.

No Place for Poetry

We have not taught the Prophet poetry; nor is it fitting for him [to be a poet]. This is but a reminder and a Qur'ān making all things clear, to warn everyone who is alive, and that the word of God be proved against the unbelievers. (Verses 69–70)

Right at the outset, the *sūrah* spoke about the question of revelation: *"Yā Sīn. By the Qur'ān, full of wisdom, you are indeed one of God's messengers, pursuing a straight way. It is a revelation by the Almighty, the Ever Merciful, so that you may warn people whose forefathers had not been warned, and who therefore are unaware [of the truth]."* (Verses 1–6) Now it is presented in this particular form to refute the allegation that the Prophet was a poet, and that the Qur'ān was mere poetry. The elders of the Quraysh were fully aware that all this was absolutely false, and that the Qur'ān Muḥammad recited was something unknown in their language. They were not so dull as to be unable to distinguish the Qur'ān from poetry. These allegations were simply part of the propaganda they launched against the new faith and the Messenger preaching it. They simply referred to the fine, inspiring style of the Qur'ān to try to make the masses confuse it with poetry.

At this point, God in all His limitless glory denies that He taught His Messenger the art of poetry. Since God did not teach him this, he will not learn it. No one will ever get to know anything other than what God teaches them.

The *sūrah* also makes it clear that poetry is not suitable for God's Messenger: *"nor is it fitting for him [to be a poet]."* Poetry takes a different line from that of prophethood. Poetry is an interaction which may change from time to time. Prophethood, on the other hand, means revelations bestowed from on high, outlining a firm system and a clear code that should be implemented as it conforms to God's law, which operates throughout the universe. Unlike poetry, it does not change to suit moods and desires.

Moreover, prophethood means constant contact with God, learning directly from what He reveals and an untiring attempt to mould human life in a way that pleases Him. In its highest standards, poetry expresses a human longing for what is perfect and beautiful, but it remains a human effort confined within man's capabilities and limitations. At lesser levels, poetry is an expression of reactions and desires that may be strongly carnal. Indeed, prophethood and poetry are far apart: one is at best a longing that issues from the earth while the other is true guidance from on high.

"*This is but a reminder and a Qur'ān making all things clear.*" (Verse 69) Both descriptions apply to the same thing: the role of revelation is to be a reminder as it works on the mind keeping it alert, and the Qur'ān is to be recited. It has been revealed to perform a particular task: "*to warn everyone who is alive, and that the word of God be proved against the unbelievers.*" (Verse 70) Here the Qur'ānic expression contrasts unbelief with life, making unbelief equal to death and propensity to faith equal to life. Thus, the Qur'ān has been revealed to the Prophet Muḥammad (peace be upon him) so as to warn those who are alive and can benefit from the warning. The unbelievers, on the other hand, are dead and cannot hear the warning. Therefore, the function of the Qur'ān, in as far as they are concerned, is to record their situation which makes them deserve punishment. God will not inflict punishment on anyone who has not received His message. Punishment is for those who did receive His message and who were determined to disbelieve in it, thereby writing their own ruin.

Just the One God

The second section of this final part of the *sūrah* addresses the question of God's oneness providing a framework for it from what people see around them and the blessings God grants them:

> Are they not aware that, among all the things Our hands have made, We have created for them cattle which they control. We have subjected these to them, so that some of them they use for riding and of some they may eat, and they have other benefits from them, and [milk] to drink. Will they not give thanks? Yet they have taken to worship deities other than God, hoping for [their] support. They are unable to support them; yet their worshippers stand like warriors to defend them.

Let not their words grieve you. We know all that they keep secret as well as all that they bring into the open. (Verses 71–76)

These verses begin with the question, '*Are they not aware…*', which could have been literally translated as 'Do they not see how…' The sign to which their attentions are drawn here is present before them. They do not have to look far for it. It is before their very eyes, requiring little contemplation. It is the cattle God has created and made subject to their control. Thus, they are able to ride them, use them for food, milk and draw various other benefits from them. All this is by God's law and the qualities He has given man and cattle. People could never have achieved any of this on their own. In fact, they cannot create a fly, even though they might muster all their resources for this purpose. They cannot control a fly unless God gave it the quality of being controlled by man. Hence the question: *"Will they not give thanks?"*

When we look at the matter in this Qur'ānic light we are bound to feel that God's blessings overflow from every corner around us. Thus, every time we ride an animal, eat a piece of meat, have a drink of milk, taste a piece of cheese or use fat for cooking, or wear a garment made of hide, wool or animal hair, we in our hearts feel God's endless blessings and infinite grace. This, then, applies to all things around us and everything we use, whether animate or inanimate. All our lives, then, become a continuous act of glorifying God and giving thanks to Him.

Yet people do not give thanks. Some of them would even attribute divinity to beings other than God. *"Yet they have taken to worship deities other than God, hoping for [their] support. They are unable to support them; yet their worshippers stand like warriors to defend them."* (Verses 74–75) In the past, such deities were statues, stones, trees, stars, angels or *jinn*. Such idolatry persists today in some areas of the world. Yet people today who do not worship such deities do not necessarily believe in God's oneness. They may associate partners with Him, in the form of believing in some alleged powers other than His, or relying on other things. What we need to understand here is that polytheism can take different forms at different times and places.

The unbelievers used to worship these deities seeking their help to win victory, yet it was they who protected those deities against assault from others: "*yet their worshippers stand like warriors to defend them.*" (Verse 75) This was absurdity of the lowest order. However, in essence, most people have not gone far above this level of absurdity; only in form. Today, people who give tyrants the status of deities are not dissimilar to those who worshipped idols and statues. They are the warriors defending the tyrants and their tyranny, yet at the same time, they humbly bow before them. Idolatry is the same, whatever form it takes. Whenever the monotheistic faith suffers any deviation, idolatry and *jāhiliyyah* creep in. The only thing that protects humanity is belief in God's absolute oneness. He is the One God, to whom all worship must be addressed. He is the One to be obeyed and on whom all must rely.

"*Let not their words grieve you. We know all that they keep secret as well as all that they bring into the open.*" (Verse 76) This is an address to the Prophet as he confronted those worshipping deities other than God. He should not be concerned about them. God knows all about them and what they scheme. They represent no danger to any believer who places his trust in God.

A Second Life for All

The third section of this final passage raises the question of resurrection and reckoning:

> Is man, then, not aware that it is We who create him out of a gamete; and then he becomes flagrantly contentious. He comes up with arguments against Us, forgetting how he himself was created. He asks: 'Who could give life to bones that have crumbled to dust?' Say: 'He who brought them into being in the first instance will give them life again. He has full knowledge of every act of creation; He who produces for you fire out of the green tree, and from this you kindle your fires.' Is, then, He who has created the heavens and the earth unable to create their like? Of course He can. He alone is the supreme Creator, the All-Knowing. When He intends something to be, He only says to it, 'Be,' and it is. (Verses 77–82)

289

This section looks first at man's own position, describing his origins and ends, putting it all before him so that he looks at it as a reality taking place all the time. Yet man neither appreciates its significance nor takes it as evidence confirming the realization of God's promise to resurrect all humanity. "*Is man, then, not aware that it is We who create him out of a gamete; and then he becomes flagrantly contentious.*" (Verse 77) Man does not doubt that his immediate origin is a gamete. It is no more than a tiny drop of worthless fluid; a drop containing countless thousands of cells, one of which then becomes an embryo, which later grows into a contentious person, arguing with his Lord and demanding proof and evidence from Him.

It is the creative power of God that transforms that gamete into this quarrelsome, contentious person. What a gulf between origin and end! Yet man finds it difficult to believe that this power can bring him back to life after death. "*He comes up with arguments against Us, forgetting how he himself was created. He asks: 'Who could give life to bones that have crumbled to dust?' Say: 'He who brought them into being in the first instance will give them life again. He has full knowledge of every act of creation.*" (Verses 78–79) How simple, using the logic of nature and obvious reality!

Does a gamete have greater life, power or value than a crumbled bone? Is not man originated from a gamete? Is the One who made an argumentative man out of a gamete unable to produce a new creation out of a crumbled bone? This is too easy and obvious to merit any lengthy discussion: "*He who brought them into being in the first instance will give them life again. He has full knowledge of every act of creation.*" (Verse 79) They are then given further clarification of God's creative power. Again the clarification uses something they always see with their own eyes: "*He who produces for you fire out of the green tree, and from this you kindle your fires.*" (Verse 80)

A casual look at this remarkable phenomena, to which they are often oblivious, is sufficient as convincing proof. Green trees laden with water often produce fire through friction, and then become fuel to this same fire. However, scientific understanding of the nature of the heat green trees receive as they absorb solar energy and retain it while they are full of water can only enhance the significance of this phenomena. It is God who has given trees their characteristics, and who created all things. However, we seldom look at things with such awareness. As a result, they do not reveal to us their amazing secrets nor do they point us to the Creator of the universe. We only need to open our hearts to them and they will tell us their secrets. We will then live with them in a permanent state of worship and glorification of God.

The *surah* then further examines the question of man's initial creation and his subsequent resurrection: *"Is, then, He who has created the heavens and the earth unable to create their like? Of course He can. He alone is the supreme Creator, the All-Knowing."* (Verse 81)

The heavens and the earth are great and wonderful creations. This earth where we live with millions of other species, and compared to which we are very little in size, and about which our knowledge remains scanty, is no more than a small satellite of the sun. Our earth depends totally on the light and heat it receives from the sun. However, the sun is only one out of a hundred million suns in this galaxy which forms our neighbouring world. The universe includes numerous other galaxies. Using their best, but limited observatories, astronomers estimate that there are one hundred million galaxies, but they could discover more if they used more powerful telescopes. The distance between our galaxy and the next is estimated at 750,000 light years. In addition, there are also vast nebula containing distant clusters of stars. But this is as far as our limited knowledge can reach.

Most of these countless stars have planets like our own star, and each planet and star has its own orbit in which it moves according to an accurate system which allows no stoppage or deviation. Otherwise, collisions would occur in outer space. We simply cannot try to describe what this great expanse contains: it is simply beyond our imagination. However, the question remains: *"Is, then, He who has created the heavens and the earth unable to create their like?"* How do people compare with such great, unimaginable creation? *"Of course He can. He alone is the supreme Creator, the All-Knowing."* (Verse 81)

The truth is that God creates this and that, as well as other types of creation, effortlessly. It is all the same to Him whether the creature He wants to bring into life is large or small: *"When He intends something*

291

to be, He only says to it, 'Be,' and it is. (Verse 82) This *'something'* could be a galaxy, an earth, an ant or a mosquito. It is all the same, requiring no more than a simple word, *'Be'*, and it is there. Nothing is easier or more difficult, near or far. Once God's will intends something, it exists whatever it may be. However, God tells us of this fact in a way we understand. This is why He expresses it in this way: saying, *'Be'*, to His intended creation.

At this point, the *sūrah* gives its final beat, describing the relation between the universe and its Creator: *"Limitless, then, in His glory is He in whose hand rests the mighty dominion over all things, and to Him you all will be brought back."* (Verse 83) The term *'mighty dominion'* describes this relation in its majestic reality of absolute ownership and complete authority over everything in the universe. Then to Him all will return.

SŪRAH 37

Al-Ṣāffāt

(Ranged in Ranks)

Prologue

This Makkan *sūrah*, like the one before it, is composed of short verses and is characterized by fast beats, successive scenes and a myriad of images. Indeed, the effect it produces is at times very intense. Like all Makkan revelations, its aim is to establish the Islamic faith firmly in people's hearts, purging it of any traces of idolatry and polytheism. In this respect, however, it addresses a particular form of polytheism which prevailed in Arabian society at the time, pausing long to expose its falsehood. All this is summed up in the allegation that God married the *jinn*, who subsequently gave Him the angels as His daughters.

The *sūrah* attacks this superstition heavily, exposing its stupidity and lack of substance. Furthermore, because this topic is given prominence, the *sūrah* begins by mentioning some types of angels: *"By the [angels] ranged in ranks, who rebuke reproachfully, and recite God's word."* (Verses 1–3) This is followed by mention of the devils and how they are targeted by piercing flames to prevent them from eavesdropping on those on high. Had they been in the position given them in ignorant superstitions, they would not have been chased in this way. The fruit of the tree growing in the midst of hell is likened to devils' heads. At the end, this superstition is strongly and decisively refuted: *"Now ask the unbelievers if it be true that your Lord has daughters, while they would have sons? Or is it that We have created the angels female in their presence? Out of their falsehood they say: 'God has begotten children.' They are lying indeed. Would He then choose daughters in preference to sons? What is the matter with you? How do you make your judgement? Do you not reflect? Or do you, perhaps, have a clear authority? Bring your scriptures, if you are speaking the truth! They claim that He has kinship with the* jinn; *yet the* jinn *themselves know that they will be brought [before God] for judgement. Limitless is God in His glory, above all what people attribute to Him.*" (Verses 149–159)

In addition to dealing with this particular form of idolatry, the *sūrah* tackles the same issues of faith discussed in other Makkan *sūrahs*. It confirms God's oneness, citing evidence from the universe: "*Most certainly your God is One, Lord of the heavens and the earth and everything between them, Lord of all the points of sunrise.*" (Verses 4–5) As it draws a scene of the Day of Judgement, it specifies that idolatry is the reason why those punished in the hereafter receive their punishment: "*On that day, they all will share in the common suffering. Thus shall We deal with all the guilty ones. Whenever they were told, 'there is no deity other than God,' they would turn away in arrogance, and would say: 'Are we to forsake our deities for the sake of a mad poet?' For certain, he has brought the truth, and confirmed the earlier messengers. You will indeed taste grievous suffering, being requited only for what you used to do.*" (Verses 33–39)

The *sūrah* also speaks about resurrection, reckoning and reward. Referring to the idolaters' reaction when they are told that they will be brought back to life, it states that they say: "*This is nothing but plain sorcery. What! After we have died and become mere dust and bones, shall we be raised back to life? And perhaps our forefathers?*" (Verses 15–17) It follows this with a detailed scene of the Day of Judgement, full of images, movements, reactions and surprises.

Reference is also made to the question of revelation and the message, quoting the unbelievers as saying: "*Are we to forsake our deities for the sake of a mad poet?*" (Verse 36) It states the true nature of prophethood: "*For certain, he has brought the truth, and confirmed the earlier messengers.*" (Verse 37)

As the *sūrah* describes the attitude of the idolaters, how far astray they go, as well as their rejection of the truth, it mentions a series of earlier messengers: Noah, Abraham and his sons, Moses and Aaron, Elijah, Lot and Jonah. These accounts show clearly how God grants His grace to His messengers, how He supports them against their enemies and how He inflicts punishment on those who deny the truth: *"Most of the people of old went astray before them; although We had sent them warners. Behold what happened in the end to those that had been warned. Not so God's true servants."* (Verses 71–74) The story of Abraham and his son Ishmael, the sacrifice and the ransom, is given special prominence as it paints obedience and submission to God in their most profound form. Indeed, such submission equates with attaining the summit that can only be reached through pure faith, one which elevates people to a splendid horizon.

A wide range of effects accompany the presentation of different issues in the *sūrah*. To mention but a few, we see the skies, stars, planets and piercing flames: *"We have adorned the skies nearest to the earth with stars, and have made them secure against every rebellious devil. Thus, they cannot eavesdrop on the ones on high, but shall be repelled from all sides, driven away, with lasting suffering in store for them. If any of them stealthily snatches away a fragment, he will be pursued by a piercing flame."* (Verses 6–10)

Special effects are also provided in the scenes that portray the Day of Judgement, its surprises and the strong reactions that ensue. These scenes are rather unique and this aspect will be highlighted later when we discuss those verses in detail.

Further effects are provided by the stories the *sūrah* relates, most particularly that of Abraham and his son Ishmael as they proceed to give the sacrifice. Here, the effects are at their highest, strongly shaking our hearts.

The *sūrah* is also characterized by its distinctive rhythm which is most suited to the images and scenes it portrays as also to the style it adopts and the meanings it wants to emphasize.

The *sūrah* can be divided into three parts. The first includes the opening describing the three types of angels who glorify God, the Lord of all points of sunrise, who adorned the skies with stars. It then mentions the *jinn* and how they try to eavesdrop on those on high and who are then targeted by piercing flames. A question is then put to them: are they more difficult to create than the other beings God created, including angels, the skies, the *jinn*, planets and flames? This leads to a refutation of what they used to say about resurrection, showing its absurdity, and confirming what they used to find difficult to believe. This is followed by a long and unique image of resurrection, reckoning, reward and punishment.

The second part mentions how those who were erroneous only followed in the footsteps of the unbelievers of old who received warnings, but paid no heed. It gives accounts of the people's of Noah, Abraham, Moses, Aaron, Elijah, Lot and Jonah, showing the ends met by the two parties in each respect.

In the last part, the superstition concerning the *jinn* and the angels is brought into focus. It states clearly God's promise of victory to His messengers: "*Our word has already been given to Our servants the messengers: it is they who will be helped, and it is Our forces who will surely be victorious.*" (Verses 171–173) The *sūrah* closes on a special note glorifying God, denying all false claims about Him, greeting His messengers and praising Him as the Supreme Lord: "*Limitless in His glory is your Lord, the Lord of almightiness, above all what people attribute to Him. And peace be upon all His messengers. All praise is due to God, the Lord of all the worlds.*" (Verses 180–182)

I

Will You Have a Look?

Al-Ṣaffāt (Ranged in Ranks)

In the Name of God, the Lord of Grace, the Ever Merciful

By the [angels] ranged in ranks, (1)

who rebuke reproachfully (2)

and recite God's word (3)

most certainly your God is One, (4)

Lord of the heavens and the earth and everything between them, Lord of all the points of sunrise. (5)

We have adorned the skies nearest to the earth with stars, (6) and have made them secure against every rebellious devil. (7)

وَحِفْظًا مِّن كُلِّ شَيْطَنٍ مَّارِدٍ ۝

Thus, they cannot eavesdrop on the ones on high, but shall be repelled from all sides, (8)

لَّا يَسَّمَّعُونَ إِلَى ٱلْمَلَإِ ٱلْأَعْلَىٰ وَيُقْذَفُونَ مِن كُلِّ جَانِبٍ ۝

driven away, with lasting suffering in store for them. (9)

دُحُورًا وَلَهُمْ عَذَابٌ وَاصِبٌ ۝

If any of them stealthily snatches away a fragment, he will be pursued by a piercing flame. (10)

إِلَّا مَنْ خَطِفَ ٱلْخَطْفَةَ فَأَتْبَعَهُ شِهَابٌ ثَاقِبٌ ۝

Now ask those [unbelievers]: Are they more difficult to create, or the other beings We have created? Them have We created out of a sticky clay. (11)

فَٱسْتَفْتِهِمْ أَهُمْ أَشَدُّ خَلْقًا أَم مَّنْ خَلَقْنَآ إِنَّا خَلَقْنَهُم مِّن طِينٍ لَّازِبٍ ۝

Whereas you marvel, they scoff; (12)

بَلْ عَجِبْتَ وَيَسْخَرُونَ ۝

and when they are reminded of the truth, they pay no heed; (13)

وَإِذَا ذُكِّرُوا لَا يَذْكُرُونَ ۝

and when they see a sign, they resort to ridicule; (14)

وَإِذَا رَأَوْا ءَايَةً يَسْتَسْخِرُونَ ۝

and say: 'This is nothing but plain sorcery. (15)

وَقَالُوٓا إِنْ هَٰذَآ إِلَّا سِحْرٌ مُّبِينٌ ۝

What! After we have died and become mere dust and bones, shall we be raised back to life? (16)

أَءِذَا مِتْنَا وَكُنَّا تُرَابًا وَعِظَٰمًا أَءِنَّا لَمَبْعُوثُونَ ۝

And perhaps our forefathers?'
(17)

أَوَءَابَآؤُنَا ٱلْأَوَّلُونَ ﴿١٧﴾

Say: 'Yes, indeed! And you shall
be utterly humbled.' (18)

قُلْ نَعَمْ وَأَنتُمْ دَٰخِرُونَ ﴿١٨﴾

There will be just one single cry,
and they will all begin to see, (19)

فَإِنَّمَا هِيَ زَجْرَةٌ وَٰحِدَةٌ فَإِذَا هُمْ يَنظُرُونَ ﴿١٩﴾

and will say: 'Woe betide us! This
is the Day of Judgement!' (20)

وَقَالُوا۟ يَٰوَيْلَنَا هَٰذَا يَوْمُ ٱلدِّينِ ﴿٢٠﴾

This is indeed the Day of
Decision which you used to call
a lie! (21)

هَٰذَا يَوْمُ ٱلْفَصْلِ ٱلَّذِى كُنتُم بِهِۦ
تُكَذِّبُونَ ﴿٢١﴾

Gather together all those who
were bent on wrongdoing, their
ilk, and all that they used to
worship (22)

ٱحْشُرُوا۟ ٱلَّذِينَ ظَلَمُوا۟ وَأَزْوَٰجَهُمْ
وَمَا كَانُوا۟ يَعْبُدُونَ ﴿٢٢﴾

instead of God, and guide them
all to the path of hell, (23)

مِن دُونِ ٱللَّهِ فَٱهْدُوهُمْ إِلَىٰ صِرَٰطِ
ٱلْجَحِيمِ ﴿٢٣﴾

but halt them a while, for they
shall be asked: (24)

وَقِفُوهُمْ إِنَّهُم مَّسْـُٔولُونَ ﴿٢٤﴾

'How is it that you do not help
one another?' (25)

مَا لَكُمْ لَا تَنَاصَرُونَ ﴿٢٥﴾

Indeed, on that day they will be
in complete submission. (26)

بَلْ هُمُ ٱلْيَوْمَ مُسْتَسْلِمُونَ ﴿٢٦﴾

They will turn upon one another
accusingly. (27)

وَأَقْبَلَ بَعْضُهُمْ عَلَىٰ بَعْضٍ يَتَسَآءَلُونَ ﴿٢٧﴾

Some [of them] will say: 'You used to [whisper to us] approaching us from the right!' (28)

قَالُوٓاْ إِنَّكُمْ كُنتُمْ تَأْتُونَنَا عَنِ ٱلْيَمِينِ ۝

The others will reply: 'No! It was you who would not believe. (29)

قَالُواْ بَل لَّمْ تَكُونُواْ مُؤْمِنِينَ ۝

We had no power over you; but you were willing to exceed all limits. (30)

وَمَا كَانَ لَنَا عَلَيْكُم مِّن سُلْطَٰنٍ بَلْ كُنتُمْ قَوْمًا طَٰغِينَ ۝

Now our Lord's word has come true against us, and we are bound to taste [the punishment]; (31)

فَحَقَّ عَلَيْنَا قَوْلُ رَبِّنَآ إِنَّا لَذَآئِقُونَ ۝

If we led you astray, we ourselves were astray.' (32)

فَأَغْوَيْنَٰكُمْ إِنَّا كُنَّا غَٰوِينَ ۝

On that day, they all will share in the common suffering. (33)

فَإِنَّهُمْ يَوْمَئِذٍ فِي ٱلْعَذَابِ مُشْتَرِكُونَ ۝

Thus shall We deal with all the guilty ones. (34)

إِنَّا كَذَٰلِكَ نَفْعَلُ بِٱلْمُجْرِمِينَ ۝

Whenever they were told, 'there is no deity other than God,' they would turn away in arrogance, (35)

إِنَّهُمْ كَانُوٓاْ إِذَا قِيلَ لَهُمْ لَآ إِلَٰهَ إِلَّا ٱللَّهُ يَسْتَكْبِرُونَ ۝

and would say: 'Are we to forsake our deities for the sake of a mad poet?' (36)

وَيَقُولُونَ أَئِنَّا لَتَارِكُوٓاْ ءَالِهَتِنَا لِشَاعِرٍ مَّجْنُونٍۭ ۝

For certain, he has brought the truth, and confirmed the earlier messengers. (37)

بَلْ جَآءَ بِٱلْحَقِّ وَصَدَّقَ ٱلْمُرْسَلِينَ ۝

You will indeed taste grievous suffering, (38)

إِنَّكُمْ لَذَآئِقُوا الْعَذَابِ الْأَلِيمِ ﴿٣٨﴾

being requited only for what you used to do. (39)

وَمَا تُجْزَوْنَ إِلَّا مَا كُنتُمْ تَعْمَلُونَ ﴿٣٩﴾

Not so God's true servants. (40)

إِلَّا عِبَادَ اللَّهِ الْمُخْلَصِينَ ﴿٤٠﴾

Theirs shall be a predetermined sustenance: (41)

أُوْلَٰئِكَ لَهُمْ رِزْقٌ مَّعْلُومٌ ﴿٤١﴾

fruits; and they will be honoured (42)

فَوَاكِهُ وَهُم مُّكْرَمُونَ ﴿٤٢﴾

in gardens of bliss, (43)

فِي جَنَّاتِ النَّعِيمِ ﴿٤٣﴾

seated on soft couches, facing one another. (44)

عَلَىٰ سُرُرٍ مُّتَقَابِلِينَ ﴿٤٤﴾

A cup will be passed round among them with a drink from a flowing spring: (45)

يُطَافُ عَلَيْهِم بِكَأْسٍ مِّن مَّعِينٍ ﴿٤٥﴾

clear, delicious to those who drink it, (46)

بَيْضَآءَ لَذَّةٍ لِّلشَّارِبِينَ ﴿٤٦﴾

causing no headiness or intoxication. (47)

لَا فِيهَا غَوْلٌ وَلَا هُمْ عَنْهَا يُنزَفُونَ ﴿٤٧﴾

With them will be mates of modest gaze, most beautiful of eye, (48)

وَعِندَهُمْ قَاصِرَاتُ الطَّرْفِ عِينٌ ﴿٤٨﴾

as if they were hidden eggs. (49)

كَأَنَّهُنَّ بَيْضٌ مَّكْنُونٌ ﴿٤٩﴾

And they will turn to one another with questions. (50)

فَأَقْبَلَ بَعْضُهُمْ عَلَىٰ بَعْضٍ يَتَسَآءَلُونَ ۞

One of them will say: I had a close companion on earth (51)

قَالَ قَآئِلٌ مِّنْهُمْ إِنِّي كَانَ لِي قَرِينٌ ۞

who used to ask me: 'Do you really believe (52)

يَقُولُ أَءِنَّكَ لَمِنَ ٱلْمُصَدِّقِينَ ۞

that after we have died and become mere dust and bones we shall be brought for judgement?' (53)

أَءِذَا مِتْنَا وَكُنَّا تُرَابًا وَعِظَامًا أَءِنَّا لَمَدِينُونَ ۞

He adds: 'Would you like to look down?' (54)

قَالَ هَلْ أَنتُم مُّطَّلِعُونَ ۞

Then he looks and sees him in the midst of the fire. (55)

فَٱطَّلَعَ فَرَءَاهُ فِي سَوَآءِ ٱلْجَحِيمِ ۞

He will then say: 'By God! You almost brought me to ruin! (56)

قَالَ تَٱللَّهِ إِن كِدتَّ لَتُرْدِينِ ۞

But for the grace of God I should have also been brought there.' (57)

وَلَوْلَا نِعْمَةُ رَبِّي لَكُنتُ مِنَ ٱلْمُحْضَرِينَ ۞

'But then is it truly so, that we are not to die (58)

أَفَمَا نَحْنُ بِمَيِّتِينَ ۞

except for our first death, and that we are not to suffer? (59)

إِلَّا مَوْتَتَنَا ٱلْأُولَىٰ وَمَا نَحْنُ بِمُعَذَّبِينَ ۞

This is indeed the supreme triumph.' (60)

إِنَّ هَٰذَا لَهُوَ ٱلْفَوْزُ ٱلْعَظِيمُ ۞

Everyone should strive to attain this goal. (61)

لِمِثْلِ هَٰذَا فَلْيَعْمَلِ الْعَٰمِلُونَ ﴿٦١﴾

Is this the better welcome, or the Zaqqūm tree? (62)

أَذَٰلِكَ خَيْرٌ نُّزُلًا أَمْ شَجَرَةُ الزَّقُّومِ ﴿٦٢﴾

We have made it a test for the wrongdoers. (63)

إِنَّا جَعَلْنَٰهَا فِتْنَةً لِّلظَّٰلِمِينَ ﴿٦٣﴾

It is a tree that grows in the very heart of the blazing fire of hell. (64)

إِنَّهَا شَجَرَةٌ تَخْرُجُ فِىٓ أَصْلِ الْجَحِيمِ ﴿٦٤﴾

Its fruit is like devils' heads. (65)

طَلْعُهَا كَأَنَّهُۥ رُءُوسُ الشَّيَٰطِينِ ﴿٦٥﴾

They will indeed eat of it, filling their bellies. (66)

فَإِنَّهُمْ لَءَاكِلُونَ مِنْهَا فَمَالِـُٔونَ مِنْهَا الْبُطُونَ ﴿٦٦﴾

Then on top of it, they will be given polluted, scalding water to drink. (67)

ثُمَّ إِنَّ لَهُمْ عَلَيْهَا لَشَوْبًا مِّنْ حَمِيمٍ ﴿٦٧﴾

Then again, their ultimate goal is hell. (68)

ثُمَّ إِنَّ مَرْجِعَهُمْ لَإِلَى الْجَحِيمِ ﴿٦٨﴾

A Sky Adorned with Stars

By the [angels] ranged in ranks, who rebuke reproachfully and recite God's word most certainly your God is One, Lord of the heavens and the earth and everything between them, Lord of all the points of sunrise. (Verses 1–5)

The *sūrah* begins by mentioning three groups of people, identifying what they do. The first description may mean that they range themselves in rows as they pray, or range their wings, awaiting God's commands. The second group rebukes whoever deserves rebuke, perhaps at the time when the angels gather their souls when they die, or at the time of resurrection, or when they are driven into hell, or in any position or situation. The third group recite God's word, which may be the Qur'ān or other scriptures or they may recite glorifications of God. They are mentioned in the form of an oath made by God confirming His oneness: "*Your God is One.*" (Verse 4) As we have already stated, the occasion here is the mention of the superstition circulated in ignorant Arabia alleging that the angels were God's daughters, and as such, they too were deities.

God then mentions to His servants something about Himself that is suited to the truth of His oneness: He is the "*Lord of the heavens and the earth and everything between them, Lord of all the points of sunrise.*" (Verse 5) The heavens and the earth stand before us, speaking to us about the Creator who controls everything in this universe. No one else claims the ability to create and control the universe, and no one can deny that the One who created the universe is the true Lord who has absolute power. He also created and controls "*everything between them,*" including the air, clouds, light, as well as tiny little creatures which man comes to know from time to time, but much more remains unknown to man. It is impossible to look with an alert mind at the heavens and the earth and what is between them without being profoundly affected by the greatness, accuracy, variety, beauty, harmony and coherence between all these creatures. Only a dead heart can look at them without genuine interaction.

"*Lord of all points of sunrise.*" (Verse 5) The translation of this verse is far from adequate, as the verse not only refers to the rising of the sun, but of every star and planet. Each has its time and point of rising. Therefore, the number of such points in all the corners of the universe is beyond imagination. At the same time, the phrase refers to the fact that as the earth turns round the sun, every point of it has its own sunrise, and its point of sunset. Whenever a point of earth is facing the sun, it has its sunrise, and the opposite point on the surface of the earth has its sunset. People did not know this at the time of the revelation of the Qur'ān, but God told them about it. This precise system that makes such successive sunrises over the earth, and the splendid beauty that so permeates our planet beckons us to reflect on the superb beauty of God's creation and to believe in His oneness. How could such beauty, accuracy and consistency have been achieved unless the Maker is One?

This is the reason why this particular attribute of God's is mentioned on this occasion. We will see that there will be another occasion in the *sūrah* which recalls the mention of the heavens and sunrises, as it refers to planets, flames, devils and their destruction.

> *We have adorned the skies nearest to the earth with stars, and have made them secure against every rebellious devil. Thus, they cannot eavesdrop on the ones on high, but shall be repelled from all sides, driven away, with lasting suffering in store for them. If any of them stealthily snatches away a fragment, he will be pursued by a piercing flame.* (Verses 6–10)

At the outset, the *sūrah* touches on the part of the superstition that relates to angels. Now it touches on the part that relates to the *jinn*. In pre-Islamic days, some Arabs alleged that the *jinn* were related to God. Indeed, some of them worshipped the *jinn* for this reason, and because they attributed to them knowledge of the world beyond human perception.

"*We have adorned the skies nearest to the earth with stars.*" (Verse 6) One look at the sky is sufficient to realize that the element of beauty is purposely incorporated into the making of the universe: its very make up is beautiful, well proportioned and harmonious. In fact, beauty is an essential part of its nature. Its design gives equal importance to beautiful appearance and perfect functioning. Therefore, everything in it is made according to an accurate measure, performing its role to perfection and adding to its overall beauty.

The sky and its stars is the most beautiful scene around us. We never tire of it. Every star and planet sends its flickering light, like a damsel's eye looking shyly at you. When you look straight at her, she turns her eye away; but when you take your glance away, her eyes brighten. To look at these stars and planets as they change position night after night gives endless pleasure.

Another function of the stars and their satellites is also mentioned in the *sūrah*, demonstrating how some of them are shooting stars and piercing flames that target the *jinn*, preventing them from getting close to those on high: We *"have made them secure against every rebellious devil. Thus, they cannot eavesdrop on the ones on high, but shall be repelled from all sides, driven away, with lasting suffering in store for them. If any of them stealthily snatches away a fragment, he will be pursued by a piercing flame."* (Verses 7–10) This means that some of the shooting stars we see guard the skies against rebellious devils to prevent them from eavesdropping on those on high. Such devils on the Day of Judgement will be punished further. However, a rebellious devil might stealthily snatch something of what goes on among the angels on high, but as this devil descends, a piercing flame pursues and burns him.

We have no idea how the rebellious devil tries to eavesdrop, how he snatches a fragment, or how he is pursued by the piercing flame. All these are beyond the limits of our human nature and its power of imagination. The only way open to us is to believe what we are told by God and accept it as it is stated. We should remember that our knowledge of the universe is only superficial. What is important to understand here is that those devils who are prevented from eavesdropping on what takes place on high are the ones whom the idolaters alleged to be related to God. Had anything of the sort been true, the whole story would have been totally different. Such alleged relatives would not have suffered the burning fate that pursues them.

Receiving the Message with Ridicule

The Prophet is then instructed to question them about whether they considered their own creation to be more difficult or the creation of the heavens, earth and all creation in the universe? If they agree that man's creation is less difficult, why should they then disbelieve in resurrection, meeting it with derision and considering it impossible, when it is nothing compared to creating the universe?

Now ask those [unbelievers]: Are they more difficult to create, or the other beings We have created? Them have We created out of a sticky clay. Whereas you marvel, they scoff; and when they are reminded of the truth, they pay no heed; and when they see a sign, they resort to ridicule; and say: 'This is nothing but plain sorcery. What! After we have died and become mere dust and bones, shall we be raised back to life? And perhaps our forefathers?' (Verses 11–17)

The other created beings in this respect include the angels, heavens, the earth and all between them, the *jinn*, stars, planets and piercing flames. They acknowledge that these are created by God. No answer, however, is expected to the question. This is simply a rhetorical device inviting amazement at their lack of understanding of what is around them. It derides the way they look at things. Leaving the question unanswered, the *sūrah* shows them the substance from which they were created in the first place: it is soft, sticky clay made of material from this earth, which is itself one of God's creatures: "*Them have We created out of a sticky clay.*" (Verse 11) It is abundantly clear then that they are not the more difficult to create. Hence, their making fun of God's signs and His promise to bring them back to life is nothing less than absurd.

Their attitude makes the Prophet wonder: "*Whereas you marvel, they scoff; and when they are reminded of the truth, they pay no heed; and when they see a sign, they resort to ridicule.*" (Verses 12–14) It is only right that the Prophet should wonder at them. A believer who recognizes God with all his faculties as Muḥammad (peace be upon him) did, and who sees in full clarity the numerous signs in the universe pointing to Him, is bound to wonder and marvel at how people can remain oblivious to them. In short, how can they adopt such an attitude?

As the Prophet looked at them with amazement, they continued ridiculing the truth he presented to them, speaking of God's oneness and their own resurrection. They preferred to remain blind, with their hearts sealed. Hence they scoffed at God's revelations and signs, wondered at the Prophet who presented these to them and made that the material for further ridicule. Part of this was how they described the Qur'ān: "*This is nothing but plain sorcery. What! After we have died and become mere dust and bones, shall we be raised back to life? And perhaps our forefathers?"* (Verses 15–17) They are oblivious to everything around them that reminds them of God's power and ability, claiming that He would not return them to life after they and their forefathers had died and perished. Yet such return is nothing to marvel at, if we would only look at the universe around us and see what God has created.

Since they would not reflect quietly and calmly on what they saw, they are strongly jolted such that they see their own agitated state in the life to come: *"Say: Yes, indeed! And you shall be utterly humbled."* (Verse 18) Yes, indeed, you and your forefathers will be resurrected and utterly humiliated, unable to put up any opposition. It is not merely that God emphatically confirms their resurrection, but He shows them how it is done. This is depicted in a long scene describing resurrection in different ways, presenting lively images and successive movements. The whole account employs the narrative style first, then changes to dialogue, and in between they see events and actions and hear comments on these. Thus, the whole scene comes alive.

"There will be just one single cry, and they will all begin to see." (Verse 19) It is all just a glimpse, taking no more than a single cry, which is described in Arabic as *zajrah*, to indicate that it is exceedingly strong and coming from a superior source. This single cry is made *"and they will all begin to see,"* suddenly, without any preparation. Surprised so violently, they cry out: *"Woe betide us! This is the Day of Judgement!"* (Verse 20) In the midst of their shock, a voice will unexpectedly make it clear that whatever happens to them is through their own making: *"This is indeed the Day of Decision which you used to call a lie!"* (Verse 21) Here we see how the *sūrah* changes its style from the narrative to directly address those who used to deny that there would ever be such a day when all mankind would be resurrected and their fate determined.

It takes only one decisive sentence of blame before the orders are issued to those whose task it is to carry them out: *"Gather together all those who were bent on wrongdoing, their ilk, and all that they used to worship instead of God, and guide them all to the path of hell, but halt them a while, for they shall be asked."* (Verses 22–24) So the wrongdoers and their like are to be gathered together. Although the order is clear and decisive, it also carries much sarcasm in the expression, *'guide them all to the path of hell.'* This is certainly a strange type of guidance, worse than going astray. Yet it is the perfect retort to their straying from the path of divine guidance. Since they did not benefit in this present world from guidance to the straight path, guidance will be given to them in the life to come, but this time to the path of hell.

Having been given such guidance, we then see them halted for questioning. Again the address turns to them with blame, even though it is delivered through a simple and innocent question: "*How is it that you do not help one another?*" (Verse 25) Why do you not support one another when you are all here and in need of any help you can get? You also have here with you the deities you used to worship. Needless to say, none of them ventures an answer. What follows this rhetorical questioning is a comment describing their condition: "*Indeed, on that day they will be in complete submission.*" (Verse 26) Both the worshippers and the worshipped are in a state of complete submission to God.

Once more, the *sūrah* picks up the narrative style, portraying them as they argue with one another: "*They will turn upon one another accusingly. Some [of them] will say: You used to [whisper to us] approaching us from the right!*" (Verses 27–28) This describes the normal condition of whispering, coming from the right. Thus, they blame the whisperers, saying they are responsible for their present ordeal. Those accused will immediately deny responsibility, putting it squarely on their accusers: "*The others will reply: No! It was you who would not believe.*" (Verse 29) It was not our whisper that took you from faith into disbelief. You were not following guidance and we led you astray by whispering. Indeed, "*We had no power over you.*" (Verse 30) We could not impose our views on you, forcing you to follow us against your will: "*but you were willing to exceed all limits.*" (Verse 30) You would not abide by any limit. "*Now our Lord's word has come true against us, and we are bound to taste [the punishment].*" (Verse 31) Both you and us are in the same position, deserving of God's punishment for not heeding the warnings. You joined us because of your propensity to follow error. We did nothing to you, instead you followed us in our error: "*If we led you astray, we ourselves were astray.*" (Verse 32)

At this point, another comment is made, but this time it sounds like a sentence announced before all, making its grounds clear and revealing what they did in this world to bring about their condemnation in the next: "*On that day, they all will share in the common suffering. Thus shall We deal with all the guilty ones. Whenever they were told, 'there is no deity other than God,' they would turn away in arrogance, and would say: 'Are we to forsake our deities for the sake of a mad poet?'*" (Verses 33–36) A further comment carries clear censure of those who say such monstrous words: "*For certain, he has brought the truth, and confirmed the earlier messengers. You will indeed taste grievous suffering, being requited only for what you used to do. Not so God's true servants.*" (Verses 37–40)

Since God's true servants are mentioned here, making it clear that they will not suffer, their condition on the Day of Judgement is also shown. Once more this comes in narrative style, describing the happiness and bliss they will enjoy to the full and contrasting it with the suffering the other party endures:

> *Theirs shall be a predetermined sustenance: fruits; and they will be honoured in gardens of bliss, seated on soft couches, facing one another. A cup will be passed round among them with a drink from a flowing spring: clear, delicious to those who drink it, causing no headiness or intoxication. With them will be mates of modest gaze, most beautiful of eye, as if they were hidden eggs.* (Verses 41–49)

This is happiness pure and perfect, combining all that is enjoyable, physically and spiritually. Everyone finds in it whatever they want of happiness. To start with, the people enjoying this happiness are God's true servants, a description that signifies they are held in high regard. They are also '*honoured*' among those on high, and this is the highest honour. They have '*fruit*' and they sit '*on soft couches facing one another.*' They will be served so that they need not exert any effort for anything. What they drink is also described in detail: "*A cup will be passed round among them with a drink from a flowing spring: clear, delicious to those who drink it, causing no headiness or intoxication.*" (Verses 45–47) These are the best qualities in any drink, giving the pleasure without negative consequences. Thus they do not fear that it will be used up, and it gives them no unpleasant side effects. They have companions who are described as follows: "*With them will be mates of modest gaze, most*

310

beautiful of eye." (Verse 48) Their modesty means that they do not look up to anyone other than their mates, despite being very pretty. They are chaste and gentle, "*as if they were hidden eggs,*" untouched by anyone.

As the story unfolds we see these true servants of God engaged in pleasant conversation, recalling things from their past lives and looking at what they now enjoy. This image contrasts with the contentious arguments the others have in their place of suffering. One of the believers then relates to his brethren something that he recalls from his first life: "*One of them will say: I had a close companion on earth who used to ask me: 'Do you really believe that after we have died and become mere dust and bones we shall be brought for judgement?'*" (Verses 51–53) His friend did not believe in the Day of Judgement, and he asked him in amazement whether he truly believed in resurrection after death. As he is speaking about his friend, this believer wishes to know what happened to him. He looks for him and calls on his brothers to look as well: "*He adds: 'Would you like to look down?' Then he looks and sees him in the midst of the fire.*" (Verses 54–55)

When he sees him in his suffering, he turns to him and says: You could have led me astray and ruined me by what you whispered in my ear. It was only through God's favour that I did not listen to you: "*He will then say: 'By God! You almost brought me to ruin! But for the grace of God I should have also been brought there.*" (Verses 56–57) I could have ended up in the same position and been driven with the herd to the same position you now are in.

His awareness of what happened to his friend makes him feel more acutely the great blessing he and his fellow believers are experiencing. Therefore, he wants to assert it and be reassured that it will last: "*But then is it truly so, that we are not to die except for our first death, and that we are not to suffer? This is indeed the supreme triumph.*" (Verses 58–60)

A short comment is made here, alerting hearts to the need to work hard in order to achieve such a goal. "*Everyone should strive to attain this goal.*" (Verse 61) The goal is a pure and everlasting happiness that cannot be ended by death or prevented by torture. It is the type of goal that deserves hard effort. Compared to this, other goals people strive for seem worthless.

In order to highlight the great gulf between this everlasting, pure happiness and the other destiny awaiting the unbelievers, the *sūrah* explains what awaits the latter after they have been held to account:

> *Is this the better welcome, or the Zaqqūm tree? We have made it a test for the wrongdoers. It is a tree that grows in the very heart of the blazing fire of hell. Its fruit is like devils' heads. They will indeed eat of it, filling their bellies. Then on top of it, they will be given polluted scalding water to drink. Then again, their ultimate goal is hell.* (Verses 62–68)

Rhetorically they are asked whether the pure endless bliss is a better position and place or the Zaqqūm tree. What is this tree, then? The answer is simple: "*It is a tree that grows in the very heart of the blazing fire of hell. Its fruit is like devils' heads.*" (Verses 64–65) Needless to say, people do not know how devils' heads look. Nevertheless, it is a frightening image. It is sufficient only to think of these heads to be scared. How, then, would they countenance the prospect of these very heads becoming the food with which they fill their bellies?

God made this tree a test for the wrongdoers. When they heard its name, they made fun of it, saying: 'How could a tree grow in hell without being burnt?' One of them, Abū Jahl, said in sarcasm: "People of the Quraysh! Do you know what the Zaqqūm tree is that Muḥammad holds up to scare you with? It is the dates of Madinah cooked with butter. Should we get it, we will swallow it without hesitation."

The fact is, however, that the Zaqqūm tree was something different from the food they knew: "*They will indeed eat of it, filling their bellies.*" (Verse 66) When it stings their throats and burns their bellies – as it grows in the fire it is of the same substance – they will look for a cool drink to stop the burning. However, they will only drink contaminated, boiling water: "*Then on top of it, they will be given polluted, scalding water to drink.*" (Verse 67)

After this meal, they leave the table to return to their permanent abode, which is far from welcoming: "*Then again, their ultimate goal is hell.*" (Verse 68)

2

Abraham's Sacrifice

They found their forefathers astray, (69)

إِنَّهُمْ أَلْفَوْاءَابَاءَهُمْ ضَالِّينَ ﴿٦٩﴾

and rushed to follow in their footsteps. (70)

فَهُمْ عَلَىٰٓ ءَاثَٰرِهِمْ يُهْرَعُونَ ﴿٧٠﴾

Most of the people of old went astray before them; (71)

وَلَقَدْ ضَلَّ قَبْلَهُمْ أَكْثَرُ ٱلْأَوَّلِينَ ﴿٧١﴾

although We had sent them warners. (72)

وَلَقَدْ أَرْسَلْنَا فِيهِم مُّنذِرِينَ ﴿٧٢﴾

Behold what happened in the end to those that had been warned. (73)

فَٱنظُرْ كَيْفَ كَانَ عَٰقِبَةُ ٱلْمُنذَرِينَ ﴿٧٣﴾

Not so God's true servants. (74)

إِلَّا عِبَادَ ٱللَّهِ ٱلْمُخْلَصِينَ ﴿٧٤﴾

Noah cried to Us, and We are the best to answer prayer: (75)

وَلَقَدْ نَادَىٰنَا نُوحٌ فَلَنِعْمَ ٱلْمُجِيبُونَ ﴿٧٥﴾

We saved him and his household from great distress; (76)

وَنَجَّيْنَٰهُ وَأَهْلَهُۥ مِنَ ٱلْكَرْبِ ٱلْعَظِيمِ ﴿٧٦﴾

and caused his offspring to be the survivors. (77)

وَجَعَلْنَا ذُرِّيَّتَهُۥ هُمُ ٱلْبَاقِينَ ﴿٧٧﴾

We caused him to be praised by later generations: (78)

وَتَرَكْنَا عَلَيْهِ فِي ٱلْآخِرِينَ ۝

Peace be upon Noah in all the worlds! (79)

سَلَامٌ عَلَىٰ نُوحٍ فِي ٱلْعَٰلَمِينَ ۝

Thus do We reward those who do good. (80)

إِنَّا كَذَٰلِكَ نَجْزِي ٱلْمُحْسِنِينَ ۝

He was truly one of Our believing servants. (81)

إِنَّهُۥ مِنْ عِبَادِنَا ٱلْمُؤْمِنِينَ ۝

Then We caused the others to drown. (82)

ثُمَّ أَغْرَقْنَا ٱلْآخَرِينَ ۝

Among those who followed his way was Abraham. (83)

وَإِنَّ مِن شِيعَتِهِۦ لَإِبْرَٰهِيمَ ۝

He turned to his Lord with a sound heart. (84)

إِذْ جَآءَ رَبَّهُۥ بِقَلْبٍ سَلِيمٍ ۝

He said to his father and his people: 'What is this that you worship? (85)

إِذْ قَالَ لِأَبِيهِ وَقَوْمِهِۦ مَاذَا تَعْبُدُونَ ۝

Do you choose false deities instead of God? (86)

أَئِفْكًا ءَالِهَةً دُونَ ٱللَّهِ تُرِيدُونَ ۝

What, then, do you think of the Lord of all the worlds?' (87)

فَمَا ظَنُّكُم بِرَبِّ ٱلْعَٰلَمِينَ ۝

Then he cast a glance at the stars, (88)

فَنَظَرَ نَظْرَةً فِي ٱلنُّجُومِ ۝

and said: 'Indeed I am sick.' (89)

فَقَالَ إِنِّي سَقِيمٌ ۝

So his people turned away from him and left. (90)

فَتَوَلَّوْاْ عَنْهُ مُدْبِرِينَ ﴿٩٠﴾

He then approached their deities stealthily and said: 'Will you not eat [your offerings]? (91)

فَرَاغَ إِلَىٰٓ ءَالِهَتِهِمْ فَقَالَ أَلَا تَأْكُلُونَ ﴿٩١﴾

What is the matter with you that you do not speak?' (92)

مَا لَكُمْ لَا تَنطِقُونَ ﴿٩٢﴾

And then he fell upon them, smiting them with his right hand. (93)

فَرَاغَ عَلَيْهِمْ ضَرْبًا بِٱلْيَمِينِ ﴿٩٣﴾

His people came to him hurriedly, (94)

فَأَقْبَلُوٓاْ إِلَيْهِ يَزِفُّونَ ﴿٩٤﴾

but he said: 'Do you worship something that you yourselves have carved, (95)

قَالَ أَتَعْبُدُونَ مَا تَنْحِتُونَ ﴿٩٥﴾

while it is God who has created you and all your handiwork?' (96)

وَٱللَّهُ خَلَقَكُمْ وَمَا تَعْمَلُونَ ﴿٩٦﴾

They said: 'Build him a pyre and throw him into the blazing fire.' (97)

قَالُواْ ٱبْنُواْ لَهُۥ بُنْيَٰنًا فَأَلْقُوهُ فِى ٱلْجَحِيمِ ﴿٩٧﴾

They schemed to harm him, but We caused them to be humiliated. (98)

فَأَرَادُواْ بِهِۦ كَيْدًا فَجَعَلْنَٰهُمُ ٱلْأَسْفَلِينَ ﴿٩٨﴾

And Abraham said: 'I will go to my Lord: He is sure to guide me. (99)

وَقَالَ إِنِّى ذَاهِبٌ إِلَىٰ رَبِّى سَيَهْدِينِ ﴿٩٩﴾

315

Lord! Grant me a righteous son.' (100)

رَبِّ هَبْ لِى مِنَ ٱلصَّالِحِينَ ۝

We gave him the happy news that he will have a forbearing son. (101)

فَبَشَّرْنَهُ بِغُلَمٍ حَلِيمٍ ۝

When the boy was old enough to work with his father, Abraham said: 'My son! I have seen in a dream that I must sacrifice you. Tell me, then, what you think.' [Ishmael] said: 'My father! Do as you are bidden, and, God willing, you will find me to be patient in adversity.' (102)

فَلَمَّا بَلَغَ مَعَهُ ٱلسَّعْىَ قَالَ يَبُنَىَّ إِنِّى أَرَىٰ فِى ٱلْمَنَامِ أَنِّى أَذْبَحُكَ فَٱنظُرْ مَاذَا تَرَىٰ قَالَ يَٰٓأَبَتِ ٱفْعَلْ مَا تُؤْمَرُ سَتَجِدُنِى إِن شَآءَ ٱللَّهُ مِنَ ٱلصَّٰبِرِينَ ۝

When the two of them had surrendered themselves to the will of God, and Abraham laid him prostrate on his forehead, (103)

فَلَمَّآ أَسْلَمَا وَتَلَّهُ لِلْجَبِينِ ۝

We called to him: 'Abraham! (104)

وَنَٰدَيْنَٰهُ أَن يَٰٓإِبْرَٰهِيمُ ۝

You have already fulfilled the dream.' Thus do We reward those who do good. (105)

قَدْ صَدَّقْتَ ٱلرُّءْيَآ إِنَّا كَذَٰلِكَ نَجْزِى ٱلْمُحْسِنِينَ ۝

All this was indeed a momentous trial. (106)

إِنَّ هَٰذَا لَهُوَ ٱلْبَلَٰٓؤُا۟ ٱلْمُبِينُ ۝

We ransomed [Ishmael] with a noble sacrifice, (107)

وَفَدَيْنَٰهُ بِذِبْحٍ عَظِيمٍ ۝

We caused him to be praised by later generations: (108)

وَتَرَكْنَا عَلَيْهِ فِي ٱلْأَخِرِينَ ۝

Peace be upon Abraham! (109)

سَلَٰمٌ عَلَىٰٓ إِبْرَٰهِيمَ ۝

Thus do we reward those who do good. (110)

كَذَٰلِكَ نَجْزِى ٱلْمُحْسِنِينَ ۝

He was truly one of our believing servants. (111)

إِنَّهُۥ مِنْ عِبَادِنَا ٱلْمُؤْمِنِينَ ۝

We gave Abraham the happy news of Isaac, a prophet and a righteous man; (112)

وَبَشَّرْنَٰهُ بِإِسْحَٰقَ نَبِيًّا مِّنَ ٱلصَّٰلِحِينَ ۝

and We blessed him and Isaac; but among their offspring there were those who do good and others who would glaringly sin against their souls. (113)

وَبَٰرَكْنَا عَلَيْهِ وَعَلَىٰٓ إِسْحَٰقَ وَمِن ذُرِّيَّتِهِمَا مُحْسِنٌ وَظَالِمٌ لِّنَفْسِهِۦ مُبِينٌ ۝

We also bestowed Our favour on Moses and Aaron; (114)

وَلَقَدْ مَنَنَّا عَلَىٰ مُوسَىٰ وَهَٰرُونَ ۝

We saved them and their people from great distress; (115)

وَنَجَّيْنَٰهُمَا وَقَوْمَهُمَا مِنَ ٱلْكَرْبِ ٱلْعَظِيمِ ۝

We gave them support, so that it was they who achieved victory. (116)

وَنَصَرْنَٰهُمْ فَكَانُوا۟ هُمُ ٱلْغَٰلِبِينَ ۝

We gave them the Scripture which made things clear; (117)

وَءَاتَيْنَٰهُمَا ٱلْكِتَٰبَ ٱلْمُسْتَبِينَ ۝

We guided them to the right path; (118)

وَهَدَيْنَاهُمَا ٱلصِّرَاطَ ٱلْمُسْتَقِيمَ ۝

We caused them to be praised by later generations: (119)

وَتَرَكْنَا عَلَيْهِمَا فِي ٱلْآخِرِينَ ۝

Peace be upon Moses and Aaron! (120)

سَلَـٰمٌ عَلَىٰ مُوسَىٰ وَهَـٰرُونَ ۝

Thus do We reward those who do good. (121)

إِنَّا كَذَٰلِكَ نَجْزِي ٱلْمُحْسِنِينَ ۝

Both were among Our believing servants. (122)

إِنَّهُمَا مِنْ عِبَادِنَا ٱلْمُؤْمِنِينَ ۝

Elijah too was one of Our messengers. (123)

وَإِنَّ إِلْيَاسَ لَمِنَ ٱلْمُرْسَلِينَ ۝

He said to his people: 'Have you no fear of God? (124)

إِذْ قَالَ لِقَوْمِهِ أَلَا تَتَّقُونَ ۝

How can you invoke Baal and forsake the best of creators, (125)

أَتَدْعُونَ بَعْلًا وَتَذَرُونَ أَحْسَنَ ٱلْخَالِقِينَ ۝

God, your Lord and the Lord of your forefathers?' (126)

ٱللَّهَ رَبَّكُمْ وَرَبَّ ءَابَآئِكُمُ ٱلْأَوَّلِينَ ۝

But they accused him of lying. Therefore, they will certainly be brought [for punishment]. (127)

فَكَذَّبُوهُ فَإِنَّهُمْ لَمُحْضَرُونَ ۝

Not so God's true servants. (128)

إِلَّا عِبَادَ ٱللَّهِ ٱلْمُخْلَصِينَ ۝

We caused him to be praised by later generations: (129)

وَتَرَكْنَا عَلَيْهِ فِي ٱلْآخِرِينَ ۝

Peace be upon Elijah! (130)

سَلَمٌ عَلَىٰٓ إِلْ يَاسِينَ ۝

Thus do We reward those who do good. (131)

إِنَّا كَذَٰلِكَ نَجْزِى ٱلْمُحْسِنِينَ ۝

He was truly one of Our believing servants. (132)

إِنَّهُۥ مِنْ عِبَادِنَا ٱلْمُؤْمِنِينَ ۝

Lot was also one of Our messengers. (133)

وَإِنَّ لُوطًا لَّمِنَ ٱلْمُرْسَلِينَ ۝

We saved him and all his household, (134)

إِذْ نَجَّيْنَٰهُ وَأَهْلَهُۥٓ أَجْمَعِينَ ۝

except for an old woman who stayed behind. (135)

إِلَّا عَجُوزًا فِى ٱلْغَٰبِرِينَ ۝

Then We utterly destroyed the others. (136)

ثُمَّ دَمَّرْنَا ٱلْءَاخَرِينَ ۝

Surely you pass by their ruins at morning-time, (137)

وَإِنَّكُمْ لَتَمُرُّونَ عَلَيْهِم مُّصْبِحِينَ ۝

as also by night. Will you not, then, use your reason? (138)

وَبِٱلَّيْلِ أَفَلَا تَعْقِلُونَ ۝

Jonah too was one of Our messengers. (139)

وَإِنَّ يُونُسَ لَمِنَ ٱلْمُرْسَلِينَ ۝

He deserted, going on the laden ship. (140)

إِذْ أَبَقَ إِلَى ٱلْفُلْكِ ٱلْمَشْحُونِ ۝

They cast lots, and he was the one who lost. (141)

فَسَاهَمَ فَكَانَ مِنَ ٱلْمُدْحَضِينَ ۝

319

The whale swallowed him, for he was to blame. (142)

فَٱلۡتَقَمَهُ ٱلۡحُوتُ وَهُوَ مُلِيمٌ ﴿١٤٢﴾

Had he not been of those who truly glorified God, (143)

فَلَوۡلَآ أَنَّهُۥ كَانَ مِنَ ٱلۡمُسَبِّحِينَ ﴿١٤٣﴾

he would have remained in the whale's belly till Resurrection Day. (144)

لَلَبِثَ فِى بَطۡنِهِۦٓ إِلَىٰ يَوۡمِ يُبۡعَثُونَ ﴿١٤٤﴾

We caused him to be cast out, sick, on a barren shore, (145)

فَنَبَذۡنَٰهُ بِٱلۡعَرَآءِ وَهُوَ سَقِيمٌ ﴿١٤٥﴾

and caused a gourd tree to grow over him. (146)

وَأَنۢبَتۡنَا عَلَيۡهِ شَجَرَةً مِّن يَقۡطِينٍ ﴿١٤٦﴾

Then We sent him to [a community of] one hundred thousand or more. (147)

وَأَرۡسَلۡنَٰهُ إِلَىٰ مِائَةِ أَلۡفٍ أَوۡ يَزِيدُونَ ﴿١٤٧﴾

They believed, so We let them enjoy life for a while. (148)

فَـَٔامَنُوا۟ فَمَتَّعۡنَٰهُمۡ إِلَىٰ حِينٍ ﴿١٤٨﴾

Overview

In this second part, the *sūrah* picks up the lessons of history as it mentions communities going back to the early days of humanity and their attitudes towards divine guidance. We find the story frequently repeating itself. Indeed, the people who persisted in disbelief in Makkah, taking a hostile attitude to the Prophet Muḥammad (peace be upon him), appear to be an offshoot of those earlier communities that went astray. The fates of those earlier communities are mentioned, putting before the Arab unbelievers certain historical events for them to reflect upon as also to reassure the believers that divine care, which never deserted the believers of old, would also not fail them.

The *sūrah* gives brief accounts of Noah, Abraham, Ishmael and Isaac, Moses and Aaron, Elijah, Lot and Jonah. It dwells more on Abraham's and Ishmael's story as it puts before us an example of supreme faith and sacrifice showing us the nature of true surrender to God's will. This particular episode is not mentioned anywhere else in the *Qur'ān*. Together, these stories make up the entire passage.

The Fate of Noah's People

They found their forefathers astray, and rushed to follow in their footsteps. Most of the people of old went astray before them; although We had sent them warners. Behold what happened in the end to those that had been warned. Not so God's true servants. (Verses 69–74)

These people are hardened in following error, but at the same time they are simply following the footsteps of others, without thinking or reflection. They rush to follow their fathers' lead taking no opportunity to question or examine: "*They found their forefathers astray, and rushed to follow in their footsteps.*" (Verses 69–70) Both they and their fathers are examples of going astray, which was also the case of the majority of earlier communities: "*Most of the people of old went astray before them.*" (Verse 71) Yet they did receive warnings, but paid no heed: "*although We had sent them warners.*" (Verse 72) What did this lead to in the end? What was the outcome of the unbelievers' attitude, as compared with the outcome of heeding the warnings and accepting the faith? This is shown in the stories that follow. The verses that ensue serve as a mere announcement of what is to come: "*Behold what happened in the end to those that had been warned. Not so God's true servants.*" (Verses 73–74)

The first story is Noah's, but the account here dwells only briefly on the outcome, highlighting the care God took of His true servants:

Noah cried to Us, and We are the best to answer prayer: We saved him and his household from great distress; and caused his offspring to be the survivors. We caused him to be praised by later generations: Peace be upon Noah in all the worlds! Thus do we reward those

321

who do good. He was truly one of Our believing servants. Then We caused the others to drown. (Verses 75–82)

This reference to Noah includes his appeal to God and the full answer to his prayer by the best to give such an answer. It also tells of the fact that he and his household were saved from the great floods that drowned all except those whom God willed to be saved. It speaks of God's will to make of his offspring communities which build the earth and establish its heritage, while he himself, would be remembered by future generations until the end of time. *"We caused him to be praised by later generations."* (Verse 78) It declares to all the worlds God's greeting to Noah, as he was one who fulfilled well the assignment given him: *"Peace be upon Noah in all the worlds! Thus do We reward those who do good."* (Verses 79–80) What reward could anyone wish for when he has received God's own greetings and is to be remembered for the rest of time? The mark of Noah's doing well that so ensured his great reward was his unshakeable faith: *"He was truly one of Our believing servants."* (Verse 81) This outcome is brought about by faith. The unbelievers among Noah's people met their own ruin: *"Then We caused the others to drown."* (Verse 82) This has set the rule ever since the dawn of history. It is the pattern given in general terms immediately before these stories: *"We had sent them warners. Behold what happened in the end to those that had been warned. Not so God's true servants."* (Verses 72–74)

Abraham and the Idols

The *sūrah* then depicts two of the main episodes from Abraham's story. The first shows him advocating faith among his people and destroying their idols, followed by their attempt to kill him and God saving him. This episode is also described in other *sūrahs*. The second episode however, is only mentioned here. It speaks of Abraham's dream, his sacrifice and how God released his son. This story is given in detail, speaking of stages and attitudes in a remarkably fine and effective style. It shows the most sublime example of obedience to God, sacrifice and self surrender:

*Among those who followed his way was Abraham. He turned to
his Lord with a sound heart. He said to his father and his people:
What is this that you worship? Do you choose false deities instead
of God? What, then, do you think of the Lord of all the worlds?*
(Verses 83–87)

Thus the story opens, moving from Noah to Abraham and making
it clear that they were related in faith and its advocacy. Thus Abraham
is said to belong to Noah's community despite the long time gap
between them. Nonetheless they shared the same divine constitution
and message.

Abraham's quality highlighted here is his sound heart, which makes
him a man of true faith and clear conscience: "*He turned to his Lord
with a sound heart.*" (Verse 84) This is an image of complete submission
as represented in Abraham's turning to his Lord. Use of the adjective
'sound' gives clear impressions, and at the same time it is easy and
clear, giving strong connotations of purity, sincerity and straightforward
behaviour.

Because he had a sound heart, Abraham took exception to the practices
of his people. This was motivated by his sound sense which recoiled
from any idea or behaviour that conflicted with essential human nature:
"*He said to his father and his people: What is this that you worship? Do
you choose false deities instead of God? What, then, do you think of the
Lord of all the worlds?*" (Verses 85–87) As he saw them worshipping
statues and idols, he disapprovingly asked: '*What is this that you worship?*'
This thing that you worship is not worthy of what you do. In fact, there
is no trace of truth in such worship: it is sheer falsehood: "*Do you choose
false deities instead of God?*" (Verse 86) What concept do you have of
God? Is it so low that human nature looks with abhorrence at its first
sight? "*What, then, do you think of the Lord of all the worlds?*" (Verse 87)

The *sūrah* does not report their answer or their argument with him.
Instead, it moves straight to the second scene, showing what he
determined to do to confront this flagrant falsehood:

*Then he cast a glance at the stars, and said: 'Indeed I am sick.' So
his people turned away from him and left. He then approached*

their deities stealthily and said: 'Will you not eat [your offerings]? What is the matter with you that you do not speak?' And then he fell upon them, smiting them with his right hand. (Verses 88–93)

It is said that Abraham's people were in the midst of a special festive occasion, which might have been their new year's day, when they went out to spend the day in gardens and parks. They started, however, by placing fruit in front of their deities for blessing. When they returned, having had their fun, they took their blessed food. Abraham, who had despaired of ever receiving a reasonable response from them, realized that they had gone too far astray, and had made up his mind with regard to his next move. Indeed, he waited until the day when they were sure to be away from their temples. He was so fed up with their error that it pained his heart. Therefore, when he was invited to join them, he looked at the sky and said: 'I am sick, I cannot join in your festivity. If I come with you, I may spoil your occasion.'

He was simply expressing his distress at their practices, so that they would leave him alone. What he said was true; it was no lie. Distress can leave real feelings of illness. Since the people were busy preparing for their celebration, they did not stop to examine his claims. Rather, they left him alone and went away. This was the chance Abraham had waited for.

He went straight to their false deities and saw splendid varieties of food and fruit placed in front of them. He said sarcastically: "*Will you not eat?*" (Verse 91) Needless to say, the statues and idols made no reply. He continued with his sarcasm, while also expressing irritation: "*What is the matter with you that you do not speak?*" (Verse 92) This is a common psychological situation: a man addressing his words to something he knows will not hear or answer him. It was, however, merely an expression of what Abraham felt towards his people as they engaged in absurd falsehood. Once more, the idols gave him no answer. At this point he moved swiftly to pour out all his frustration in action, not just in mere words: "*And then he fell upon them, smiting them with his right hand.*" (Verse 93) Thus he cleared his illness and distress by solid action.

With this scene over, the *sūrah* paints a new one. The people return from their festivities and see their deities destroyed. Here we do not have the details given in *Sūrah* 21, The Prophets, about their asking as to what had happened and determining who was the perpetrator. Instead, the *sūrah* moves straight to their confrontation with Abraham.

"*His people came to him hurriedly.*" (Verse 94) The news circulated quickly among them, and they unflinchingly sought to confront him. They were angry, agitated and numerous, while he was alone. Yet he had his faith: he knew its simple details, recognizing its soundness within himself and seeing its evidence in the universe around him. This made him stronger than this agitated, angry multitude with its confused beliefs and stupid concepts. Therefore, he put his argument straight, caring little for their number and anger: "*He said: Do you worship something that you yourselves have carved, while it is God who has created you and all your handiwork?*" (Verses 95–96)

It is the logic of a simple and sound nature putting the case starkly and clearly to others: how come you worship what you carve with your own hands, when worship should be addressed to the Maker, not to what is made: "*It is God who has created you and all your handiwork.*" (Verse 96) He is the Maker of all, and He is the One to be worshipped.

Although Abraham's argument was clear and logical, in their blind anger, the people did not listen. When did falsehood ever listen to simple truth? Therefore, their leaders retaliated by exercizing a crude tyranny: "*They said: Build him a pyre and throw him into the blazing fire.*" (Verse 97) This is the only logic tyranny knows. It cares little for argument and proof. Tyrants know that they cannot face the word of truth, with its overpowering appeal.

The *sūrah* gives no details of what happened after they issued their orders. It simply shows the outcome with the fulfilment of God's promise to His true servants and His warnings to the unbelievers: "*They schemed to harm him, but We caused them to be humiliated.*" (Verse 98) What chance has such scheming when God wants it to be foiled? What can frail and powerless tyrants who cling to power do when God takes care of His true servants?

The Great Sacrifice

The *sūrah* moves on to the second episode it relates of Abraham's history. After he was saved from the fire, he closed that chapter of his life to begin a new phase: "*And Abraham said: I will go to my Lord: He is sure to guide me.*" (Verse 99) His words indicate that he was migrating, this in both a mental and physical sense. He was abandoning everything: his father, family, home, people and land, leaving them all behind and going to his Lord, free of all concerns. He thus surrendered himself to his Lord, assured that He would give him guidance and care, setting him on the right path. It is a migration from one state to another, abandoning all ties and bonds in favour of one bond that remains pure and strong. His words express complete faith and unqualified surrender.

Until that moment, Abraham was without children. He had left behind his relations, friends and all that was familiar to him. Needless to say, his relations with those who threw him in the fire suffered a final breakdown. Therefore, he went to his Lord, praying to Him to grant him believing offspring: "*Lord! Grant me a righteous son.*" (Verse 100) And God answered his true servant's prayer: "*We gave him the happy news that he will have a forbearing son.*" (Verse 101) The son was most probably Ishmael, as clearly inferred from his life story and from the *sūrah* itself. Indeed, we can see the mark of his forbearance in his youth. We can also imagine the delight experienced by Abraham in his new abode, where he was a stranger, at the birth of this son described by God as a '*forbearing son.*'

It is time for us now to look at the glorious attitude that Abraham's life story represents, drawing from it an inspiring lesson as presented by God Almighty to the Muslim community.

> When the boy was old enough to work with his father, Abraham said: 'My son! I have seen in a dream that I must sacrifice you. Tell me, then, what you think.' [Ishmael] said: 'My father! Do as you are bidden, and, God willing, you will find me to be patient in adversity.' (Verse 102)

What effect will faith not produce? We see here Abraham in his old age, cut off in a foreign land, having deserted his homeland and his

326

people, being given a child. The child turns out to be a model son, with his forbearance confirmed by God Himself. Hardly had Abraham enjoyed his son's company and seen his youth blooming so as to become his companion and assistant, when he sees in his dream that he should slaughter him. He understands that it is a sign from God requiring sacrifice. What is his attitude now? He does not hesitate for a moment. The thought of disobedience does not even occur to him. He thinks only of submission. It is true that the dream was only a signal, not a clear and direct order issued through revelation. It was a signal by his Lord though, and that was enough for Abraham to comply, not to delay, and not even to ask why.

Moreover, his compliance did not betray any feeling of distress, horror or panic; it was marked by calm acceptance and reassurance, reflected in his words as he put this most grave matter to his son: "*My son! I have seen in a dream that I must sacrifice you. Tell me, then, what you think.*" (Verse 102) These are the words of a man in full control of himself and his feelings, knowing that he is only doing his duty and trusting that it behoves him to comply. We do not see any element of panic driving a person to do even what he feels to be repugnant, in order to get it done and finished with.

That it was hard for Abraham is beyond doubt. He was not required to send his only son to war, nor to put him to a task that would end in his death. Nothing of the sort. Instead he was required to undertake the task himself, by his own hand. And what task was that? It was to slaughter his own son by way of sacrifice. This was the order he received calmly, the one that he put to his son and asked him to consider carefully. He did not take his son by surprise and do what was bidden. Rather, he puts the question to him as if it were both normal and familiar. To Abraham, the question was one of obedience. Since his Lord wanted something, so be it, without hesitation. His son should also know and accept it willingly, with submission so that he too would earn the reward of obeying God and experience the pleasure of submission to Him. He himself had known that pleasure and now wants his son to feel it as the pure goodness that surpasses all else that life can offer.

What does the son say as his father proposes to slaughter him in fulfilment of what he saw in a dream? The son also rises to the sublime standard his father had earlier attained: "*He said: My father! Do as you are bidden, and, God willing, you will find me to be patient in adversity.*" (Verse 102) This is not a response of mere obedience and resignation. It is a response marked with acceptance and certainty. His reply begins with, *'My father!'* The prospect of his death does not cause him to panic or to forget his manners and love of his father. "*Do as you are bidden.*" He also feels the same as his father, taking the dream as a signal, which means an order. This is sufficient to make him willing to carry it out without hesitation.

Furthermore, we see in Ishmael's response proper manners with his Lord, and recognition of the limits of his ability in the face of hardship. Therefore, he seeks his Lord's help to overcome his weakness. He attributes to God the grace of helping him to obey and make the sacrifice: "*God willing, you will find me to be patient in adversity.*" (Verse 102) He does not press the matter as a heroic act on his part. Nor does he describe it as facing the danger and caring little for the consequences. He does not give himself any credit in the matter; he simply attributes it all to God who has helped him in carrying out His orders with patience in adversity. This is an example of perfect humility before God, trust in Him, combined with complete obedience and submission to His will.

The scene moves further to show us the order being carried out: "*When the two of them had surrendered themselves to the will of God, and Abraham laid him prostrate on his forehead.*" (Verse 103) Once more, obedience, faith and acceptance of God's will rise to a far nobler standard than anything known to humanity. The father puts his son prostrate before him and the son submits and shows no resistance. All this takes place in reality. Such is self surrender, which is the essence of Islam: complete trust, obedience, certainty, acceptance, submission and action. Both father and son experience nothing other than pure faith.

The point here is not one of bravery, courage, enthusiasm or heroic action which a warrior might feel in battle. A committed fighter may undertake a task knowing that his chance of survival is negligible. However, this is totally different from what Abraham and Ishmael were doing: for them, there is no boiling situation, no rush of enthusiasm prompting hasty action before weakness or hesitation can creep in. Theirs is a rational self surrender, with full knowledge of what they want, and complete reassurance about what will take place. More than that, they coolly appreciate the pleasure of obeying God's orders.

At this stage, Abraham and Ishmael have done all that is required of them. They have submitted themselves and carried out the order. All that remained was the actual shedding of Ishmael's blood and his death, which, in God's scales, counted for little, compared with the energy, feelings and determination both father and son put into what was bidden of them. By this time, the test had reached its climax, its results were known and its objectives fulfilled. What remained was physical pain and a dead body, but God does not want His servants to endure suffering. He does not require them to torment or kill themselves. Once they have submitted themselves and shown their true willingness to do what He bids, then they have fulfilled what is required and passed the test successfully.

Deliverance

God witnessed the sincerity shown by both Abraham and Ishmael, and He considered them to have fulfilled all that was required of them:

> *We called to him: 'Abraham! You have already fulfilled the dream.' Thus do We reward those who do good. All this was indeed a momentous trial. We ransomed [Ishmael] with a noble sacrifice.* (Verses 104–107)

You have indeed fulfilled all you needed to fulfil. God wants nothing from His servants other than that they submit themselves to Him totally, so that they have nothing which they consider too dear or too precious to give up, not even an only son, or their own lives. You, Abraham, have done this, offering everything dear, with certainty and acceptance. What was left was flesh and blood, which could be substituted by any type of flesh and blood. Thus, God ransomed this young man who had submitted himself to His will by a great and noble sacrifice. It is reported that the sacrifice was a ram which Abraham found ready by God's will and that he sacrificed this ram in place of Ishmael.

Abraham was then told: *"Thus do We reward those who do good."* (Verse 105) We reward them by choosing them for such a test, directing their minds and hearts to rise to the necessary level, helping them in such fulfilment and then giving them the reward they deserve.

It is to commemorate this great event which serves as a symbol of true faith and submission to God that Muslims celebrate the 'Īd of Sacrifice, or *al-Aḍḥā*. This event serves as a reference point for the Muslim community to know their first father, Abraham, whose faith it follows and to whom it traces its ancestry. It thus understands the nature of its faith, based on submission to God's will with perfect acceptance and reassurance. It will never need to ask God why. It will never hesitate to do His bidding, once it realizes what He wants of it. It gives its all, withholding nothing, and choosing no particular way or form of offering. It simply does what He bids it to do. The Muslim community also knows that God does not wish to overburden it with the test, nor put it to hardship. All He needs is that Muslims should be ready to give whatever they are required to give, in full obedience and commitment, without hesitation. Once they prove such complete dedication, He will remove the need for their sacrifice and pain. He will consider that they have fulfilled their duty and reward them for that, replacing their sacrifice and honouring them as He honoured their father, Abraham.

"We caused him to be praised by later generations." (Verse 108) He is remembered by one generation after another. He is the father of all prophets, and the founding father of the Muslim community which inherits his faith. God has assigned to the Muslim community the task of leading humanity on the basis of Abraham's faith. In so doing, God has made the Muslim community Abraham's descendants for the rest of human life.

"Peace be upon Abraham." (Verse 109) It is a greeting of peace by his Lord, recorded in His book and engraved in the book of the universe. *"Thus do We reward those who do good."* (Verse 110) We reward them

after testing them, and We fulfil Our promise to them and honour them. "*He was truly one of our believing servants.*" (Verse 111) Such is the reward of faith, and such is its nature as revealed by the momentous test.

God's grace is bestowed once more on Abraham, as He gave him Isaac in his old age. He further blesses him and his son, making Isaac a prophet: "*We gave Abraham the happy news of Isaac, a prophet and a righteous man; and We blessed him and Isaac.*" (Verses 112–113) Their offspring goes on through generations, but its main criterion is not the relation of blood, but the relation of faith and a code of living: whoever follows in their footsteps does good, and whoever deviates wrongs himself and cannot benefit from this blood relation: "*Among their offspring there were those who do good and others who would glaringly sin against their souls.*" (Verse 113)

Abraham's Descendants

The descendants of Abraham and Isaac included Moses and Aaron:

> We also bestowed Our favour on Moses and Aaron; We saved them and their people from great distress; We gave them support, so that it was they who achieved victory. We gave them the Scripture which made things clear; We guided them to the right path; We caused them to be praised by later generations: Peace be upon Moses and Aaron! Thus do We reward those who do good. Both were among Our believing servants. (Verses 114–122)

Here we only have a glimpse of the story of Moses and Aaron, highlighting God's favours bestowed on them first in being chosen to deliver His message, then in saving them and their people from great distress, which is recounted in detail in other *sūrahs*. God's favours on them also included their victory over their enemies, Pharaoh and his people, as also giving them the Scriptures and guiding them to the right path. It should be clear that God guides to this right path only those who believe in Him. He further ensured that they would be praised by future generations. This glimpse concludes with a greeting and blessing of peace from God to Moses and Aaron. Again the type of reward given to those who do good and the great value of faith, for which believers are held in honour, is repeated here.

A similar glimpse of the story of Elijah, a prophet mentioned in the Old Testament, is given here. Elijah was a messenger to people in Syria who worshipped a statue called Baal. The ruins of the city of Baalbek in Lebanon retain traces of such worship:

> *Elijah too was one of Our messengers. He said to his people: 'Have you no fear of God? How can you invoke Baal and forsake the best of creators, God, your Lord and the Lord of your forefathers?' But they accused him of lying. Therefore, they will certainly be brought [for punishment]. Not so God's true servants. We caused him to be praised by later generations: Peace be upon Elijah! Thus do We reward those who do good. He was truly one of Our believing servants.* (Verses 123–132)

Elijah called on his people to believe in God's oneness, denouncing their practice of worshipping Baal in preference to God, the best of creators. Thus, he followed the same line as Abraham when he denounced his people's idolatrous worship. The same stance was taken by every messenger when they encountered idol worship. The wrongdoers' response was to accuse Elijah of lying and to reject his message. God confirms here that they too will be brought before Him for punishment, except for those of them who believed in the message of the truth. This snippet ends in the same way as other historical accounts in this *sūrah* by emphasizing the honour God grants to His messengers: this by giving them the greeting and blessing of peace, outlining the reward of people who do good and the great value of faith. This is the only occasion that an account of Elijah is given in the *Qur'ān*.

Then we take a brief look at Lot, whose story occurs after Abraham's story in other *sūrahs*:

> *Lot was also one of Our messengers. We saved him and all his household, except for an old woman who stayed behind. Then We utterly destroyed the others. Surely you pass by their ruins at morning-time, as also by night. Will you not, then, use your reason?* (Verses 133–138)

The depiction here is similar to that given of Noah. It refers to the fact that Lot was God's messenger, and that he was saved with his family, except his wife, while the hardened unbelievers were destroyed. This is followed by a reminder to the Arabs who used to pass by the area where Lot's people lived without heeding the lesson their ruins told, and without fearing that they would be destroyed in similar fashion.

Jonah and the Whale

The last of these glimpses from the history of earlier messengers concerns Jonah:

> Jonah too was one of Our messengers. He deserted, going on the laden ship. They cast lots, and he was the one who lost. The whale swallowed him, for he was to blame. Had he not been of those who truly glorified God, he would have remained in the whale's belly till Resurrection Day. We caused him to be cast out, sick, on a barren shore, and caused a gourd tree to grow over him. Then We sent him to [a community of] one hundred thousand or more. They believed, so We let them enjoy life for a while. (Verses 139–148)

The *Qur'ān* does not mention where Jonah's people lived, but it is understood that they were not far from the sea. Reports tell us that Jonah was frustrated by his people's continued denial of his message and the truth it made clear. He warned them against God's impending punishment, and then abandoned them in anger. His anger led him to the sea-shore, where he boarded a laden ship. When the ship was in the middle of the sea, it was hit by a raging storm. It was widely believed at that time that such a disaster signalled that among the passengers there must be someone who had incurred God's anger. For the ship to withstand the storm that person had to be thrown overboard. They, thus, drew lots and Jonah was the one who lost. Although they knew him to be a virtuous and God-fearing man, the drawing of his lot was confirmed. Therefore, they threw him into the sea, or he might have jumped himself. Nonetheless, he was swallowed by the whale, deserving of blame, because he had abandoned the assignment God had given him, leaving his people in anger before seeking God's permission. When he felt acute distress inside the whale's belly, he glorified God and prayed for His forgiveness, stating that he had wronged himself. He said in his prayer: "*There is no deity other than You! Limitless are You in Your glory! I have done wrong indeed!*" (21: 87) God answered his prayer, and the whale cast him out.

The *sūrah* makes it clear that "*had he not been of those who truly glorified God, he would have remained in the whale's belly till Resurrection Day.*" (Verses 143–144) When he was cast out, he was both sick and naked. Therefore God "*caused a gourd tree to grow over him,*" its broad leaves covering him. It also protected him against flies, which are said not to come near this plant. This was part of the favour God bestowed on him. When he had recovered, God returned him to the people whom he had left in anger. In turn, they feared that his warnings would come true, and they believed, praying for God's forgiveness. God thus accepted them, sparing them the punishment He inflicts on people who deny His message: "*They believed, so We let them enjoy life for a while.*" (Verse 148) They numbered a hundred thousand or more, and all of them became believers.[1]

This brief account of Jonah's story explains the fate of those who believe, so contrasting the fate of the unbelievers in the other stories. Let the Arabs, who received Muḥammad's message, choose which fate they prefer.

---

1. Other references to Jonah's story are discussed in Vol. 9, pp. 144–145, and Vol. 12, pp. 65–68. – Editor's note.

3

To Whom Victory is Guaranteed

Now ask the unbelievers if it be true that your Lord has daughters, while they would have sons? (149)

فَٱسْتَفْتِهِمْ أَلِرَبِّكَ ٱلْبَنَاتُ وَلَهُمُ ٱلْبَنُونَ ۝

Or is it that We have created the angels female in their presence? (150)

أَمْ خَلَقْنَا ٱلْمَلَٰٓئِكَةَ إِنَٰثًا وَهُمْ شَٰهِدُونَ ۝

Out of their falsehood they say: (151)

أَلَآ إِنَّهُم مِّنْ إِفْكِهِمْ لَيَقُولُونَ ۝

'God has begotten children.' They are lying indeed. (152)

وَلَدَ ٱللَّهُ وَإِنَّهُمْ لَكَٰذِبُونَ ۝

Would He then choose daughters in preference to sons? (153)

أَصْطَفَى ٱلْبَنَاتِ عَلَى ٱلْبَنِينَ ۝

What is the matter with you? How do you make your judgement? (154)

مَا لَكُمْ كَيْفَ تَحْكُمُونَ ۝

Do you not reflect? (155)

أَفَلَا تَذَكَّرُونَ ۝

Or do you, perhaps, have a clear authority? (156)

أَمْ لَكُمْ سُلْطَٰنٌ مُّبِينٌ ۝

Bring your scriptures, if you are speaking the truth! (157)

فَأْتُوا۟ بِكِتَٰبِكُمْ إِن كُنتُمْ صَٰدِقِينَ ۝

They claim that He has kinship with the *jinn*; yet the *jinn* themselves know that they will be brought [before God] for judgement. (158)

وَجَعَلُوا۟ بَيْنَهُۥ وَبَيْنَ ٱلْجِنَّةِ نَسَبًا ۚ وَلَقَدْ عَلِمَتِ ٱلْجِنَّةُ إِنَّهُمْ لَمُحْضَرُونَ ۝

Limitless is God in His glory, above all what people attribute to Him. (159)

سُبْحَٰنَ ٱللَّهِ عَمَّا يَصِفُونَ ۝

Not so God's true servants. (160)

إِلَّا عِبَادَ ٱللَّهِ ٱلْمُخْلَصِينَ ۝

Neither you nor what you worship (161)

فَإِنَّكُمْ وَمَا تَعْبُدُونَ ۝

can lure away from God any (162)

مَآ أَنتُمْ عَلَيْهِ بِفَٰتِنِينَ ۝

except one who is destined for hell. (163)

إِلَّا مَنْ هُوَ صَالِ ٱلْجَحِيمِ ۝

Every single one of us has his appointed place: (164)

وَمَا مِنَّآ إِلَّا لَهُۥ مَقَامٌ مَّعْلُومٌ ۝

we are ranged in ranks, (165)

وَإِنَّا لَنَحْنُ ٱلصَّآفُّونَ ۝

and we too extol His limitless glory. (166)

وَإِنَّا لَنَحْنُ ٱلْمُسَبِّحُونَ ۝

They have long been saying: (167)

وَإِن كَانُوا۟ لَيَقُولُونَ ۝

'If only we had before us a tradition from those of old, (168)

we would certainly be true servants of God.' (169)

لَوۡ أَنَّ عِندَنَا ذِكۡرٗا مِّنَ ٱلۡأَوَّلِينَ ۝

لَكُنَّا عِبَادَ ٱللَّهِ ٱلۡمُخۡلَصِينَ ۝

Yet they reject it. In time, they will come to know. (170)

فَكَفَرُواْ بِهِۦۖ فَسَوۡفَ يَعۡلَمُونَ ۝

Our word has already been given to Our servants the messengers: (171)

وَلَقَدۡ سَبَقَتۡ كَلِمَتُنَا لِعِبَادِنَا ٱلۡمُرۡسَلِينَ ۝

it is they who will be helped, (172)

إِنَّهُمۡ لَهُمُ ٱلۡمَنصُورُونَ ۝

and it is Our forces who will surely be victorious. (173)

وَإِنَّ جُندَنَا لَهُمُ ٱلۡغَٰلِبُونَ ۝

So, turn away from them for a while, (174)

فَتَوَلَّ عَنۡهُمۡ حَتَّىٰ حِينٖ ۝

and watch them; in time, they too will come to see. (175)

وَأَبۡصِرۡهُمۡ فَسَوۡفَ يُبۡصِرُونَ ۝

Do they really wish to hasten Our punishment? (176)

أَفَبِعَذَابِنَا يَسۡتَعۡجِلُونَ ۝

When it strikes in their midst, terrible will be the morning of those who were already warned. (177)

فَإِذَا نَزَلَ بِسَاحَتِهِمۡ فَسَآءَ صَبَاحُ ٱلۡمُنذَرِينَ ۝

And again, turn away from them for a while, (178)

وَتَوَلَّ عَنۡهُمۡ حَتَّىٰ حِينٖ ۝

and watch them; in time, they too will come to see. (179)

وَأَبْصِرْ فَسَوْفَ يُبْصِرُونَ ﴿١٧٩﴾

Limitless in His glory is your Lord, the Lord of almightiness, above all what people attribute to Him. (180)

سُبْحَانَ رَبِّكَ رَبِّ الْعِزَّةِ عَمَّا يَصِفُونَ ﴿١٨٠﴾

And peace be upon all His messengers. (181)

وَسَلَامٌ عَلَى الْمُرْسَلِينَ ﴿١٨١﴾

All praise is due to God, the Lord of all the worlds. (182)

وَالْحَمْدُ لِلَّهِ رَبِّ الْعَالَمِينَ ﴿١٨٢﴾

Overview

This last part of the *sūrah* builds on the main themes already discussed, particularly the historical accounts given in the second part which explain the true nature of the relation between God and His servants to refute the superstitions circulated among the Arabs. In one such superstition the Arabs claimed that the angels were God's daughters, and in another they alleged that a marriage relation existed between God and the *jinn*. The *sūrah* now puts before them what they said before God's message was delivered to them. This was when they expressed dear hopes that God would send them a messenger and when they emphasized that they would follow the guidance such a messenger provided. Yet when God sent them the Messenger they asked for they resorted to disbelief. The *sūrah* concludes by stating God's promise to His messengers that they will end victorious, disassociating God from all the unbelievers' claims, and praising God, the Lord of all the worlds.

Superstitious Beliefs

Now ask the unbelievers if it be true that your Lord has daughters, while they would have sons? Or is it that We have created the angels female in their presence? Out of their falsehood they say: 'God has begotten children.' They are lying indeed. Would He then choose daughters in preference to sons? What is the matter with you? How do you make your judgement? Do you not reflect? Or do you, perhaps, have a clear authority? Bring your scriptures, if you are speaking the truth! (Verses 149–157)

The *sūrah* uses every means to refute the unbelievers' claims; it shows their false superstition for what it is, draws its argument on the basis of their own logic and how it works in their own environment. They used to prefer boys to girls, considering the birth of a girl something of a tragedy. Yet they allege at the same time that the angels were female and that they were God's daughters. Therefore, the *sūrah* takes up the argument, using their own standards to show how stupid their claims were: *"Now ask the unbelievers if it be true that your Lord has daughters, while they would have sons?"* If females are of a lesser rank, how could they assign daughters to their Lord and keep sons for themselves? Or was it that He chose for Himself daughters and gave them sons? Neither possibility stands to reason. The Prophet is instructed to question them about this worthless claim. He is also to ask them about the source of the superstition and how it came about. In other words, where did they get the idea that the angels were females? Did they witness their creation in order to know their sex? *"Or is it that We have created the angels female in their presence?"* (Verse 150)

The *sūrah* gives the exact wording of their fabricated lies about God: *"Out of their falsehood they say: 'God has begotten children.' They are lying indeed."* (Verses 151–152) They are liars even according to their own tradition which prefers sons to daughters. How could it be, then, that God would choose daughters for Himself? *"Would He then choose daughters in preference to sons?"* (Verse 153) It wonders at their judgement which ignores their own logic: *"What is the matter with you? How do you make your judgement? Do you not reflect?"* (Verses 154–155) Where do you get the evidence on which you base your judgement? *"Or do you, perhaps, have a clear authority? Bring your scriptures, if you are speaking the truth!"* (Verses 156–157)

The *sūrah* moves on to refute the other superstition which alleged that some relationship existed between God and the *jinn: "They claim that He has kinship with the* jinn; *yet the* jinn *themselves know that they will be brought [before God] for judgement."* (Verse 158) The allegation being that the angels were God's daughters born to Him by the *jinn!* The unbelievers claimed that this is how the relation started. The *jinn*, however, know for certain that they are created by God, like all other creation, and they also know that they will be brought before Him for judgement. Had they been related to Him, they would be due different treatment.

God places Himself far above this worthless fabrication: *"Limitless is God in His glory, above all what people attribute to Him."* (Verse 159) He also makes clear that the believers among the *jinn* would not be driven to suffer their punishment. *"Not so God's true servants."* (Verse 160)

The *sūrah* then quotes an address made to the idolaters, their alleged deities and their deviant beliefs. Apparently, the address is made by the angels:

> *Neither you nor what you worship can lure away from God any except one who is destined for hell. Every single one of us has his appointed place: we are ranged in ranks, and we too extol His limitless glory.* (Verses 161–166)

What this address means is that neither the unbelievers, nor the deities they worship could turn anyone away from God's path except one who is considered to belong to the people of hell and destined for it. They cannot lead astray a believer who is God's obedient servant. Hell has its own people who are of a known type. These respond to temptations and listen to those who try to lead them astray.

The angels also refute this superstition, making it clear that each one of them has his own position which he does not exceed. They are a type of God's creation who worship Him alone. They are assigned certain tasks and they fulfil them, ranging themselves in rows for prayer and extolling God's glory.

An Unfailing Promise

The *sūrah* then speaks about the idolaters who circulate such superstitions, mentioning the promises they made when they envied the people of earlier revelations for receiving such messages. They used to say that had they had some sort of traditional beliefs inherited from Abraham or later prophets, they would have had a degree of faith that would have enhanced their position with God: "*They have long been saying: If only we had before us a tradition from those of old, we would certainly be true servants of God.*" (Verses 167–169) Yet when they received the best revelations ever bestowed from on high, they turned away and forgot their promises: "*Yet they reject it. In time, they will come to know.*" (Verse 170) The verse carries an implicit threat, which is suitable for those who persist in disbelief, going back on expressed wishes and promises: "*They will come to know.*"

At this point the *sūrah* states God's promise to His messengers of His assured help. In this way victory is assured them: "*Our word has already been given to Our servants the messengers: it is they who will be helped, and it is Our forces who will surely be victorious.*" (Verses 171–173)

The promise is a true promise, and God's word is fulfilled. The roots of true faith have been firmly established on earth and its structure is raised despite the unbelievers' rejection, the persecution to which believers are subjected as well as many other obstacles and barriers. The beliefs of idolaters and unbelievers have disappeared, their power has dwindled while the faith preached by God's messengers appeals to people's minds and hearts. In fact, its appeal remains strong in spite of all the opposing factors. All the attempts to suppress divine faith in favour of any other philosophy or ideology have failed, even in those areas where these started. God's promise to His messengers has come true. This is a universal phenomenon that has remained true throughout the world and in all generations.

It is also true for every movement that aims to revive the divine message, provided that its advocates are sincere and dedicated. It will be triumphant no matter what obstacles are put in its way. Falsehood may mobilize all its powers of persecution, torture, open warfare as well as propaganda that relies on fabricated lies, but all to no avail. The removal of such calumny may entail fighting a few battles, perhaps with different results, but eventually God's promise to His messengers will be fulfilled. This is a promise of ultimate victory that will see them established on earth and having power. This promise will be fulfilled even though all the powers on earth are ranged to stop it.

This promise is one of God's universal laws which operates just like the stars and planets follow their cycles, the night and day alternate, and like a dead land coming to life when rain falls on it. However, this law follows God's will and works according to His planning. It may appear slow in relation to people's limited life spans, but it will never fail. In fact it may be fulfilled in a way that people do not appreciate, because they always look for the form of victory they know. Indeed, they may not readily appreciate that victory comes in a new form and they may need time to appreciate this.

People may want to see a particular form of victory for the advocates of the divine faith who follow His messengers, but God wishes to accomplish a different form which is greater and longer lasting. What takes place, then, is what God wants, even if this means that these advocates will have to endure greater troubles, exert more effort and strive for much longer than they expected. Before the Battle of Badr, the Prophet's Companions hoped to take the Quraysh's trade caravan, but God wanted that they miss it and instead engage their enemy, with its superior forces, in battle. What God wanted ensured a much better outcome for them and for Islam. That was the victory God wanted to give His Messenger, a victory for His message with lasting effects.

The advocates of God's faith may lose a battle, and may even suffer very hard times, but this is because God is preparing them to achieve victory in a greater battle. He thus brings about circumstances that make their victory yield fruit on a wider scale and for a longer period.

God's word has gone forth, and His promise has been given by His will. His law will take effect without fail: *"Our word has already been given to Our servants the messengers: it is they who will be helped, and it is Our forces who will surely be victorious."* (Verses 171–173)

When this true promise has been declared, God orders His Messenger to turn away from unbelievers, leaving them to God's word and promise to take effect. He should, however, watch them as the word proves true, for they will see with their own eyes how this comes about:

> *So, turn away from them for a while, and watch them; in time, they too will come to see. Do they really wish to hasten Our punishment? When it strikes in their midst, terrible will be the morning of those who were already warned. And again, turn away from them for a while, and watch them; in time, they too will come to see.* (Verses 174–179)

The Prophet is told to leave them alone and not care for them. He is further told to wait for the day when he and they will see what God's promise means for him and them. If they hasten His punishment, they will suffer greatly when it falls upon them. Should this strike a community, they will have got what is certain to grieve them. Again, the Prophet is told to abandon them to their fate. This order implies further warning to them, and again the *sūrah* advises that the outcome will be terrible: *"And again, turn away from them for a while, and watch them; in time, they too will come to see."* (Verses 178–179) What will happen is left unspecified, implying great terror.

The *sūrah* concludes with extolling God's glory, stating that all might belongs to Him alone. It adds the blessing and greeting of peace to God's messengers, and declares that all praise is due to God, the Lord of all, who has no partners whatsoever:

> *Limitless in His glory is your Lord, the Lord of almightiness, above all what people attribute to Him. And peace be upon all His messengers. All praise is due to God, the Lord of all the worlds.* (Verses 180–182)

It is indeed a fitting ending that sums up the main issues discussed in the *sūrah* as a whole.

SŪRAH 38

Ṣād

Prologue

Revealed in Makkah, this *surah* addresses three issues: God's oneness, revelation, and the reckoning on the Day of Judgement. These three issues are discussed in its first part comprising 16 verses. Here the Makkan elders' amazement at the Prophet's call on them to believe in God's oneness and that he was chosen by God to be His Messenger is described. "*They deem it strange that one from among them has come to warn them. The unbelievers say: 'This is a sorcerer telling lies. Does he make all the gods into one God? This is indeed most strange!' Their leaders go about saying: 'Walk away, and hold steadfastly to your deities: this is the only thing to do. Never did we hear of a claim like this in any faith of latter days! It is all an invention. Was the message given to him alone out of all of us?'*" (Verses 4–8) In these verses we are also told how they met God's warnings of punishment in the life to come: "*They say: Our Lord! Hasten to us our share of punishment even before the Day of Reckoning.*" (Verse 16)

Basically, they found it impossible to believe that God would choose one of their own number to deliver His message and moreover that this person should be Muḥammad ibn 'Abdullāh who had not held a position of authority among them. Therefore, in reply to their question about His choice, God too questions them: "*Or do they own the treasures of your Lord's grace, the Almighty, the Munificent? Or do they have control over the heavens and the earth and all that is between them? Let them, then, try to ascend by all conceivable means."* (Verses 9–10) This tells them that when God wishes to open the gates of His mercy to anyone, nothing can withhold it. They are further told that human beings own nothing in the heavens and earth; it is a matter of God's sustenance and mercy, which He bestows on whomever He wishes. It is He who chooses those He knows to deserve His bounty and bestows on them whatever He will, without limit or restriction.

Within this context the *sūrah* gives an account of David and Solomon and the favours God blessed them with, including prophethood, kingdom, and the fact that the mountains, birds, *jinn* and wind were subjected to them. Yet they were ordinary human beings afflicted by the same type of human weakness as anyone else. They too then needed God's mercy and care to overcome such weaknesses. In this respect, their repentance is accepted and they are set on the way to God's pleasure.

By means of both stories the Prophet is instructed to persevere in the face of all the opposition the unbelievers put up against him. He should look to God's grace and care as demonstrated to David and Solomon: *"Bear with patience whatever they say, and remember Our servant David who was endowed with strength. He always turned to Us."* (Verse 17)

The *sūrah* also gives a brief account of the Prophet Job, describing how God may test His true servants with hardship and affliction. The patience Job showed in adversity provides a splendid example of how to remain steadfast. The account also describes the good end Job experienced as God bestowed His mercy on him, dispelling all his pain. The Muslims in Makkah are thus shown how to find solace amidst the constant hardship the unbelievers try to inflict on them. They are reminded that such hardship invariably opens the way to God's mercy, which is inexhaustible.

These stories form the second and major part of the *sūrah*. It also includes a reply to the unbelievers' hastening of God's punishment, presenting a scene from the Day of Judgement, describing the happiness that awaits the God-fearing and the blazing fire that awaits those who reject the truth. The values of truth are well established in the life to come, providing the criterion for judgement. The arrogant Makkan chiefs will realize this when they see their fate and compare it with that of the weak elements on whom they poured their derision, claiming that God's mercy would never be shown to those so weak. The scene so described provides contrasting images: "*The God-fearing will certainly have a good place to return to: gardens of perpetual bliss, with gates wide open to them. They will be comfortably seated there, and they will call for abundant fruit and drink, having beside them well-matched mates of modest gaze.*" (Verses 49–52) On the other hand, "*those who transgress the bounds of what is right will have the most evil place to return to: hell will they have to endure; and how evil a resting place. Let them, then, taste this: a scalding fluid and a dark, disgusting food, and coupled with it, further [suffering] of a similar nature.*" (Verses 55–58) They will argue, quarrel and curse one another in hell, and they will remember how they used to ridicule the believers: "*They will say: How is it that we do not see here men whom we considered to be wicked, and whom we made the target of our derision? Or is it that our eyes have missed them?*" (Verses 62–63) They cannot find such people in hell, because they are the ones who belong to heaven. This then is the answer to both their hastening of God's punishment and their ridicule of the believers. This scene forms the third part of the *sūrah*.

In reply to their disbelieving reaction to what the Prophet had told them of the revelations he received from on high, he tells them about Adam and what happened on high. The Prophet was not present when this took place; he was only told about it by God. Indeed no human being, other than Adam, was present. From this account we learn about *Iblīs'* condemnation and that it was his envy at God's preference for Adam that brought about his expulsion from heaven. Since the unbelievers thought it was too big a favour for God to choose Muhammad from among them, their attitude is not dissimilar to that of *Iblīs*. This last part of the *sūrah* concludes with a clear statement from the Prophet: "*Say: No reward do I ask of you for this, and I am not one to claim what I am not. This is no less than a reminder to all the worlds, and in time you will certainly come to know its truth.*" (Verses 86–88)

The *sūrah*, in all its four parts, depicts the destruction of earlier communities when they resorted to arrogance, accusing God's messengers of lying and holding the believers in contempt. In short, they themselves sealed their own defeat and humiliation: *"Whatever hosts, of any affiliation, may be raised will suffer defeat. Before their time, the truth was rejected by Noah's people, the 'Ād, Pharaoh of the tent-pegs, the Thamūd, Lot's people and the dwellers of the wooded dales: these were different groupings; yet each one of them accused God's messengers of lying. Therefore, My retribution fell due."* (Verses 11–14) The *sūrah* contrasts this with the favours God bestows on His chosen servants, giving them power and taking good care of them. This is made abundantly clear in the stories about David, Solomon and Job.

The *sūrah* also takes us on a round in which we see what lies in store beyond the Day of Judgement, giving us images of happiness and bliss on the one hand, and torment on the other. The last round in the *sūrah* gives the story of the first human being and the hostility shown by his first enemy, the one who deliberately leads people astray, and who they follow unaware of his designs.

The *sūrah* also includes a special touch that is meant to alert hearts to the truth reflected in the creation of the heavens and earth. This is the truth that God wants to establish on earth through the messengers He sends. The two are interrelated: *"We have not created heaven and earth and all that is between them without a purpose."* (Verse 27)

I

Unjustifiable Reaction

Ṣād

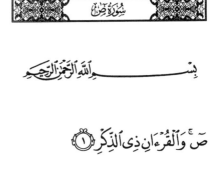

In the Name of God, the Lord of Grace, the Ever Merciful

Ṣād. By the Qur'ān, full of admonition. (1)

But the unbelievers are steeped in arrogance and hostility. (2)

How many a generation have We destroyed before their time? They all cried out [for mercy], but it was too late to escape. (3)

They deem it strange that one from among them has come to warn them. The unbelievers say: 'This is a sorcerer telling lies. (4)

Does he make all the gods into one God? This is indeed most strange!' (5)

Their leaders go about saying: 'Walk away, and hold steadfastly to your deities: this is an intended design. (6)

وَٱنطَلَقَ ٱلْمَلَأُ مِنْهُمْ أَنِ ٱمْشُوا۟ وَٱصْبِرُوا۟ عَلَىٰٓ ءَالِهَتِكُمْ ۖ إِنَّ هَٰذَا لَشَىْءٌ يُرَادُ ٦

Never did we hear of a claim like this in any faith of latter days! It is all an invention. (7)

مَا سَمِعْنَا بِهَٰذَا فِى ٱلْمِلَّةِ ٱلْأَخِرَةِ إِنْ هَٰذَآ إِلَّا ٱخْتِلَٰقٌ ٧

Was the message given to him alone out of all of us?' In fact they are in doubt concerning My reminder; they have not yet tasted My punishment. (8)

أَءُنزِلَ عَلَيْهِ ٱلذِّكْرُ مِنۢ بَيْنِنَا ۚ بَلْ هُمْ فِى شَكٍّ مِّن ذِكْرِى ۖ بَل لَّمَّا يَذُوقُوا۟ عَذَابِ ٨

Or do they own the treasures of your Lord's grace, the Almighty, the Munificent? (9)

أَمْ عِندَهُمْ خَزَآئِنُ رَحْمَةِ رَبِّكَ ٱلْعَزِيزِ ٱلْوَهَّابِ ٩

Or do they have dominion over the heavens and the earth and all that is between them? Let them, then, try to ascend by all conceivable means. (10)

أَمْ لَهُم مُّلْكُ ٱلسَّمَٰوَٰتِ وَٱلْأَرْضِ وَمَا بَيْنَهُمَا ۖ فَلْيَرْتَقُوا۟ فِى ٱلْأَسْبَٰبِ ١٠

Whatever hosts, of any affiliation, may be raised will suffer defeat. (11)

جُندٌ مَّا هُنَالِكَ مَهْزُومٌ مِّنَ ٱلْأَحْزَابِ ١١

Before their time, the truth was rejected by Noah's people, the 'Ād, Pharaoh of the tent-pegs, (12)

كَذَّبَتْ قَبْلَهُمْ قَوْمُ نُوحٍ وَعَادٌ وَفِرْعَوْنُ ذُو ٱلْأَوْتَادِ ١٢

350

the Thamūd, Lot's people and the dwellers of the wooded dales: these were different groupings; (13)

وَثَمُودُ وَقَوْمُ لُوطٍ وَأَصْحَٰبُ لَّئَيْكَةِ أُوْلَٰٓئِكَ ٱلْأَحْزَابُ ۝

yet each one of them accused God's messengers of lying. Therefore, My retribution fell due. (14)

إِن كُلٌّ إِلَّا كَذَّبَ ٱلرُّسُلَ فَحَقَّ عِقَابِ ۝

These, too, have but to wait for one single blast; and it shall not be delayed. (15)

وَمَا يَنظُرُ هَٰٓؤُلَآءِ إِلَّا صَيْحَةً وَٰحِدَةً مَّا لَهَا مِن فَوَاقٍ ۝

They say: 'Our Lord! Hasten to us our share of punishment even before the Day of Reckoning.' (16)

وَقَالُوا۟ رَبَّنَا عَجِّل لَّنَا قِطَّنَا قَبْلَ يَوْمِ ٱلْحِسَابِ ۝

Arrogance and Hostility

Ṣād. By the Qur'ān, full of admonition. The unbelievers are steeped in arrogance and hostility. How many a generation have We destroyed before their time? They all cried out [for mercy], but it was too late to escape. (Verses 1–3)

God states an oath by an Arabic letter of the alphabet, *Ṣād*,[1] as well as by the Qur'ān, which He describes here as *'full of admonition.'* This letter is made by God, who created it as a sound when it is spoken by people. It is also one letter of the alphabet that makes up the Qur'ānic style and address. The complete alphabet has always been available to

---

1. This letter is pronounced as a velarized variation of 's', sharing its other features of friction and voicelessness, and having the same place of articulation. – Editor's note.

people, but the Qur'ān has never been within their ability to produce, because it is God's book, which He made. Humans are incapable of producing anything like that which God makes, be that with regard to the Qur'ān or to anything else. The sound symbolized by the letter *Ṣād* is vocalized by people without effort, but it is also by God's will. For it is He who made the larynx tract and all the sounds it voices. If people only contemplated this one small but miraculous aspect of their own creation they would realize there is nothing unusual in God choosing one of their own number to receive His revelations. To reveal a message from on high is no more amazing than giving them such miracles as are contained within themselves.

"*Ṣād. By the Qur'ān, full of admonition.*" The Qur'ān includes admonition as well as other things, such as legal provisions, stories, and instruction on how to refine manners. Admonition as well as reminding people of their need to turn to God and seek His favours are the primary purposes of the Qur'ān. Indeed, the stories and legal provisions are part of the admonition and the remembrance of God. It should be said that the Arabic text uses the word *dhikr*, which is rendered in the translation as '*full of admonition*'. However, the word also means 'to be well known'. The verse could then be rendered as '*Ṣād By the Qur'ān, a widely known divine Book.*" This is also a true description of the Qur'ān.

"*But the unbelievers are steeped in arrogance and hostility.*" (Verse 2) The verse begins with the word, '*but*', which suggests that there is a move away from the initial subject matter: the oath by the letter *Ṣād* and the Qur'ān. The oath sounds incomplete because what it intends to affirm is not mentioned. The *sūrah* simply states the oath and talks about the idolaters and their profound hostility. Yet this very departure from the initial issue heightens our interest in the next. The very fact that an oath by the letter *Ṣād* and the Qur'ān is made indicates the intention to discuss something of great importance, one that merits an oath by God Almighty. Yet next to this, the *sūrah* mentions the idolaters' arrogance and hostility to the Qur'ān, indicating that the issue remains the same both before and after the conjunction, '*but*'. This departure in the mode of address focuses our attention on the great gulf that lies between the immense status God attaches to the Qur'ān and the idolaters' arrogance and hostility to it.

Mention of the fate of those before them who held a similar attitude then follows. It shows such people appealing for help, but none was forthcoming. Their cries mark a radical change in their attitude, but it is all too late to be of any significance: "*How many a generation have We destroyed before their time? They all cried out [for mercy], but it was too late to escape.*" (Verse 3) Their end is shown to the new unbelievers so that they may change their attitude of hostility and arrogance while there is still time for them to do so. Otherwise, they will end up in the same position: appealing for mercy, but none will be shown.

A Strange Amazement

This initial shock is intended to awaken their hearts. Details of their arrogance then follow:

> *They deem it strange that one from among them has come to warn them. The unbelievers say: 'This is a sorcerer telling lies. Does he make all the gods into one God? This is indeed most strange!' Their leaders go about saying: 'Walk away, and hold steadfastly to your deities: this is the only thing to do. Never did we hear of a claim like this in any faith of latter days! It is all an invention. Was the message given to him alone out of all of us?"* (Verses 4–8)

Such is the arrogance: "*Was the message given to him alone out of all of us?*" And such is the hostility: "*Does he make all the gods into one God?... Never did we hear of a claim like this in any faith of latter days!... This is a sorcerer telling lies... It is all an invention.*" Amazement that God's messenger should be human is an oft-repeated story. Since the beginning of divine messages every community took the same stance. Every new messenger was human, yet their fellow men continued to express amazement at this.

"*They deem it strange that one from among them has come to warn them.*" (Verse 4) Yet the most natural and logical thing is that the messenger who warns them should be human who thinks and feels like them: a man who appreciates what thoughts they may harbour, their weaknesses, desires, abilities and what obstacles they may encounter or influences they may fall under. When a man is given the message to warn them, he lives among them, setting a practical example for them to follow. They know that he is one of them and that they are required to follow the life system he endorses. It is not difficult for them to do so, since a man like them has set the example. Moreover, he is of their own generation, speaking their language, knowing their traditions and the way they go about their affairs. Mutual response is easily established between them. There is no thought of him being alien to them or to their lives.

Yet this most natural and logical situation was always the cause of amazement and the basis for levelling accusations at God's messengers. The unbelievers simply did not appreciate the purpose behind such a choice, nor did they understand the nature of the divine message. To them, it should not provide practical leadership on the way to God; rather, it should be mysterious, full of secret, an enigma. They wanted it to be engulfed in obscurity, removed from practical life. Then they could treat it as just another legend or superstition that formed the basis of their unsound beliefs.

God, however, wanted something different for humanity, especially in the case of His last message, Islam. He wanted it to be the norm for human society: for it to provide a clean, pure and sublime way of life that is practical, free of mystery as also one that is easy to implement.

"The unbelievers say: This is a sorcerer telling lies." They said this, discounting the possibility that God might have sent His revelations to one of them. In saying so, they hoped to turn ordinary people away from the Prophet, to cause confusion and mar the clear truth that was being stated by the man who was known for his honesty, integrity and truthfulness.

The plain fact is that the Quraysh elders did not for an instant believe that Muḥammad, whom they knew very well, was a sorcerer or a liar, as they alleged. Their allegations were simply propaganda tools aimed at misleading people. The Quraysh elders recognized that the truth Muḥammad preached would do away with all their privileges; privileges that relied on deception and false values. On one occasion the Quraysh elders held a conference on how to counter the effects of what the Prophet said to people, and how to turn pilgrims from other tribes away from him. It is useful to quote this again here. Al-Walīd ibn al-Mughīrah, a distinguished figure among the Quraysh chaired that conference:

> In his opening address, al-Walīd said: "Now that the pilgrimage season is approaching, people will start arriving from all over the place. They must have heard about your friend [meaning the Prophet]. So you had better agree what to say when you are asked about him. We must guard against having too many opinions, particularly if they are mutually contradictory."
>
> When his audience asked his advice as to what they should say, he preferred to listen to their suggestions first. What concerned al-Walid most was that the opinion they would come out with should take account of the fact that Muḥammad was asking people to listen to the Qur'ān, God's message, expressed in beautiful language and a powerful style. The description they would attach to Muḥammad should also account for his persuasive, eloquent argument.
>
> Descriptions like 'fortune-teller', 'madman', 'poet' and 'magician' were proposed. None was considered convincing by al-Walīd, who pointed out weaknesses in each, one after the other. He told his people that what Muḥammad said was nothing like what was said by such men. When nobody could suggest anything more plausible, they asked al-Walīd if he had a better suggestion.
>
> He said: "What Muḥammad says is certainly beautiful. It is like a date tree with solid roots and rich fruit. Every one of these suggestions you have made is bound to be recognized as false. The least disputable one is to claim that he is a magician who repeats magic words which make a man fall out with his father, mother, wife and clan." They all approved of al-Walīd's suggestion and set about preparing their propaganda campaign to make the pilgrims wary of Muḥammad and unwilling to meet him.[2]

---

2. The translated text differs slightly from the one quoted by the author as I preferred to quote it from my own rendering of the report of this misrepresentation conference. See my book, *Muhammad: Man and Prophet*, Leicester, 2002, pp. 119–120. – Editor's Note.

Such was the scheming of the Quraysh elders and such was their agreed strategy whereby they would accuse the Prophet of sorcery and lying. They said this deliberately even though they knew it was all a lie. They were fully aware that Muḥammad, (peace be upon him), was neither a sorcerer nor a liar.

They were also amazed at him calling on them to worship God alone, which is the most truthful statement anyone can make: "*Does he make all the gods into one God? This is indeed most strange! Their leaders go about saying: Walk away, and hold steadfastly to your deities: this is the only thing to do. Never did we hear of a claim like this in any faith of latter days! It is all an invention.*" (Verses 5–7)

The Qur'ān describes their great surprise at this basic truth: "*Does he make all the gods into one God?*" (Verse 5) The question is asked in such a way that makes it sound as if no one could have ever thought it possible. "*This is indeed most strange!*" (Verse 5) In Arabic, the *sūrah* uses the word *'ujāb*, which is an unusual derivative of *'ajīb*, meaning strange, to emphasize the peculiarity of the claim. The *sūrah* also describes the method they employed to neutralize the effects of the divine message among their people seeking to ensure that they would stick to their traditional beliefs. They implied that the new message contained something highly suspicious, and that in their high positions, they knew this and were intent on countering it: "*Their leaders go about saying: Walk away, and hold steadfastly to your deities: this is an intended design.*" (Verse 6) This is not a question of religion and faith, although there is something different about it. Hence, ordinary people should attend to their business, maintain their traditions and let the leaders uncover this new plot, because it is only they who can establish what is concealed behind outward appearances. Basically, then, they sought to reassure people that they would look after their interests.

This is a well known device that those in power use to divert peoples' interest in public affairs or their searching for the truth. To allow the public to search for the truth by themselves would represent a serious threat to authority, as ultimately it leads to the exposure of false leadership.

The Quraysh elders also tried to deceive people by pointing to the faiths of the people of earlier revelations who had allowed superstitions to creep into their faith, diverting it from the pure concept of God's oneness: "*Never did we hear of a claim like this in any faith of latter days! It is all an invention.*" (Verse 7) By that time, the concept of trinity had spread among the Christians while the legend of Ezra being God's son had infiltrated Judaism. Hence the elders specifically referred to these, saying: "*Never did we hear of a claim like this in any faith of latter days!*" They claimed to have never before heard anyone advocate God's absolute oneness as did Muḥammad. Hence, it could only be fabrication.

Islam has always sought to purge the monotheistic faith from all traces of legend, alien elements and the deviation that affected earlier religions, because monotheism is the fundamental truth that forms the basis of all existence. Indeed, the whole universe confirms this truth, providing evidence in support of it. Moreover, unless human life is based on monotheism it cannot be sound either in its fundamentals or its details. As we consider the resistance of the Quraysh, as well as earlier communities of unbelievers, to the monotheistic principle, it is fitting that we should briefly outline its importance.

The unity of the general laws that operate in this universe which we behold is clear, testifying to the fact that the will that set these laws in operation must by necessity be a single will. Wherever we look around us in this universe we find this fact staring us in the face. Everything in the universe is in constant and regular movement. The atom, which is the basic unit of everything in the universe, animate or inanimate, is in motion, as it consists of electrons that move around the nucleus composed of protons just as the planets move in orbit around the sun in our own solar system, and like the galaxy composed of numerous solar systems and celestial mass rotate. All planets, the sun, and the larger galaxy move in one anticlockwise direction, from west to east. The elements which make up the earth, other planets and the stars are the same, and they are all made of atoms composed of electrons, protons and neutrons. Indeed, these are the bricks that make up all these planets and stars.

While all matter is made of three bricks, scientists believe that all powers: light, heat, x-rays, wireless waves, gamma rays and all types of radiation are in fact different forms of electromagnetic power. They all travel at the same speed, but the difference between them is the difference in wavelength. Matter, then, is made of three bricks, and power is in essence waves. In his special relativity theory, Einstein equates matter with energy. Experiments endorsed his claims. In recent times, an experiment endorsed it in the loudest sound ever heard in this world, produced by nuclear fission in an atom bomb.[3]

Such is the unity in the make-up of the universe, as man has come to learn through physical experiment. We also know how this unity is reflected in the law of continuous motion common to all things in a coherent and balanced way so that no object interferes or collides with another. The clearest example is the countless number of planets, stars and galaxies floating in space. *"Each floats in its own orbit."* (36: 40) They all testify to the truth that they are set in their respective positions in space and given their movements, dimensions and coordinates by One who is fully aware of their nature, determining all this in His overall design of this wonderful universe.

This brief word here about the overall unity of the universe is sufficient for it testifies that human life can only be set right on this basis. When this fact is clearly understood, people formulate a sound concept of the universe around them, their position in it, their interrelation with other beings, as also their relation with the One God and with everything else in the universe. This is exceedingly important in shaping people's emotions and understanding of all that life entails.

A person who believes in God's oneness and understands the meaning of His oneness, sets his relation with his Lord on this basis, and puts his relations with everyone and everything other than God in their respective positions. Thus, his energy and feelings are not manipulated by a host of other different deities nor are other people able to impose themselves on him.

---

3. Ahmad Zaki, *Ma'a Allāh fī al-Samā'*, Cairo, 1965

A believer who knows that God, the One, is the originator of this universe deals with the universe and all that exists in it on the basis of cooperation and friendship. This gives life a taste and vitality that are totally different from that which is felt by those who do not believe in any of this.

Anyone who believes in the unity of the system God has set for the universe will receive His orders and legislation in a special way, knowing that the implementation of God's law in human life will provide harmony between all that exists. This truth necessarily sets human conscience on a sound footing, giving it consistency and enlightenment. It also clarifies the bonds between man and his Creator on the one hand and between man and the universe on the other. This then has clear effects on the practical, moral, social and behavioural aspects of human life.

The Qur'ān places much emphasis on the concept of God's oneness, and persistently clarifies this and what it entails. This is particularly true in Makkan *sūrahs*, but it is also true in *sūrahs* revealed in Madinah, although the way it is presented in the latter changes so as to fit the subject matter of these *sūrahs*.

Yet this is the truth the unbelievers were most amazed at, endlessly debating this with the Prophet, and wondering at his insistence on it. They also called on people to express amazement at it, doing their utmost to turn them away from it. Indeed, they went even further, expressing amazement that the Prophet was chosen to be entrusted with God's message to mankind: "*Was the message given to him alone out of all of us?*" (Verse 8) This is nothing but plain envy, a trait that motivated their hostility to his message despite their awareness that this was the truth.

> The Qur'ān had its attraction even to the most outspoken enemies of Islam. They realized that Muḥammad spent some time every night in worship reading the Qur'ān in prayer. Therefore, protected by the cover of darkness, some of them sat just outside his house, listening to the Qur'ān being recited inside. Every one of them was on his own, thinking that no one would know about his action. One can only assume that the motivation was either to try to judge the message of Muḥammad objectively, or to learn

the truth about it, or to listen to the superb literary style of the Qur'ān. As the day began to break, each one of them went back so that no one could find out about his action. Soon, the three of them: Abū Jahl himself, Abū Sufyān and al-Akhnas ibn Sharīq met. There was no need to ask each other what they were doing. There was only one reason for their presence there at that particular time. Therefore, they counselled each other against such action: "Should some of your followers see you," one of them said, "you would stir doubts in their minds."

The following night they did the same, and once again they met at the break of day. Again they counselled each other against their 'irresponsible' action. Nevertheless, the third night each of them went to sit outside the Prophet's home and listen to the Qur'ān. When they met in the morning, they felt ashamed of themselves. One of them suggested that they should give each other their word of honour not to come again. They did so before going home.

Later that morning al-Akhnas ibn Sharīq went to see Abū Sufyān in his home. He asked him what he thought about what he heard Muḥammad reciting. Abū Sufyān said: "I heard things which I know and recognize to be true, but I also heard things whose nature I cannot understand." Al-Akhnas said that he felt the same. He then left and went to Abū Jahl's home to put the same question to him.

Abū Jahl's answer was totally different. For once, he was candid and honest with himself and his interlocuter: "I will tell you about what I heard! We have competed with the clan of 'Abd Manāf for honours: they fed the poor, and we did the same; they provided generous support to those who needed it and we did the same. When we were together on the same level, like two racehorses running neck and neck, they said that one of their number was a Prophet receiving revelations from on high! When can we attain such an honour? By God, we shall never believe in him."[4]

---

4. This report is quoted as in Adil Salahi, *Muhammad: Man and Prophet*, Leicester, 2002, pp. 173–174. – Editor's note.

We see clearly that nothing stopped Abū Jahl from admitting the truth with which he wrestled on three consecutive nights, being beaten every time, except his envy. He was envious that Muḥammad should have attained a position to which no one else can aspire. This was indeed the secret motivation behind those who said: "*Was the message given to him alone out of all of us?*" (Verse 8) They were the ones who repeatedly said: "*Why was not this Qur'ān bestowed from on high on some great man of the two cities?*" (43: 31) The two cities were Makkah and Ṭā'if where the Arab elders and noblemen lived. Whenever they heard about a new prophet, such people sought to gain power through religion. They were thus extremely shocked and envious when God chose Muḥammad (peace be upon him), bestowing on him of His grace what He knew Muḥammad alone deserved.

The answer the *sūrah* gives to their question is laden with sarcasm and warning: "*In fact they are in doubt concerning My reminder; they have not yet tasted My punishment.*" (Verse 8) They had asked: "*Was the message given to him alone out of all of us.*" This when they doubted the very message itself and were unable to accept that it was from God, even though they realized no human being could have produced anything like it.

The *sūrah* sets aside what they said about the Qur'ān to issue them with a warning: "*they have not yet tasted My punishment.*" (Verse 8) It is as if the *sūrah* is stating that they say whatever they say because they are still safe, not having tasted anything of God's punishment. When they do experience this, they will say nothing of it because then they will know.

The *sūrah* then comments on their wonder at God's choice of Muḥammad to be His Messenger. It asks them whether they control God's mercy: "*Or do they own the treasures of your Lord's grace, the Almighty, the Munificent?*" (Verse 9) Do they seek to interfere with what belongs to God to decide? It is God who gives whatever He wishes to any of His servants and who withholds it from anyone He wishes. He is the Almighty whose will applies to all and cannot be resisted, and whose grace is limitless. If they find it hard to accept that God has chosen Muḥammad (peace be upon him) for his role, by what right and in what capacity can they decide how God's favours be granted when they do not own the treasures of His grace?

"*Or do they have dominion over the heavens and the earth and all that is between them?*" (Verse 10) This is something that they do not dare to claim. It is the One who owns and controls the heavens and the earth who decides who should receive what and who should be assigned to what role. If they do not have dominion over the heavens and the earth and all that is between them, how come they interfere with the decisions of the One who has this dominion? A sarcastic and reproachful comment then follows: "*Let them, then, try to ascend by all conceivable means.*" (Verse 10) If that is the case, let them take control of the universe and administer the treasures of God's grace. Let them decide who should receive such favours and who should be deprived.

This sarcastic remark is followed by a statement of fact describing their real status: "*Whatever hosts, of any affiliation, may be raised will suffer defeat.*" (Verse 11) They are no more than the remnants of a defeated army left aside. They have no ability to change or object to God's will. The phraseology of this verse makes it hard to capture its sense in translation. The subject, '*whatever hosts*', refers to something insignificant that no identity can be assigned to. The verbal phrase, '*will suffer defeat*', is expressed in the Arabic original in one adjectival word, *mahzūm*, which suggests that defeat is an essential characteristic of such hosts and that they cannot get rid of it. This is a very true description. God's enemies can never be in any position other than the one indicated by this Qur'ānic expression which connotes powerlessness and absolute lack of control, no matter how mighty they may appear or when they appear.

The *sūrah* gives examples of former communities who treaded the same course, and we discover that they all faced utter defeat: "*Before their time, the truth was rejected by Noah's people, the 'Ād, Pharaoh of the tent-pegs, the Thamūd, Lot's people and the dwellers of the wooded dales: these were different groupings; yet each one of them accused God's messengers of lying. Therefore, My retribution fell due.*" (Verses 12–14) These communities were the Quraysh's predecessors. All of them, including Pharaoh who built the pyramids that stand firm like tent pegs, and Shu'ayb's people who dwelled in the wooded dales, rejected God's messages. What eventually happened to these tyrannical peoples?

God's retribution fell due and they were all decimated. There is nothing left of them except the ruins that tell of their defeat.

Such was the fate of past communities of unbelievers. As for the present ones, they are, generally, left until a blast brings about the end of life on earth just before the Day of Judgement: *"These, too, have but to wait for one single blast; and it shall not be delayed."* (Verse 15) Once this blast falls due, it will not be delayed even for a short moment. It occurs at its appointed time. God has willed that this community of the last message will be given its time, and that He will not destroy it as He did past communities. This is an act of grace, but they do not appreciate this or thank God for it. On the contrary, they hasten their own punishment, asking God to give them their lot now, before the day He has appointed: *"They say: Our Lord! Hasten to us our share of punishment even before the Day of Reckoning."* (Verse 16)

At this point the *sūrah* ends its reference to the unbelievers and turns instead to the Prophet. He is comforted and directed to remember what happened to earlier messengers, the hard tests they went through and the grace God bestowed on them when they proved themselves.

2

Tests for Prophets

Bear with patience whatever they say, and remember Our servant David who was endowed with strength. He always turned to Us. (17)

أَصْبِرْ عَلَىٰ مَا يَقُولُونَ وَاذْكُرْ عَبْدَنَا دَاوُدَ ذَا الْأَيْدِ إِنَّهُ أَوَّابٌ ۝

We caused the mountains to join him in extolling Our limitless glory in the evening and at sunrise, (18)

إِنَّا سَخَّرْنَا الْجِبَالَ مَعَهُ يُسَبِّحْنَ بِالْعَشِيِّ وَالْإِشْرَاقِ ۝

and likewise the birds in flocks: they all would echo his praise. (19)

وَالطَّيْرَ مَحْشُورَةً كُلٌّ لَّهُ أَوَّابٌ ۝

We strengthened his kingdom; We endowed him with wisdom and decisive judgement. (20)

وَشَدَدْنَا مُلْكَهُ وَآتَيْنَاهُ الْحِكْمَةَ وَفَصْلَ الْخِطَابِ ۝

Have you heard the story of the litigants who surmounted the walls of the sanctuary? (21)

وَهَلْ أَتَاكَ نَبَأُ الْخَصْمِ إِذْ تَسَوَّرُوا الْمِحْرَابَ ۝

When they went in to David, he was alarmed. They said: 'Have no fear. We are but two litigants: one of us has wronged the other; so judge between us with justice, and do not be unfair. Show us the way to rectitude. (22)

إِذْ دَخَلُوا۟ عَلَىٰ دَاوُۥدَ فَفَزِعَ مِنْهُمْ قَالُوا۟ لَا تَخَفْ خَصْمَانِ بَغَىٰ بَعْضُنَا عَلَىٰ بَعْضٍ فَٱحْكُم بَيْنَنَا بِٱلْحَقِّ وَلَا تُشْطِطْ وَٱهْدِنَآ إِلَىٰ سَوَآءِ ٱلصِّرَٰطِ ۝

This is my brother: he has ninety-nine ewes and I have only one ewe. Yet he said: "Let me take charge of her," and has been hard on me in his speech.' (23)

إِنَّ هَٰذَآ أَخِى لَهُۥ تِسْعٌ وَتِسْعُونَ نَعْجَةً وَلِىَ نَعْجَةٌ وَٰحِدَةٌ فَقَالَ أَكْفِلْنِيهَا وَعَزَّنِى فِى ٱلْخِطَابِ ۝

Said [David]: 'He has certainly wronged you by demanding that your ewe be added to his ewes! Thus do many partners wrong one another, except for those who believe and do righteous deeds, but how few are they!' Then David realized that We were only testing him. He prayed for his Lord's forgiveness, fell down in prostration and turned to God in repentance. (24)

قَالَ لَقَدْ ظَلَمَكَ بِسُؤَالِ نَعْجَتِكَ إِلَىٰ نِعَاجِهِۦ وَإِنَّ كَثِيرًا مِّنَ ٱلْخُلَطَآءِ لَيَبْغِى بَعْضُهُمْ عَلَىٰ بَعْضٍ إِلَّا ٱلَّذِينَ ءَامَنُوا۟ وَعَمِلُوا۟ ٱلصَّٰلِحَٰتِ وَقَلِيلٌ مَّا هُمْ وَظَنَّ دَاوُۥدُ أَنَّمَا فَتَنَّٰهُ فَٱسْتَغْفَرَ رَبَّهُۥ وَخَرَّ رَاكِعًا وَأَنَابَ ۩ ۝

We forgave him that, and in the life to come he is to be close to Us and will be well received. (25)

فَغَفَرْنَا لَهُۥ ذَٰلِكَ وَإِنَّ لَهُۥ عِندَنَا لَزُلْفَىٰ وَحُسْنَ مَـَٔابٍ ۝

David! We have made you a vicegerent on earth: judge, then, between people with justice, and do not follow vain desire, lest it leads you astray from the path of

يَٰدَاوُۥدُ إِنَّا جَعَلْنَٰكَ خَلِيفَةً فِى ٱلْأَرْضِ فَٱحْكُم بَيْنَ ٱلنَّاسِ بِٱلْحَقِّ وَلَا تَتَّبِعِ ٱلْهَوَىٰ فَيُضِلَّكَ عَن سَبِيلِ ٱللَّهِ إِنَّ ٱلَّذِينَ يَضِلُّونَ

God. Those who go astray from the path of God will have a severe punishment for having ignored the Day of Reckoning. (26)

عَنْ سَبِيلِ ٱللَّهِ لَهُمْ عَذَابٌ شَدِيدٌ بِمَا نَسُوا۟ يَوْمَ ٱلْحِسَابِ ﴿٢٦﴾

We have not created heaven and earth and all that is between them without a purpose. That is what the unbelievers assume. Woe betide the unbelievers when they are cast in the fire. (27)

وَمَا خَلَقْنَا ٱلسَّمَآءَ وَٱلْأَرْضَ وَمَا بَيْنَهُمَا بَٰطِلًا ذَٰلِكَ ظَنُّ ٱلَّذِينَ كَفَرُوا۟ فَوَيْلٌ لِّلَّذِينَ كَفَرُوا۟ مِنَ ٱلنَّارِ ﴿٢٧﴾

Are We to equate those who believe and do righteous deeds with those who spread corruption in the land? Are We to equate the God-fearing with the wicked? (28)

أَمْ نَجْعَلُ ٱلَّذِينَ ءَامَنُوا۟ وَعَمِلُوا۟ ٱلصَّٰلِحَٰتِ كَٱلْمُفْسِدِينَ فِى ٱلْأَرْضِ أَمْ نَجْعَلُ ٱلْمُتَّقِينَ كَٱلْفُجَّارِ ﴿٢٨﴾

This is a blessed book which We have revealed to you so that people may ponder over its message, and that those endowed with insight may take it to heart. (29)

كِتَٰبٌ أَنزَلْنَٰهُ إِلَيْكَ مُبَٰرَكٌ لِّيَدَّبَّرُوٓا۟ ءَايَٰتِهِۦ وَلِيَتَذَكَّرَ أُو۟لُوا۟ ٱلْأَلْبَٰبِ ﴿٢٩﴾

To David We gave Solomon: how excellent a servant of Ours; he would always turn to Us. (30)

وَوَهَبْنَا لِدَاوُۥدَ سُلَيْمَٰنَ نِعْمَ ٱلْعَبْدُ إِنَّهُۥٓ أَوَّابٌ ﴿٣٠﴾

When, one evening, nobly-bred, swift-footed steeds were brought before him, (31)

إِذْ عُرِضَ عَلَيْهِ بِٱلْعَشِىِّ ٱلصَّٰفِنَٰتُ ٱلْجِيَادُ ﴿٣١﴾

he kept saying: 'My love of good things is part of my remembering my Lord!' until they disappeared from sight. (32)

فَقَالَ إِنِّي أَحْبَبْتُ حُبَّ الْخَيْرِ عَن ذِكْرِ رَبِّي حَتَّىٰ تَوَارَتْ بِالْحِجَابِ ﴿٣٢﴾

'Bring them back to me!' He then stroked their legs and their necks. (33)

رُدُّوهَا عَلَيَّ فَطَفِقَ مَسْحًا بِالسُّوقِ وَالْأَعْنَاقِ ﴿٣٣﴾

We had tried Solomon, and placed a body on his throne. He then turned to Us, (34)

وَلَقَدْ فَتَنَّا سُلَيْمَانَ وَأَلْقَيْنَا عَلَىٰ كُرْسِيِّهِ جَسَدًا ثُمَّ أَنَابَ ﴿٣٤﴾

and prayed: 'My Lord! Forgive me my sins, and bestow upon me such power as shall belong to no one after me. You are indeed the bountiful giver.' (35)

قَالَ رَبِّ اغْفِرْ لِي وَهَبْ لِي مُلْكًا لَّا يَنبَغِي لِأَحَدٍ مِّن بَعْدِي إِنَّكَ أَنتَ الْوَهَّابُ ﴿٣٥﴾

We made the wind subservient to him, so that it gently sped at his command wherever he wished, (36)

فَسَخَّرْنَا لَهُ الرِّيحَ تَجْرِي بِأَمْرِهِ رُخَاءً حَيْثُ أَصَابَ ﴿٣٦﴾

and the jinn, including every kind of builder and diver, (37)

وَالشَّيَاطِينَ كُلَّ بَنَّاءٍ وَغَوَّاصٍ ﴿٣٧﴾

and others bound together in fetters. (38)

وَآخَرِينَ مُقَرَّنِينَ فِي الْأَصْفَادِ ﴿٣٨﴾

This is Our gift; so give or withhold as you please, without account. (39)

هَٰذَا عَطَاؤُنَا فَامْنُنْ أَوْ أَمْسِكْ بِغَيْرِ حِسَابٍ ﴿٣٩﴾

In the life to come he is to be close to Us and will be well received. (40)

وَإِنَّ لَهُۥ عِندَنَا لَزُلْفَىٰ وَحُسْنَ مَـَٔابٍ ۝

Remember Our servant Job who cried out to his Lord: 'Satan has afflicted me with weariness and suffering!' (41)

وَٱذْكُرْ عَبْدَنَآ أَيُّوبَ إِذْ نَادَىٰ رَبَّهُۥٓ أَنِّى مَسَّنِىَ ٱلشَّيْطَـٰنُ بِنُصْبٍ وَعَذَابٍ ۝

'Strike [the ground] with your foot! Here is cool water for you to wash with and to drink.' (42)

ٱرْكُضْ بِرِجْلِكَ هَـٰذَا مُغْتَسَلٌ بَارِدٌ وَشَرَابٌ ۝

We restored his family to him, and doubled their number as an act of grace from Us, and as a reminder to those who are endowed with insight. (43)

وَوَهَبْنَا لَهُۥٓ أَهْلَهُۥ وَمِثْلَهُم مَّعَهُمْ رَحْمَةً مِّنَّا وَذِكْرَىٰ لِأُوْلِى ٱلْأَلْبَـٰبِ ۝

'Take in your hand a bunch of grass and strike with it, and you will not then break your oath.' We found him patient in adversity. How excellent a servant of Ours; he would always turn to Us. (44)

وَخُذْ بِيَدِكَ ضِغْثًا فَٱضْرِب بِّهِۦ وَلَا تَحْنَثْ إِنَّا وَجَدْنَـٰهُ صَابِرًا نِّعْمَ ٱلْعَبْدُ إِنَّهُۥٓ أَوَّابٌ ۝

Remember Our servants Abraham, Isaac and Jacob: all men of strength and vision. (45)

وَٱذْكُرْ عِبَـٰدَنَآ إِبْرَٰهِيمَ وَإِسْحَـٰقَ وَيَعْقُوبَ أُوْلِى ٱلْأَيْدِى وَٱلْأَبْصَـٰرِ ۝

We gave them a specially distinctive quality: the remembrance of the life to come. (46)

إِنَّآ أَخْلَصْنَـٰهُم بِخَالِصَةٍ ذِكْرَى ٱلدَّارِ ۝

In Our sight, they were indeed among the elect, the truly good. (47)	وَإِنَّهُمْ عِندَنَا لَمِنَ ٱلْمُصْطَفَيْنَ ٱلْأَخْيَارِ ۝
And remember Ishmael, Elisha and Dhu'l-Kifl: each belonged to the truly good. (48)	وَٱذْكُرْ إِسْمَٰعِيلَ وَٱلْيَسَعَ وَذَا ٱلْكِفْلِ وَكُلٌّ مِّنَ ٱلْأَخْيَارِ ۝

Overview

This long passage is devoted to aspects of the histories of earlier messengers so that the Prophet Muḥammad (peace be upon him) would remember them and disregard all the rejections, accusations, amazement and fabrications the unbelievers levelled at him. All this was certain to weigh hard on anyone, but the Prophet is told to bear it all and remain patient in adversity.

At the same time, the stories present the effects of God's grace as it was bestowed on earlier messengers. It shows how God granted them favours of all sorts, including power, authority, care and blessings. This contrasts with the amazement expressed by the Quraysh at God's favouring the Prophet (peace be upon him) with His message. He was not a unique case among God's messengers. To some of them God granted a kingdom, in addition to their being His messengers. Among them one was favoured with the mountains and birds echoing his glorification and praise of God, and to another the wind and *jinn* were made subservient. Such were David and Solomon. What is strange, then, for God to have chosen from among all the Quraysh, Muḥammad, the man of truth, upon whom to bestow His revelations?

These stories describe the care God always took of His messengers and how He instructed them so that they became worthy of their mission. Like Muḥammad, they were ordinary human beings, experiencing the weaknesses all people do. God took care of them so that their weaknesses did not get the better of them. He explained things to them and gave them directives. He also tested them so that

He would forgive them their errors and grant them favours. This was bound to reassure the Prophet that God would take care of him at every step.

David Ruling in a Dispute

> *Bear with patience whatever they say, and remember Our servant David who was endowed with strength. He always turned to Us. We caused the mountains to join him in extolling Our limitless glory in the evening and at sunrise, and likewise the birds in flocks: they all would echo his praise. We strengthened his kingdom; We endowed him with wisdom and decisive judgement.* (Verses 17–20)

'*Bear with patience...*' This is a reference to the road taken by all God's messengers. It groups them together. Everyone of them took it: everyone suffered, was tested and remained patient in adversity; each at his own step in the lofty ladder of prophethood. The life of each one of them was a series of tests, each bearing much pain. Even when things were pleasant and comfortable, this represented a different form of test so as to ensure that they remained patient when life was easy in the same way as they were patient in adversity. Both situations require endurance. When we contemplate the lives of all God's messengers, as told to us in the Qur'ān, we realize that patience was the most prominent element. In essence, their lives were a long series of trials and tests.

The lives of God's messengers were in fact an open book for all humanity to read, with every page speaking about trials, afflictions and patience. The records show how the human soul triumphs over pain and necessity. How it rises above all that to which the present world attaches value, and how it discards desires and temptations, so as to achieve full dedication to God, and in so doing passes the test He has set. It shows the meaning of choosing Him over everything else so as to say to mankind: 'This is the way to rise; it is the only way leading to God's acceptance.'

"*Bear with patience whatever they say.*" (Verse 17) They said much, such as: "*This is a sorcerer telling lies.*" (Verse 4) "*Does he make all the gods into one God? This is indeed most strange."* (Verse 5) *"Was the message given to him alone out of all of us?"* (Verse 8) Indeed they said much more. God directs the Prophet to bear their statements with patience, and tells him that in his mind and heart he should live with a different type of people: the select few, God's messengers with whom he has a strong affinity and close relationship. Indeed, he used to refer to them as though they were his immediate relatives, saying: 'May God have mercy on my brother Joseph,' and 'I have a stronger bond with my brother Moses,' etc.

"Bear with patience whatever they say, and remember Our servant David who was endowed with strength. He always turned to Us." (Verse 17) David is referred to here as a strong person who turned to God. The *sūrah* earlier mentioned (Verses 12–13) the peoples of Noah, the 'Ād, Thamūd, Pharaoh, Lot's people and the community that lived in the wooded dale near Madyan. All of these were tyrannical, and it was such tyranny that gave them the impression of power. David, on the other hand, was a man of strength, but he always turned to God, repenting of his sins, glorifying God and worshipping Him. He did so when he was truly powerful, with a kingdom to rule.

In *Sūrah* 2, The Cow, we have an account of David in his youth, when he was a soldier in Saul's army. At the time, which was long after Moses, the Israelites asked one of their prophets to assign one of them as king and they promised that they would fight for God's cause under his leadership. God appointed Saul as their king and he marshalled them to face Goliath's mighty army. It was David who killed Goliath. From that day, his standing was enhanced, such that, in turn, he became king. Yet having a throne did not lead him astray. He continued to turn to God in repentance, glorifying and worshipping Him.

Apart from prophethood and a kingdom, God also blessed David with an alert heart and a melodious voice, which he used to good effect as he sang his psalms and hymns. He would be so absorbed in his devotion that barriers between him and the universe would disappear and the mountains would echo his glorification, while birds gathered around him, all glorifying the Lord Creator. *"We caused the mountains to join him in extolling Our limitless glory in the evening and at sunrise, and likewise the birds in flocks: they all would echo his praise.*" (Verses 18–19) People may be speechless when they hear that the mountains, inanimate entities, should join David in his constant glorification of God as he chants his songs of praise. Not only that but the birds also flock to him, listen and join in with the chorus to his hymns. Their surprise results from the fact that it runs counter to everything they have been used to. They only know that man, birds and mountains belong to totally separate realms.

Yet, why should anyone be surprised? All these creatures, different as their races, shapes, forms and characteristics are, share in one fundamental fact: they turn to the Lord who created the whole universe with all its animate and inanimate objects. When man's relation with his Lord attains sublime purity, barriers between different elements are removed. The whole matter is simple: God gave His servant David this unique characteristic, and caused the mountains to join him in extolling His glory morning and evening, and gathered the birds around him to echo his praises. This was simply an additional gift by virtue of God's grace.

"*We strengthened his kingdom; We endowed him with wisdom and decisive judgement.*" (Verse 20) Thus, his kingdom was strong and well established. He administered his government with wisdom and clear, decisive vision. The phrase '*decisive judgement*' means that his views were clear, not subject to hesitation. When this is coupled with wisdom, it makes for perfect government within man's world. However, this did not spare David from being subjected to tests and trials. Nevertheless, God continued to take care of him and guided his footsteps:

> *Have you heard the story of the litigants who surmounted the walls of the sanctuary? When they went in to David, he was alarmed. They said: 'Have no fear. We are but two litigants: one of us has wronged the other; so judge between us with justice, and do not be unfair. Show us the way to rectitude. This is my brother: he has ninety-nine ewes and I have only one ewe. Yet he said: "Let me take charge of her," and has been hard on me in his speech.' Said [David]: 'He has certainly wronged you by demanding that your*

ewe be added to his ewes! Thus do many partners wrong one another, except for those who believe and do righteous deeds, but how few are they!' Then David realized that We were only testing him. He prayed for his Lord's forgiveness, fell down in prostration and turned to God in repentance. (Verses 21–24)

These verses tell of a test to which David was subjected. David used to devote some of his time to conducting the affairs of his kingdom and to judge in people's disputes. The rest of his time he devoted to his worship, preferring seclusion when he sang his psalms. When he went into the sanctuary, no one was allowed in.

One day, David was surprised when he saw two people climbing over the wall into the sanctuary. He was alarmed. No good believer or trustworthy person would enter in this way. Therefore, they immediately tried to reassure him, saying that they were in dispute and wanted him to judge between them in fairness, showing them the way to justice. One of them immediately started putting his case forward, saying that the other man, his brother, had 99 ewes while he only had one. Yet he insisted on taking charge of his single ewe, placing it with his 99.

As stated by one of the disputants, the case is one of gross injustice that cannot be condoned. Hence, David immediately started to give his judgement without speaking to the other man or asking him to give his side of the story. Instead, he told the first man that the other had been unfair in his demands, and that many people behave in this way, except those who are good believers and do righteous deeds. These, however, are few in number.

It seems that at this stage the two men disappeared. In fact, they were two angels who had come to test David, the prophet God had placed in a position of authority to judge between people in fairness, making sure who is right before passing judgement. They had put the case to him in a very sentimental way, one that invited immediate sympathy. However, a judge must not allow sentiment to take charge. He must not be hasty. Above all, he must not rely on the statement of one party, without allowing the other party to present his case and submit his evidence. Some aspects of the case, if not all of it, may then be seen in a different light. In other words, appearances can often be deceptive or incomplete.

At this point David realized that this was a test: "*Then David realized that We were only testing him.*" (Verse 24) His good nature surfaced again, because he was a man always ready to accept what is right: "*He prayed for his Lord's forgiveness, fell down in prostration and turned to God in repentance.*" (Verse 24)

God's response was to accept his repentance: "*We forgave him that, and in the life to come he is to be close to Us and will be well received.*" (Verse 25) Some commentators on the Qur'ān picked up some Israelite reports and made much of these which cannot be acceptable because they are incompatible and irreconcilable with the nature of prophethood. Even the reports that tried to moderate these legends accept certain parts of them. The fact is that these legends do not merit consideration, because they cannot fit with God's assertion in reference to David: "*He is to be close to Us and will be well received.*" (Verse 25)

The Qur'ānic comments given after the story explain the nature of the test and specify the line God wants His servant to whom He assigned judgement between people to take:

> *David! We have made you a vicegerent on earth: judge, then, between people with justice, and do not follow vain desire, lest it leads you astray from the path of God. Those who go astray from the path of God will have a severe punishment for having ignored the Day of Reckoning.* (Verse 26)

It is then a case of David being given the position of vicegerent on earth, one whereby he is required to judge between people in all fairness. He is told not to follow vain desires, which means in the case of a prophet, not to be hasty in one's first reaction. For this can easily lead to going astray from God's path. Rather, he must make sure of all the facts before passing judgement. The concluding sentence in the verse gives a general rule that applies to all cases of going astray from God's path. It exposes the person concerned to severe punishment on the Day of Reckoning.

One aspect of the care God took of His servant David is that He drew his attention at the first hurdle, and put him back on the right track at the first rash move, warning him of the ultimate result, when he had not even made one step towards it. Such is God's favour that He bestows on His chosen servants. Since they are human, they may slip when they travel an uneven patch of the road, but God takes them by the hand putting them back on course and teaching them how to repent. Then He forgives them and bestows even greater favours on them.

A Reminder to Grasp

Having stated the main principle in conducting the position of vicegerent on earth and in judging people's disputes, the context of the truth on which the whole system that sustains the universe is based is then stated. Broader as it is than man's whole world and role, this basic truth deals with the very existence of the universe and with the life to come. Furthermore, the last divine message to mankind is based on this truth. Indeed, the Qur'ān is the book that explains this great truth:

> We have not created heaven and earth and all that is between them without a purpose. That is what the unbelievers assume. Woe betide the unbelievers when they are cast in the fire. Are We to equate those who believe and do righteous deeds with those who spread corruption in the land? Are We to equate the God-fearing with the wicked? This is a blessed book which We have revealed to you so that people may ponder over its message, and that those endowed with insight may take it to heart. (Verses 27–29)

These three verses set this great truth, one that is profound and accurate. For certain, the creation of the heavens and the earth and all that is between them was not without purpose. Their creation is based on the truth and for a definite intent. It is from this great truth that all else stems whether it be man's vicegerency on earth, the right to judge between people, or setting feelings and actions on the right course so that those who do good deeds are not equated with those who spread corruption on earth, and that the God-fearing are not grouped together with the wicked. The truth embodied in God's blessed book is given to people with insight and understanding so that they can study its verses and reflect on the essential facts of existence. Such truth and facts cannot even be imagined by unbelievers, because they do not relate to the great truth on which the universe is based. Hence, they entertain ill thoughts about their Lord and will not understand the truth: *"That is what the unbelievers assume. Woe betide the unbelievers when they are cast in the fire."* (Verse 27)

The law God has laid down for human life is part of His law for the universe. His revealed book, the Qur'ān, explains the truth on which His universal law is based. The justice required of those who are in authority, i.e. vicegerents, and those who judge between people are part of the total truth. People's lives cannot be properly established unless this part is in harmony with the rest of the parts. This means that deviation from the divine law, the truth in discharging the responsibilities of man's vicegerency on earth and from fairness when judging disputes is in effect a deviation from the universal law that sustains the universe. It is, therefore, a very serious and grave matter, one that leads to a collision with the immense universal forces. Anyone heading for such a collision will end in ruin. No wrongdoing tyrant can withstand such crushing forces. This must always be remembered and reflected upon by people endowed with insight.

A Test for Solomon

The *sūrah* picks up the thread of the story to show us the favour God granted David as He gave him Solomon for a son. It also speaks of the great favours He bestowed on Solomon, the test he was subjected to, the care God took of him and the blessings showered on him when the test was over:

> *To David We gave Solomon: how excellent a servant of Ours; he would always turn to Us. When, one evening, nobly-bred, swift-footed steeds were brought before him, he kept saying: 'My love of*

good things is part of my remembering my Lord!' until they
disappeared from sight. 'Bring them back to me!' He then stroked
their legs and their necks. We had tried Solomon, and placed a body
on his throne. He then turned to Us, and prayed: 'My Lord! Forgive
me my sins, and bestow upon me such power as shall belong to no
one after me. You are indeed the bountiful giver.' We made the
wind subservient to him, so that it gently sped at his command
wherever he wished, and the jinn, *including every kind of builder*
and diver, and others bound together in fetters. This is Our gift; so
give or withhold as you please, without account. In the life to come
he is to be close to Us and will be well received. (Verses 30–40)

The references in the story to nobly-bred steeds and the body placed
on his throne have been interpreted in a variety of ways. However, I
do not feel comfortable with any such interpretation considering them
either unfounded reports from Israelite sources or else lacking any
supporting evidence. I cannot visualize the two incidents in any
satisfactory way so as to explain them to my reader. Nor can I find any
authentic report to rely upon in interpreting them. The only authentic
ḥadīth I have found may or may not relate to either event. This *ḥadīth*,
related by al-Bukhārī on Abū Hurayrah's authority, says: "Solomon
said: 'I will consort tonight with 70 women, so that each one of them
will give birth to a warrior who fights for God's cause,' but he did not
add, 'God willing.' He consorted with them, but only one of them
became pregnant, and then she gave birth to half a person. By Him
who holds my soul in His hand, had he said, 'God willing,' they would
have been warriors fighting for God's cause." It is possible that this
was the test which Solomon had to go through and to which these
verses refer. It is also possible that the body placed on his throne was
this half person. This, however, is only a possibility. As for the story
about the horses, it is said that Solomon reviewed some of his horses
towards the end of the day. This caused him to miss an evening prayer
which he used to offer before sunset. Upset, he asked for the horses to
be brought back. When they were, he hit their necks and legs as
punishment for diverting his attention from worship. In a different
report, it is suggested that he rubbed their necks and legs because they

were kept for fighting for God's cause. Neither version, however, has much to support it, and it is thus impossible to ascertain the truth of either one.

Thus anyone who is careful about what he says cannot give any details of these two incidents with any degree of certainty. All he can say is that Solomon underwent some test concerning the way he conducted his kingdom's affairs, just as God tests prophets to guide them and keep them from error. We also learn that Solomon turned to his Lord in submission and sought His forgiveness.

He then prayed with hope and dedication: "*My Lord! Forgive me my sins, and bestow upon me such power as shall belong to no one after me. You are indeed the bountiful giver.*" (Verse 35) The proper interpretation of Solomon's request is that he did not ask for something to show that he was the most favoured person, but that he asked instead for a special thing, to distinguish him from any future king and master. It was to be of a special nature, not repeated for others. It should also be something not normally possessed by kings.

God answered his prayer: "*We made the wind subservient to him, so that it gently sped at his command wherever he wished, and the* jinn, *including every kind of builder and diver, and others bound together in fetters.*" (Verses 36–38) That God made the wind subservient to one of His servants, is nothing extraordinary because the wind is undoubtedly subservient to His will: it runs by His command in accordance with His laws. If at any time God facilitates one of His servants to express His will, in this case allowing the wind to run with ease wherever Solomon wished, it is nothing strange for God Almighty. Similar things occur in a variety of ways. God also said to the Prophet Muḥammad in the Qur'ān: "*If the hypocrites, those who are sick at heart and those who spread lies in the city do not desist, We will rouse you against them, and then they will not be your neighbours in this city except for a little while.*" (33: 60) What does this mean? It means that unless they change their ways, Our will is going to give you power over them so as to drive them out of Madinah. This will take the form of making you desirous to fight and drive them out. Thus, our will concerning them will be made to take effect through you. This is one way of making God's will and the Prophet's will identical, but it is through God's will that it is done. We, however, see it through what the Prophet wishes and does. In this way we can also understand how the wind was made subservient to Solomon as this was identical with God's command.

God also made the *jinn* subservient to him. They built whatever he wished them to build, and they also dived into the earth and the sea to bring him whatever he wished. He further gave him the authority to punish anyone who disobeyed him or who caused corruption and to chain them by their hands and feet, or every two or more together, as he deemed fit or needed.

Solomon was then told that he had full authority over whatever favours God granted him. He could give to anyone or withhold from anyone as he wished: "*This is Our gift; so give or withhold as you please, without account.*" (Verse 39) This was a further honour granted him by God. Added to all of this, Solomon is told that he has been given closeness to God in this present life and that he will be granted a warm welcome in the life to come: "*In the life to come he is to be close to Us and will be well received.*" (Verse 40) Thus did God grant Solomon a very high standard of care, blessing and favour.

The Symbol of Patience in Adversity

We are then given more of the story of tests, patience in adversity, followed by favours bestowed from on high. This time, the prophet who is tested is Job:

> *Remember Our servant Job who cried out to his Lord: 'Satan has afflicted me with weariness and suffering!' 'Strike [the ground] with your foot! Here is cool water for you to wash with and to drink.' We restored his family to him, and doubled their number as an act of grace from Us, and as a reminder to those who are endowed with insight. 'Take in your hand a bunch of grass and strike with it, and you will not then break your oath.' We found him patient in adversity. How excellent a servant of Ours; he would always turn to Us.* (Verses 41–44)

The story of Job and his steadfastness in face of a severe test is well known, and often cited as an example of patience in adversity. However, it is also coloured with Israelite distortions. The part that sounds correct in the story is that Job was God's good servant who always turned to Him in humility and submission. God tested him and he remained patient. It seems that the test he endured entailed the loss of his wealth, family and health. Nevertheless, he maintained his bond with God, trusting to Him, and was satisfied with what God had given him.

He had a few well-wishers who remained faithful to him, including his wife, but Satan tried to convince these that had God loved Job, He would not have subjected him to such a severe situation. When they told him this, it was harder for him than the test itself. His wife spoke to him repeating some such whispers, and Job was very upset. He swore that should God restore his health, he would beat her up, specifying the number of times he would hit her, which is said to be one hundred.

At this point Job complained to God about the trouble Satan's schemes and whispers were causing him: "*Satan has afflicted me with weariness and suffering!*" (Verse 41) When he had proved his sincerity beyond any doubt, and when he had rejected all Satan's attempts to weaken him, complaining that these were hard for him, God bestowed His grace on him, ending his test, and restoring his health. He ordered him to hit the ground with his leg, and a cool spring would gush forth. He was to wash himself with its water and drink from it. This was enough for him to recover his health: "*Strike [the ground] with your foot! Here is cool water for you to wash with and to drink.*" (Verse 42)

The *sūrah* states: "*We restored his family to him, and doubled their number as an act of grace from Us, and as a reminder to those who are endowed with insight.*" (Verse 43) Some reports suggest that God brought back to life his sons who had died earlier or that He gave him a similar number of sons. However, there is nothing in the Qur'ānic text to suggest that He brought anyone back to life. It may actually be that the Qur'ānic statement means that when his health was restored, he regained his family that had almost been lost to him. He also gave him more as additional favours. This serves as a reminder to those who have insight and understanding.

What is important in the stories related in this *sūrah* is that they show how God bestows favours and grace on His servants. Although He subjects them to tests they remain patient in adversity, bearing their hardship with assured resignation, knowing that whatever God decides is ultimately good.

God also bestowed His grace on Job and his wife with regard to the oath he had made about beating her. She had looked after him during his days of hardship and was also patient during their adversity. Therefore, God ordered Job to take in his hand a bunch of dried sticks, in the number he had stated in his oath, and hit her with the bunch once only. In this way, he would fulfil his oath: "*Take in your hand a bunch of grass and strike with it, and you will not then break your oath.*" (Verse 44) Such care and blessings were in return for what God knew of Job's patience in adversity, his being a model of obedience, always turning to Him for support: "*We found him patient in adversity. How excellent a servant of Ours; he would always turn to Us.*" (Verse 44)

Other Prophets

Having related these three stories in some detail, to remind the Prophet that he too should remain steadfast in the face of opposition, the *sūrah* makes a very brief reference to other prophets. They too endured tests and remained patient; they also received God's favours as a result. Some of these lived earlier than David, Solomon and Job, and we know the periods they lived in, while we do not know the others' time of life, because the Qur'ān and other sources available to us have not specified it.

> *Remember Our servants Abraham, Isaac and Jacob: all men of strength and vision. We gave them a specially distinctive quality: the remembrance of the life to come. In Our sight, they were indeed among the elect, the truly good. And remember Ishmael, Elisha and Dhu'l-Kifl: each belonged to the truly good. (Verses 45–48)*

Abraham, Isaac, Jacob, as well as Ishmael, undoubtedly lived earlier than David and Solomon, but we do not know in what time relation they were to Job. Elisha and Dhu'l-Kifl are mentioned only very briefly in the Qur'ān. The Arabic name given to the first of these two is Alyasaʿ, which is closer to the Hebrew version of Elisha. Most probably they refer to the same person. As for Dhu'l-Kifl, we know nothing of him apart from how he is described here: he *'belonged to the truly good.'*

God, limitless is He in His glory, describes Abraham, Isaac and Jacob as *'men of strength and vision'*, which refers to their good actions, whether physical, done by hand, or mental, relying on sound vision and good judgement. This implies that a person who does not do good deeds is without a hand, and the one who does not think well is without a mind or a vision.

Another of their good characteristics is that God gave them a distinctive quality to remember the life to come. This they did with complete disregard for everything else: *"We gave them a specially distinctive quality: the remembrance of the life to come."* (Verse 46) This is the quality that gave them their distinction and choice position: *"In Our sight, they were indeed among the elect, the truly good."* (Verse 47)

Similarly, God states that Ishmael, Elisha and Dhu'l-Kifl were truly good. He instructs His last messenger to remember them and to contemplate their patience in adversity and the grace He bestowed on them. He too should remain patient in the face of denial and rejection. Steadfastness and patience is the proper course for all advocates of the divine message, particularly God's messengers. God will not abandon such servants. Instead, He will reward them for their patience. What He has for them is certainly better than anything else. When compared with God's grace and care, the schemings and rejections of the unbelievers are of little significance.

3

Contrasting Ends

Let all this be a reminder. The God-fearing will certainly have a good place to return to: (49)

هَٰذَا ذِكْرٌ ۚ وَإِنَّ لِلْمُتَّقِينَ لَحُسْنَ مَـَٔابٍ ﴿٤٩﴾

gardens of perpetual bliss, with gates wide open to them. (50)

جَنَّـٰتِ عَدْنٍ مُّفَتَّحَةً لَّهُمُ ٱلْأَبْوَٰبُ ﴿٥٠﴾

They will be comfortably seated there, and they will call for abundant fruit and drink, (51)

مُتَّكِئِينَ فِيهَا يَدْعُونَ فِيهَا بِفَـٰكِهَةٍ كَثِيرَةٍ وَشَرَابٍ ﴿٥١﴾

having beside them well-matched mates of modest gaze. (52)

وَعِندَهُمْ قَـٰصِرَٰتُ ٱلطَّرْفِ أَتْرَابٌ ﴿٥٢﴾

This is what you are promised for the Day of Reckoning: (53)

هَٰذَا مَا تُوعَدُونَ لِيَوْمِ ٱلْحِسَابِ ﴿٥٣﴾

this, Our provision for you will never end. (54)

إِنَّ هَٰذَا لَرِزْقُنَا مَا لَهُ مِن نَّفَادٍ ﴿٥٤﴾

This is so! Indeed those who transgress the bounds of what is right will have the most evil place to return to: (55)

هَٰذَا ۚ وَإِنَّ لِلطَّـٰغِينَ لَشَرَّ مَـَٔابٍ ﴿٥٥﴾

hell will they have to endure; and how evil a resting place. (56)

جَهَنَّمَ يَصْلَوْنَهَا فَبِئْسَ الْمِهَادُ ۝

Let them, then, taste this: a scalding fluid and a dark, disgusting food, (57)

هَٰذَا فَلْيَذُوقُوهُ حَمِيمٌ وَغَسَّاقٌ ۝

and coupled with it, further [suffering] of a similar nature. (58)

وَءَاخَرُ مِن شَكْلِهِۦٓ أَزْوَٰجٌ ۝

Here is another crowd of people rushing headlong to join you. No welcome to them! They too shall burn in the fire. (59)

هَٰذَا فَوْجٌ مُّقْتَحِمٌ مَّعَكُمْ لَا مَرْحَبًا بِهِمْ إِنَّهُمْ صَالُوا۟ النَّارِ ۝

These others will say: 'No, but it is you! No welcome to you either! It is you who brought this on us! How vile a place to be in!' (60)

قَالُوا۟ بَلْ أَنتُمْ لَا مَرْحَبًا بِكُمْ أَنتُمْ قَدَّمْتُمُوهُ لَنَا فَبِئْسَ الْقَرَارُ ۝

They will say: 'Our Lord! Give double punishment in the fire to whomever has brought this on us.' (61)

قَالُوا۟ رَبَّنَا مَن قَدَّمَ لَنَا هَٰذَا فَزِدْهُ عَذَابًا ضِعْفًا فِى النَّارِ ۝

They will say: 'How is it that we do not see here men whom we considered to be wicked, (62)

وَقَالُوا۟ مَا لَنَا لَا نَرَىٰ رِجَالًا كُنَّا نَعُدُّهُم مِّنَ الْأَشْرَارِ ۝

and whom we made the target of our derision? Or is it that our eyes have missed them?' (63)

أَتَّخَذْنَٰهُمْ سِخْرِيًّا أَمْ زَاغَتْ عَنْهُمُ الْأَبْصَٰرُ ۝

This is in truth how it will be: the people of the fire will quarrel among themselves. (64)	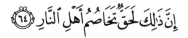

A Quarrel in Hell

The previous passage presented a taste of the life of some of God's chosen people, as they were tested and endured hardship with patience and resignation. They were then granted God's favours and grace. In this way some of the most noble lives in this present world were depicted. Now the *surah* continues its discourse, speaking about God-fearing people in contrast to those who are tyrannical and commit excesses. It shows them however in the next world, where life is everlasting. Thus it paints a scene of the Day of Judgement.

First, a picture is drawn of two completely contrasting images, both in their general outlook and detail. Thus, the God-fearing will have '*a good place to return to,*' while the transgressors will have '*the most evil place to return to.*' The former will be in gardens of perpetual bliss, with gates wide open, where every comfort is available and they are well seated, enjoying all the food and drink they desire, as also female companions of the same age. Although they are still young women, they are '*of modest gaze,*' which means that they are not looking around for anything or coveting what others have. This is all part of what God will provide them with, and whatever He provides will never be exhausted.

As for the others, they have a place where they will be stationed, but there is no rest there, for it is hell, which is described as '*how evil a resting place.*' They have scalding hot drinks, and food that fills them with disgust. It is what flows and seeps through those who occupy hell. Or they have something else of the same type, which is described here as ensuring similar suffering.

The scene is completed with a third image that comes alive with the dialogue it reports. A group of transgressors who used to have close ties in this world are shown to be exchanging accusations and insults. Some used to tempt others into further error, while others behaved arrogantly towards believers, ridiculing their faith and their belief in heaven. Indeed they were no different to those among the Quraysh who used to refer to the Prophet and wonder: "*Was the message given to him alone out of all of us?*" (Verse 8)

Now they are depicted as going straight to hell, one lot after another, with some referring to others and saying: "*Here is another crowd of people rushing headlong to join you.*" (Verse 59) What answer do they receive? It is an angry and rash one: "*No welcome to them! They too shall burn in the fire.*" (Verse 59) Would those who heard this insult take it in silence? Not they! Their response comes quickly: "*No, but it is you! No welcome to you either! It is you who brought this on us! How vile a place to be in!*" (Verse 60) This is a direct accusation, blaming them for bringing about such a fate. They follow this accusation with a prayer that reveals how angry they are, wishing to wreak revenge on the others: "*They will say: Our Lord! Give double punishment in the fire to whomever has brought this on us.*" (Verse 61)

What happens next? They look around searching for the believers whom they treated with arrogance in their first life, thinking ill of them and ridiculing their claims. They do not see them rushing into the fire alongside them. Hence, they ask: Where are they? Where have they gone? Or could it be that they are here but our vision is impaired so we do not see them: "*They will say: How is it that we do not see here men whom we considered to be wicked, and whom we made the target of our derision? Or is it that our eyes have missed them?*" (Verses 62–63) Yet those who are missed by the dwellers of hell are enjoying their abode in heaven.

The scene concludes with a statement about the actual situation of the people of hell: "*This is in truth how it will be: the people of the fire will quarrel among themselves.*" (Verse 64) There is a wide gulf between their fate and that of the believers whom they ridiculed and refused to believe would be God's chosen ones. How miserable is their own lot which they were once keen to hasten: "*Our Lord! Hasten to us our share of punishment even before the Day of Reckoning.*" (Verse 16)

4

Man's First Creation

Say: 'I am but a warner; and there is no deity other than God, the One who conquers all, (65)

the Lord of the heaven and the earth and all that is between, the Almighty, the All-Forgiving!' (66)

Say: 'This is a great message; (67)

yet you turn away from it. (68)

No knowledge would I have of what those on high argue. (69)

It is only revealed to me that I am here to give clear warning.' (70)

Your Lord said to the angels: 'I am about to create a human being out of clay; (71)

قُلۡ إِنَّمَآ أَنَا۠ مُنذِرٞۖ وَمَا مِنۡ إِلَٰهٍ إِلَّا ٱللَّهُ ٱلۡوَٰحِدُ ٱلۡقَهَّارُ ٦٥

رَبُّ ٱلسَّمَٰوَٰتِ وَٱلۡأَرۡضِ وَمَا بَيۡنَهُمَا ٱلۡعَزِيزُ ٱلۡغَفَّٰرُ ٦٦

قُلۡ هُوَ نَبَؤٌاْ عَظِيمٌ ٦٧

أَنتُمۡ عَنۡهُ مُعۡرِضُونَ ٦٨

مَا كَانَ لِيَ مِنۡ عِلۡمٍۭ بِٱلۡمَلَإِ ٱلۡأَعۡلَىٰٓ إِذۡ يَخۡتَصِمُونَ ٦٩

إِن يُوحَىٰٓ إِلَيَّ إِلَّآ أَنَّمَآ أَنَا۠ نَذِيرٞ مُّبِينٌ ٧٠

إِذۡ قَالَ رَبُّكَ لِلۡمَلَٰٓئِكَةِ إِنِّي خَٰلِقُۢ بَشَرٗا مِّن طِينٖ ٧١

when I have fashioned him and breathed of My spirit into him, kneel down before him in prostration.' (72)

فَإِذَا سَوَّيْتُهُ وَنَفَخْتُ فِيهِ مِن رُّوحِي فَقَعُوا لَهُۥ سَٰجِدِينَ ۝

The angels prostrated themselves, all of them together. (73)

فَسَجَدَ ٱلْمَلَٰئِكَةُ كُلُّهُمْ أَجْمَعُونَ ۝

Not so *Iblīs*. He gloried in his arrogance and was one of those who reject the truth. (74)

إِلَّا إِبْلِيسَ ٱسْتَكْبَرَ وَكَانَ مِنَ ٱلْكَٰفِرِينَ ۝

Said [God]: '*Iblīs*! What prevents you from bowing down to one whom I have created with My hands? Are you too proud, or do you deem yourself superior?' (75)

قَالَ يَٰإِبْلِيسُ مَا مَنَعَكَ أَن تَسْجُدَ لِمَا خَلَقْتُ بِيَدَيَّ أَسْتَكْبَرْتَ أَمْ كُنتَ مِنَ ٱلْعَالِينَ ۝

Answered [*Iblīs*]: 'I am better than he: You have created me out of fire, but created him from clay.' (76)

قَالَ أَنَا۠ خَيْرٌ مِّنْهُ خَلَقْتَنِي مِن نَّارٍ وَخَلَقْتَهُۥ مِن طِينٍ ۝

Said He: 'Then get out from it: you are accursed; (77)

قَالَ فَٱخْرُجْ مِنْهَا فَإِنَّكَ رَجِيمٌ ۝

My rejection shall follow you until the Day of Judgement.' (78)

وَإِنَّ عَلَيْكَ لَعْنَتِي إِلَىٰ يَوْمِ ٱلدِّينِ ۝

Said [*Iblīs*]: 'My Lord! Grant me a respite till Resurrection Day.' (79)

قَالَ رَبِّ فَأَنظِرْنِي إِلَىٰ يَوْمِ يُبْعَثُونَ ۝

Said He: 'You are one of those granted respite (80)

قَالَ فَإِنَّكَ مِنَ ٱلْمُنظَرِينَ ۝

till the day of the appointed time.' (81)

إِلَىٰ يَوْمِ ٱلْوَقْتِ ٱلْمَعْلُومِ ۝

[*Iblīs*] then said: 'I swear by Your very might: I shall certainly tempt them all (82)

قَالَ فَبِعِزَّتِكَ لَأُغْوِيَنَّهُمْ أَجْمَعِينَ ۝

except Your true servants.' (83)

إِلَّا عِبَادَكَ مِنْهُمُ ٱلْمُخْلَصِينَ ۝

[And God] said: 'This, then, is the truth! And the truth do I state: (84)

قَالَ فَٱلْحَقُّ وَٱلْحَقَّ أَقُولُ ۝

I will most certainly fill hell with you and such of them as shall follow you.' (85)

لَأَمْلَأَنَّ جَهَنَّمَ مِنكَ وَمِمَّن تَبِعَكَ مِنْهُمْ أَجْمَعِينَ ۝

Say: 'No reward do I ask of you for this, and I am not one to claim what I am not. (86)

قُلْ مَا أَسْأَلُكُمْ عَلَيْهِ مِنْ أَجْرٍ وَمَا أَنَا مِنَ ٱلْمُتَكَلِّفِينَ ۝

This is no less than a reminder to all the worlds, (87)

إِنْ هُوَ إِلَّا ذِكْرٌ لِّلْعَالَمِينَ ۝

and in time you will certainly come to know its truth.' (88)

وَلَتَعْلَمُنَّ نَبَأَهُ بَعْدَ حِينٍ ۝

Overview

This last passage of the *sūrah* reaffirms the issues presented at its outset: God's oneness, revelations and requital in the life to come. It mentions Adam's story as evidence of the truth of revelation, citing in support what took place on high and what was determined then of accountability for man's actions on the Day of Reckoning. The story shows an aspect of Satan's envy which caused his ruin and expulsion from God's mercy. This was when he envied Adam what God had bestowed on him of His favours. The passage also depicts the ever-raging battle between Satan and mankind. His aim is to tempt and seduce the largest number of people possible so that they will join him in hell; this to avenge himself on Adam whom he blamed for his expulsion. It is a battle with well defined objectives. Yet still people surrender to their old enemy.

The *sūrah* concludes by reconfirming the fact of revelation, and the great issue behind it. Needless to say, the unbelievers remain oblivious to these facts.

A Plain Warning

> *Say: I am but a warner; and there is no deity other than God, the One who conquers all the Lord of the heaven and the earth and all that is between, the Almighty, the All-Forgiving!* (Verses 65–66)

The Prophet is given instructions as to what to say to the idolaters who were surprised and amazed at what he preached, wondering: "*Does he make all the gods into one God? This is indeed most strange!*" (Verse 5) He is to say to them that this is the plain truth: "*There is no deity other than God, the One who conquers all.*" He is to further inform them that he himself has no say in all this, apart from giving warnings and leaving people to their Lord to judge. He is "*the Lord of the heavens and the earth and all that is between.*" He has no partners. No one can find shelter against His will whether it be in the heavens and the earth, or in between them. For He is "*the Almighty, the All-Forgiving.*" He has all power and He forgives anyone seeking forgiveness and who turns back to Him in repentance.

The Prophet's instructions make it clear that what he has brought people is far greater than what they think, and that it is a prelude to something they choose to remain oblivious of: "*Say: This is a great message; yet you turn away from it.*" (Verses 67–68) It is indeed far greater than it appears at first sight. It is part of God's will that applies to the entire universe and its system. It cannot be separated from the creation of the heavens and the earth, or from the distant past and the far away future.

This message is addressed to people far beyond the Quraysh in Makkah, the Arabs in their Peninsula and the generation that witnessed its revelation. It transcends the boundaries of place and time to address humanity across all generations, shaping its destiny, from the time of its revelation until God inherits the earth and all those living on it. It came at its appropriate time to fulfil its mission in the time set for it by God.

Mankind's course has been changed with this great message: it is now set on a path demarcated by God. This is true both with regard to those who accept it or reject it, fight for or against it, and in its then current generation or subsequent ones. Nothing and no event in the history of mankind has had greater influence on man than this message. It laid down concepts, rules and systems and set values that apply to the whole earth, for all times. The Arabs could not have imagined anything like this to be possible, not even in their dreams. How could they have imagined that this message, initially addressed to them, would change the face of the earth and the course of history. How could they have thought that it would influence the conscience and life of humanity, accomplish God's will with regard to human destiny and link all these to universal existence and to the truth inherent in the creation of the heavens and the earth. Nor could they have thought for one moment that it was a message that would remain valid for all time, fulfilling its role in directing people's lives.

Today, Muslims adopt the same attitude towards this message as the Arabs of old: they do not understand its nature or its link with the whole universe. They do not recognize the truth inherent in it as part of the truth inherent in the universe. Nor do they look at its influence on human history in a realistic, objective way that is not borrowed from the enemies of this faith who always try to belittle Islam and its effects. This makes Muslims today totally unaware of their true role in the past, present or future, or that they are required to play this role to the end of time.

The Arabs of old thought that the matter concerned them and Muḥammad, not least the fact that it was he who was chosen to receive revelations. All their worry focused on this question. Therefore, the Qur'ān tells them that the matter is far greater than this issue. It is greater than them and Muḥammad who is no more than a messenger delivering what was entrusted to him. He did not invent it, and he could not have learnt what lies beyond it until God had taught him. He was not present with those on high when it all began. It was God who told him of it: *"No knowledge would I have of what those on high argue. It is only revealed to me that I am here to give clear warning.'* (Verses 69–70)

How it All Started

At this point, the *sūrah* tells us how the human story first began and what happened on high. This defines its course as well as its fate and destination. Muḥammad was sent at the end of time to warn people of all this:

> *Your Lord said to the angels: I am about to create a human being out of clay; when I have fashioned him and breathed of My spirit into him, kneel down before him in prostration.* (Verses 71–72)

We do not know how God said this to the angels or how He speaks to them. Nor do we know how the angels receive what God imparts to them. We do not know anything of the angels' nature except what God has told us about them in His revealed book. Therefore, it is useless to try to delve further into this. We should instead consider the significance of the story as told in the Qur'ān.

God created man out of clay, just like the rest of living things on earth. All the elements in their constitutions are derived from clay, with the exception of the secret of life, about which we do not know how or where it came from. Apart from this secret and the breathing of a soul into man, all the constituents of his body stem from mother earth. He will be transformed again into these constituents when the unknown secret departs from his body together with the effects of the sublime breath of soul which defined his course in life.

Again we do not know the nature of the sublime breathing of a soul into man, but we know its effects which distinguished man from the rest of creation on earth. It distinguished him with the quality of aspiring to the sublime, with mind and spirit, which allowed him to look at past experiences and make future plans, and facilitated his spirit to go beyond what is received by his senses and understood by his mind to reach to what neither the senses nor the mind can comprehend. This quality of aspiring to the sublime is unique to man, shared by no other living creature on earth. It never happened in the long history of the earth that any species, or any individual from any species, made this leap even when we accept that physical evolution occurs.

God breathed of His soul into man because His will wished to place him in charge of the earth, managing its affairs within the limits He set, so that he would build human life on it. God gave man the ability to gain higher knowledge. Ever since, man has risen higher whenever he is in contact with the source of his soul, deriving his values from there and maintaining a straight course. When he deviates from this source, the knowledge within him will be in discordance, unable to follow a coherent, progressive, and forward movement. In fact, these discordant trends will threaten his course and may lead to a setback in his human quality, pulling him down, even though his scientific knowledge and experience in some areas at least are well advanced.

This creature of small stature, limited ability, short life duration and basic knowledge could not have attained such honour except for this aspect of divine grace bestowed on him. Otherwise, what is man? He is this small, weak creature living on earth alongside millions of other species. The earth is only a small satellite of a mere star of which there are millions and millions in the great space whose boundaries are known only to God. Who is this creature, man, before whom the angels are required to prostrate? It is because of this subtle, yet great secret that man deserves his position of honour. When this is discarded, man goes back to his origin, the clay of the earth.

The angels acted on God's orders, as they naturally do: "*The angels prostrated themselves, all of them together.*" (Verse 73) How, when and where? All this is part of God's knowledge. To know does not add significance to the story. Instead, the significance is seen in the position and value given to man, a creature made of clay, when he rose above his origin through this breath of God's soul. The angels prostrated themselves in compliance with God's order, knowing that His wisdom is infinite.

"*Not so* Iblīs. *He gloried in his arrogance and was one of those who reject the truth.*" (Verse 74) Was *Iblīs* one of the angels? Most probably not, because if he were an angel, he would not have disobeyed God. Angels do not disobey any order issued to them by God, and they always do what they are bidden. It is mentioned in the Qur'ān that he was created of fire, while it is known that the angels were created from light. Yet he was with the angels and the order to prostrate before Adam included him. He is not specifically mentioned in connection with the order so as to belittle his position. Yet we know that the order applied to him because of the reproach he received as a result of his disobedience.

"*Said [God]:* Iblīs! *What prevents you from bowing down to one whom I have created with My hands? Are you too proud, or do you deem yourself superior?*" (Verse 75) God is the Creator of all. Therefore, the mention that He has created man is particularly significant because it refers to the special care given to this creature who has been given a breath of His soul. Are you too proud to obey My orders? Or do you deem yourself superior like all others who refuse to submit?

"*Answered* [Iblīs]: *I am better than he: You have created me out of fire, but created him from clay.*" (Verse 76) The answer overflows with envy. It also ignores the noble element that Adam has in addition to his creation from clay. Thus, it is a rude retort stemming from a nature that had abandoned all goodness.

At this point, the divine order was issued expelling this rebellious creature: "*Said He: Then get out from it: you are accursed; My rejection shall follow you until the Day of Judgement.*" (Verses 77–78) We cannot define the referent of the pronoun 'it'. It could refer either to heaven, or to God's grace. Both interpretations are possible. There need be no argument over this. In both cases the meaning is clear: *Iblīs* was expelled and cursed as he incurred God's displeasure by rebelling against His orders.

However, *Iblīs's* envy turned into a grudge and determination to avenge himself on Adam and his progeny: "*Said* [Iblīs]: *My Lord! Grant me a respite till Resurrection Day.*" (Verse 79) For some purpose, God granted *Iblīs* his request, allowing him the chance he wanted: "*Said He: You are one of those granted respite till the day of the appointed time.*" (Verse 81) Satan then revealed his goal which summed up his grudge: "[Iblīs] *then said: I swear by Your very might: I shall certainly tempt them all except Your true servants.*" (Verses 82–83) Thus *Iblīs* defined his plan of action. He swore by the Lord of power that he would tempt all human beings, except those over whom he had no power. This was not a gesture of nobility on his part; but rather an acknowledgement of the uselessness of his efforts. Thus he told us about the barrier between him and those who are safe from, and immune to his temptation. It is their worship of God that makes them safe. This is in accordance with God's design and will. God declares His will, defining the way ahead: "*[And God] said: This, then, is the truth! And the truth do I state: I will most certainly fill hell with you and such of them as shall follow you.*" (Verses 84–85)

God always states the truth. The Qur'ān repeatedly states this fact and re-emphasizes it in a variety of ways. In this *sūrah* there are several references to different aspects of the truth, such as the demand of the disputants who climbed the walls of David's sanctuary that he should judge between them in fairness. The Arabic text adds clear connotations that the judgement should be made on the basis of truth. Similarly, the comments on David's story refer to the creation of the heavens and the earth on the basis of the truth. Now, God Almighty reaffirms the truth, saying: "*This, then, is the truth! And the truth do I state.*" (Verse 84) Thus, these references emphasize different aspects of the truth, but its nature is always the same. It includes this true promise: "*I will most certainly fill hell with you and such of them as shall follow you.*" (Verse 85)

It is, then, a battle between Satan and Adam's children: they go into it with full knowledge, aware of the consequences which are made clear in this true promise. They bear responsibility for their choices. Yet in His mercy, God has decided not to leave them without enlightenment. Therefore, he sent them His messengers to warn them.

At the end of the *sūrah*, the Prophet is instructed to say his final word:

> *Say: No reward do I ask of you for this, and I am not one to claim what I am not. This is no less than a reminder to all the worlds, and in time you will certainly come to know its truth.* (Verses 86–88)

It is a sincere call to them to save themselves when the warning has been given and the fate has been shown. The caller, advocating the truth, plain and simple, makes no false claims or pretensions, demanding no reward from anyone. He orders nothing except what sound human nature readily endorses. He simply delivers a reminder to all the worlds, since people may forget or choose to be oblivious. They may ignore the great message that has been delivered to them, but they will eventually come to know its truth. Indeed within a few years of receiving this address, the Arabs knew the truth of this message, and they will come to know it on Judgement Day, when God's promise will be fulfilled: "*I will most certainly fill hell with you and such of them as shall follow you.*" (Verse 85)

Thus, the ending of the *sūrah* is in full harmony with its beginning as also with the themes and issues it has tackled. It is given in a powerful note suggesting that what is to come is grave indeed: "*in time you will certainly come to know its truth.*" (Verse 88)

SŪRAH 39

Al-Zumar

(The Throngs)

Prologue

This *sūrah* deals almost exclusively with the issue of God's oneness. It varies its address to the human heart, striking the full range of tones on its instrument so as to produce a sustained and profound effect. This it does to firmly establish the roots of the principle of God's oneness, purging the heart of anything that could mar its image. Thus, from start to finish, the *sūrah* variously deals with just one subject.

From the very outset, this issue is given immediate prominence: "*This book is bestowed from on high by God, the Almighty, the Wise. It is We who have bestowed on you this revelation from on high, stating the truth. Therefore, worship God alone, sincere in your faith in Him. True devotion is due to God alone.*" (Verses 1–3) It comes again with regular frequency, either expressly stated or as a concept to contemplate. Examples of the first type are: "*Say: 'I am commanded to worship God, sincere in my faith in Him alone; and I am commanded to be the first to submit myself to Him.' Say: 'Indeed I would dread, were I to disobey my Lord, the suffering of an awesome day.' Say: 'God alone do I worship, sincere in my faith in Him alone. You can worship whatever you please instead of Him.'*" (Verses 11–15) "*Say: 'You ignorant people! Would you bid me worship anyone other than God?' It has been revealed to you, and to those before you, that if you ever associate partners with God, all your works shall certainly come to nothing, and you shall certainly be among the lost. You shall worship God alone, and be one of those who give thanks [to Him]."* (Verses 64–66) Two examples now follow of the second type: *"God cites the case of a man who has for his masters several partners at odds with each other, and a man belonging wholly to one person? Can they be deemed equal? All praise is due to God alone, but most of them do not understand."* (Verse 29) *"Is not God sufficient for His servant. Yet they would try to frighten you with those [they worship] other than Him. He whom God lets go astray can never find any guide; whereas he whom God guides aright can never be led astray. Is God not mighty, capable of inflicting retribution?"* (Verses 36–37)

Alongside stating the truth of God's oneness the *sūrah* provides numerous guidelines and inspiring touches to alert our hearts. This serves to fine tune our responses so that we can make the right response to the divine address. For example: *"There is good news for those who shun the worship of false deities and turn to God, so give good news to My servants, who listen carefully to what is said and follow the best of it. These are the ones whom God has graced with His guidance, and these are the ones endowed with insight."* (Verses 17–18) *"God has bestowed from on high the best of all teachings: a book that is consistent within itself, repeating its statements [of the truth] in manifold forms. It causes the skins of those who stand in awe of their Lord to shiver, but then their skins and hearts soften at the mention of God. Such is God's guidance: He guides with it him that wills, whereas the one whom God lets go astray can never find any guide."* (Verse 23) *"When man suffers affliction, he cries out to his Lord, turning to Him for help; but once He bestows upon him a favour by His grace, he forgets what he cried and prayed for earlier, and claims that others are equal to God, thus leading others astray from His path. Say [to him]: 'Enjoy yourself for a while in your disbelief, for you are one of those destined to the fire.'"* (Verse 8)

A prominent feature of the whole *sūrah* is the way in which the air of the life to come spreads over it. Every short passage takes us there. Indeed, the hereafter is its stage. Again, a few examples suffice by way of illustration: *"How about one who devoutly worships God during the hours of the night prostrating himself or standing in prayer, ever mindful of the life to come, and hoping for his Lord's mercy?"* (Verse 9) *"Say:*

Indeed I would dread, were I to disobey my Lord, the suffering of an awesome day." (Verse 13) "*How about one on whom God's sentence of punishment has been passed? Can you rescue those who are already in the fire?*" (Verse 19) "*How about one who shall have nothing but his bare face to protect him from the awful suffering on Resurrection Day.*" (Verse 24) "*Yet much greater will be the suffering of the life to come, if they but knew it.*" (Verse 26) "*Is not there in hell a proper abode for the unbelievers?*" (Verse 32) "*If the wrongdoers possessed all that is on earth, and twice as much, they would surely offer it all as ransom from the awful suffering on the Day of Resurrection. For God will have made obvious to them something they have never reckoned with.*" (Verse 47) "*Turn towards your Lord and submit to Him before the suffering comes upon you, for then you cannot be helped. Follow the best that has been revealed to you by your Lord before the suffering comes upon you of a sudden, without your being aware of it, lest anyone should say: 'Woe is me for having neglected what is due to God, and for having been one of those who scoffed [at the truth]'; or lest he should say: 'If God had but guided me, I would surely have been among the God-fearing'; or lest he should say, when faced by the suffering [that awaits him]: 'If only I could have a second chance in life, I will be among those who do good.'*" (Verses 54–58) Moreover, a large part of the *sūrah* draws complete scenes of the hereafter, thereby adding to its overall ambience.

Scenes of the universe which are varied and frequent in Makkan *sūrahs* are few here. We have one at the opening: "*He has created the heavens and the earth in accordance with the truth. He causes the night to flow into the day, and the day to flow into the night; and He has made the sun and the moon subservient [to His laws]: each running its course for a set term. He is indeed the Almighty, the All-Forgiving.*" (Verse 5) One more such scene is given in the middle of the *sūrah*: "*Have you not considered how God sends down water from the skies, and then causes it to travel through the earth to form springs? He then brings with it vegetation of different colours; and then it withers and you can see it turning yellow. In the end He causes it to crumble to dust. In all this there is indeed a reminder for those endowed with insight.*" (Verse 21) Apart from these expressions we have a number of other quick references to the creation of the heavens and the earth.

The *surah* also includes references to practical life and human nature. Thus, early in the *surah* there is a reference to the origins of humanity: "*He has created you all from a single soul, and from it He fashioned its mate; and He has bestowed on you four kinds of cattle in pairs; and He creates you in your mothers' wombs, one act of creation after another, in threefold depths of darkness. Such is God, your Lord: to Him belongs all dominion. There is no deity other than Him. How, then, can you lose sight of the truth?*" (Verse 6) On the nature of human reactions in situations of both adversity and pleasant ease there are the following two examples: "*When man suffers affliction, he cries out to his Lord, turning to Him for help; but once He bestows upon him a favour by His grace, he forgets what he cried and prayed for earlier.*" (Verse 8) "*When man suffers affliction, he cries out to Us; but once We bestow upon him a favour by Our grace, he says: 'I have been given all this by virtue of my knowledge.' By no means! It is but a test.*" (Verse 49) The fact that people's souls are always in God's grasp is also highlighted: "*God takes away people's souls upon their death, and the souls of the living during their sleep. He keeps with Him the souls of those whose death He has ordained and sends back the others until their appointed time. In all this there are signs for people who reflect.*" (Verse 42)

However, the ambience of the *surah* is derived from its discourse on the Day of Judgement and the life to come. This permeates the *surah* until its conclusion with a scene of devoted worship giving us a clear impression of the atmosphere on that day: "*You will see the angels surrounding the Throne, extolling their Lord's glory and praise. Judgement will have been passed on all in justice, and it will be said: All praise is due to God, the Lord of all the worlds.*" (Verse 75)

This impression fits perfectly with the ambience of the *surah* and the effect it has on our hearts. It emphasizes feelings of awe, fear of God and apprehension over one's fate in the hereafter. Hence, the images it presents to us are those of a trembling, anxious and apprehensive heart. Take for example the image in verse 9 painting a devout worshipper spending hours at night in prayer with his mind fixed on his destiny in the life to come, hoping for God's mercy. Or take the image in verse 23 depicting good believers listening to the Qur'ān, yet they are shivering, though it is not long before their hearts and skins soften at the mention of God. The *sūrah* is full of directives drawing people's attentions to the need to fear God and to be fully aware of what may happen to them on the Day of Resurrection: "*You servants of Mine who believe! Fear your Lord!*" (Verse 10) "*Say: Indeed I would dread, were I to disobey my Lord, the suffering of an awesome day.*" (Verse 13) "*Above them there shall be layers of fire, and layers of fire shall be beneath them. In this way God puts fear into His servants' hearts: 'My servants! Fear Me!'*" (Verse 16) Additionally there are scenes of the Day of Judgement which emphasize our feelings of awe and apprehension.

The *sūrah* deals with its main theme in quick, short rounds, each one of which concludes with an image of the Day of Resurrection. We will discuss these separately, as they are presented in the *sūrah*, because it is difficult to break this down into main passages. Indeed every few verses can be treated as a distinct entity for all address one major truism, God's oneness.

I

The Diversity of God's Creation

Al-Zumar (The Throngs)

In the Name of God, the Lord of Grace, the Ever Merciful

بِسۡمِ ٱللَّهِ ٱلرَّحۡمَٰنِ ٱلرَّحِيمِ

This book is bestowed from on high by God, the Almighty, the Wise. (1)

تَنزِيلُ ٱلۡكِتَٰبِ مِنَ ٱللَّهِ ٱلۡعَزِيزِ ٱلۡحَكِيمِ ۝

It is We who have bestowed on you this revelation from on high, stating the truth. Therefore, worship God alone, sincere in your faith in Him. (2)

إِنَّآ أَنزَلۡنَآ إِلَيۡكَ ٱلۡكِتَٰبَ بِٱلۡحَقِّ فَٱعۡبُدِ ٱللَّهَ مُخۡلِصٗا لَّهُ ٱلدِّينَ ۝

True devotion is due to God alone. Those who take others besides Him as their protectors say: 'We worship them for no reason other than that they would bring us nearer to God.' God will judge between them

أَلَا لِلَّهِ ٱلدِّينُ ٱلۡخَالِصُۚ وَٱلَّذِينَ ٱتَّخَذُواْ مِن دُونِهِۦٓ أَوۡلِيَآءَ مَا نَعۡبُدُهُمۡ إِلَّا لِيُقَرِّبُونَآ إِلَى ٱللَّهِ زُلۡفَىٰٓ إِنَّ ٱللَّهَ يَحۡكُمُ بَيۡنَهُمۡ فِ

concerning all matters on which they differ. God will not grace with guidance anyone who is an ungrateful liar. (3)

مَاهُمْ فِيهِ يَخْتَلِفُونَ إِنَّ ٱللَّهَ لَا يَهْدِى مَنْ هُوَ كَـٰذِبٌ كَفَّارٌ ٣

Had God wished to take to Himself a son, He could have chosen anyone He wanted from whatever He creates. Limitless is He in His glory: the One God who conquers all. (4)

لَوْ أَرَادَ ٱللَّهُ أَن يَتَّخِذَ وَلَدًا لَّٱصْطَفَىٰ مِمَّا يَخْلُقُ مَا يَشَآءُ سُبْحَـٰنَهُۥ هُوَ ٱللَّهُ ٱلْوَٰحِدُ ٱلْقَهَّارُ ٤

He has created the heavens and the earth in accordance with the truth. He causes the night to flow into the day, and the day to flow into the night; and He has made the sun and the moon subservient [to His laws]: each running its course for a set term. He is indeed the Almighty, the All-Forgiving. (5)

خَلَقَ ٱلسَّمَـٰوَٰتِ وَٱلْأَرْضَ بِٱلْحَقِّ يُكَوِّرُ ٱلَّيْلَ عَلَى ٱلنَّهَارِ وَيُكَوِّرُ ٱلنَّهَارَ عَلَى ٱلَّيْلِ وَسَخَّرَ ٱلشَّمْسَ وَٱلْقَمَرَ كُلٌّ يَجْرِى لِأَجَلٍ مُّسَمًّى أَلَا هُوَ ٱلْعَزِيزُ ٱلْغَفَّـٰرُ ٥

He has created you all from a single soul, and from it He fashioned its mate; and He has bestowed on you four kinds of cattle in pairs; and He creates you in your mothers' wombs, one act of creation after another, in threefold depths of darkness. Such is God, your Lord: to Him belongs all dominion. There is no deity other than Him. How, then, can you lose sight of the truth? (6)

خَلَقَكُم مِّن نَّفْسٍ وَٰحِدَةٍ ثُمَّ جَعَلَ مِنْهَا زَوْجَهَا وَأَنزَلَ لَكُم مِّنَ ٱلْأَنْعَـٰمِ ثَمَـٰنِيَةَ أَزْوَٰجٍ يَخْلُقُكُمْ فِى بُطُونِ أُمَّهَـٰتِكُمْ خَلْقًا مِّنۢ بَعْدِ خَلْقٍ فِى ظُلُمَـٰتٍ ثَلَـٰثٍ ذَٰلِكُمُ ٱللَّهُ رَبُّكُمْ لَهُ ٱلْمُلْكُ لَا إِلَـٰهَ إِلَّا هُوَ فَأَنَّىٰ تُصْرَفُونَ ٦

If you disbelieve, God has no need of you; nor is He pleased with disbelief by His servants. If you give thanks, He is pleased with you. No soul will bear the burden of another. In time, to your Lord you all must return, and then He will tell you the truth of all you did. He has full knowledge of what is in people's hearts. (7)

إِن تَكْفُرُوا فَإِنَّ ٱللَّهَ غَنِيٌّ عَنكُمْ وَلَا يَرْضَىٰ لِعِبَادِهِ ٱلْكُفْرَ وَإِن تَشْكُرُوا يَرْضَهُ لَكُمْ وَلَا تَزِرُ وَازِرَةٌ وِزْرَ أُخْرَىٰ ثُمَّ إِلَىٰ رَبِّكُم مَّرْجِعُكُمْ فَيُنَبِّئُكُم بِمَا كُنتُمْ تَعْمَلُونَ إِنَّهُ عَلِيمٌ بِذَاتِ ٱلصُّدُورِ ۝

Maintaining Sincerity in Faith

The *sūrah* begins with a clear, emphatic statement: "*This book is bestowed from on high by God, the Almighty, the Wise.*" (Verse 1) As He is Almighty, He is able to bestow it from on high, and as He is wise, He knows the purpose of bestowing it, ensuring that it is all done in accordance with wise and elaborate planning.

The *sūrah*, however, does not dwell on this fact. It is only a prelude to its main theme, which this book has been revealed to establish, namely, God's oneness, addressing all worship to Him alone, ensuring sincerity in faith, eliminating all traces of any alleged partnership with God and establishing direct contact with Him without any intermediary or need for intercession.

"*It is We who have bestowed on you this revelation from on high, stating the truth.*" (Verse 2) The essence of the truth with which the book has been revealed is the absolute oneness of God, which forms the foundation of all existence. In verse 5 the *sūrah* states: "*He has created the heavens and the earth in accordance with the truth.*" It is all the same truth that makes up the foundation of the universe and provides the purpose for revealing the Qur'ān. It is a single, consistent truth confirmed by the unity of the system that controls the heavens and the earth, and expressed in human language through this book. It is the truth that puts the seal on everything made by the only Creator.

"Therefore, worship God alone, sincere in your faith in Him." (Verse 2) The address here is to the Prophet, the recipient of the book as it is bestowed from on high. It embodies the constitution which he advocates, calling on all mankind to adopt it: to worship God alone, sincere in our devotion, and to conduct human life, in all spheres, on this basis. These are not mere statements. It is a complete system, starting with a firm belief that is translated into an all-embracing way of life for both the individual and the community.

A believer in God's oneness submits only to God, bowing his head to none other, and asking nothing from others. For him only God is powerful and holds sway. Indeed, all other creatures are weak, unable to do him, or themselves, either harm or good. It is God alone who gives, bestows favours or withholds them. What is the use, then, of turning to anyone other than God for help when all are weak and God alone holds all power?

A true believer recognizes the unity of the system that conducts all affairs in the universe, realizes that the code of living God has chosen for mankind is part of that system, specially moulded to achieve harmony between human life and the universe. Hence, a believer does not choose any system or legal code other than that which God has laid down. A believer in God's oneness also feels that there is a bond between him and all that God has created in this universe, and that all creatures are friendly towards him. He feels that all around him have been put in place by God's hand. Hence, he warms to everything that comes his way of God's creation. He does not hurt, destroy or waste anyone or anything, or use it in any way other than what God has sanctioned.

Similarly, the effects of believing in God's oneness are apparent in believers' concepts and feelings just as they are reflected in their actions and behaviour. Thus, belief in God's oneness is not merely a verbal utterance. Hence why it is given such emphasis in God's book, and hence why it is repeated and explained in a great variety of ways. Each and everyone of us needs to study and reflect upon God's oneness so that this truth is perfectly ingrained in our own essence.

"True devotion is due to God alone." (Verse 3) In Arabic this statement has added emphasis provided by certain characteristics of the sentence

structure, which is peculiar to Arabic and difficult to capture in translation. It gives the statement the sense of a declaration producing a loud but clear echo. Thus sound, structure and meaning combine to strongly emphasize this basic truth upon which all life, throughout the universe, is based.

Who Deserves Guidance?

Then a refutation of the complex superstition the idolaters presented in opposition to belief in God's oneness follows: "*Those who take others besides Him as their protectors say: 'We worship them for no reason other than that they would bring us nearer to God.' God will judge between them concerning all matters on which they differ. God will not grace with guidance anyone who is an ungrateful liar.*" (Verse 3)

Although they declared that God created them and the heavens and earth, they would not carry this belief to its natural and logical consequence which required that they devote all their worship and submission to Him alone. Instead they invented the superstition that the angels were God's daughters and even carved statues representing angels so that they could worship these. They then claimed that their worship of these statues, such as al-Lāt, al-'Uzzā and Manāt, was not in essence devotion to them. It was merely a gesture to bring them closer to God, in the hope that these statues or what they represented would eventually intercede with God on their behalf.

Thus, deviation from simple, natural logic landed them in such a medley of falsehood: for the angels are not God's daughters, nor do the idols represent angels. God does not accept such deviation. He neither accepts intercession on people's behalf nor allows them to draw closer to Him in this way. Humanity deviates from the logic of its own nature whenever it moves away from the simple faith of God's oneness, which is the essence of Islam, as it was the essence of divine religion, preached by every messenger of God. Nowadays, we see in different parts of the world worship of saints, which is similar in essence to the practice of the Arabs of old who worshipped angels, or statues representing angels, to draw closer to God. God, in His limitless glory, defines the way that brings people close to Him: this is belief in God's oneness without intermediaries or intercessors of any sort.

"*God will not grace with guidance anyone who is an ungrateful liar.*" (Verse 3) They lie to God when they allege that the angels are His daughters. They also lie to Him when they claim that such worship of the angels will plead with Him on their behalf. In fact this worship makes them unbelievers, disobedient of God's express orders. Needless to say, God does not give His guidance to one who lies to Him, let alone disbelieves in Him. Guidance is granted as a reward for turning to Him, sincerity in worship, and diligently seeking the right way.

The *sūrah* then shows their belief to be erroneous, indeed otiose: "*Had God wished to take to Himself a son, He could have chosen anyone He wanted from whatever He creates. Limitless is He in His glory: the One God who conquers all.*" (Verse 4) This is a supposition made for the sake of argument and to correct concepts. Had God wished for a son, He could have chosen any of His creatures. His will is free, unrestricted. However, He, in His limitless glory, has made Himself free of any such need. Hence, no one can attribute to Him a son. Such is His will and determination: "*Limitless is He in His glory: the One God who conquers all.*" (Verse 4)

Why would He need a son when He is the Creator and Originator of all who controls everything. Indeed everything in the universe belongs to Him and He can do with it all whatever He wants: "*He has created the heavens and the earth in accordance with the truth. He causes the night to flow into the day, and the day to flow into the night; and He has made the sun and the moon subservient [to His laws]: each running its course for a set term. He is indeed the Almighty, the All-Forgiving.*" (Verse 5) This reference to the great universe and the phenomena of night and day, and the subjecting of the sun and moon to God's law, puts the truth of the One God clearer before human nature. The One who creates all this from nothing does not need a son or a partner.

Clear evidence of God's oneness is seen in the way the heavens and the earth are created, and in the law controlling the universe. Indeed, to merely look at the skies and the earth gives us a clear sense of the oneness of the will that has created all and controls all. It has now become clear that the entire world known to man is composed of atoms made of the same matter, consisting of rays that have the same nature. It is also known that all atoms and the bodies composed of such atoms, including the earth in which we live and all planets and stars, are in perpetual motion dictated by a consistent law that operates without fail in the tiny atom as well as in the huge star. Furthermore, it has now been clearly established that this perpetual motion is in accordance with another constant law that further stresses the unity of creation and the unity of control. Every day, man discovers something new testifying to the unity of design throughout the universe.

"*He has created the heavens and the earth in accordance with the truth.*" (Verse 5) Likewise, He bestowed His book from on high to state the truth. It is the same truth in the universe and in this book, the Qur'ān. Both originate from the same source, and both are evidence of the oneness of their Maker, the Almighty, the Wise.

"*He causes the night to flow into the day, and the day to flow into the night.*" (Verse 5) This is indeed an amazing statement that forces anyone who carefully looks at it to consider what has now been established of the earth's nature and its circular shape. Throughout this commentary on the Qur'ān, I have been keen not to look at its verses and statements from the angle of any theory science advances, because such theories may be right or they may be wrong. They may be proven today to be true but something may be discovered tomorrow to render them false. By contrast, the Qur'ān is the word of truth, and it carries its own proof. It needs no supporting evidence from what human beings may or may not discover. Yet the statement included in this verse forces me to relate it to the fact that the earth is circular, because it describes a fact we all notice. As the earth rotates, the part of it facing the sun receives its light and this is daytime. However, this part is not stationary because the earth continues to rotate. As it does, the night begins to spread over the part that had had the day. This part is in a rounded shape, and the day spreads over it in a flowing movement, followed by the night also in a flowing movement. After a while the day begins to flow again over the night from the other side, in never-ceasing motion: "*He causes the night to flow into the day, and the day to flow into the night.*" (Verse 5) The statement draws the design, defines the position and specifies the nature of the earth and its movement. Its circular shape and rotation give this statement its most accurate interpretation.

"*He has made the sun and the moon subservient [to His laws]: each running its course for a set term.*" (Verse 5) The sun and the moon run in their respective orbits. They are under God's control. No one claims to set them in motion. By natural logic, they cannot run without someone setting them to do so, controlling them by a system that does not deviate by a hair's breadth across countless centuries. Yet both the sun and the moon continue to run their courses '*for a set term,*' which is known only to God.

"*He is indeed the Almighty, the All-Forgiving.*" (Verse 5) His might and power are coupled with His forgiveness of anyone who turns to Him. Thus, those who lie to Him, disbelieve in His oneness, attribute partners to Him or allege that He has a son are made aware that the way is open to them to return to the right way and to believe in the One who is Almighty, Much-Forgiving.

Three Depths of Darkness

The *sūrah* then seeks to touch people's hearts. It refers them to the evidence of life close by them, and in fact derived from their own creation and from the animals made subservient to them:

> *He has created you all from a single soul, and from it He fashioned its mate; and He has bestowed on you four kinds of cattle in pairs; and He creates you in your mothers' wombs, one act of creation after another, in threefold depths of darkness. Such is God, your Lord: to Him belongs all dominion. There is no deity other than Him. How, then, can you lose sight of the truth?* (Verse 6)

Let man look at his own self. He has not created himself, nor does he know who created the human entity except for what God has told him. Yet we all originate from one soul, with one nature and the same characteristics that distinguish us from the rest of creation. Moreover, every human individual shares in these characteristics, because the human soul is one in the countless millions of humans across all generations and all communities. Moreover, its mate or spouse is also made from the same essence. Thus, despite all differences of detail between men and women, they share all these characteristics. This again confirms the unity of the original design for mankind, male and female, and the unity of the Will that created this single soul with its two manifestations.

The reference to the fact of human spouses is coupled by a reference to the same phenomenon in cattle, which in turn suggests that it applies to all living creatures: "*He has bestowed on you four kinds of cattle in pairs.*" The Arabic phrase states 'eight *zawj*,' but this word means both 'couple' and 'spouse'. Hence, the way it is rendered in translation. The eight are made up of a male and a female of sheep, goats, bovine and camels. The verse mentions that they have been bestowed by God, which means that it is God who has made them subservient to man. It is their subservience that is bestowed from on high and effected in man's world. Thus, man is given God's permission to use cattle for the benefit of human life.

The verse continues its discussion of man's creation, referring to various growth stages of the embryo: "*He creates you in your mothers' wombs, one act of creation after another.*" These stages of creation begin with the gamete, then a clinging cell mass, then an embryo, then the bones, and then to a creation that indicates its human status. "*in threefold depths of darkness.*" (Verse 6) There is the darkness of the placenta in which the embryo grows, the darkness of the uterus, and the darkness inside the mother's body. It is God's hand that takes the single cell through these stages of creation, one after another, looking after it and giving it the ability to grow and develop until it is formed in a complete human being as God has determined.

Anyone who looks carefully at this journey, which covers a huge gulf traversed in a short period of time, and who reflects on these stages of development, and on how this simple cell is guided along its remarkable journey in these depths of darkness, beyond man's knowledge, will inevitably recognize the Creator and His handiwork. How, then, is man turned away from the true faith: "*Such is God, your Lord: to Him belongs all dominion. There is no deity other than Him. How, then, can you lose sight of the truth?*" (Verse 6)

Having outlined this clear vision of the signs testifying to God's absolute oneness and all encompassing power, the *sūrah* shows people's positions at the parting of the ways between belief and disbelief. It makes it clear that responsibility rests with each individual. It tells them about the end of their lives' journey and the reckoning that awaits them. It will be administered by the One who created them under three depths of darkness and who knows their innermost thoughts and feelings:

> *If you disbelieve, God has no need of you; nor is He pleased with disbelief by His servants. If you give thanks, He is pleased with you. No soul will bear the burden of another. In time, to your Lord you all must return, and then He will tell you the truth of all you did. He has full knowledge of what is in people's hearts.* (Verse 7)

The journey inside the mother's belly is merely one stage of a long journey. The second stage is life in this world and the final stage is that of reckoning and reward. All this takes place according to God's design who knows all. He does not need any of His servants. They are essentially weak and powerless, but He bestows on them an abundance of His grace.

"*If you disbelieve, God has no need of you.*" (Verse 7) If you believe, you will not increase His kingdom in any way. If you disbelieve, this too will not affect His kingdom in any adverse way. He, however, does not like people to disbelieve: "*nor is He pleased with disbelief by His servants.*" (Verse 7) By contrast, "*If you give thanks, He is pleased with you.*" He will accept this from you and reward you generously for it. Everyone is accountable for their own deeds, and none will be held responsible for another, nor will he be allowed to take upon himself part of another's burden: "*No soul will bear the burden of another.*" (Verse 7) The ultimate end of the journey is to God. There can be neither escape from Him nor refuge with anyone else: "*In time, to your Lord you all must return, and then He will tell you the truth of all you did.*" (Verse 7) You can hide nothing from Him: "*He has full knowledge of what is in people's hearts.*" (Verse 7)

2

As Comfort Replaces Affliction

When man suffers affliction, he cries out to his Lord, turning to Him for help; but once He bestows upon him a favour by His grace, he forgets what he cried and prayed for earlier, and claims that others are equal to God, thus leading others astray from His path. Say [to him]: 'Enjoy yourself for a while in your disbelief, for you are one of those destined to the fire.' (8)

وَإِذَا مَسَّ ٱلْإِنسَٰنَ ضُرٌّ دَعَا رَبَّهُۥ مُنِيبًا إِلَيْهِ ثُمَّ إِذَا خَوَّلَهُۥ نِعْمَةً مِّنْهُ نَسِىَ مَا كَانَ يَدْعُوٓاْ إِلَيْهِ مِن قَبْلُ وَجَعَلَ لِلَّهِ أَندَادًا لِّيُضِلَّ عَن سَبِيلِهِۦ قُلْ تَمَتَّعْ بِكُفْرِكَ قَلِيلًا إِنَّكَ مِنْ أَصْحَٰبِ ٱلنَّارِ ۝

How about one who devoutly worships God during the hours of the night prostrating himself or standing in prayer, ever mindful of the life to come, and hoping for his Lord's mercy? Say: 'Can those who know and those who do not know be deemed equal?' Only those who are endowed with insight will take heed. (9)

أَمَّنْ هُوَ قَٰنِتٌ ءَانَآءَ ٱلَّيْلِ سَاجِدًا وَقَآئِمًا يَحْذَرُ ٱلْءَاخِرَةَ وَيَرْجُواْ رَحْمَةَ رَبِّهِۦ قُلْ هَلْ يَسْتَوِى ٱلَّذِينَ يَعْلَمُونَ وَٱلَّذِينَ لَا يَعْلَمُونَ إِنَّمَا يَتَذَكَّرُ أُوْلُواْ ٱلْأَلْبَٰبِ ۝

Say: '[Thus speaks God:] You servants of Mine who believe! Fear your Lord! Those who do good in this world will have a good reward. Wide is God's earth. Those who are patient in adversity will be given their reward in full, beyond reckoning.' (10)

قُل يَٰعِبَادِ ٱلَّذِينَ ءَامَنُوا ٱتَّقُوا رَبَّكُمْ لِلَّذِينَ أَحْسَنُوا فِي هَٰذِهِ ٱلدُّنْيَا حَسَنَةٌ وَأَرْضُ ٱللَّهِ وَٰسِعَةٌ إِنَّمَا يُوَفَّى ٱلصَّٰبِرُونَ أَجْرَهُم بِغَيْرِ حِسَابٍ ۝

Overview

The first passage touched people's hearts by telling them about their existence, how they are all created from a single soul and how its mate was also created from it. It told them about the creation of animals in pairs, and how man is created in three depths of darkness inside the mother's belly. It touched on how God's hand gave them their human characteristics and their ability to grow and develop.

Now the *sūrah* touches their hearts again as it shows them their conditions in times of hardship and times of ease. It shows them how they boast and how, in their weakness, they swing from one condition to another. They are consistent only when they maintain their bond with God and humble themselves before Him. They will then know the truth and know their way. They will also then be able to benefit from their human characteristics.

Brief Enjoyment

When man suffers affliction, he cries out to his Lord, turning to Him for help; but once He bestows upon him a favour by His grace, he forgets what he cried and prayed for earlier, and claims that others are equal to God, thus leading others astray from His path. Say [to him]: 'Enjoy yourself for a while in your disbelief, for you are one of those destined to the fire.' (Verse 8)

Human nature appears naked when man suffers affliction. Masks are torn off, covers are removed and disillusionment disappears. At this point, human nature turns to its Lord alone knowing that only He can remove affliction. It realizes that all its claims about God having partners are false.

When affliction is gone and man finds himself enjoying an abundance of God's favours, he again burdens his nature with heaps of false influences. He forgets his earnest pleas to God during the time of his affliction, choosing now to overlook his acknowledgement of God's oneness and that it is He alone who can relieve his hardship. He forgets all this and begins to claim that others are equal to God. These alleged equals may be deities man worships just like in the early days of *jāhiliyyah*, or they may be in the shape of values, persons, or situations to which he gives in his consciousness a share of what belongs exclusively to God. We see this in many of the *jāhiliyyah* situations we encounter everywhere. Thus man may worship his desires, inclinations, hopes, fears, wealth, children, rulers and chiefs in the same way as he worships God or even in greater devotion. In fact, he may love them more than he loves God. Polytheism can take different forms, some of which are subtle. People may not think of these as polytheism because they do not take the familiar form of acknowledging multiple deities; yet they are essentially polytheistic.

The result is to go astray, moving away from God's way which has one form, namely, acknowledging His oneness and addressing worship and love to Him alone. Believing in God does not admit any partnership in man's heart, be that a partnership of wealth, children, home country, land, friend or relative. Should such a partnership be found in man's heart, it means acknowledging some beings as equal to God. Thus it allows a brief enjoyment in this life and ends in the fire of hell: "*Say [to him]: Enjoy yourself for a while in your disbelief, for you are one of those destined to the fire.*" (Verse 8) Every enjoyment in this life is small no matter how long it endures. Furthermore, anyone's span of life is brief no matter to what old age he attains. Indeed, the life of the entire human race on this earth is merely a brief enjoyment when compared to God's days.

Juxtaposed with this depressing picture of man is another showing him standing in awe, remembering God in all situations, pleasant or distressing. He goes through his life on earth without ever losing consciousness of the Day of Judgement. He always looks up to his Lord, hoping for His grace. It is from such a bond with God that true knowledge emerges, providing full awareness of the truth:

> How about one who devoutly worships God during the hours of the night prostrating himself or standing in prayer, ever mindful of the life to come, and hoping for his Lord's mercy? Say: 'Can those who know and those who do not know be deemed equal?' Only those who are endowed with insight will take heed. (Verse 9)

All the elements provided here, sincere devotion, the dread of what may happen in the life to come, the hope for God's grace, the purity of heart that opens the locks that prevent understanding, giving our hearts the blessing of clear perception all draw a bright picture which is the opposite of the one drawn in the previous verse. Hence, it is necessary to draw the comparison: "Can those who know and those who do not know be deemed equal?" (Verse 9) True knowledge is that which understands the truth and opens one's mind to the need to be in touch with the fundamental truths in the universe. True knowledge is not a host of pieces of information that clutter the mind without leading to any understanding of the fundamentals of existence.

The way to true knowledge and enlightened information then is devout worship, a sensitive heart, being mindful of the life to come, entertaining strong hopes of benefiting from God's mercy and of being conscious of God. Those who limit themselves to individual experiences and superficial vision are no more than collectors of information. They will never attain the rank of people with knowledge. "Only those who are endowed with insight will take heed." (Verse 9)

It's a Wide Earth

The *sūrah* then addresses the believers, requiring them to remain God-fearing and to ensure that they always do good. They should use their life on earth, short as it is, as a means to earn everlasting reward in the life to come:

Say: [Thus speaks God:] You servants of Mine who believe! Fear your Lord! Those who do good in this world will have a good reward. Wide is God's earth. Those who are patient in adversity will be given their reward in full, beyond reckoning. (10)

It is important to note here how the Arabic text is phrased. The words between brackets, '*thus speaks God*', are not in the text. They are added to remove confusion. The text should originally read: "Say to My servants," but the Prophet is made to address them, because an address alerts the addressees and makes them more aware of what is to come. When the Prophet addresses them, he does not call them as his servants, because they are God's servants, not his. This means that he is addressing them in God's name, making the address from God directly to them. The Prophet is merely the means by which the address is given.

"*Say: [Thus speaks God:] You servants of Mine who believe! Fear your Lord!*" (Verse 10) To fear God means to have a sensitive heart and to look up to Him cautiously and with apprehension, hope, wary lest one should incur His displeasure and keen to earn His pleasure. It is seen in the bright picture drawn in the previous verse of a devout worshipper, full of humility.

"*Those who do good in this world will have a good reward.*" (Verse 10) What a great reward: a good deed in this present life, which is short and flimsy, is repaid with something good in the life to come, which is everlasting. This is certainly an act of God's grace. He knows man's weakness and small effort, so He repays him generously and takes care of him.

"*Wide is God's earth.*" (Verse 10) Your love of your land where you have relatives and friends should not prevent you from seeking a different abode if your own area is hostile to your faith and you cannot do well there. To stick to your place of habitat in such a case could present an opening for Satan. It could become a form of attributing equals to God, even though it might not be felt in this way. This is a fine point indicating that polytheism can subtly creep into our hearts. It is given within the context of belief in God's oneness and fearing Him. It should be seen as evidence of the source of the Qur'ān. No one can deal in this way with the human heart except the One who created it and knows what has an effect on it and how.

God, the Creator of mankind, knows that leaving one's land is hard. It involves abandoning one's relatives and the people with whom one has close ties, leaving the place where one can easily find work and earn a living, to go to a new place where one is a stranger. This is not an easy thing for anyone. Hence, the *sūrah* refers here to patience in adversity and how it is generously rewarded by God: "*Those who are patient in adversity will be given their reward in full, beyond reckoning.*" (Verse 10) Thus, God's servants feel His care and are touched as they see that when they have to undertake something hard God turns to them with care and grace. He opens for them what compensates for land, country, family and relatives, giving them a reward without count.

All praise is due to God who knows all that affects a human heart and is fully aware of every thought that finds its way into his mind.

3

The Losers

Say: 'I am commanded to worship God, sincere in my faith in Him alone; (11)

قُلْ إِنِّيٓ أُمِرْتُ أَنْ أَعْبُدَ ٱللَّهَ مُخْلِصًا لَّهُ ٱلدِّينَ ۝

and I am commanded to be the first to submit myself to Him.' (12)

وَأُمِرْتُ لِأَنْ أَكُونَ أَوَّلَ ٱلْمُسْلِمِينَ ۝

Say: 'Indeed I would dread, were I to disobey my Lord, the suffering of an awesome day.' (13)

قُلْ إِنِّيٓ أَخَافُ إِنْ عَصَيْتُ رَبِّي عَذَابَ يَوْمٍ عَظِيمٍ ۝

Say: 'God alone do I worship, sincere in my faith in Him alone. (14)

قُلِ ٱللَّهَ أَعْبُدُ مُخْلِصًا لَّهُۥ دِينِي ۝

You can worship whatever you please instead of Him.' Say: 'True losers indeed are those who shall have lost their own selves and their families on Resurrection Day. Such is the ultimate loss.' (15)

فَٱعْبُدُوا مَا شِئْتُم مِّن دُونِهِۦ قُلْ إِنَّ ٱلْخَاسِرِينَ ٱلَّذِينَ خَسِرُوٓا أَنفُسَهُمْ وَأَهْلِيهِمْ يَوْمَ ٱلْقِيَٰمَةِ أَلَا ذَٰلِكَ هُوَ ٱلْخُسْرَانُ ٱلْمُبِينُ ۝

Above them there shall be layers of fire, and layers of fire shall be beneath them. In this way God puts fear into His servants' hearts: 'My servants! Fear Me!' (16)

لَهُم مِّن فَوْقِهِمْ ظُلَلٌ مِّنَ ٱلنَّارِ وَمِن تَحْتِهِمْ ظُلَلٌ ذَٰلِكَ يُخَوِّفُ ٱللَّهُ بِهِ عِبَادَهُۥ يَٰعِبَادِ فَٱتَّقُونِ ۝١٦

There is good news for those who shun the worship of false deities and turn to God, so give good news to My servants, (17)

وَٱلَّذِينَ ٱجْتَنَبُواْ ٱلطَّٰغُوتَ أَن يَعْبُدُوهَا وَأَنَابُوٓاْ إِلَى ٱللَّهِ لَهُمُ ٱلْبُشْرَىٰ فَبَشِّرْ عِبَادِ ۝١٧

who listen carefully to what is said and follow the best of it. These are the ones whom God has graced with His guidance, and these are the ones endowed with insight. (18)

ٱلَّذِينَ يَسْتَمِعُونَ ٱلْقَوْلَ فَيَتَّبِعُونَ أَحْسَنَهُۥٓ أُوْلَٰٓئِكَ ٱلَّذِينَ هَدَىٰهُمُ ٱللَّهُ وَأُوْلَٰٓئِكَ هُمْ أُوْلُواْ ٱلْأَلْبَٰبِ ۝١٨

How about one on whom God's sentence of punishment has been passed? Can you rescue those who are already in the fire? (19)

أَفَمَنْ حَقَّ عَلَيْهِ كَلِمَةُ ٱلْعَذَابِ أَفَأَنتَ تُنقِذُ مَن فِى ٱلنَّارِ ۝١٩

As against this, those who are God-fearing will have lofty mansions raised upon mansions high, beneath which running waters flow. This is God's promise. Never does God fail to fulfil His promise. (20)

لَٰكِنِ ٱلَّذِينَ ٱتَّقَوْاْ رَبَّهُمْ لَهُمْ غُرَفٌ مِّن فَوْقِهَا غُرَفٌ مَّبْنِيَّةٌ تَجْرِى مِن تَحْتِهَا ٱلْأَنْهَٰرُ وَعْدَ ٱللَّهِ لَا يُخْلِفُ ٱللَّهُ ٱلْمِيعَادَ ۝٢٠

Overview

This passage has the air of the hereafter stamped on it from start to finish: it highlights the fear of its punishment and the hope for its reward. It begins by a directive to the Prophet to declare God's oneness fully and without a trace of ambiguity. He further declares that he, a Prophet and a Messenger of God, dreads the consequences of any deviation from it. He unequivocally states his determination to follow his course, leaving the unbelievers to choose whatever method they want to follow, outlining the results to which each of the two ways leads.

The First to Submit to God

> *Say: I am commanded to worship God, sincere in my faith in Him alone; and I am commanded to be the first to submit myself to Him. Say: Indeed I would dread, were I to disobey my Lord, the suffering of an awesome day.* (Verses 11–13)

This declaration by the Prophet outlining what he is commanded to do with regard to worship, devotion and submission is very important in keeping the belief in God's oneness pure, as Islam wants it to be. In this respect, the Prophet is one of God's servants. He does not exceed that position. In their servitude to God, all people stand in one rank, while God has His sublime position over all creation.

Thus the two concepts of Godhead and servitude are well established and clearly distinguished. There can be no confusion between the two. Oneness is clearly seen as an attribute of God alone, in which no one else has any share. When Muḥammad (peace be upon him) stands in the position of God's servant making this clear declaration, fearing to commit any disobedience of God, there can be no room for any claim of intercession by idols or angels granted through addressing worship to them instead of God.

The declaration is made once more, with the Prophet's announcement that he will stick to his way, leaving the idolaters to their way and the painful end to which that leads:

Say: God alone do I worship, sincere in my faith in Him alone. You can worship whatever you please instead of Him. Say: True losers indeed are those who shall have lost their own selves and their families on Resurrection Day. Such is the ultimate loss. (Verses 14–15)

Once more the Prophet announces: I am unwavering in following my way, addressing all worship to God and submitting myself to Him alone. As for you, you can follow any way you want, worship whomever you wish, but this will lead you to the worst imaginable loss: a loss of oneself as one goes to hell, and the loss of family and kin, be they believers or unbelievers. If those relatives are believers, the idolaters will have lost them as each group goes their separate ways, and if they are unbelievers, the loss is the same as they all will have lost themselves in hell: "*Such is the ultimate loss.*" (Verse 15)

We then have a picture showing the extent of the loss: "*Above them there shall be layers of fire, and layers of fire shall be beneath them. In this way God puts fear into His servants' hearts: 'My servants! Fear Me!'*" (Verse 16) It is a scene that strikes real fear in people's hearts, showing the fire in layers that engulfs people from above and below. They are seen within these layers as they close in on them from all sides. Yet these layers are fire. God shows this picture to His servants while they are on earth and still have the chance to change their ways: "*In this way God puts fear into His servants' hearts.*" (Verse 16) He calls on them warning them so that they may choose the way to safety: "*My servants! Fear Me!*" (Verse 16)

On the other side stand those who are safe, having feared this fate and done what is necessary to avoid it:

There is good news for those who shun the worship of false deities and turn to God, so give good news to My servants, who listen carefully to what is said and follow the best of it. These are the ones whom God has graced with His guidance, and these are the ones endowed with insight. (Verses 17–18)

'*False deities*' are referred to here by the word *ṭāghūt*, which implies an exaggerated sense of exceeding the bounds. Those who shun the worship of *ṭāghūt* are the ones who reject the worship of anyone other than God in any form whatsoever. They are the ones who turn to God, stand in front of Him and worship Him alone. These have good news issued to them directly from on high. The Prophet is giving them this good news by God's order: "*So give good news to My servants.*" The fact that this news comes from on high and is delivered by the noble Messenger is in itself a great blessing.

One quality of such people is that they listen to whatever is being said, but their hearts and minds pick up only the best of it and discard the rest. Thus, the only words that they actually receive are the best words that improve and purify people's hearts and souls. A good soul is always ready to receive good words and respond to them, while the one which is foul receives only what is foul. "*These are the ones whom God has graced with His guidance.*" (Verse 18) He knows that they are genuinely good in their hearts and souls and He, therefore, guided them to listen and respond to the best of what is said. Guidance comes only from God.

"*And these are the ones endowed with insight.*" (Verse 18) It is a sound mind that leads a person to self-purification and safety. Anyone who does not follow the way that ensures such safety appears to be deprived of a sound mind and insight, which are blessings given by God.

Before showing us the blessings these people enjoy in the life to come, the *sūrah* states that those who worshipped false deities have already reached hell. Who can save them from its fire, then? "*How about one on whom God's sentence of punishment has been passed? Can you rescue those who are already in the fire?*" (Verse 19) This address is made to the Prophet (peace be upon him). If he cannot save them from the fire, who else can?

They are pictured here as if they are already in the fire, since the sentence of punishment has been passed on them. Juxtaposed with this is the image of those who truly feared God:

> As against this, those who are God-fearing will have lofty mansions raised upon mansions high, beneath which running waters flow. This is God's promise. Never does God fail to fulfil His promise. (Verse 20)

425

The scene depicts mansions raised upon high mansions, with streams flowing below. All this contrasts with the image of layers of fire engulfing the other group from above and below. Drawing such contrasts is a characteristic of the Qur'ānic style. Such is God's promise, which will always come true.

Those Muslims who were the first to receive the Qur'ān interacted with these scenes in their practical lives. To them, they were not mere promises or threats issued from afar, speaking about a distant future; they were a reality they saw and felt. Hence, they were truly influenced by them. Their lives on earth reflected the reality of the Hereafter which they felt and almost experienced while still extant in this life. It is in this way that a Muslim should receive God's promise.

4

The Best of All Discourses

Have you not considered how God sends down water from the skies, and then causes it to travel through the earth to form springs? He then brings with it vegetation of different colours; and then it withers and you can see it turning yellow. In the end He causes it to crumble to dust. In all this there is indeed a reminder for those endowed with insight. (21)

أَلَمْ تَرَ أَنَّ اللَّهَ أَنزَلَ مِنَ السَّمَاءِ مَآءً فَسَلَكَهُ يَنَابِيعَ فِي الْأَرْضِ ثُمَّ يُخْرِجُ بِهِ زَرْعًا مُخْتَلِفًا أَلْوَانُهُ ثُمَّ يَهِيجُ فَتَرَاهُ مُصْفَرًّا ثُمَّ يَجْعَلُهُ حُطَامًا إِنَّ فِي ذَٰلِكَ لَذِكْرَىٰ لِأُولِي الْأَلْبَابِ ﴿٢١﴾

How about one whose heart God has opened to Islam, and thus receives light from his Lord? Woe, then, betide those whose hearts harden at the mention of God. These are most obviously in error. (22)

أَفَمَن شَرَحَ اللَّهُ صَدْرَهُ لِلْإِسْلَامِ فَهُوَ عَلَىٰ نُورٍ مِّن رَّبِّهِ فَوَيْلٌ لِّلْقَاسِيَةِ قُلُوبُهُم مِّن ذِكْرِ اللَّهِ أُوْلَٰئِكَ فِي ضَلَالٍ مُّبِينٍ ﴿٢٢﴾

God has bestowed from on high the best of all teachings: a book that is consistent within itself, repeating its statements [of the truth] in manifold forms. It causes the skins of those who

اللَّهُ نَزَّلَ أَحْسَنَ الْحَدِيثِ كِتَابًا مُّتَشَابِهًا مَّثَانِيَ تَقْشَعِرُّ مِنْهُ جُلُودُ

stand in awe of their Lord to shiver, but then their skins and hearts soften at the mention of God. Such is God's guidance: He guides with it him that wills, whereas the one whom God lets go astray can never find any guide. (23)

اَلَّذِينَ يَخْشَوْنَ رَبَّهُمْ ثُمَّ تَلِينُ جُلُودُهُمْ وَقُلُوبُهُمْ إِلَىٰ ذِكْرِ ٱللَّهِ ذَٰلِكَ هُدَى ٱللَّهِ يَهْدِى بِهِۦ مَن يَشَآءُ وَمَن يُضْلِلِ ٱللَّهُ فَمَا لَهُۥ مِنْ هَادٍ ٢٣

How about one who shall have nothing but his bare face to protect him from the awful suffering on Resurrection Day? It will be said to the wrongdoers: 'Taste now what you have earned.' (24)

أَفَمَن يَتَّقِى بِوَجْهِهِۦ سُوٓءَ ٱلْعَذَابِ يَوْمَ ٱلْقِيَـٰمَةِ وَقِيلَ لِلظَّـٰلِمِينَ ذُوقُوا۟ مَا كُنتُمْ تَكْسِبُونَ ٢٤

Those who lived before them also disbelieved, and so suffering befell them from where they could not perceive. (25)

كَذَّبَ ٱلَّذِينَ مِن قَبْلِهِمْ فَأَتَىٰهُمُ ٱلْعَذَابُ مِنْ حَيْثُ لَا يَشْعُرُونَ ٢٥

God gave them a taste of humiliation in this world. Yet much greater will be the suffering of the life to come, if they but knew it! (26)

فَأَذَاقَهُمُ ٱللَّهُ ٱلْخِزْىَ فِى ٱلْحَيَوٰةِ ٱلدُّنْيَا وَلَعَذَابُ ٱلْءَاخِرَةِ أَكْبَرُ لَوْ كَانُوا۟ يَعْلَمُونَ ٢٦

We have set for people in this Qur'ān all sorts of illustrations, so that they may reflect. (27)

وَلَقَدْ ضَرَبْنَا لِلنَّاسِ فِى هَـٰذَا ٱلْقُرْءَانِ مِن كُلِّ مَثَلٍ لَّعَلَّهُمْ يَتَذَكَّرُونَ ٢٧

It is an Arabic Qur'ān, free from distortion, so that people may become conscious of God. (28)

قُرْءَانًا عَرَبِيًّا غَيْرَ ذِى عِوَجٍ لَّعَلَّهُمْ يَتَّقُونَ ٢٨

God cites the case of a man who has for his masters several partners at odds with each other, and a man belonging wholly to one person. Can they be deemed equal? All praise is due to God alone, but most of them do not understand. (29)

ضَرَبَ ٱللَّهُ مَثَلاً رَّجُلاً فِيهِ شُرَكَآءُ
مُتَشَٰكِسُونَ وَرَجُلاً سَلَماً لِّرَجُلٍ هَلْ
يَسْتَوِيَانِ مَثَلاً ٱلْحَمْدُ لِلَّهِ بَلْ أَكْثَرُهُمْ
لَا يَعْلَمُونَ ۝

Overview

In this passage the *sūrah* draws attention to the life of plants after rainfall, and then how the water courses to its end. The Qur'ān often draws a comparison between the life of plants and this present life of ours, highlighting the fact that it is of short duration. It urges people with insight to reflect on this comparison. In connection with the water being poured from the skies, the *sūrah* also refers to the Qur'ān, the book sent down from heaven to breathe life into people's hearts and souls. It gives an inspiring description of the response of those whose hearts are open to it, and how they experience a mixture of awe, fear, comfort and reassurance. It then describes the respective fates of those who respond to God's message and those whose hearts are hardened. At the end of the passage, the *sūrah* cites examples of one who worships the One God, and the one who worships multiple deities. The two cannot be equal and cannot hold the same position, in the same way as two slaves one serving one master and the other having several masters, who are in dispute with one another cannot be considered the same.

Rain Bringing Life

Have you not considered how God sends down water from the skies, and then causes it to travel through the earth to form springs? He then brings with it vegetation of different colours; and then it withers and you can see it turning yellow. In the end He causes it to crumble to dust. In all this there is indeed a reminder for those endowed with insight. (Verse 21)

The Qur'ān draws attention to a phenomenon that takes place everywhere on earth. Its familiarity, however, tends to make people overlook it. Yet it is remarkable in every step. The Qur'ān directs us to look at how God's hand directs it step by step to produce its desired effects. The water that comes down from the sky: what is it, and how does it descend? This is a remarkable phenomenon, but we tend not to reflect on it because it is so familiar. The very creation of water is indeed a miracle. We know that it comes into existence when two hydrogen atoms combine with one oxygen atom under certain conditions. Our knowledge, however, should alert us to the fact that it is God's hand that made the universe, allowing the hydrogen and the oxygen to be available and to provide the conditions that allow them to combine and produce water, which is essential for life to emerge. In fact, without water, no life could have emerged. Thus we see how a series of measures culminated in the existence of water and the emergence of life. All this is of God's own making. Moreover, the very fall of rain, after the creation of water, is in itself a miraculous phenomenon, brought about by the system that operates the universe and the earth, allowing the formation of water and its fall by God's will.

That which follows such rainfall is described thus: God *"causes it to travel through the earth to form springs."* (Verse 21) This applies to the rivers running on the surface of the earth as well as the rivers that run underneath its surface when water seeps underground. It then forms springs or wells. It is God's hand that prevents it from going too far into the earth making it impossible to bring up again.

"He then brings with it vegetation of different colours." (Verse 21) The emergence of vegetation after rain is again a miraculous phenomenon that man can never emulate, no matter how hard he tries. Look at the young shoot as it splits the earth and removes the heavy layers above it, seeking space, light and fresh air, and growing slowly and gradually. Looking at it invites contemplation and fills our hearts with feelings of the greatness of God who *"gives everything its*

distinctive nature and form, and further guides them." (20: 50) Plants vary in colour at the same spot, on the same plant, and indeed in just one such flower there is a great exhibition of marvellous creation. Man stands in front of this with great awe, aware that he cannot produce anything like it.

This growing, fresh plant that is full of life attains its full growth and completes its life cycle, *"then it withers and you can see it turning yellow."* (Verse 21) It has completed its life as ordained in the system of the universe. It is now ripe for harvest. *"In the end He causes it to crumble to dust."* (Verse 21) Its role in life is now completed as it was determined by the Giver of life. *"In all this there is indeed a reminder for those endowed with insight."* (Verse 21) These are the ones who reflect, making use of the insight God has granted them.

Two Types of Heart

How about one whose heart God has opened to Islam, and thus receives light from his Lord? Woe, then, betide those whose hearts harden at the mention of God. These are most obviously in error. God has bestowed from on high the best of all teachings: a book that is consistent within itself, repeating its statements [of the truth] in manifold forms. It causes the skins of those who stand in awe of their Lord to shiver, but then their skins and hearts soften at the mention of God. Such is God's guidance: He guides with it him that wills, whereas the one whom God lets go astray can never find any guide. (Verses 22–23)

Just like He sends water from the skies to cause vegetation of various colours and forms to grow, God bestows from on high a reminder which is received by hearts that are alive, and that open up and react to such life. By contrast, hardened hearts receive it like a rock that cannot embrace life. God opens to Islam those hearts that He knows to be good. These hearts receive the light of Islam and they shine and radiate. The gulf between these hearts and the ones that are hardened is wide indeed: *"Woe, then, betide those whose hearts harden at the mention of God. These are most obviously in error."* (Verse 22)

This verse depicts the nature of the hearts that receive Islam and warm to it, becoming full of life. It describes how they blossom, becoming fresh and radiant. It also describes the other type of hearts which are hard, dark and lifeless. Needless to say, the hearts that open up to Islam, receive and reflect its light are totally different from those which are hardened at the mention of God's name. The gap between the two is enormous.

The next verse describes how the believers receive the Qur'ān, a book that is fully coherent in nature, direction, message and characteristics. Thus, it is *'consistent within itself,'* and it *'repeats its statements of the truth in manifold forms,'* giving consistent directives and varying the ways it presents its images and stories without causing any contradiction. They are repeated at different places for a purpose that can be best served through such repetition. Such repetition does not detract from the harmony and consistency of the basic truth stated throughout the Qur'ān.

Those who stand in awe of God maintain an attitude that mixes fear of God with hope of His mercy. They are the ones who are very strongly influenced when they receive God's word to the extent that their skins shiver. They later soften and their hearts find reassurance as they listen to God's words. This is a very vivid image giving in words a description that is full of movement and action.

"Such is God's guidance: He guides with it him that wills." (Verse 23) Hearts do not shiver in this way unless God's guidance prompts them to respond. God knows the true feelings of these hearts and rewards them with either His guidance or by letting them go astray: *"whereas the one whom God lets go astray can never find any guide."* (Verse 23) He allows such people to go astray because He knows that they have gone so far into error that they will never respond to guidance.

The *sūrah* then shows what awaits those who chose to go astray on the Day of Judgement. It paints a very depressing picture at the time when results are given:

> *How about one who shall have nothing but his bare face to protect him from the awful suffering on Resurrection Day? It will be said to the wrongdoers: 'Taste now what you have earned.'* (Verse 24)

Normally a person uses his hands and body to protect his face from fire or harmful objects. In this case, however, he cannot use his hands or legs to save himself from the fire; instead, he uses his face for protection, which describes a case of great confusion and hardship. In the midst of all this difficulty and suffering they are faced with strong censure and given the results of their lives' actions. What a terrible result they have to face: "*It will be said to the wrongdoers: Taste now what you have earned.*" (Verse 24)

The *sūrah* then speaks about the unbelievers who stood in opposition to the Prophet, showing them what happened to the unbelievers of earlier communities, so that they may save themselves from a similar fate:

> *Those who lived before them also disbelieved, and so suffering befell them from where they could not perceive. God gave them a taste of humiliation in this world. Yet much greater will be the suffering of the life to come, if they but knew it!* (Verses 25–26)

Such is the outcome faced by the unbelievers in both lives, in this world and the next. In this life, God made them taste humiliation, and in the life to come they will face a greater suffering. God's law will continue to operate, the fates of past generations remain witnesses to the truth, God's warnings concerning the Day of Judgement remain in force, their chance to save themselves continues, and this Qur'ān remains available to those who will heed the warnings.

Unequal Situations

> *We have set for people in this Qur'ān all sorts of illustrations, so that they may reflect. It is an Arabic Qur'ān, free from distortion, so that people may become conscious of God. God cites the case of a man who has for his masters several partners at odds with each other, and a man belonging wholly to one person. Can they be deemed equal? All praise is due to God alone, but most of them do not understand.* (Verses 27–29)

God draws an analogy citing the examples of two of His servants: one believes in His Oneness and one ascribes divinity to others beside God. He compares them to two slaves: one is owned by several people who are at odds with each other about who owns him; he is caught between them, while each of them requires him to do certain things. He is at a loss, not knowing which way to turn and cannot manage to satisfy them all because of their contradictory orders. The other is owned by one master, and he knows what his master wants and is clear about his desires and requirements.

"*Can they be deemed equal?*" (Verse 29) They are definitely unequal. The one who has one master enjoys consistency and knows what is expected of him. His energy is spent in a consistent way and the road ahead of him is clear. The other, who has several masters, is always suffering anxiety and worry. He does not feel settled. He is unable to satisfy even one of his masters, let alone them all.

This comparison accurately describes the nature of believing in God's oneness as opposed to the nature of idolatry. The one who believes in God's oneness goes along his earth's journey equipped with clear guidance, because his eyes are looking up to one guiding star in the sky. Thus his way is straight. He knows one source for life, strength and sustenance; harm and benefit; grace and deprivation. He sets on his straight way to this source, strengthening his ties with it. He is assured of his single goal and does not lose sight of it. Thus, his energy is streamlined, assured of his work's objective. His feet are set firm on the ground while his gaze looks to God in heaven.

This telling analogy is followed by a comment praising God who has chosen for His servants what gives them comfort, safety, security and contentment. Yet they deviate from the truth, and most of them do not even know it.

This is but one of the numerous examples the Qur'ān gives people so that they may reflect. It is a clear Qur'ān in the Arabic tongue. It addresses human nature with simple logic. In it there is no ambiguity, equivocation or deviation.

5

The People of the Truth

Indeed you are bound to die, and they too are bound to die; (30)

إِنَّكَ مَيِّتٌ وَإِنَّهُم مَّيِّتُونَ ﴿٣٠﴾

and then on the Day of Resurrection you all will dispute with one another in the presence of your Lord. (31)

ثُمَّ إِنَّكُمْ يَوْمَ ٱلْقِيَـٰمَةِ عِندَ رَبِّكُمْ تَخْتَصِمُونَ ﴿٣١﴾

Who could be more wrong than one who invents a lie about God and rejects the truth when it comes to him? Is not there in hell a proper abode for the unbelievers? (32)

فَمَنْ أَظْلَمُ مِمَّن كَذَبَ عَلَى ٱللَّهِ وَكَذَّبَ بِٱلصِّدْقِ إِذْ جَآءَهُۥٓ أَلَيْسَ فِى جَهَنَّمَ مَثْوًى لِّلْكَـٰفِرِينَ ﴿٣٢﴾

It is the one who brings the truth and the one who accepts it as true that are God-fearing. (33)

وَٱلَّذِى جَآءَ بِٱلصِّدْقِ وَصَدَّقَ بِهِۦٓ أُوْلَـٰٓئِكَ هُمُ ٱلْمُتَّقُونَ ﴿٣٣﴾

They will have all that they wish for with their Lord: such is the reward of those who do good. (34)

لَهُم مَّا يَشَآءُونَ عِندَ رَبِّهِمْ ذَٰلِكَ جَزَآءُ ٱلْمُحْسِنِينَ ﴿٣٤﴾

God will expunge the worst of their deeds and will give them their reward in accordance with the best that they did. (35)

Widely Different Rewards

Commenting on the preceding passage, the *sūrah* states that the dispute between the Prophet and his opponents is left to God for judgement, which will occur after they have all died. He will requite the liars as they deserve and give generous reward to the people of the truth.

Indeed you are bound to die, and they too are bound to die; and then on the Day of Resurrection you all will dispute with one another in the presence of your Lord. (Verses 30–31)

Death is the end of every living thing. Only God remains. In death all people share the same end, including Muḥammad, God's last Messenger. Mention of this fact here comes within the framework of the great truth the *sūrah* emphasizes, namely, God's absolute oneness. This is followed by stating what comes after death, because death is not the final end: it is a link in the chain of life that has been so ordained that no part of it passes in vain. On the Day of Judgement people will stand in front of God disputing with one another over what they used to claim, and how they reacted to the guidance God sent them.

Who could be more wrong than one who invents a lie about God and rejects the truth when it comes to him? Is not there in hell a proper abode for the unbelievers? (Verse 32)

These are facts stated in the form of questions. None is more wrong than the person who makes false claims about God, alleging that He has daughters and partners, and who then rejects the truth preached by God's Messenger, refusing to believe in God's oneness. This is unbelief, and in hell there is a proper abode for all unbelievers. The interrogative form given to these two statements makes them clearer and more emphatic.

This is one party to the dispute. The other party is the one who brings the message of truth given him by God, believes in it and delivers it fully convinced of its truth. That is God's Messenger. Sharing with him in this description are all earlier messengers of God, as well as everyone who advocates this message, fully convinced that it is true. These are indeed God-fearing.

The *sūrah* speaks further about these people and the reward God has in store for them: "*They will have all that they wish for with their Lord: such is the reward of those who do good.*" (Verse 34) This is an all-embracing statement that includes all the desires that a believing soul may entertain. The verse states that this is theirs, ready for them with their Lord. This means that they have a rightful claim to it which will not be lost or denied: "*Such is the reward of those who do good.*" (Verse 34)

Thus God gives them all that He wishes to give them of honour and blessing, which is in excess of their fair reward. Thus, He bestows on them an abundance of His grace: "*God will expunge the worst of their deeds and will give them their reward in accordance with the best that they did.*" (Verse 35) Fairness requires that good deeds are set against bad ones and reward is determined on that basis. God's grace, however, is that which God grants to His servants who feared Him: He writes off the worst of their deeds, so that they are not taken into account when their deeds are reckoned, and then He rewards them on the basis of the best they ever did. Thus their good deeds are made to grow and become preponderant.

Such is God's grace which He bestows on whomever He wills. He has committed Himself to do this, giving a promise to this effect. Thus, it is a fact of which the God-fearing are certain.

6

Signs to Reflect Upon

Is not God sufficient for His servant? Yet they would try to frighten you with those who are inferior to Him. He whom God lets go astray can never find any guide; (36)

أَلَيْسَ ٱللَّهُ بِكَافٍ عَبْدَهُۥ وَيُخَوِّفُونَكَ بِٱلَّذِينَ مِن دُونِهِۦ وَمَن يُضْلِلِ ٱللَّهُ فَمَا لَهُۥ مِنْ هَادٍ ٣٦

whereas he whom God guides aright can never be led astray. Is God not mighty, capable of inflicting retribution? (37)

وَمَن يَهْدِ ٱللَّهُ فَمَا لَهُۥ مِن مُّضِلٍّ أَلَيْسَ ٱللَّهُ بِعَزِيزٍ ذِى ٱنتِقَامٍ ٣٧

If you ask them who created the heavens and the earth, they will answer: 'God.' Say: 'Consider these beings you invoke beside Him: if God wills harm to befall me, could they remove the harm He has inflicted? Or, if He wills that mercy should be bestowed on me, could they withhold His mercy?' Say: 'God is enough for me: In Him place their trust those who have a trust to place.' (38)

وَلَئِن سَأَلْتَهُم مَّنْ خَلَقَ ٱلسَّمَٰوَٰتِ وَٱلْأَرْضَ لَيَقُولُنَّ ٱللَّهُ قُلْ أَفَرَءَيْتُم مَّا تَدْعُونَ مِن دُونِ ٱللَّهِ إِنْ أَرَادَنِيَ ٱللَّهُ بِضُرٍّ هَلْ هُنَّ كَٰشِفَٰتُ ضُرِّهِۦٓ أَوْ أَرَادَنِي بِرَحْمَةٍ هَلْ هُنَّ مُمْسِكَٰتُ رَحْمَتِهِۦ قُلْ حَسْبِىَ ٱللَّهُ عَلَيْهِ يَتَوَكَّلُ ٱلْمُتَوَكِّلُونَ ٣٨

Say: 'My people! Do all that may be in your power, and I will do what I can. You shall come to know (39)

قُل يَـٰقَوْمِ ٱعْمَلُوا عَلَىٰ مَكَانَتِكُمْ إِنِّي عَـٰمِلٌ فَسَوْفَ تَعْلَمُونَ ﴿٣٩﴾

who will be visited with humiliating suffering and who shall be smitten by long-lasting suffering. (40)

مَن يَأْتِيهِ عَذَابٌ يُخْزِيهِ وَيَحِلُّ عَلَيْهِ عَذَابٌ مُّقِيمٌ ﴿٤٠﴾

We have bestowed on you this book from on high, setting out the truth for mankind. Whoever follows its guidance does so for his own good, and whoever goes astray shall do so at his own peril. You are not responsible for them.' (41)

إِنَّا أَنزَلْنَا عَلَيْكَ ٱلْكِتَـٰبَ لِلنَّاسِ بِٱلْحَقِّ فَمَنِ ٱهْتَدَىٰ فَلِنَفْسِهِ وَمَن ضَلَّ فَإِنَّمَا يَضِلُّ عَلَيْهَا وَمَآ أَنتَ عَلَيْهِم بِوَكِيلٍ ﴿٤١﴾

God takes away people's souls upon their death, and the souls of the living during their sleep. He keeps with Him the souls of those whose death He has ordained and sends back the others until their appointed time. In all this there are signs for people who reflect. (42)

ٱللَّهُ يَتَوَفَّى ٱلْأَنفُسَ حِينَ مَوْتِهَا وَٱلَّتِي لَمْ تَمُتْ فِى مَنَامِهَا فَيُمْسِكُ ٱلَّتِي قَضَىٰ عَلَيْهَا ٱلْمَوْتَ وَيُرْسِلُ ٱلْأُخْرَىٰٓ إِلَىٰٓ أَجَلٍ مُّسَمًّى إِنَّ فِى ذَٰلِكَ لَآيَـٰتٍ لِّقَوْمٍ يَتَفَكَّرُونَ ﴿٤٢﴾

Have they chosen others besides God to intercede for them? Say: 'Why, even though they have no power over anything and no understanding?' (43)

أَمِ ٱتَّخَذُوا مِن دُونِ ٱللَّهِ شُفَعَآءَ قُلْ أَوَلَوْ كَانُوا لَا يَمْلِكُونَ شَيْـًٔا وَلَا يَعْقِلُونَ ﴿٤٣﴾

Say: 'All intercession belongs to God alone. His alone is the dominion over the heavens and the earth; and to Him you will all in the end return.' (44)

قُل لِّلَّهِ ٱلشَّفَٰعَةُ جَمِيعًا لَّهُۥ مُلْكُ ٱلسَّمَٰوَٰتِ وَٱلْأَرْضِ ثُمَّ إِلَيْهِ تُرْجَعُونَ ﴿٤٤﴾

Whenever God alone is mentioned, the hearts of those who will not believe in the life to come shrink with aversion; but when others are mentioned side by side with Him, they rejoice. (45)

وَإِذَا ذُكِرَ ٱللَّهُ وَحْدَهُ ٱشْمَأَزَّتْ قُلُوبُ ٱلَّذِينَ لَا يُؤْمِنُونَ بِٱلْءَاخِرَةِ وَإِذَا ذُكِرَ ٱلَّذِينَ مِن دُونِهِۦٓ إِذَا هُمْ يَسْتَبْشِرُونَ ﴿٤٥﴾

Say: 'God! Originator of the heavens and the earth! You have knowledge of all that is imperceptible and all that is present. It is You who will judge between Your servants concerning all that over which they differ.' (46)

قُلِ ٱللَّهُمَّ فَاطِرَ ٱلسَّمَٰوَٰتِ وَٱلْأَرْضِ عَٰلِمَ ٱلْغَيْبِ وَٱلشَّهَٰدَةِ أَنتَ تَحْكُمُ بَيْنَ عِبَادِكَ فِى مَا كَانُوا۟ فِيهِ يَخْتَلِفُونَ ﴿٤٦﴾

If the wrongdoers possessed all that is on earth, and twice as much, they would surely offer it all as ransom from the awful suffering on the Day of Resurrection. For God will have made obvious to them something they have never reckoned with. (47)

وَلَوْ أَنَّ لِلَّذِينَ ظَلَمُوا۟ مَا فِى ٱلْأَرْضِ جَمِيعًا وَمِثْلَهُۥ مَعَهُۥ لَٱفْتَدَوْا۟ بِهِۦ مِن سُوٓءِ ٱلْعَذَابِ يَوْمَ ٱلْقِيَٰمَةِ وَبَدَا لَهُم مِّنَ ٱللَّهِ مَا لَمْ يَكُونُوا۟ يَحْتَسِبُونَ ﴿٤٧﴾

Obvious to them will have become the evil of what they had done; and they will be overwhelmed by that which they used to deride. (48)

وَبَدَا لَهُمْ سَيِّئَاتُ مَا كَسَبُواْ وَحَاقَ بِهِم مَّا كَانُواْ بِهِۦ يَسْتَهْزِءُونَ ۝

When man suffers affliction, he cries out to Us; but once We bestow upon him a favour by Our grace, he says: 'I have been given all this by virtue of my knowledge.' By no means! It is but a test, yet most of them do not understand. (49)

فَإِذَا مَسَّ ٱلْإِنسَٰنَ ضُرٌّ دَعَانَا ثُمَّ إِذَا خَوَّلْنَٰهُ نِعْمَةً مِّنَّا قَالَ إِنَّمَا أُوتِيتُهُۥ عَلَىٰ عِلْمٍ بَلْ هِيَ فِتْنَةٌ وَلَٰكِنَّ أَكْثَرَهُمْ لَا يَعْلَمُونَ ۝

Those who lived before their time said the same, but of no avail to them was all that they had ever done: (50)

قَدْ قَالَهَا ٱلَّذِينَ مِن قَبْلِهِمْ فَمَا أَغْنَىٰ عَنْهُم مَّا كَانُواْ يَكْسِبُونَ ۝

for the very evil of their deeds recoiled upon them. Similarly, the wrongdoers among these present people will have the evil of their deeds recoil upon them. They will never be able to frustrate [God's purpose]. (51)

فَأَصَابَهُمْ سَيِّئَاتُ مَا كَسَبُواْ وَٱلَّذِينَ ظَلَمُواْ مِنْ هَٰؤُلَآءِ سَيُصِيبُهُمْ سَيِّئَاتُ مَا كَسَبُواْ وَمَا هُم بِمُعْجِزِينَ ۝

Are they not aware that it is God who grants sustenance in abundance, or gives it sparingly, to whomever He wills? In this there are signs to those who believe. (52)

أَوَلَمْ يَعْلَمُواْ أَنَّ ٱللَّهَ يَبْسُطُ ٱلرِّزْقَ لِمَن يَشَآءُ وَيَقْدِرُ إِنَّ فِي ذَٰلِكَ لَءَايَٰتٍ لِّقَوْمٍ يُؤْمِنُونَ ۝

Overview

This is the longest passage in the *sūrah*. It tackles the issue of God's oneness from several angles, starting with a statement about the attitude a believer adopts towards all earthly powers, relying only on the one true power, caring little for anything else. Therefore, he disregards all such imaginary forces, trusting to God's judgement between him and those who dispute with him. He goes along his way firm and reassured about his destiny.

This is followed by a clear statement about the role and responsibility of God's Messenger, making it clear that he is not responsible for others, whether they choose to follow divine guidance or go astray. It is God who has power over them in all situations. They have no one to intercede with Him, for it is to God alone that all intercession belongs. His is the kingdom of the heavens and earth, and with Him all journeys end.

The *sūrah* then describes how the idolaters feel depressed when God's oneness is mentioned, while they delight when idolatry is discussed. This is followed by an invitation to the Prophet to declare God's oneness in the clearest of terms, leaving the idolaters to God. It describes how they will gladly give all that the earth contains, and twice as much, if only it will be accepted from them. This is how they feel once they realize how God may deal with them.

Such is the case, yet they still appeal to God alone when they are in a situation of distress. Should God grant them a favour, they make all sorts of wild claims. Any of them could say about God's favours: "I have been given this through my knowledge." This echoes what was said by others in former times, but God Almighty took them to task, and He is able to deal with these present unbelievers in the same way. They cannot defy God. Whether God gives provisions in abundance or in stinted measure in accordance with His wisdom and will: "*In this there are signs to those who believe.*" (Verse 52)

To Do All in One's Power

Is not God sufficient for His servant? Yet they would try to frighten you with those who are inferior to Him. He whom God lets go astray can never find any guide; whereas he whom God guides aright can never be led astray. Is God not mighty, capable of inflicting retribution? If you ask them who created the heavens and the earth, they will answer: 'God.' Say: 'Consider these beings you invoke beside Him: if God wills harm to befall me, could they remove the harm He has inflicted? Or, if He wills that mercy should be bestowed on me, could they withhold His mercy?' Say: 'God is enough for me: In Him place their trust those who have a trust to place.' Say: 'My people! Do all that may be in your power, and I will do what I can. You shall come to know who will be visited with humiliating suffering and who shall be smitten by long-lasting suffering.' (Verses 36–40)

These five verses epitomize the logic of faith: simple, clear, forceful and profound. Thus it was in the Prophet's heart, and thus it should be in every heart that advocates a cause. These verses represent the line that such a believer should follow. They provide his light as he goes along his clear and straight way.

It is reported that these verses were revealed as a result of the unbelievers trying to scare the Prophet, claiming that their deities, which he described in disrespectful terms, would be sure to harm him. They warned him that unless he desisted, their gods would cause him much trouble. However, the significance of these verses is far broader than this. They describe the true nature of the battle between an advocate of the truth and all the forces that line up against him. They show the confidence and reassurance a believer feels as he gives these forces their true measure.

"*Is not God sufficient for His servant?*" (Verse 36) Yes, indeed. So, what can scare him when God is with him? What can generate any feeling of fear in him after he has taken the position of a servant of God and fulfilled the responsibilities that such a position confers? Who can doubt God's sufficiency for His servants when He is the Almighty who holds sway over all His creation?

"*Yet they would try to frighten you with those who are inferior to Him.*" (Verse 36) How could he be frightened when those inferiors do not frighten one who is protected by God? Is there anyone on earth who is not inferior to God? It is a very simple issue. It requires no argument or hard thinking. It is God opposed by some who are inferior to Him. This leaves no room for doubt concerning the outcome.

God's will is the one that is done. He determines everything for His servants, including what takes place within them, their inner thoughts and feelings: "*He whom God lets go astray can never find any guide; whereas he whom God guides aright can never be led astray.*" (Verses 36–37) He knows who deserves to go astray and who deserves to be guided. He lets them have what they deserve. When He has made His judgement, no one can alter it.

"*Is God not mighty, capable of inflicting retribution?*" (Verse 37) Yes, indeed, He is. He requites everyone as they deserve, inflicting retribution on those who deserve it. When anyone fulfils the duties incumbent on God's servants, He extends His protection to them. How can such a person, then, fear anyone?

The same truth is then re-emphasized in a different way, using their own logic and what they, by their very nature, acknowledge of God's attributes: "*If you ask them who created the heavens and the earth, they will answer: 'God.' Say: 'Consider these beings you invoke beside Him: if God wills harm to befall me, could they remove the harm He has inflicted? Or, if He wills that mercy should be bestowed on me, could they withhold His mercy?' Say: 'God is enough for me: In Him place their trust those who have a trust to place.'*" (Verse 38)

Whenever they were asked, they would readily state that God is the Creator of the heavens and the earth. No human nature could say anything else. No rational being could explain the existence of the heavens and the earth except through a supreme will. Therefore, the *sūrah* uses this natural acceptance to ask every reasonable human being: since God is the Creator of the heavens and the earth, can anyone anywhere in the heavens and the earth remove harm from anyone if God wills that harm afflict that person? By the same token, can anyone withhold mercy from anyone if God wishes it to be bestowed on that person? The clear and decisive answer to these questions is in the negative. So, why should an advocate of God's cause fear anything? What can he fear, and what can he hope for, when no one can remove harm from him or withhold grace?

When this notion is firmly planted in a believer's heart, the matter is settled. There is no more argument. The only fear or hope such a believer may have is centred on what comes from God. It is He who is sufficient for His servants, and in Him all trust is placed: "*Say: God is enough for me: In Him place their trust those who have a trust to place.*" (Verse 38)

This gives believers all they need of trust and reassurance, leaving no room for worry or fear of anything. They go along their way in full confidence as to the end they will meet: "*Say: My people! Do all that may be in your power, and I will do what I can. You shall come to know who will be visited with humiliating suffering and who shall be smitten by long-lasting suffering.*" (Verses 39–40) Do what you can, the way you wish. I am going my way entertaining no desire to change or deviate even slightly from it, free from worry or anxiety. You will come to know who will suffer humiliation in this life and everlasting punishment in the life to come.

Once this simple truth testified by both human nature and the universe at large has been presented, confirming that God is the Creator of the heavens and earth, and that the message advocated by prophets and their followers comes from Him, who in the whole universe can affect anything? Who can protect others from harm or withhold mercy from them? Since no one has any power to do so, what would they fear, and what would they hope for?

What Intercession?

Such is the reality of the situation between God's messengers and all earthly forces opposing them. The question then is what is their message, and how should they react towards those who deny them?

> *We have bestowed on you this book from on high, setting out the truth for mankind. Whoever follows its guidance does so for his own good, and whoever goes astray shall do so at his own peril. You are*

not responsible for them. God takes away people's souls upon their death, and the souls of the living during their sleep. He keeps with Him the souls of those whose death He has ordained and sends back the others until their appointed time. In all this there are signs for people who reflect. Have they chosen others besides God to intercede for them? Say: 'Why, even though they have no power over anything and no understanding?' Say: 'All intercession belongs to God alone. His alone is the dominion over the heavens and the earth; and to Him you will all in the end return.' (Verses 41–44)

"We have bestowed on you this book from on high, setting out the truth for mankind." (Verse 41) The truth is the nature of this book: it is clear in the law it sets out and in its system: it is on the basis of this truth that the universe is sustained; the truth that links the code of human life outlined in this book to the system of the universe. This truth has now been bestowed on mankind giving them guidance on how to live by its provisions. You, Prophet, are only the means to deliver it to them. It is up to them to choose what they wish for and how to deal with it. Each one of them can choose either guidance or error, and each will define his or her own fate. No responsibility attaches to you for what they choose: *"Whoever follows its guidance does so for his own good, and whoever goes astray shall do so at his own peril. You are not responsible for them."* (Verse 41)

It is God who has power over them. They are in His hands when they are asleep or awake, or indeed in all situations and conditions. He determines what to do with them: *"God takes away people's souls upon their death, and the souls of the living during their sleep. He keeps with Him the souls of those whose death He has ordained and sends back the others until their appointed time."* (Verse 42) God gathers the souls of those who die, and He also takes away people's souls when they are asleep, even though they are not dead. During sleep, these souls are temporarily removed. If the term of some is over, God will retain their souls and they cannot wake up. Those whose term of life continues will have their souls returned and they will wake up. Thus, people's souls are in God's hands whether they are asleep or awake: *"In all this there are signs for people who reflect."* (Verse 42)

Such being the case, with the Prophet having no responsibility for others, it is up to each of them individually: if they follow divine guidance, they benefit themselves; and if they choose error, they bear the responsibility for their choice. They will have to face the reckoning, for they will not be left unaccountable. What hope, then, do they have for salvation? *"Have they chosen others besides God to intercede for them? Say: Why, even though they have no power over anything and no understanding? Say: All intercession belongs to God alone. His alone is the dominion over the heavens and the earth; and to Him you will all in the end return."* (Verses 43–44) The question here is sarcastic, referring to their claims that they worship the statues of angels in order that these bring them closer to God. They are asked: *"Why, even though they have no power over anything and no understanding?"* The question is followed by an emphatic statement that all intercession belongs to God: it is He who permits whomever He wishes to intercede. Do they think that attributing partners to God is the way to achieve intercession?

"His alone is the dominion over the heavens and the earth." (Verse 44) No one can defy His will in His kingdom, where all dominion belongs to Him alone. *"And to Him you will all in the end return."* (Verse 44) There is no escape, simple.

The *sūrah* then describes how strongly they dislike any statement about God's oneness, while they delight in the attribution of partners with Him, when everything around them in the universe rejects such polytheism:

> *Whenever God alone is mentioned, the hearts of those who will not believe in the life to come shrink with aversion; but when others are mentioned side by side with Him, they rejoice.* (Verse 45)

The verse describes a real situation during the Prophet's time, when the unbelievers delighted at the mention of their false deities, but showed clear dislike when God's oneness was asserted. Yet the verse also describes a state of affairs that takes place in all environments. Some people do express dislike when they are asked to believe in God alone and to implement His law and code of living. When other systems and laws are mentioned, they demonstrate happiness and delight. Only then are they ready to discuss and argue. It is these very people that God is describing in this verse: they are the ones, in all communities and generations, who trample over sound human nature, choose deviation, go and lead others astray.

The reply to all such deviation is taught by God to His Messenger whereby the latter says:

> Say: God! Originator of the heavens and the earth! You have knowledge of all that is imperceptible and all that is present. It is You who will judge between Your servants concerning all that over which they differ. (Verse 46)

It is a simple prayer that comes from sound human nature looking at the heavens and the earth, that cannot find anyone other than God who could have created them, that acknowledges His creation, and addresses Him by the quality that fits the Originator of the universe, i.e. His knowledge of the imperceptible and all that anyone witnesses. It is He who is fully aware of what is present and what is absent, what is hidden and what is manifest. "It is You who will judge between Your servants concerning all that over which they differ." (Verse 46) He is the only judge and arbiter when they all return to Him, as return they must.

As Man Suffers Affliction

The *sūrah* then shows their miserable state when they return for judgement:

> If the wrongdoers possessed all that is on earth, and twice as much, they would surely offer it all as ransom from the awful suffering on the Day of Resurrection. For God will have made obvious to them something they have never reckoned with. Obvious to them will have become the evil of what they had done; and they will be overwhelmed by that which they used to deride. (Verses 47–48)

449

The verse makes an implicit threat within a statement that strikes fear into the hearts of those described as 'wrongdoers', which refers to everyone who associates partners, of any type, with God. If those people had in their possession 'all that is on earth,' including everything to which they attach high value and fear to lose should they accept Islam, indeed, if they had 'twice as much', they would willingly offer it all just to be spared the awful suffering they will see with their own eyes on the Day of Resurrection. Added to this is another implicit threat that is equally fearful: "For God will have made obvious to them something they have never reckoned with." (Verse 47) The sūrah does not specify what will become obvious to them, but it is clearly understood that it is terrible, to be feared. It comes from God, and He shows them what they could never have expected.

"Obvious to them will have become the evil of what they had done; and they will be overwhelmed by that which they used to deride." (Verse 48) Again this aggravates their position, because they will see for themselves how evil their deeds were, and they will find themselves engulfed with the warnings that they used to deride and ridicule.

Then follows a description of an ironic situation: they are outspoken in denying God's oneness, yet when they suffer affliction they turn to none but Him, praying earnestly for His help. When He bestows His grace on them and removes their affliction they revert to their boastful claims and deny His favours:

> When man suffers affliction, he cries out to Us; but once We bestow upon him a favour by Our grace, he says: 'I have been given all this by virtue of my knowledge.' By no means! It is but a test, yet most of them do not understand. (Verse 49)

This verse describes man if he does not accept the truth and turn back to his true Lord, following the path leading to Him and remaining on that path in all situations of strength or weakness. Affliction purges human nature of the desires and ambitions that blur its vision. It removes from it all alien influences that place a barrier between it and the truth. Therefore, when afflicted, it can easily recognize God and turn to Him alone. Yet when the testing times are over, and human nature again finds itself in easy and comfortable circumstances, man forgets what he said only a short while earlier. His nature is again turned away from the truth under the influence of his desires, and he looks at God's favours and provisions only to say: *"I have been given all this by virtue of my knowledge."* (Verse 49) This was said by Qārūn, or Korah, in former times, and it is said by everyone who admires what he is able to obtain of wealth or position through some sort of ability or knowledge, forgetting who grants him these, namely the One who has made causes produce their effects and who grants everyone their provisions.

"By no means! It is but a test, yet most of them do not understand." (Verse 49) It is all just a test. Man either proves himself, shows that he is grateful to God and sets himself on the right way or he denies God's favours, takes the wrong way and goes astray.

By an act of God's grace, the Qur'ān reveals this secret to us. It alerts us to the source of danger, warns us against failure in the test, and thus leaves us no excuse or argument. It reminds us of the fates of those who lived long before us, which were the result of something like the words spoken by many an unbeliever in the past: *"I have been given all this by virtue of my knowledge."* (Verse 49)

> *Those who lived before their time said the same, but of no avail to them was all that they had ever done: for the very evil of their deeds recoiled upon them. Similarly, the wrongdoers among these present people will have the evil of their deeds recoil upon them. They will never be able to frustrate [God's purpose].* (Verses 50–51)

They are the same deviant words spoken by earlier peoples and which led them to ruin. Nothing of their knowledge, wealth or positions were of benefit to them. The same rule will apply to the present unbelievers, because God's law will never change. *"They will never be able to frustrate God's purpose."* (Verse 51) Indeed, God cannot be defied by His creation who remain weak, despite any appearance of power they may enjoy. As for what God has granted them of His favours and provisions, it is all subject to His will. He gives all His creation whatever He may determine for them, according to His wisdom, making it all a test for them which ensures that His will is done: *"Are they not aware that it is God who grants sustenance in abundance, or gives it sparingly, to whomever He wills? In this there are signs to those who believe."* (Verse 52) God's signs are given to people so that they will benefit by the guidance they provide and will be led to faith. They must not turn them into causes of unbelief and rejection of the truth.

7

The Gates of Mercy

Say: '[Thus speaks God]: You servants of Mine who have transgressed against their own souls! Do not despair of God's mercy: God forgives all sins; He alone is Much-Forgiving, Merciful.' (53)

قُلْ يَٰعِبَادِىَ ٱلَّذِينَ أَسْرَفُوا۟ عَلَىٰ أَنفُسِهِمْ لَا تَقْنَطُوا۟ مِن رَّحْمَةِ ٱللَّهِ إِنَّ ٱللَّهَ يَغْفِرُ ٱلذُّنُوبَ جَمِيعًا إِنَّهُۥ هُوَ ٱلْغَفُورُ ٱلرَّحِيمُ ﴿٥٣﴾

Turn towards your Lord and submit to Him before the suffering comes upon you, for then you cannot be helped. (54)

وَأَنِيبُوٓا۟ إِلَىٰ رَبِّكُمْ وَأَسْلِمُوا۟ لَهُۥ مِن قَبْلِ أَن يَأْتِيَكُمُ ٱلْعَذَابُ ثُمَّ لَا تُنصَرُونَ ﴿٥٤﴾

Follow the best that has been revealed to you by your Lord before the suffering comes upon you of a sudden, without your being aware of it, (55)

وَٱتَّبِعُوٓا۟ أَحْسَنَ مَآ أُنزِلَ إِلَيْكُم مِّن رَّبِّكُم مِّن قَبْلِ أَن يَأْتِيَكُمُ ٱلْعَذَابُ بَغْتَةً وَأَنتُمْ لَا تَشْعُرُونَ ﴿٥٥﴾

lest anyone should say: 'Woe is me for having neglected what is due to God, and for having been one of those who scoffed [at the truth]; (56)

أَن تَقُولَ نَفْسٌ يَٰحَسْرَتَىٰ عَلَىٰ مَا فَرَّطتُ فِى جَنۢبِ ٱللَّهِ وَإِن كُنتُ لَمِنَ ٱلسَّٰخِرِينَ ﴿٥٦﴾

or lest he should say: 'If God had but guided me, I would surely have been among the God-fearing;' (57)

أَوْ تَقُولَ لَوْ أَنَّ اللَّهَ هَدَىٰنِي لَكُنتُ مِنَ ٱلْمُتَّقِينَ ﴿٥٧﴾

or lest he should say, when faced by the suffering [that awaits him]: 'If only I could have a second chance in life, I will be among those who do good.' (58)

أَوْ تَقُولَ حِينَ تَرَى ٱلْعَذَابَ لَوْ أَنَّ لِي كَرَّةً فَأَكُونَ مِنَ ٱلْمُحْسِنِينَ ﴿٥٨﴾

[God will say]: 'Yes, indeed! My revelations did come to you, but you rejected them. You were filled with false pride and had no faith at all.' (59)

بَلَىٰ قَدْ جَآءَتْكَ ءَايَٰتِي فَكَذَّبْتَ بِهَا وَٱسْتَكْبَرْتَ وَكُنتَ مِنَ ٱلْكَٰفِرِينَ ﴿٥٩﴾

On the Day of Resurrection you will see those who invented lies about God with their faces darkened. Is not there in hell a proper abode for the arrogant? (60)

وَيَوْمَ ٱلْقِيَٰمَةِ تَرَى ٱلَّذِينَ كَذَبُوا۟ عَلَى ٱللَّهِ وُجُوهُهُم مُّسْوَدَّةٌ أَلَيْسَ فِي جَهَنَّمَ مَثْوًى لِّلْمُتَكَبِّرِينَ ﴿٦٠﴾

But God will deliver those who are God-fearing to their place of safety: no harm shall afflict them, nor shall they grieve. (61)

وَيُنَجِّي ٱللَّهُ ٱلَّذِينَ ٱتَّقَوْا۟ بِمَفَازَتِهِمْ لَا يَمَسُّهُمُ ٱلسُّوٓءُ وَلَا هُمْ يَحْزَنُونَ ﴿٦١﴾

Overview

The previous passage included a description of the terrible situations in which the wrongdoers find themselves on the Day of Judgement: *"If the wrongdoers possessed all that is on earth, and twice as much, they would surely offer it all as ransom from the awful suffering on the Day of Resurrection. For God will have made obvious to them something they have never reckoned with. Obvious to them will have become the evil of what they had done; and they will be overwhelmed by that which they used to deride."* (Verses 47–48) Now the *sūrah* shows the way back leaving the gates of God's mercy wide open, requiring nothing for admittance except sincere repentance. At this point, God shows the prospect of His forgiveness and mercy available to all those who have transgressed no matter how great the sins they have committed are. He invites them all to turn back to Him with repentance, entertaining no feeling of despair. This invitation to benefit by God's grace is coupled with an image of what awaits them of suffering if they do not take this opportunity to repent before it is too late.

Mercy Available to All

Say: [Thus speaks God]: You servants of Mine who have transgressed against their own souls! Do not despair of God's mercy: God forgives all sins; He alone is Much-Forgiving, Merciful. (Verse 53)

It is divine mercy that will erase every transgression, whatever it happens to be. It is an invitation to all those who have gone far into error and led a life that has taken them far astray, telling them hope still remains available and God's mercy and forgiveness are not far from them. God is most merciful to His servants. He knows their weaknesses and the factors that work on them, whether these are within themselves or in society. He is aware that Satan sets traps for them at every corner, using a great variety of forces, never tiring of his attempt to seduce them. Moreover, God knows that man can easily fall when he lets his bond to the truth weaken, and that his desires and aspirations can easily disturb his equilibrium, pulling him this way or that, leading him into error.

As God knows all this about man, He provides him with ample help, opening the gates of His mercy. He does not take him to task for his sin until He has facilitated for him all the ways and means to rectify his error and mend his ways. Nevertheless, when man goes deep into sin, thinking that he is totally rejected by God and that all is lost, he hears at this point of utter despair a fine address expressing the unlimited mercy available to him: "*Say: [Thus speaks God]: You servants of Mine who have transgressed against their own souls! Do not despair of God's mercy: God forgives all sins; He alone is Much-Forgiving, Merciful.*" (Verse 53)

This means that despite his repeated sins, going far into disobedience of God, all he needs to receive God's grace that revives all that is good in him is to repent. All he needs to do is turn back to God through the gate that is left wide open, without a guard, and with no need for any special permission:

> *Turn towards your Lord and submit to Him before the suffering comes upon you, for then you cannot be helped. Follow the best that has been revealed to you by your Lord before the suffering comes upon you of a sudden, without your being aware of it.* (Verses 54–55)

To turn to God in true submission and to surrender oneself once more to Him is all that is needed. No rituals, no barriers, no intermediaries, no intercessors. It is a direct link between servant and Master, creature and Creator: whoever wishes to return, stop rebellion and approach in full submission may do so. What he will receive is acceptance, a warm welcome and grace beyond measure.

Come on all of you, then! Come on "*before the suffering comes upon you, for then you cannot be helped.*" (Verse 54) Should the chance be missed, there can be no help. The chance is open now, but its duration cannot be guaranteed. In fact, it can terminate at any moment of the night and day. Therefore, come on and "*Follow the best that has been revealed to you by your Lord,*" which is this Qur'ān that you now have at your fingertips, "*before the suffering comes upon you of a sudden, without your being aware of it.*" (Verse 55) Come on now before it is too late. Otherwise you will regret missing the chance and ridiculing God's promise: "*lest anyone should say: Woe is me for having neglected what is due to God, and for having been one of those who scoffed [at the truth].*" (Verse 56) Alternatively, someone may say that God condemned him to be in error: had He decreed that he would follow divine guidance, he would have been a God-fearing person: "*or lest he should say: If God had but guided me, I would surely have been among the God-fearing.*" (Verse 57) This is a baseless excuse: the chance is offered to everyone, the means are available to all, and the gates are wide open. Yet people deliberately miss out: "*Or lest he should say, when faced by the suffering [that awaits him]: If only I could have a second chance in life, I will be among those who do good.*" (Verse 58) This is something that will never be given. Once this life is over, no return is allowed. All people are now at the stage when they can do what they want. If they miss this chance, all is lost. They will be held to account, and they will be rebuked: "*Yes, indeed! My revelations did come to you, but you rejected them. You were filled with false pride and had no faith at all.*" (Verse 59)

At this point, when the *sūrah* has brought our feelings and hearts to the Day of Judgement, it shows us the two contrasting images of the unbelievers and the God-fearing on that momentous day:

> *On the Day of Resurrection you will see those who invented lies about God with their faces darkened. Is not there in hell a proper abode for the arrogant? But God will deliver those who are God-fearing to their place of safety: no harm shall afflict them, nor shall they grieve.* (Verses 60–61)

This is the final end: one group have faces darkened by humiliation, sorrow and the scorches of hell. These are the arrogant who, during their lives in this world, were called to turn to God and believe in Him, and the chance was kept open for them even after they went far into sin, but they refused to pay heed. Now, on the Day of Judgement, they are left in utter humiliation that shows in their faces. The other group are the winners who will not be touched

457

by grief or affliction. These are the God-fearing who, during their lives on earth, paid heed to God's warnings and hoped for His mercy. They are the ones who will be safe: "*no harm shall afflict them, nor shall they grieve.*" (Verse 61)

With all issues made abundantly clear, let everyone choose what they want. They can either respond to the call and enjoy God's grace they are certain to find just behind the open gate of repentance, or they can persist in disobedience until the suffering takes them unawares.

8

Driven in Throngs

God is the Creator of everything, and of all things He is the Guardian. (62)

اللَّهُ خَٰلِقُ كُلِّ شَىْءٍ وَهُوَ عَلَىٰ كُلِّ شَىْءٍ وَكِيلٌ ۝

His are the keys of the heavens and the earth. Those who deny God's revelations will surely be the losers. (63)

لَّهُۥ مَقَالِيدُ ٱلسَّمَٰوَٰتِ وَٱلْأَرْضِ وَٱلَّذِينَ كَفَرُواْ بِـَٔايَٰتِ ٱللَّهِ أُوْلَٰٓئِكَ هُمُ ٱلْخَٰسِرُونَ ۝

Say: 'You ignorant people! Would you bid me worship anyone other than God?' (64)

قُلْ أَفَغَيْرَ ٱللَّهِ تَأْمُرُوٓنِّيٓ أَعْبُدُ أَيُّهَا ٱلْجَٰهِلُونَ ۝

It has been revealed to you, and to those before you, that if you ever associate partners with God, all your works shall certainly come to nothing, and you shall certainly be among the lost. (65)

وَلَقَدْ أُوحِىَ إِلَيْكَ وَإِلَى ٱلَّذِينَ مِن قَبْلِكَ لَئِنْ أَشْرَكْتَ لَيَحْبَطَنَّ عَمَلُكَ وَلَتَكُونَنَّ مِنَ ٱلْخَٰسِرِينَ ۝

You shall worship God alone, and be one of those who give thanks [to Him]. (66)

بَلِ ٱللَّهَ فَٱعْبُدْ وَكُن مِّنَ ٱلشَّٰكِرِينَ ۝

No true understanding of God have they: on the Day of Resurrection, the whole earth will be a mere handful to Him, and the heavens will be rolled up in His right hand. Limitless is He in His glory, and sublimely exalted above anything which they associate as partner with Him. (67)

وَمَا قَدَرُوا اللَّهَ حَقَّ قَدْرِهِ وَالْأَرْضُ جَمِيعًا قَبْضَتُهُ يَوْمَ الْقِيَامَةِ وَالسَّمَاوَاتُ مَطْوِيَّاتٌ بِيَمِينِهِ سُبْحَانَهُ وَتَعَالَى عَمَّا يُشْرِكُونَ ۝

The trumpet will be sounded, and all creatures that are in the heavens and the earth will fall down senseless, except those God wills to be spared. It will then be sounded a second time, and they will rise and look around them. (68)

وَنُفِخَ فِي الصُّورِ فَصَعِقَ مَن فِي السَّمَاوَاتِ وَمَن فِي الْأَرْضِ إِلَّا مَن شَاءَ اللَّهُ ثُمَّ نُفِخَ فِيهِ أُخْرَى فَإِذَا هُمْ قِيَامٌ يَنظُرُونَ ۝

The earth will shine bright with the light of its Lord; the Record of Deeds will be laid open; all the prophets and the witnesses will be brought in. Judgement will be passed on them all in justice, and they will not be wronged; (69)

وَأَشْرَقَتِ الْأَرْضُ بِنُورِ رَبِّهَا وَوُضِعَ الْكِتَابُ وَجِايءَ بِالنَّبِيِّينَ وَالشُّهَدَاءِ وَقُضِيَ بَيْنَهُم بِالْحَقِّ وَهُمْ لَا يُظْلَمُونَ ۝

for every human being will be repaid in full for whatever they have done. He is fully aware of all that they do. (70)

وَوُفِّيَتْ كُلُّ نَفْسٍ مَّا عَمِلَتْ وَهُوَ أَعْلَمُ بِمَا يَفْعَلُونَ ۝

The unbelievers will be led to hell in throngs. When they reach it, its gates will be opened, and its keepers will ask them: 'Did there not come to you messengers from among yourselves, who recited to you your Lord's revelations and forewarned you of this day?' They will answer: 'Yes, indeed.' But the sentence of suffering will have already been passed against the unbelievers. (71)

وَسِيقَ ٱلَّذِينَ كَفَرُوٓاْ إِلَىٰ جَهَنَّمَ زُمَرًا ۖ حَتَّىٰٓ إِذَا جَآءُوهَا فُتِحَتْ أَبْوَٰبُهَا وَقَالَ لَهُمْ خَزَنَتُهَآ أَلَمْ يَأْتِكُمْ رُسُلٌ مِّنكُمْ يَتْلُونَ عَلَيْكُمْ ءَايَٰتِ رَبِّكُمْ وَيُنذِرُونَكُمْ لِقَآءَ يَوْمِكُمْ هَٰذَا ۚ قَالُواْ بَلَىٰ وَلَٰكِنْ حَقَّتْ كَلِمَةُ ٱلْعَذَابِ عَلَى ٱلْكَٰفِرِينَ ﴿٧١﴾

They will be told: 'Enter the gates of hell; there you will abide.' How vile an abode for the arrogant! (72)

قِيلَ ٱدْخُلُوٓاْ أَبْوَٰبَ جَهَنَّمَ خَٰلِدِينَ فِيهَا ۖ فَبِئْسَ مَثْوَى ٱلْمُتَكَبِّرِينَ ﴿٧٢﴾

And the believers will be led to paradise in throngs. When they reach it, they shall find its gates wide open; and its keepers will say to them: 'Peace be to you! Well have you done. Come in: you are here to stay.' (73)

وَسِيقَ ٱلَّذِينَ ٱتَّقَوْاْ رَبَّهُمْ إِلَى ٱلْجَنَّةِ زُمَرًا ۖ حَتَّىٰٓ إِذَا جَآءُوهَا وَفُتِحَتْ أَبْوَٰبُهَا وَقَالَ لَهُمْ خَزَنَتُهَا سَلَٰمٌ عَلَيْكُمْ طِبْتُمْ فَٱدْخُلُوهَا خَٰلِدِينَ ﴿٧٣﴾

They will say: 'All praise is due to God who has made His promise to us come true and given us this land as our own. Now we may dwell in paradise as we please.' How excellent is the reward of those who worked hard. (74)

وَقَالُواْ ٱلْحَمْدُ لِلَّهِ ٱلَّذِى صَدَقَنَا وَعْدَهُ وَأَوْرَثَنَا ٱلْأَرْضَ نَتَبَوَّأُ مِنَ ٱلْجَنَّةِ حَيْثُ نَشَآءُ ۖ فَنِعْمَ أَجْرُ ٱلْعَٰمِلِينَ ﴿٧٤﴾

You will see the angels surrounding the Throne, extolling their Lord's glory and praise. Judgement will have been passed on all in justice, and it will be said: 'All praise is due to God, the Lord of all the worlds.' (75)

وَتَرَى ٱلْمَلَٰٓئِكَةَ حَآفِّينَ مِنْ حَوْلِ ٱلْعَرْشِ يُسَبِّحُونَ بِحَمْدِ رَبِّهِمْ وَقُضِىَ بَيْنَهُم بِٱلْحَقِّ وَقِيلَ ٱلْحَمْدُ لِلَّهِ رَبِّ ٱلْعَٰلَمِينَ ۝

Overview

This final part of the *sūrah* presents its main theme, God's oneness, from the angle of the oneness of the Creator who created and controls everything. This serves to show how singular the unbelievers' offer to the Prophet was that he should join them in worshipping their idols in return for them joining him in worshipping God. Since God is the Creator and Controller of all, how could anyone be worshipped alongside Him? "*No true understanding of God have they,*" when they associate partners with Him when He has sway over all and everything, subjecting them all to His will: "*on the Day of Resurrection, the whole earth will be a mere handful to Him, and the heavens will be rolled up in His right hand.*" (Verse 67) As this image of the Day of Judgement is shown here, the *sūrah* presents a unique scene of that day, culminating with the angels surrounding God's throne, extolling their Lord's glory and praise. The entire universe joins them in their praises: "*All praise is due to God, the Lord of all the worlds.*" (Verse 75) This is, then, the decisive word on the issue of God's oneness.

False Understanding

God is the Creator of everything, and of all things He is the Guardian. His are the keys of the heavens and the earth. Those who deny God's revelations will surely be the losers. (Verses 62–63)

This is the truth that everything in the universe confirms. No one can ever claim to create anything. No rational being can claim that this

462

universe came into existence without a creator, when everything in it testifies to elaborate planning and a clear purpose behind creation. Nothing in it, from the very small to the very large, is left to chance: "*Of all things He is the Guardian.*" (Verse 62) Into His control the heavens and the earth are placed. He conducts their affairs the way He chooses. They operate in accordance with the system He put in place for them. No will other than His interferes with anything. This is acknowledged by human nature, confirmed by practical fact and endorsed by reason and conscience.

"*Those who deny God's revelations will surely be the losers.*" (Verse 63) They have lost the understanding that makes their lives on earth consistent and harmonious with the life of the universe. They have lost the comfort of divine guidance, the beauty of faith, the reassurance of belief and the sweetness of certainty. On the Day of Judgement they will lose their own souls and their families. Hence, the term 'losers' applies to them in all its shades and connotations.

In the light of this truth, testified to by the heavens, the earth and every creature in the universe, the Prophet is instructed in how to reply to the idolaters' offer of both parties joining together in the worship of their idols and God Almighty at the same time. It is as if the whole question is a bargain to be struck by compromise: "*Say: You ignorant people! Would you bid me worship anyone other than God?*" (Verse 64) This is the natural reaction to such a stupid offer that betrays nothing but ignorance.

This is followed with a clear warning against associating partners with God, beginning with the prophets and God's messengers who would never entertain even the slightest thought of such association. This, however, serves to alert all others to the truth that in the question of who is to be worshipped, God stands alone without partners, while in the question of offering worship, all mankind, including the prophets and God's messengers, are in the same position as God's servants: "*It has been revealed to you, and to those before you, that if you ever associate partners with God, all your works shall certainly come to nothing, and you shall certainly be among the lost.*" (Verse 65)

This warning against associating partners with God concludes with an order to worship God alone. We are to show gratitude to Him for providing us with guidance to the path to certainty. We should also thank Him for all His countless favours which He bestows on us and which we all enjoy at every moment of our lives: "*You shall worship God alone, and be one of those who give thanks.*" (Verse 66)

"*No true understanding of God have they.*" (Verse 67) Indeed, they have no clear or true understanding of Him when they associate with Him some of His creatures. Nor do they worship Him as He should be worshipped. They do not appreciate His oneness, greatness, majesty and power. Therefore, the *sūrah* reveals to us an aspect of God's great power in the normal Qur'ānic way of drawing images that place before our eyes a fundamental truth: "*On the Day of Resurrection, the whole earth will be a mere handful to Him, and the heavens will be rolled up in His right hand. Limitless is He in His glory, and sublimely exalted above anything which they associate as partner with Him.*" (Verse 67)

All that we read in the Qur'ān or in *Ḥadīth* of such images and scenes are given in order to present fundamental truths that we would otherwise not comprehend. In other words we need images we can visualize. Here we have an example of this method, portraying for us an aspect of God's absolute power that cannot be limited to one form, placed within one area or confined within certain boundaries.

A Majestic Scene

We now have a scene of the Day of Judgement that begins with the first blowing of the trumpet and ends when the judgement is passed and people are being led to their respective places, either heaven or hell. God Almighty stands in His greatness while the entire universe repeats His glorification and praise. It is a unique scene which is, as it starts, full of life and movement, but one which then slows down until every movement ceases and all stand still. Thus, complete stillness covers the place where all are brought for judgement, standing humbly before God Almighty.

The first blow on the trumpet is made, and all creatures who until that moment remained alive on earth and in the heavens fall senseless, except those God spares. We do not know how much time elapses before the second blow is sounded on the trumpet: "*The trumpet will be sounded, and all creatures that are in the heavens and the earth will fall down senseless, except those God wills to be spared. It will then be sounded a second time, and they will rise and look around them."* (Verse 68) The third blow of gathering them all is not mentioned here. Nor is there mention of the bustling and the crowding, because the scene here is a quiet one, where all move very gradually.

"The earth will shine bright with the light of its Lord." (Verse 69) This is the earth where all action will take place. Needless to say, there is no light other than the light of its Lord Almighty. *"The Record of Deeds will be laid open."* It is the book in which all deeds by all creatures are entered. *"All the prophets and the witnesses will be brought in."* They will testify stating the truth they know. No argument or dispute is mentioned here so as to maintain the atmosphere of majesty and humility before God that permeates the entire scene. *"Judgement will be passed on them all in justice, and they will not be wronged; for every human being will be repaid in full for whatever they have done. He is fully aware of all that they do."* (Verses 69–70) There is no need for a word to be said or a voice to be raised. The whole picture of reckoning, questions asked and answers given, is folded without mention because it does not fit with the ambience of majesty expressed.

The Ultimate Destination

"The unbelievers will be led to hell in throngs. When they reach it, its gates will be opened." (Verse 71) The angels keeping guard will receive them there with a statement that they deserve their lot, reminding them of the reasons why they have ended up there: *"its keepers will ask them: 'Did there not come to you messengers from among yourselves, who recited to you your Lord's revelations and forewarned you of this day? They will answer: 'Yes, indeed.' But the sentence of suffering will have already been passed against the unbelievers."* (Verse 71) The position is one of submission, without any argument or dispute. They accept their lot and submit to their fate: *"They will be told: 'Enter the gates of hell; there you will abide.' How vile an abode for the arrogant!"* (Verse 72)

Such is the fate of the arrogant party, destined for hell. How about the other party, the God-fearing who are destined for heaven?

And the believers will be led to paradise in throngs. When they reach it, they shall find its gates wide open; and its keepers will say to them: Peace be to you! Well have you done. Come in: you are here to stay. (Verse 73)

It is a warm welcome, coupled with pleasant praise of the recipients and an outline of the reasons for which they deserved their reward: "*Well have you done.*" You purified yourselves of sin, lived a pure life and came here with such purity. None but the pure enter heaven. Therefore, you are to remain here forever.

At this point, the voices of the people of heaven are raised high in glorifying and praising God: "*They will say: All praise is due to God who has made His promise to us come true and given us this land as our own.*" (Verse 74) This is the land worth inheriting. They live in it wherever they wish, taking from it whatever they want. "*How excellent is the reward of those who worked hard.*" (Verse 74)

The scene is given a finale that fills our hearts with awe and majesty. It too is in complete harmony with the ambience of the whole *sūrah* devoted to the theme of God's oneness. The entire universe is in complete submission to God Almighty, and praises of God are uttered by every living soul and all existence:

You will see the angels surrounding the Throne, extolling their Lord's glory and praise. Judgement will have been passed on all in justice, and it will be said: All praise is due to God, the Lord of all the worlds. (Verse 75)

Index

bounty, 231; caring hand, 277; chosen people, 387; command(s), 146, 304, 380; consistent law, 90; control, 412; creation, 122, 220, 276, 408; creatures, 120, 122, 307; daughters,157, 304, 338, 339, 340, 409; design, 397, 414; decree, 1, 4, 10, 19, 21, 23, 211; decision, 6; different attributes, 185; displeasure, 277; dominion, 32; endless blessings, 288; express orders, 410; favours, 38, 95, 126, 128, 149, 220, 228, 243, 331, 361, 382, 387, 417, 443, 451; forbearance, 243; forgiveness, 120, 137, 334; glory, 341, 343; grace, 35, 51, 62, 67, 92, 93, 94, 101, 112, 145, 146, 147, 170, 191, 192, 193, 194, 220, 232, 237, 276, 331, 346, 362, 370, 373, 383, 397, 418, 419, 437, 451, 455, 456, 458; grasp, 184; great care, 95; guidance, 86, 168, 200, 400, 428, 431, 432; Godhead, 246, 285, 423; help, 22, 48, 49, 76, 201; judgement, 247, 443; kingdom, 220; knowledge, 124, 127, 134, 136, 137, 153, 210, 228, 396; law(s), 76, 121, 214, 237, 241, 242, 278, 286, 288, 359, 410, 433, 451; leave, 94, 112, 147, 194, 226, 232; limitless knowledge, 126; mercy, 107, 110, 192, 193, 346, 347, 361, 392, 402, 418, 453, 455, 456; mercy and care, 346; message(s), 23, 52, 80, 82, 87, 90, 125, 128, 165, 175, 176, 219, 224, 255, 261, 338, 355, 359, 362, 429; message to mankind, 52, 359; Messenger, 5, 6, 27, 31, 33, 34, 35, 45, 47, 52, 55, 72, 74, 80, 83, 87, 90, 91, 94, 99, 104, 106, 109, 116, 129, 159, 175, 201, 224, 254, 259, 286, 333, 353, 436, 437, 443; oneness, 89, 123, 125, 133, 156, 165, 248, 287, 288, 294, 307, 332, 345, 357, 358, 359, 392, 399, 400, 403, 407, 408, 409, 410, 417, 420, 423, 434, 436, 443, 448, 450, 462, 466; order, 134, 396, 425; partners, 125, 160, 237, 239; path, 73, 375; pleasure, 46, 64, 118, 169, 281, 346; power, 190, 237, 240, 308; power and ability, 308; promise, 135, 422, 425, 426; punishment, 117, 177, 361; purpose, 88,

115, 137, 442, 451; requital, 127; revelations, 60, 67, 75, 76, 122, 175, 225, 307, 459, 462, 463; ruling, 4; servants, 149, 419, 420, 423, 445, 463; supervision, 180; throne, 462; true servants, 295, 301, 310, 313, 318, 321, 322, 332, 336, 340; unlimited favours, 147; universal laws, 342; warnings, 345, 433, 458; way, 80, 87, 90, 101, 112, 236, 241, 242, 417; word, 293, 297, 303, 304, 341, 342, 343, 432; will, 4, 6, 11, 23, 36, 43, 50, 68, 79, 80, 85, 86, 87, 88, 89, 90, 137, 144, 164, 166, 180, 190, 193, 212, 224, 276, 278, 292, 321, 322, 328, 330, 342, 352, 362, 379, 380, 393, 430, 445; wisdom, 65, 90, 135, 136, 171, 278

Goliath, 372

Good manners, 106

Gratitude, 76, 126, 128, 144, 147, 148, 149, 150, 151, 152, 170, 194, 195, 205, 231, 234, 463

Guidance, 23, 44, 73, 74, 86, 121, 124, 137, 153, 159, 162, 166, 167, 168, 169, 179, 180, 184, 195, 200, 201, 202, 205, 207, 216, 219, 220, 221, 222, 224, 236, 241, 247, 256, 257, 260, 287, 308, 309, 320, 326, 338, 400, 406, 409, 410, 422, 424, 425, 428, 431, 432, 434, 436, 440, 443, 446, 447, 448, 452, 457, 463, 464

H

Ḥadīth, 22, 23, 40, 63, 66, 71, 91, 116, 144, 178, 179, 190, 378, 464

Ḥafṣah, 63, 65

Al-Ḥākim, 15

Ḥakīm ibn Ḥizām, 16

Ḥamzah, 40

Ḥārithah clan, 41, 42

Al-Ḥārith ibn ʿAwf, 32, 34

Hāshimite clan, 83

Hawathah ibn Qays, 31

Heaven, 2, 8, 30, 35, 48, 50, 64, 90, 114, 115, 120, 121, 124, 125, 126, 127, 128, 131, 132, 133, 134, 135, 136, 140, 155, 156, 157, 158, 184, 185, 187, 188, 189, 191, 195, 196, 227, 232, 233, 234, 235, 236, 237, 239, 240, 242, 243, 244, 248,

253, 259, 264, 281, 285, 289, 291, 294, 297, 303, 304, 305, 306, 307, 346, 347, 348, 362, 367, 376, 388, 389, 392, 393, 397, 401, 406, 407, 409, 410, 411, 429, 434, 439, 441, 443, 444, 445, 446, 447, 448, 449, 459, 460, 462, 463, 464, 465, 466

Heavens and the earth, 2, 8, 114, 120, 125, 128, 131, 155, 158, 184, 185, 187, 188, 189, 236, 239, 240, 242, 243, 244, 248, 285, 289, 291, 294, 297, 303, 304, 346, 350, 362, 376, 392, 393, 397, 401, 406, 407, 410, 411, 439, 441, 444, 445, 447, 448, 449, 459, 460, 462, 463, 465

Hell, 32, 69, 190, 198, 223, 227, 233, 269, 281, 293, 299, 303, 304, 308, 309, 312, 336, 340, 347, 386, 387, 388, 391, 392, 397, 398, 401, 417, 424, 425, 435, 436, 437, 454, 457, 461, 464, 465

Hereafter, 59, 61, 63, 127, 133, 139, 164, 167, 169, 184, 282, 294, 400, 401, 402, 423, 426

Holy Land, 146

Hubayrah ibn Wahb, 39

Al-Ḥudaybiyah Peace Treaty, 1, 83

Ḥudhayfah ibn al-Yamān, 35, 48

Human nature, 4, 17, 94, 135, 138, 178, 261, 262, 263, 306, 323, 398, 402, 410, 417, 434, 445, 446, 449, 450, 463

Humanity, 8, 71, 73, 83, 91, 138, 209, 237, 238, 289, 290, 320, 328, 330, 354, 371, 393, 402, 409

Humility before God, 75, 76, 328, 465

Ḥuyay ibn Akhṭab, 31, 33, 54, 55, 57

Hypocrites, 1, 2, 3, 5, 7, 8, 9, 11, 12, 13, 25, 28, 33, 37, 38, 39, 40, 41, 45, 50, 51, 52, 53, 54, 57, 58, 81, 90, 94, 95, 101, 106, 109, 111, 112, 115, 118, 119, 122, 379

Hypocrisy, 13, 55, 57

I

Iblīs, 143, 152, 153, 347, 390, 391, 396, 397

Ibn 'Abbās, 83

Ibn Abī al-Ḥuqayq, 31, 54

Ibn Hishām, 42, 53

Ibn Isḥāq, 31, 35, 47, 53, 55, 63

Ibn Kathīr, 72, 83

Ibn Mājah , 15, 92

Ibn Umm Maktūm, 56

'Īd of Sacrifice, or *al-Aḍḥā*, 330

Idolaters, 34, 38, 39, 40, 57, 58, 128, 133, 144, 147, 159, 175, 207, 239, 241, 270, 294, 295, 306, 340, 341, 352, 392, 409, 423, 424, 443, 463

Idolatrous beliefs, 207

Idolatry, 195, 207, 288, 289, 293, 294, 434, 443

Iḥsān, 116

'Ikrimah ibn Abī Jahl, 39

Īmān, 75, 116

'Imārah ibn Ḥazm, 46

Imtā' al-Asmā', 39, 47

Individual responsibility, 217, 221, 238

Inheritance, 3, 4, 18, 20, 21

Intercession, 54, 123, 125, 127, 155, 157, 158, 246, 252, 261, 262, 263, 407, 409, 423, 441, 443, 446, 447, 448

'Ishā', 39

Ishmael, 256, 295, 316, 321, 326, 328, 329, 330, 370, 382, 383

Islam, 2, 8, 11, 12, 13, 14, 16, 17, 18, 19, 20, 21, 29, 34, 40, 42, 48, 50, 51, 52, 53, 54, 56, 58, 62, 67, 68, 69, 71, 73, 74, 75, 76, 84, 89, 104, 116, 159, 193, 199, 201, 237, 270, 278, 328, 342, 354, 357, 359, 394, 409, 423, 427, 431, 432, 450

Islamic: brotherhood, 20; character, 2, 77; code, 4, 87; concept of God, 3; concept of life, 2, 102; faith, 85, 86, 116, 198, 207, 293; features, 2; legislation, 4, 68; message, 255; moral standards, 2; social order, 12; teachings, 2, 3, 81

Israelites, 119, 372

J

Jābir, 40, 62

Jāhiliyyah, 73, 289, 417

Jerusalem, 151

Jesus son of Mary, 2, 11, 24

Jews, 2, 7, 31, 32, 36, 38, 40, 51, 52, 53, 54, 55, 56, 57, 58, 241

Jihād, 22, 42, 43